Essential Law
for Marketers

To my wonderful wife Fenella

Essential Law
for Marketers

Second Edition

Ardi Kolah

KoganPage

LONDON PHILADELPHIA NEW DELHI

Publisher's note

Every possible effort has been made to ensure that the information contained in this book is accurate at the time of going to press, and the publishers and author cannot accept responsibility for any errors or omissions, however caused. No responsibility for loss or damage occasioned to any person acting, or refraining from action, as a result of the material in this publication can be accepted by the editor, the publisher or the author.

First published in 2002 by Butterworth-Heinemann
Second edition published in Great Britain and the United States in 2013 by Kogan Page Limited

120 Pentonville Road	1518 Walnut Street, Suite 1100	4737/23 Ansari Road
London N1 9JN	Philadelphia PA 19102	Daryaganj
United Kingdom	USA	New Delhi 110002
www.koganpage.com		India

© Ardi Kolah, 2002, 2013

ISBN   978 0 7494 6450 9
E-ISBN   978 0 7494 6451 6

British Library Cataloguing-in-Publication Data

A CIP record for this book is available from the British Library.

Library of Congress Cataloging-in-Publication Data

Kolah, Ardi.
     Essential law for marketers / Ardi Kolah.
       p. cm. – (Guru in a bottle)
     ISBN 978-0-7494-6450-9 (pbk.) – ISBN 978-0-7494-6451-6 ( )   1. Marketing–Law and legislation–England.   2. Marketing–Law and legislation–Wales.   3. Sales–England.
4. Sales–Wales.   5. Marketing–Law and legislation–European Union countries.   I. Title.
     KD2206.K65 2012
     343.4208–dc23
                                                                                          2012029007

Typeset by Graphicraft Limited, Hong Kong
Print production managed by Jellyfish
Printed and bound in Great Britain by CPI Group (UK) Ltd, Croydon, CR0 4YY

Contents

3 Legal barriers to market entry 85

4 Legal requirements for sales and marketing activities 131

5 Law as a weapon for competitive sales and marketing advantage 183

6 Direct marketing and direct selling   211

7 The EU Privacy and Electronic Communications Regulations   243

8 Sales and price promotions   259

About the author

Ardi Kolah, BA, LLM, FCIM, FCIPR, FRSA, is director of communications for a financial services Fortune 500 company in Europe.

He began his career as a TV and radio reporter and producer at the BBC in network news and current affairs and the BBC World Service before embarking on a career within public relations, marketing and sponsorship working with some of the world's most successful brands including Accenture, Logica plc, Disney, Ford of Europe, Speedo, Standard Chartered Bank, Shell, Procter & Gamble, Yahoo, Reebok, Pepsi, Reliance, Emirates, Great Wheel Corporation, MOBO, YouGov, QBE, Brit Insurance, WHO, Royal Navy and Royal Air Force.

He's a former visiting lecturer on MBA programmes at Cranfield School of Management, Imperial College Business School and Judge Business School, Cambridge University.

A prolific author, he's written some of the leading works on brand marketing, public relations, sponsorship and the legal aspects of marketing, with combined sales in excess of £2.5 million worldwide. He writes a regular blog for the UK's leading sales and marketing portal Brand Republic and has been a regular contributor to *Sponsorship News*, the *FT*, the *Wall Street Journal*, *Bloomberg News*, *CNN* and *BBC World Business Report* and is on the editorial board of the *Journal of Brand Strategy*.

He holds several industry awards, including the Hollis Award for Best Low Budget Sponsorship for his work on the British Independent Film Awards and CIPR Excellence Award for Outstanding Individual in education and training.

He's a Fellow of the Chartered Institute of Marketing and of the Chartered Institute of Public Relations, a Member of the Public Relations Consultants Association, a Liveryman of the Worshipful Company of Marketors, an elected member of BAFTA and a member of the Society of Authors.

In 2003 Ardi was independently ranked by the CIM as one of the top 50 gurus in the world – and he's been trying to live this down ever since!

He's a frequent speaker at conferences around the world and has been a judge on numerous industry panels, including CIPR Excellence Awards, New Media Age Awards, National Business Awards and Scottish Newspaper of the Year Awards.

A former board director of the CIPR and the European Sponsorship Association.

He studied law at Kingston University London and then was awarded a scholarship to study for an international master's degree in law at King's College London and University College London.

He lives in Wimbledon, South-West London, with his wife Fenella and their two children, Zara and Aviva.

About the editor

Dr Beatriz San Martín is a senior associate at law firm Field Fisher Waterhouse, where she specializes in intellectual property rights law. She holds a doctorate from the University of Cambridge and advises clients in all aspects of intellectual property, with a particular focus on patents and life sciences. She's written numerous articles for legal and pharmaceutical publications and is on the Editorial Advisory Board of Pharmaceutical Technology Europe.

Foreword

by Jonathan Coad, Partner, Lewis Silkin

On a daily basis, media lawyers and their clients have to navigate a minefield created by domestic and EU legal authorities if they are to succeed and prosper.

Guru in a Bottle® *Essential Law for Marketers*, 2nd edition brings a degree of comprehensibility to UK and European law as it impacts the business of sales and marketing in a way that is rarely present in standard legal text books on the market.

This book contains all the laws and regulations that you really do need to know if you're in the marketing business and want to avoid the pitfalls of falling foul either of the regulations or the law which govern the industry.

It's no less essential if you want to gain the competitive advantage which knowledge of the relevant law and regulations can give you when you can deploy them positively to ensure that you are ahead of your rivals in the market.

For all those engaged in promoting brands, organizations, institutions, causes and issues, it is highly undesirable to embroil the client in a legal or regulatory dispute because of the acute embarrassment, financial risk and damage to reputation that it can cause.

Working as a specialist media litigator, I have had to tackle several disasters which have arisen from advertising and marketing activities that haven't been undertaken with sufficient knowledge and care. This is the book that can keep you out of such trouble.

There is nothing worse than being paid to promote a brand only to tarnish its image and create a negative perception around it as a result of defending an action in defamation or copyright, or having the brand owner's wrists slapped very publicly by the Advertising Standards Authority in the UK.

So this book really is 'essential' if you're in the market and presenting yourself as an expert sales and marketing practitioner, because if you're not aware of the legal framework that impacts sales and marketing practice, you'll be at a massive disadvantage compared with your peer group who do have that knowledge and understanding.

This book is going to save you time and money as it contains a wealth of material which it would otherwise cost you a great deal to access and collate. If it saves you just one trip to the ASA or the High Court then it constitutes a monumental bargain!

Ardi Kolah has not only produced a masterful digest of the legal principles that you need to know, he has set them out in a highly innovative and user-friendly way.

He manages to make complex legal and regulatory principles readable and comprehensible – as you would expect from a globally recognized authority in the area of the legal and commercial aspects of sales and marketing with many years of international experience to his credit.

Ardi has also taken careful note of customer feedback from his first edition – as every good marketing professional should – and incorporated into this fully updated second edition.

Fortunately for all of us who work within this industry, he has also taken the time to commit all this expertise into one volume which comprises a comprehensive lexicon of the UK and EU laws and regulations for sales and marketing professionals, but which also contains much invaluable practical advice.

For all these reasons, I strongly recommend Ardi's excellent law book with its passion, humour and simple English – all the hallmarks of the Guru in a Bottle® style that takes complicated subjects and makes them human.

"Anyone seen the man on the Clapham omnibus?"

Introduction

The introduction to the first edition began by saying that knowing your legal obligations as well as your rights as a marketer is fundamental. In many respects, the first edition was unique in that it was written as a law book for non-lawyers and with the 'legal virgin' in mind who wanted to get to grips with essential legal principles as they applied to professional sales and marketing in its broadest context.

Our sympathy has always been with marketers who want to use the full force of marketing firepower at their disposal but who perhaps lack the fundamental understanding of the restrictions placed on them by the law in being able to carry this out unencumbered. Knowing and understanding the 'rules of engagement' will definitely give you a competitive advantage. And of course ignorance of the law is no defence when the wheels come off the wagon of your carefully crafted marketing campaign and you find it needs to be scrapped or – worse still – it leaves you open to legal and even criminal sanctions when it's in full swing!

The first edition quickly became the recognized standard work on the subject for anyone studying marketing and communications and was the recommended textbook for those studying professional examinations regulated by the Chartered Institute of Marketing, the Chartered Institute of Public Relations and many other professional institutes.

The second edition contains many of the features of the first edition, such as avoiding jargon and over-complicated 'legalese-type' explanations that only lawyers can understand! It's also been completely updated to take account of the seismic changes that have transformed the law as it applies in England and Wales, as well as the impact of EU laws that have effectively rewritten the law on privacy, human rights, data protection and marketing across the web and mobile networks.

This book also takes account of a tremendous amount of feedback we received from readers, and so the second edition has been organized differently in light of this. Some sections, such as intellectual property rights, have been incorporated in a different way compared with the first edition, which we hope you'll find works much better in how it applies to your daily sales and marketing activities.

Fundamentally, we've looked at the law as it applies to all sales and marketing activities through three distinct lenses:

- law as a barrier to market entry;
- law as a requirement for sales and marketing activities; and
- law as a weapon for competitive advantage.

In this way, we've created a powerful tool that in the right hands will dramatically improve the performance of any sales and marketing programme.
The chapters of the book are arranged as follows:

- *Chapter 1: Making agreements.* This chapter examines the typical type of contracts you're likely to come across in sales and marketing.
- *Chapter 2: Making statements in sales and marketing.* In this chapter, we'll look at statements that you may wish to make in any sales and marketing activity to ensure that they comply with current legal best practice.
- *Chapter 3: Legal barriers to market entry.* This chapter looks at how legal barriers such as intellectual property rights can help to maintain and defend your market position.
- *Chapter 4: Legal requirements for sales and marketing activities.* In this chapter, we'll navigate you through the thicket of legal rules and regulations that surrounds a very wide variety of sales and marketing activities so you keep on the right side of the law. This includes the new CAP Code, which now extends to websites!
- *Chapter 5: Law as a weapon for competitive sales and marketing advantage.* In this chapter, we'll look at strategies for using the law for competitive sales and marketing advantage, such as the use of comparative advertising and product placement on television.
- *Chapter 6: Direct marketing and direct selling.* This chapter looks at the impact of the Data Protection Act 1998, as well as regulations that affect direct selling and distance selling.
- *Chapter 7: The EU Privacy and Electronic Communications Regulations.* In this chapter, we'll examine the extent to which the EU Privacy and Electronic Communications Regulations (PEC Directive) have changed the face of how we conduct marketing, such as the use of cookies on websites.
- *Chapter 8: Sales and price promotions.* In this chapter, we'll look at how best to implement sales and price promotions and how the CAP Code, the Gambling Act 2005 and other legislation have made an impact on these popular areas of sales and marketing activities.
- *Chapter 9: Prize promotions and incentives.* In this chapter, we'll examine prize draws, prediction competitions and skill-based competitions, as well as the potential lottery risks that are run by marketers and how to avoid these pitfalls.
- *Chapter 10: Sponsorship and hospitality.* In the final chapter, we untangle the complex web of legal issues as they affect sponsorship, as well as assess the impact of the Bribery Act 2010 on the provision of hospitality to customers, clients and prospects.

The law as it applies to England and Wales

This book covers English law and how it applies to England and Wales only. Scotland is a separate jurisdiction with its own laws and customs and, whilst there's a reasonable correlation between English and Scottish law, we're not covering the latter at any stage. Separate advice from a Scottish lawyer will be required if a sales and marketing issue has legal implications in Scotland.

Although European Union law is a highly specialized area, where possible we've also highlighted the relevance of this to sales and marketing.

All information contained in this book is for general purposes only and, where necessary, separate legal advice should be sought from a qualified lawyer who specializes in your area of sales and marketing practice.

The law stated as it applies to England and Wales is correct as of April 2012.

About Guru in a Bottle®

Guru in a Bottle® is about taking technical, high-level subjects and making them clear, human and accessible. Unlike Dummies®, which tends to treat the reader as a blank canvas for much of the content presented, the approach taken by Guru in a Bottle® is to guide the reader through technical subjects as their friend and personal guru. Buying a Guru in a Bottle® book gets the Guru out of the Bottle, empowering the business manager and student to tackle technical subjects and enhance their working and learning experience.

Ardi Kolah created the iconic character Guru in a Bottle® with cartoonist Steve Marchant, and the unique approach has helped make the Guru in a Bottle® series extremely popular throughout Europe, the United States and India.

"What the large print giveth,
the small print taketh away"

Making agreements

Introduction

The fundamental basis for all commercial relationships is a legally binding contract that confers certain rights and benefits on the parties of that agreement whilst at the same time imposing obligations, duties and responsibilities in the execution of that contract.

Commercial agreements and relationships endure where there's a mutual alignment of rights and obligations so that all parties derive economic value from the agreement. The point at which the agreement starts to unravel is where the value expected to be delivered fails to materialize and the agreement doesn't fairly benefit all parties who signed up to it. It's therefore critical that the agreement reflects the intentions of all parties so that there aren't problems further down the line that effectively derail these 'best laid plans'. The other key issue is that, having agreed the terms and conditions, one or more parties to the contract fail to deliver or are in breach of what has been agreed, which could give rise to termination of the contract and some form of compensation or remedy for the injured party.

Within the context of marketing, there are a huge number of different types of agreements, ranging from the supply of public relations or advertising services, through merchandise for a major marketing campaign, to the agreement to build a new website.

Let's take cloud computing, for example. Many businesses are currently bombarded with the opportunity to remove the requirement for storing a mountain of valuable marketing data on their in-house servers and to switch to a managed service where the data sit on a cloud. This may sound like a fantastic opportunity, but it has led to major concerns about the wide variance in the quality of cloud service providers (CSPs) and whether a new type of contract needs to be created given that an organization isn't buying a piece of technology but rather is engaged in business process re-engineering.

In a survey of 200 IT suppliers and 450 end users undertaken in 2011 by marketing consultancy Vanson Bourne, over 50 per cent of clients had agreements where the contract was set to renew automatically, making it difficult to get out of them. Other issues of concern were that 33 per cent of CSPs excluded liability for loss of data, and over 50 per cent of all clients didn't have a migration plan in place to cover the termination of the service contract. The underlying result of the research was that neither users nor service providers had given sufficient thought to the need for consistent standards in contracts.

Frank Jennings, chair of the governance board of the UK Cloud Industry Forum, sums up the situation: 'People don't even read their own contracts and there's a general assumption that suppliers "won't shaft me".'

Liabilities and indemnities can be a major cause of contractual grief, and this chapter guides you through the various legal provisions you can expect to affect many sales and marketing agreements within a business-to-consumer (B2C) and business-to-business (B2B) context.

Negotiation

Ultimately the sales and marketing contract you eventually end up with will be largely determined by how well you can negotiate the deal in the first place. See also Guru in a Bottle® *The Art of Influencing and Selling* for further discussion on how to negotiate successfully.

There has been much discussion by lawyers as to whether an obligation to negotiate a contract in 'good faith' can be legally binding.

At the time of writing, the situation appears opaque and will depend on the circumstances under which negotiations take place. The clearest and most recent steer on this point was given by the High Court in the Barbudev case (2011), which ruled that an agreement to negotiate in 'good faith' is too uncertain in terms of its application for the courts to be able to enforce it.

In an earlier ruling from the Court of Appeal in the Petrobras case (2005), the court left it open that a commitment to negotiate in 'good faith' may be legally binding in certain circumstances, so an express obligation to negotiate in 'good faith' may be held to be enforceable.

In the general context of sales and marketing agreements, it's highly unlikely that any representations to negotiate in 'good faith' could be relied on later should things go wrong. In essence, it's much safer to assume that the contractual agreement is the principal instrument that determines what the parties to the agreement intended.

Heads of terms

Establishing heads of terms is very common practice within commerce, and there's nothing technical about them. Their main purpose is to record the main points of principle on a sales and marketing deal before the fine details and small print get drafted and negotiated. Heads of terms are also known as letters of intent, memoranda of understanding, term sheets or heads of agreement.

Some of the benefits of a good set of heads of terms are:

- It provides a focus and clears up confusion. It's common for two people to leave a conversation and end up with very different interpretations as to what was agreed! Writing down the basic bones of a transaction means that those misunderstandings get spotted and resolved amicably before hours of legal drafting and expense are incurred.

- We're all human, and memory fades over time. Forgetting what you agreed in a meeting a month ago is a real possibility, so a set of heads of terms is a great aide-memoire.

- It acts like a moral commitment on both sides to observe the terms agreed.

It's also a useful discipline to have heads of terms particularly when instructing an in-house lawyer to draft a sales and marketing agreement on your behalf. In drafting an agreement, the lawyer is setting out, in legally binding words, what you've agreed with the other party. Although lawyers love to add loads of 'legal stuff' to a contract, at the end of the day it's their job to create an instrument that reflects the intentions of all parties.

'A good set of heads of terms lets us know what that is. We can then get on with "doing our bit" without having to come back to you with a whole host of irritating questions,' explains Brinsley Dresden, partner with leading media law firm Lewis Silkin.

Heads of terms generally come in two flavours: 'term sheets' and interim agreements.

'Term sheet'-type documents provide evidence of serious intent and have some moral force, but generally don't contractually require the parties to conclude the deal on the terms outlined in the heads, or even at all. Their intention is effectively to outline key terms agreed in principle, to give the parties a structured basis for negotiating the main contract. They are generally intended to be non-binding as a whole, but will often include some provisions that are intended to be binding.

Interim agreements are documents that are intended to be binding in their entirety and are therefore effectively temporary agreements. They are most often used to cover the situation common to many industries where the parties start to incur costs or perform the contract before the final contract is agreed, for example leasing a marquee or providing outside catering at a hospitality event. In such a situation, the heads of terms will assume greater importance, and additional considerations will apply.

There's no standard form for heads of terms; they can vary from a simple letter, which is probably the most common format you'll encounter, to a carefully drafted document prepared by professional advisers.

They are commonly entered into at the beginning of a transaction, once the parties have agreed preliminary terms and before the definitive agreements are drafted (which is when the parties begin to incur significant legal costs). The parties may need to enter a series of heads of terms throughout the negotiations, particularly when negotiations are prolonged.

Heads of terms in certain specific situations may fall foul of competition law rules. For example, if they have as their object or effect the restriction, prevention or distortion of competition within the UK or the EU, they may be prohibited by Chapter 1 of the Competition Act 1998 or Article 101(1) of the Treaty on the Functioning of the European Union (formerly 81(1) of the EC Treaty). In such cases, the parties should consider whether the heads of terms are exempt, for example under a block exemption, or whether the agreement qualifies for individual exemption and should seek suitably qualified legal advice in such cases.

The other danger to avoid is the case of the heads of terms being signed, work commencing, and the parties getting involved in the nitty-gritty of the day-to-day arrangements but forgetting to finalize the full agreement! This of course can store up problems for a later date, so it's preferable to get an agreement signed as soon as practicable.

Legal effect of heads of terms

The legal effect of 'non-binding' heads of terms is often one of the key concerns of the parties. They don't want the statement of the terms of the commercial transaction to be legally binding; but if, as is often the case, they include provisions in the heads of terms document dealing with issues such as confidentiality, exclusivity (lockout) or costs, they'll want those provisions to have legal effect.

The case law in this area (see also '"Subject to contract"' below) illustrates that great care must be taken when drafting heads of terms.

Where the intention of the parties is to be legally bound, then the legal requirements relating to the creation of a valid contract must be satisfied. Third-party rights may also become an issue at this point, and heads of terms can give rise to liability for misrepresentation or negligent misstatement, whether or not they are contractually binding.

Legal requirements for creating binding provisions

In the unusual situation where one of the parties wishes to rely on heads of terms as evidence of an agreement and in the absence of a properly construed contract, there are two 'tests' that the heads of terms will need to pass in order to be legally enforceable: the terms must be sufficiently certain to be enforceable; and, unless the heads of terms are executed under seal, there must be consideration flowing from the party benefiting from the agreement to the other party, in the form of a promise in return, a payment, an action or a forbearance (not doing something in return).

Third-party rights

This is where the heads of terms get much more complex and qualified legal advice will be required. The issue may arise as to whether some third party has the right to enforce a binding term. For example, the parent company or a group subsidiary of a party to the heads of terms might want to benefit from the confidentiality provisions – a term that may give them directly enforceable rights under the Contracts (Rights of Third Parties) Act 1999.

'Subject to contract'

These words are often seen on estate agents' boards in small print below the word 'SOLD'. So under what circumstances do the words 'subject to contract' actually indicate a sale?

Leaving aside the legal complexities surrounding the sale and purchase of land, which are outside the scope of this book, there's a well-established principle of English law that an agreement made on terms such that the parties don't intend to be legally bound unless and until they enter into a more formal contract isn't legally binding. After all, that's common sense.

The use of the phrase 'subject to contract' in commercial negotiations creates a strong presumption that the parties don't want to be bound but isn't immune from attack when used in heads of terms documents, particularly if the parties start to perform the contract envisaged by the heads of terms, for example providing services as described earlier, such as hospitality.

It's preferable for heads of terms to spell out the parties' intention, rather than relying on the inclusion of the words 'subject to contract', for example: 'These heads of terms are not intended to be legally binding between the parties except as specifically set out in this letter.'

If some provisions of the heads of terms are intended to be legally binding, and others are not, it's particularly important to identify the relevant provisions clearly. However, it's always preferable to have a properly executed contractual agreement rather than relying on heads of agreement as the instrument for binding the parties in a contractual sense.

Foreign jurisdictions

The 'subject to contract' wording isn't recognized in many jurisdictions outside the UK, so it shouldn't be relied on when dealing with foreign parties. In some jurisdictions, certain headings, such as 'pre-contract' or 'preliminary contract', can risk creating contractual obligations. In some continental European jurisdictions, such as France and Italy, heads of terms may be construed by the courts as a binding pre-agreement if they contain key terms such as the parties, price and conditions precedent. It's therefore essential that the language in the heads of terms is consistent throughout in expressing that the document isn't legally binding.

Most continental European jurisdictions impose a duty to negotiate in good faith, which extends to all phases of commercial relationships in both the pre-contractual and the contractual stages. Entering into a heads of terms document may help to crystallize the duty and make it easier to enforce. For example, heads of terms that set out detailed terms agreed in principle would be evidence of the closeness of the relationship and of what each party expected from the other.

Non-binding heads of terms

As a general rule, when drafting heads of terms that aren't intended to be binding as a whole, the document should cover important deal points. It's usual to find a statement that the parties intend to enter legal relations, for example sponsorship exclusivity or a television advertising campaign.

Any provisions that are intended to be legally binding must satisfy the legal requirements relating to the creation of a valid contract.

Typically, a non-binding heads of terms document should cover the following points:

- Principles underlying the agreement, leaving the detail for the formal contract.

- Governing law – if one party to the deal wants the document to be governed by foreign law, the other party should understand how this might affect its rights before making this concession.

- Key preconditions to signing the contract and the person responsible for making sure those preconditions are satisfied.

- Acknowledgement that the non-binding heads of terms are non-exhaustive. Wasted time and effort on excessive detail often occur because each side fears that the other will later try to treat any point not raised as implicitly conceded in principle. A statement that specifically leaves open the opportunity to raise subsidiary points can help keep things moving.

- Assumptions upon which the heads of terms are based, as well as the identification of areas where further information is required and reservation of the right to revisit the deal in light of any further or new information.

- An agreed formula for calculating any fees payable in order to ensure there aren't misunderstandings as to how the formula will operate under the legally binding contract.

The following can also form part of the non-binding heads of terms: provisions for scope; terms and conditions with respect to works being carried out or services rendered; limitation on liabilities; duration; payment of fees; arbitration and disputes resolution; and jurisdictional issues.

Use of standard terms of business

It's likely that you'll work for a company or organization that has standard terms of business or be dealing with companies, suppliers and consultancies that will also have standard terms of business. And of course there is likely to be more than one set of standard terms of business depending on the circumstances and nature of the agreement to be entered into.

It's important if you work to standard terms of business to keep these under constant review; for example, the sales department may be issuing sales quotations or processing orders using terms and conditions that are out of date, not fit for purpose or simply cloned from terms used by competitors!

The use of standard terms of business can help save the time and money that would be incurred in drawing up specific terms for each individual transaction that your company may wish to make. Standardization also allows more junior members of the team to be able to handle and conclude contracts that are in alignment with a company's stated policies and procedures.

In order to avoid standard terms for transactions where their use is not appropriate, a procedure could be created internally where contracts over a certain value are automatically sent to the legal department for review before they are issued, which is a prudent system that most organizations have in place, particularly if they operate in regulated industries and need to keep an audit trail available for inspection by the regulator.

Offer and acceptance

The contracting process is analysed for legal purposes in terms of offer and acceptance. From the seller's perspective, it is preferable that the offer should be made by the buyer and if appropriate be accepted by the seller. From a sales and marketing perspective, this appears to run counter to where the focus of communication has been to this point (from seller to buyer), but makes perfect legal sense.

The common law rule is that new contract terms can't be introduced after the contract has been formed by offer and acceptance between the parties.

This means that the all-too-frequent practice whereby sellers seek to impose their standard business terms by printing them on the back of an invoice generally won't be effective to incorporate the terms in the contract, because the invoice won't usually be dispatched until sometime after the contract will be held to have been entered into.

Standard terms should be drafted and contracting procedures established by the seller. The advantages to the seller are that it will then know whether and, if so, when a contract has been entered into. The rule that a valid contract can be made when acceptance of an offer is posted means that the party making the offer won't know immediately that it is contractually bound.

If the offer by the buyer is not on the seller's terms, then any purported acceptance by the seller stated to be on its own terms may in fact be a counter-offer and won't create a legally binding agreement (see '"Battle of the Forms"' below).

The seller should ensure that:

- any proposals put forward for agreement – whether in the form of a quotation or a brochure – are phrased so as not to constitute an offer, as otherwise the buyer's acceptance could form a contract before the seller's standard terms can be incorporated into it;

- the offer made by the buyer is on the seller's standard terms and conditions, which may be by way of providing the buyer with the seller's standard order form, stating that the order is an offer on the seller's standard terms and conditions; and

- the standard terms contain a clause indicating that any purported acceptance by the buyer will take effect only as an offer on the seller's standard terms and that no contract will be created until the seller issues its acknowledgement or confirmation of order.

It should be borne in mind that it's not possible to guarantee the effectiveness of such a provision. The courts might, in such circumstances, find that the seller's and the buyer's terms weren't incorporated as there was no consensus. However, the provision will at the very least strengthen the seller's negotiating position if there's a dispute later.

As a contract can be oral, any discussions with the customer or client – whether over the phone or face to face – need to be on the basis of the seller's standard terms or stated to be subject to contract (not binding until a written contract is entered into).

A buyer will seek to submit its standard purchase terms together with its purchase order so as to constitute an offer on those terms, which will be accepted by the seller delivering the goods.

Incorporation of standard terms in contracts with buyers

In order to maximize the chances of successfully incorporating the seller's standard terms in its contracts with customers or clients, the seller must ensure that standard terms are brought to the attention of customers or clients at the earliest possible opportunity.

The simplest way of doing this is expressly to state in pre-contract correspondence that the seller's standard terms will apply to the sale. However, this is likely to provoke customers or clients into seeking to negotiate the terms. The seller's desire to avoid this must be balanced against the increased risk that those terms will be considered not to have been incorporated if an express statement isn't made in the pre-contractual correspondence. The next best option is for the seller to bring the terms to the attention of customers or clients in as much pre-contract and contract documentation as possible.

This could include setting out the standard terms:

- in the seller's sales brochures, catalogues or other marketing material; or
- on the seller's quotation forms; or
- on the acknowledgement or confirmation of order issued by the seller; or
- on the seller's delivery notes.

If the standard terms appear on all or some of the above documents, there's no harm in putting them on the seller's invoices as well, because if there's a course of dealing with that particular customer or client this will assist the seller's argument that the terms had been brought to the attention of the customer over a period of time should there be a dispute later.

Conversely, a buyer's standard purchase terms should be set out on: the purchase order of the buyer; or the quotation acceptance of the buyer.

All sales and marketing employees must be made fully aware of the company or organization's sales and purchasing procedures and adhere to them at all times. They should also be given guidance where the standard contract has blank spaces that need to be completed. Any blanks completed in a way inconsistent with the printed terms have the legal effect of adding provisions that override the standard terms.

When introducing new standard terms, a copy should be sent to every customer or client stating that the new terms will apply in the future.

This is also an ideal opportunity to enclose a slip for return by which the customer signs and acknowledges receipt of the new terms. Such a confirmatory slip won't always be returned, but when it is it can be invaluable evidence of acceptance of the new terms. The use of methods to prove receipt, such as recorded delivery, may also be useful evidence, particularly if seeking to rely on a course of dealings over a period of time.

However, it should be noted that receipt doesn't necessarily indicate acceptance.

The following drafting rules should be followed with a view to ensuring, so far as possible, that terms are properly incorporated:

- Where the seller's terms are printed on the reverse of a document, the document should have a statement on the face of it clearly stating that the sale is made on the terms printed on the reverse and that they form part of the contract.

- If a term is unusual, particular attention should be drawn to it on the face of the document, since the courts require special notice to be given of any such terms (for example, many exclusion clauses fall into this category).

- If a term governs or potentially varies something on the face of the document, for example price or delivery date, it should be cross-referenced.

'Battle of the forms'

While standard terms of sale are more usual, it's becoming increasingly common to see standard terms of purchase.

If both sellers and buyers seek to impose their own standard terms, then difficulties arise in determining which terms will prevail.

The approach taken by the courts is that an acceptance that attempts to impose new terms isn't an acceptance at all, but is a counter-offer, which can be accepted by an unequivocal acceptance by the other party or by performance under the contract. This means in practice that the last set of terms dispatched before acceptance or performance – if you like, the last 'shot' fired in the 'battle of the forms' – will prevail.

There are several practical approaches that a seller may adopt when faced with a 'battle of the forms'.

The most obvious and practical way of dealing with this situation is to discuss the sale terms with the customer or client and if possible agree any variations in terms and conditions in a side letter. The disadvantage is that this involves a negotiation of the standard terms, which could result in further time and legal costs. However, where the relationship is important, such as a key account, then agreeing special terms makes commercial sense.

An alternative solution would be to include the seller's terms in as many pre-contractual documents as possible and refrain from raising the standard terms as an issue with the customer as well as firing the last 'shot' in the 'battle of the forms' by ensuring as far as possible that the terms appear on the last document passing between the parties before the delivery of the goods or services.

The advantage of this approach is that no time is wasted in negotiating amendments to the seller's terms and that, assuming that the 'battle of the forms' is won, the seller's terms will be incorporated without amendment. The disadvantage is that the risk that the customer might succeed in firing the last 'shot' can't be entirely eliminated, in which case those terms will end up being incorporated without amendment.

Representations made in sales and marketing literature

Companies or organizations may incur liabilities for statements or representations made to the buyer that they hadn't intended would form part of the contract depending on the context of the sales situation.

Indigo International case (2003)

In this case, the High Court ruled that statements in sales and marketing could lead to an action for misrepresentation if the buyer had relied on these to enter into the contract and would be entitled to damages.

In such cases, it isn't necessary that it's reasonable for the buyer to rely on such statements but merely that it did and the seller ought to have known that such statements would act as an inducement. See also Guru in a Bottle® *The Art of Influencing and Selling* on how to write effective sales materials.

Verbal statements made in sales and marketing

There is a danger that sales and marketing employees could make statements to the buyer in circumstances where those statements are inaccurate or unsustainable claims about a product.

The courts may, as in the circumstances surrounding sales and marketing literature, find that such statements are contractually binding on the company or organization whether as an additional term of the parties' contract or as a collateral contract. Alternatively, the court may decide that this amounts to a misrepresentation and gives rise to an action for damages (see 'Remedies available for breach of contract' below).

It's therefore important that sales and marketing employees are aware of their legal obligations and should always consult a suitably experienced lawyer when in any doubt about sales and marketing literature.

Relevant statutory framework for sale of goods, services or goods and services

From a legal perspective, the fork in the road for which relevant statutory framework applies in making agreements depends on whether the seller is involved in selling goods on its own, services on its own or goods and services together (Figure 1.1).

Figure 1.1 Relevant statutory framework in selling goods and services

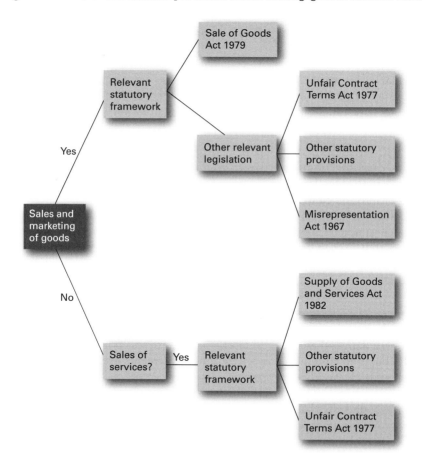

Sale of goods or goods and services

A significant number of statutes and regulations have an impact on contracts for the sale of goods:

- those statutes that regulate the supply of goods or supply of goods and services and impose implied terms and conditions in contracts of sale;
- those statutes that limit the extent to which the seller can exclude or restrict its liability; and
- statutes that specifically relate to misrepresentation, consumer credit and product liability.

The most important pieces of legislation are the Sale of Goods Act 1979 (SOGA 1979) and the Unfair Contract Terms Act 1977 (UCTA 1977) as they apply to all sale of goods contracts.

There are a number of important implied terms in sale of goods contracts by reason of the SOGA 1979, for example as to title to the goods and quality of the goods, and it provides a large number of presumptions that apply unless specifically dealt with in the contract for the sale of goods.

UCTA 1977 regulates the use of exclusion clauses that the seller may wish to rely on in order to avoid any liability at a future date for the goods sold.

With B2C transactions, the Unfair Terms in Consumer Contracts Regulations 1999 (SI 1999/2083) (Unfair Terms Regulations) also apply. These regulations impose additional restrictions on the exclusion of liability, and other regulations may also apply depending on whether the sale is online, via phone or mail order, and these include the Consumer Protection (Distance Selling) Regulations 2000 (see Chapter 6).

At the time of writing, the government has yet to reform the law by replacing UCTA and the Unfair Terms Regulations with a single statute, although the previous government did accept the need for a new Consumer Rights Bill in order to modernize and simplify consumer law as well as implement the EU Consumer Rights Directive that the EU Council of Ministers voted to adopt in October 2011. Member states have two years to implement measures into national law, which means that the law in the UK will need to change before the end of 2013. Although this has yet to happen, it's useful to outline briefly what these changes will mean for sellers and buyers in the future.

EU Consumer Rights Directive

The Consumer Rights Directive brings together a number of disparate existing rules. Currently, European rules on consumer rights are contained in four separate EU directives covering unfair contracts, distance selling, doorstep selling, and sales and guarantees respectively. The problem with these EU regulations is that they were made in a rather haphazard fashion, and many were written almost three decades ago. The Consumer Rights Directive will, it's hoped, 'harmonize' these existing regulations and give consumers more clarity about their rights when buying and selling in Europe. For further discussion, see Chapter 4.

Broadly, the purpose of the EU directive is to ensure that customers can be confident about making purchases within Europe, particularly online, and from businesses in other European countries outside of their own.

The new EU directive is also intended to apply to B2C sales. The key points include:

- An obligation for sellers to provide buyers with key information before the conclusion of a contract: main characteristics of the product, geographical address and identity of the trader, the price inclusive of taxes, and all additional freight, delivery or postal charges for all consumer contracts to help the consumer make an informed choice.
- The consumer's right to a 14-day 'cooling-off period'. This means that consumers can cancel an order, return the goods and get their money back at any point during the 14 calendar days after they make a purchase online or during the visit of a trader to their home.
- The consumer's protection against the risk of loss or damage to goods until it receives them. In practical terms this will mean that sellers will be liable for that risk – and, probably, that sellers will have to bear the cost of postal insurance or pass this on in higher prices.
- The consumer's right to have goods replaced or repaired at any time during the two years after it makes the purchase. When this isn't possible, a refund must be given.
- The seller's obligation to cover the cost of returns when that cost exceeds €40 (currently).
- The seller's obligation to sell to any and every EU country.

In light of the expected approval of the EU directive, the government has signalled its intention to merge all existing UK consumer protection laws and regulations together with the requirements of the finalized Consumer Rights Directive into a single new Consumer Bill of Rights.

In the UK, there are 12 existing laws and regulations relating to consumer protection, which the government has said are complex and confusing and not in the best interests of consumers and business. The forthcoming Consumer Bill of Rights is therefore intended to repeal and replace a number of pieces of legislation, including:

- Consumer Protection (Distance Selling) Regulations;
- Unfair Terms in Consumer Contracts Regulations 1999;
- Misrepresentation Act 1967;
- Sale of Goods Act 1979;
- Sale and Supply of Goods and Services Act 1994;
- Supply of Goods (Implied Terms) Act 1973;
- Unfair Contract Terms Act 1977.

These changes will require a radical readjustment to the many ways that businesses operate at the point of sale. In particular, technology, media and telecoms businesses that provide software and entertainment products to consumers to be downloaded at the time of sale will need to be aware of the changes that will be required.

Marketers operating in Europe should take the opportunity before the end of 2013 to review their sales and marketing practices, both online and offline, to ensure that they will be compliant when the new legislation comes into force. A government consultation process is now under way.

Unfair Terms Regulations 1999

These regulations apply to any term in a contract between a seller or supplier and a consumer that hasn't been individually negotiated and provide that any such term that is unfair isn't binding on the consumer. It should also be noted that the fact that a single term may have been individually negotiated doesn't mean that the remaining terms in a standard-form contract will escape the fairness test.

A term is 'unfair' if it causes a significant imbalance in the positions of the parties to the detriment of the consumer in a way that is contrary to the requirement of good faith. The scales of justice are therefore heavily tipped in favour of the consumer!

In assessing unfairness, regulation 6(1) of the Unfair Terms Regulations requires the following to be taken into account:

- the nature of the goods or services to which the contract relates;
- all the circumstances surrounding the conclusion of the contract at the time of entering into it; and
- all the other terms of the contract or of another contract on which it is dependent.

The 'core provisions' of a standard contract, defined as terms that define the main subject matter of the contract or concern the adequacy of price or remuneration for the goods or services sold, are excluded from the fairness test, but only in so far as they are expressed in plain and intelligible language.

What the Unfair Terms Regulations refer to as an 'indicative and non-exhaustive list' of terms that may be considered unfair is set out in Schedule 2 of the Unfair Terms Regulations.

These include:

- a clause providing for a deposit or advance payment made by a consumer that is then forfeited if the consumer cancels the contract, unless there is also a corresponding clause providing for the consumer to receive an equivalent amount if the contract is cancelled by the seller or supplier;
- a clause in a yearly agreement that provides that the consumer must give not less than six months' notice of termination, failing which the agreement is automatically extended for another year at the end of the term; and

- a clause allowing the seller to change without a valid reason features of the goods such as their size or colour.

In addition to the sanction of an unfair term being held not to be binding on an individual consumer, the Office of Fair Trading (OFT) and other qualifying bodies are given powers, following the making of a complaint (which may even be made by a business competitor!), to take action in relation to unfair terms, including applying for an injunction to prevent a business from relying on an unfair term. It sounds extreme but is true!

Qualifying bodies include the Information Commissioner; various utility regulators, the Rail Regulator, Trading Standards, the Consumers' Association and the Financial Services Authority.

Sale of Goods Act 1979

The SOGA 1979 imposes the following implied terms in contracts for the sale of goods:

- That the seller has the right to sell the goods (section 12(1), SOGA 1979).
- That the goods are free from undisclosed charges or encumbrances and that the buyer will enjoy quiet possession of the goods (section 12(2) and (3), SOGA 1979).
- Where goods are sold by description that the goods will correspond with that description (section 13, SOGA 1979).
- In consumer contracts, and subject to certain exceptions, that any lack of conformity of the goods with their description in the contract that becomes apparent within six months of delivery is presumed to have existed at the time of delivery (regulation 5, Sale and Supply of Goods to Consumers Regulations 2002). This reversed burden of proof makes it easier for consumers to bring claims in the first six months.
- Where goods are sold in the course of a business that the goods are of satisfactory quality (section 14(2), SOGA 1979). Goods are of satisfactory quality if they meet the standard that a reasonable person would regard as satisfactory, taking account of any description of the goods, price and all other relevant circumstances.

In addition, the quality of goods includes their state and condition, and the following factors among others are to be taken into account in determining whether goods are of satisfactory quality:

- fitness for all the purposes for which goods of that kind are commonly supplied;
- appearance and finish;
- freedom from minor defects;
- safety; and
- durability.

In consumer contracts, section 14(2D) of the SOGA 1979 provides that public statements made by the seller, the manufacturer or the manufacturer's representative about a product, such as in sales and marketing literature, will be used in determining whether the product is of satisfactory quality. Although there are defences to this, a retailer could potentially be held liable for promises made by a manufacturer about product performance.

Where goods are sold in the course of a business and the buyer, expressly or by implication, makes known to the seller the purpose for which it wants the goods, the goods should be reasonably fit for that purpose (section 14(3), SOGA 1979). The term doesn't apply if the buyer doesn't rely on the seller's skill or judgement or if it's unreasonable for the buyer to rely on it.

Where goods are sold by sample, they should correspond to the sample in quality, and they should be free from any defect making their quality unsatisfactory that would not be apparent on a reasonable examination of the sample.

Section 5A of the SOGA 1979 gives consumer buyers the following remedies where goods fail to conform to the contract of sale at the time of delivery: the right to require the seller to repair or replace the goods within a reasonable time and without causing significant inconvenience to the consumer; and the right to require the seller to reduce the purchase price of the goods by an appropriate amount or to rescind the contract. The consumer can exercise this right only if the repair or replacement is impossible or disproportionate, taking into account the value of the goods if they had not been faulty, the significance of the fault in the goods and the inconvenience to the consumer of other remedies, or if the seller fails to repair or replace the goods within a reasonable time and without significant inconvenience to the consumer.

Goods are deemed not to conform to the contract of sale if there is a breach of an express term of the contract or a term implied by section 13 (sale by description), section 14 (satisfactory quality and fitness for purpose) or section 15 (sale by sample) of the SOGA 1979.

Goods that don't conform to the contract of sale at any time within the period of six months starting with the date on which the goods were delivered to the consumer must be taken not to have so conformed at that date.

The burden is on the seller to establish that the goods did conform to the contract at the date of delivery, unless the application of the principle is incompatible with the nature of the goods, such as perishable foodstuffs, or the nature of the lack of conformity.

If a seller commits a breach of any condition of contract, the buyer is entitled to reject the goods and terminate the contract. However, the buyer's right to reject the goods is lost if it accepts the goods.

Under section 35 of SOGA 1979, the buyer is deemed to have accepted the goods and so loses the right to reject the goods in three situations:

- When the buyer intimates to the seller that it has accepted the goods.
- When the goods have been delivered to the buyer and it acts consistently with ownership of the goods. The buyer must be given a reasonable opportunity of examining the goods in order to check that they comply with the requirements of the contract (this can be excluded in B2B contracts under section 35(2) and (3), SOGA 1979).
- When the buyer has retained the goods after a reasonable time without intimating to the seller it has rejected them. A 'reasonable time' takes into account the time taken to ascertain what would be required to modify or repair the goods, according the judgment of the Court of Appeal in the Clegg case (2003).

UCTA 1977

This statute applies to clauses in contracts that seek to restrict or exclude business liability. UCTA 1977 doesn't apply to international supply contracts in general or where the contract is made outside of the UK jurisdiction and this has been agreed by the parties provided that the party relying on the exclusion hasn't done so simply to circumvent the implied terms of UCTA 1977.

Different controls apply according to the nature of the liability that the supplier wishes to exclude or restrict:

- A term excluding or restricting liability for death or personal injury caused by negligence is wholly ineffective (section 2(1), UCTA 1977).
- A term excluding or restricting liability for negligence is enforceable only to the extent that it satisfies the reasonableness test (section 2(2), UCTA 1977).
- Breach of statutory implied terms is ineffective.
- A term excluding or restricting liability for implied terms of good title to the goods without encumbrances is also ineffective (section 6(1), UCTA 1977).
- Any terms that seek to exclude or restrict liability for correspondence with description of the goods delivered to the customer, satisfactory quality, fitness for purpose or correspondence with a sample will be ineffective against the consumer and will be enforceable only in so far as they can satisfy the reasonableness test as against persons other than consumers (section 6(2) and (3), UCTA 1977).

These controls apply where a contract expressly excludes one or more of the implied terms or excludes one or more of them by implication, for example by means of a term that states that goods supplied will be fit only for the purpose specifically stated by the seller or will meet only certain quality standards specified by the seller.

In contracts with consumers or in contracts with another business that are on the seller's standard terms of business, additional controls also apply.

For example, any attempt to exclude or restrict liability for breach of contract will be enforceable only to the extent that it satisfies the reasonableness test (section 3, UCTA 1977).

'Reasonableness test'

In order to pass the 'reasonableness test' under UCTA 1977, a contract term must have been 'a fair and reasonable one to be included having regard to the circumstances which were, or ought reasonably to have been, known to or in the contemplation of the parties when the contract was made' (section 11(1), UCTA 1977).

Schedule 2 to UCTA 1977 contains a non-exhaustive list of guidelines in assessing reasonableness, which strictly apply only in deciding whether the exclusion or limitation of any of the implied conditions contained in sections 13, 14 or 15 of SOGA 1979 is reasonable.

The guidelines have also been applied by the courts when considering the reasonableness test in relation to the exclusion of other types of liability, in particular for breach of contract under section 3 of UCTA 1977.

In summary, the guidelines are:

- the balance in strength of the bargaining positions of the parties relative to each other (including alternatives open to customers, for example the ability to insure that could redress an imbalance in relative bargaining positions);
- whether any inducement was given to the customer or client to agree the term, or whether the customer had an opportunity of entering into a similar contract with other persons without having to accept a similar term;
- whether the customer or client knew or ought reasonably to have known of the existence of the term having regard, among other things, to any custom of the trade and any previous course of dealing between the parties;
- if a term excludes or restricts liability or if some condition isn't complied with, whether it was reasonable at the time of the contract to expect that compliance with that condition would be practicable; and
- whether the goods were manufactured, processed or adapted to the special order of the customer or client.

Misrepresentation Act 1967

A term that excludes or restricts liability for misrepresentation resulting in death or personal injury caused by negligence is unenforceable (section 2(1), UCTA 1977). In the case of other loss or damage, a term that excludes or restricts liability for misrepresentation or excludes any remedy for misrepresentation is enforceable only to the extent that it satisfies the reasonableness test (section 3, Misrepresentation Act 1967).

The Misrepresentation Act 1967 also imposes statutory liability for pre-contractual misrepresentations.

Consumer Protection Act 1987

This imposes strict liability on manufacturers, importers into the EU and own-label brands for injuries caused by goods that are unsafe and intended for consumer use. A supplier may not exclude its liability under this Act.

Consumer Protection (Distance Selling) Regulations 2000

These apply to contracts where goods are sold at a distance, for example over the internet, by phone or mail order, without the seller and buyer being in each other's physical presence.

The regulations apply only to contracts between businesses and consumers. For these purposes, a consumer is defined as 'any natural person who, in contracts to which these regulations apply, is acting for purposes which are outside his business'. This reflects the wording in the Unfair Terms Regulations (see 'Unfair Terms Regulations (1999)' above).

The Consumer Protection (Distance Selling) Regulations 2000 contain a requirement on the seller to provide the consumer with certain specified information. This includes information on the right to cancel the distance contract, the main characteristics of the goods or services, and delivery costs where appropriate.

The regulations provide for a cooling-off period, which enables a consumer to cancel the contract by providing notice of cancellation to the seller. If the contract is cancelled then it's treated as if it hadn't been made. This right of cancellation doesn't apply to certain contracts, for example where the goods are made to the consumer's specification.

Other elements of the regulations provide that: businesses selling services by the internet, phone or mail order will be able to deliver key written details, which the regulations oblige them to provide, to consumers at any time from when an order is placed until the service finishes; and, if the information to be provided isn't made available until after provision of the service has started, consumers will be able to cancel the agreement for up to seven days after the information is received (Consumer Protection (Distance Selling) (Amendment) Regulations 2005 (SI 2005/689)). See also Chapter 6 for a discussion on distance selling and direct selling.

Other regulations, such as the Financial Services (Distance Marketing) Regulations 2004 (SI 2004/2095), apply to the marketing of banking, credit, insurance, personal pensions, investment and other such products exclusively by distance means. They contain similar provisions to the Consumer Protection (Distance Selling) Regulations 2000 in that certain specified information must be given to the consumer before the conclusion of the contract, and they also provide for a cooling-off period.

The Electronic Commerce (EC Directive) Regulations 2002

These apply to businesses selling goods to other businesses or consumers on the internet or by e-mail. In essence the regulations require a seller:

- to make specific information available to customers, for example the seller's name and address;
- to inform customers how the contract is to be concluded;
- to ensure customers are able to print off and store a copy of the terms and conditions;
- to allow the customer to identify and correct input errors before an order is placed;
- to acknowledge receipt of an order; and
- to comply with any consumer contract laws in place in its home state when dealing with consumers in other European Union member states.

For a detailed discussion on these Regulations, refer to Chapter 7.

Equality Act 2006

This Act protects individuals from discrimination in the provision of goods and services on the grounds or religion or belief, or on the grounds of sexual orientation.

Consumer Protection from Unfair Trading Regulations 2008

These regulations apply to the sale or supply of products to consumers. The regulations require businesses not to mislead consumers through acts or omissions or subject them to aggressive commercial practices, whether before, during or after the sale.

Business Protection from Misleading Marketing Regulations 2008

These prohibit suppliers from advertising goods to traders in a misleading way. The regulations define advertising as:

any form of representation that is made in connection with a trade, business, craft or profession in order to promote the supply or transfer of a product, which includes pre-sales representations made to the customer by the supplier's sales team, and other marketing and promotional activities such as the provision of information of products in catalogues or on websites, and descriptions on packaging.

The regulations don't give traders or competitors a direct right of action, but these regulations are policed by designated consumer protection authorities.

Cancellation of Contracts made in a Consumer's Home or Place of Work Etc. Regulations 2008

These allow consumers who enter into a contract for goods or services during a visit by a seller to a consumer's home or place of work, or on an excursion organized by the seller, to cancel that contract within seven days of the consumer being given notice of his or her cancellation rights, whether the visit was solicited by the consumer or not.

Bribery Act 2010

The Bribery Act 2010, which came into force on 1 July 2011, replaces the existing criminal offences of bribery and introduces new offences on the statute books.

The Bribery Act 2010 creates a new corporate offence of failure to prevent bribery by an 'associated person', under which a commercial organization will be guilty of an offence if a person associated with it bribes another person intending to obtain or retain business for the commercial organization, or to obtain or retain an advantage in the conduct of business for the commercial organization (section 7, Bribery Act 2010). This is a strict liability offence, and the only defence available to the commercial organization is that it had in place 'adequate procedures' to prevent bribery by its associated persons.

Under the Bribery Act 2010, a person (A) is associated with a relevant commercial organization (C) if A performs services for or on behalf of C (section 8, Bribery Act 2010).

According to the Ministry of Justice, which has issued guidance on the adequate procedures defence, where a supplier of goods can be properly said to be performing services for its customer, rather than simply acting as the seller of the goods to the customer, it may also be an associated person of the customer.

For most supply of goods arrangements, there is unlikely to be a risk of a section 7 Bribery Act 2010 offence arising. However, the risk may arise in certain circumstances where the supplier is providing any services in addition to the goods, or the supplier is an exclusive supplier of the goods. An example of bribery in this context would be if sums are paid by a supplier of goods in order to expedite customs procedures in the country of export. In such cases, a customer should consider whether it's appropriate to deploy prescriptive anti-bribery procedures and drafting, such as due diligence on the supplier, requiring the supplier to comply with the customer's anti-bribery policies, and the inclusion of anti-bribery clauses in the supply agreement.

- Check that the agreement for the purchase of goods is set out clearly and unambiguously.
- Check that the agreement itemizes the correct products, term, price and specification.

- Ensure that there are no pre-existing arrangements such as exclusive purchase arrangements or restrictive covenants that would prevent the buyer from proceeding with the agreement.
- If acting as the seller, ensure that the buyer marks all pre-contractual correspondence 'subject to contract'.
- If as the buyer you want to incorporate your own standard terms, ensure that the agreement expressly does so and reject the seller's standard terms.
- Check the definitions of the goods in the agreement very carefully and the address to which they need to be delivered.
- If there is a conflict between the main body of the agreement and the schedules, consider which terms are to prevail.
- As a buyer, consider whether the EU procurement rules apply.

For further guidance on the Bribery Act 2010, see Chapter 10.

Supply of services

The Sale of Goods Act 1979 applies only to contracts by which a seller transfers property in goods to a buyer. It doesn't apply to contracts for the supply of services or contracts for services and materials like those that are typical within the marketing services sector.

These B2C and B2B agreements for the supply of services and/or services and materials are subject to the Supply of Goods and Services Act 1982 (SGSA 1982), which has legal protections that are very similar in scope to those under the SOGA 1979.

Supply of Goods and Services Act 1982 (SGSA 1982)

The SGSA 1982 implies into a contract for services and materials substantially the same terms as the SOGA 1979 as to:

- title (section 2, SGSA 1982);
- description (section 3, SGSA 1982);
- quality and fitness for purpose (section 4, SGSA 1982); and
- transfer by sample (section 5, SGSA 1982).

The SGSA 1982 implies three terms into contracts for the supply of services whether or not goods are also transferred:

- Where the supplier is acting in the course of a business it will carry out the service with reasonable care and skill (section 13, SGSA 1982).
- Where the supplier is acting in the course of a business and the time for the service to be carried out is not fixed by the contract; left to be fixed in a manner agreed in the contract or determined by the course of dealing between the parties.

- There is an implied term that the supplier will carry out the service within a reasonable time (section 14, SGSA 1982). What constitutes a 'reasonable time' is a question of fact (section 14(2), SGSA 1982). Where the consideration for the service isn't determined by the contract; left to be determined in a manner agreed in the contract or determined by the course of dealing between the parties.

There is an implied term that the party contracting with the supplier will pay the supplier a reasonable charge (section 15, SGSA 1982). What constitutes a 'reasonable charge' is a question of fact (section 15(2), SGSA 1982).

With the exception of the term as to title contained in section 2 of SGSA 1982, which may not be excluded (section 7(3A), Unfair Contract Terms Act 1977 (UCTA)), these terms can be excluded or varied by the express agreement of the parties to the contract or by a course of dealing (section 16, SGSA 1982).

An express term won't exclude an implied term unless it's inconsistent with the implied term (section 16(2), SGSA 1982).

Nevertheless, UCTA 1977 will apply to any attempted restriction or exclusion of these implied terms, so that persons cannot exclude or restrict their liability for death or personal injury resulting from negligence (section 2(1), UCTA 1982) or exclude or restrict their liability for other loss caused by negligence, unless the clause purporting to restrict or exclude such loss passes the test of reasonableness (section 2(2), UCTA 1982).

In this context, there is no distinction between consumer and non-consumer contracts.

Liability for fraud and fraudulent misrepresentation can't be excluded. There is case law that suggests that an exclusion clause that fails to distinguish between fraudulent and non-fraudulent misrepresentation can never be reasonable, and is consequently wholly unenforceable (see 'Misrepresentation' below).

A clause that purports to exclude one party's liability for breach of all its contractual obligations may be held by a court not to create a contract at all, but to take effect merely as a declaration of intent by the seller and not be legally binding on the buyer.

In the event that an exclusion clause is relied on and is found to be unreasonable, it will be wholly unenforceable, with the result that the seller will be liable for all of the buyer's loss recoverable as a matter of contractual law.

It may be prudent for a seller to accept liability for some losses under a contract and therefore qualify the scope of an exclusion clause it wants to rely on, rather than a blanket exclusion clause, as this will have more chance of being seen to be reasonable by the courts and therefore valid. There are two different 'tests' that an exclusion clause will need to pass depending on whether the customer is a business or a consumer (Table 1.1).

As can be seen from Table 1.1, this presents a difficulty for a company or organization that sells to both traders (B2B) and consumers (B2C). One solution favoured by lawyers is for the seller to have two different sets of standard terms and even have these printed on different-coloured paper for B2B and B2C buyers.

The danger of taking this approach revolves around determining whether any particular customer falls within the definition of 'consumer', which, to complicate matters further, is defined differently under UCTA 1977 and the Unfair Terms Regulations.

Table 1.1 Satisfying the tests of reasonableness or fairness

Relevant statutory framework	Business to business (B2B)	Business to consumer (B2C)
UCTA 1977 'reasonableness test'	*UCTA 1977 'reasonableness test' does apply.* Factors relevant to the issue of reasonableness are often specific to the circumstances surrounding each contract. A business can't exclude liability for death or personal injury caused by its negligence. In contrast, a seller could reasonably be expected to accept liability in negligence for damage to tangible property up to a specified limit, as insurance should be easily obtainable in respect of this type of loss. A total exclusion of liability for consequential, financial or indirect losses of the kind frequently used in standard terms is likely to be held unreasonable. In contrast, a clause that places an upper limit on such liability will have a good chance of being held reasonable depending on the amount of such limit.	*UCTA 1977 'reasonableness test' does apply.* However, given that that the court has regard to the circumstances of the parties in determining reasonableness, it follows that what may be reasonable in B2B agreements may not be reasonable in B2C agreements, where the courts often apply a higher or stricter standard given the relative bargaining power of the parties in order to protect the consumer.

Table 1.1 *continued*

Relevant statutory framework	Business to business (B2B)	Business to consumer (B2C)
Unfair Terms Regulations 'fairness test'	*Unfair Terms Regulations 'fairness test' doesn't apply.*	*Unfair Terms Regulations 'fairness test' does apply.* Avoid provisions that allow the seller unilaterally to vary the contract (for example, a provision allowing the seller unilaterally to vary the price of the goods delivered). Such a provision is more likely to be considered fair if it's drafted so as to give the consumer the right to back out without penalty before any variation becomes effective. Remove any restrictions or exclusions that aren't absolutely necessary for the protection of the seller, as they may make the contract as a whole appear to be balanced unduly in favour of the seller, and therefore unfair, without securing a real commercial benefit for the seller. Use plain and intelligible language in the agreement. Where appropriate, give reasons for the inclusion of exclusion clauses in the form of a recital or preamble in the agreement. Ensure that any dispute resolution procedures make it clear that the consumer will ultimately have the right to take the issue to the courts.

If the company deals predominantly with traders but there is a possibility of occasional consumer sales, then a practical approach is to incorporate the usual B2B exclusions but to include a provision stating that, in the event of a transaction with a consumer, the consumer's statutory rights aren't adversely affected.

Alternatively, where the majority of the customers of the company are consumers, it will clearly be necessary to include clauses that are designed to satisfy the 'fairness test' under the Unfair Terms Regulations and the UCTA 1977 reasonableness test as applied to consumers, notwithstanding that it would be possible to justify harsher exclusions in the case of the relatively small number of B2B customers.

Following the decision of the Court of Appeal in the Regus case (2007), an exclusion clause won't necessarily be dismissed if it doesn't exclude obvious and primary measures of loss for the breach. In the Regus case, there was a diminution in value of the services promised by the serviced office space provider.

It follows that exclusion clauses should, as far as possible, be drafted in the form of a series of clauses, sub-clauses and sub-paragraphs, as should one sub-clause be held unreasonable it can be severed from the other provisions of the exclusion clause and these could remain enforceable.

The use of a short preamble or recital at the beginning of a clause explaining the background or reasons for its insertion is likely to be helpful in convincing a court of its reasonableness. For example: 'The seller has obtained insurance cover in respect of its own legal liability for individual claims not exceeding £1,000,000 per claim. The seller's liability is therefore limited to £1,000,000 and the buyer is responsible for making its own arrangements for the insurance of any excess loss.' This assumes that the drafting objective is to produce a clause that satisfies the UCTA 1977 'reasonableness test'.

Unfair Terms in Consumer Contracts Regulations 1999

The Unfair Terms in Consumer Contracts Regulations 1999 (SI 1999/2083) (UTCCR 1999) apply to unfair terms in contracts concluded between a consumer and a seller of goods or a supplier of services.

For the purposes of the UTCCR 1999, the regulations provide that:

- a consumer means a natural person who is acting outside their trade, business or profession (regulation 1);
- a seller or supplier is a natural or legal person who acts in the course of their trade, business or profession (regulation 1); and
- an unfair term is one which hasn't been significantly negotiated and which, contrary to the requirements of good faith, causes a significant imbalance in the parties' rights and obligations under the contract, in favour of the seller or supplier (regulations 1 and 5).

Schedule 2 to UTCCR 1999 contains a list of terms that may be regarded as unfair. This list isn't exhaustive, and therefore all terms in a contract to which UTCCR 1999 applies should be reviewed with their potential unfairness in mind.

Marketing agency agreement

If you work in-house within sales and marketing, then it's likely that at some point you may need to hire an external marketing agency, such as an advertising, sponsorship, events, sales promotions, licensing, merchandising, hospitality, public relations or digital agency.

Irrespective of whether you're on the client or agency side, both parties need to reach a workable agreement that is proportionate to the value of the agreement for the marketing services to be delivered.

Contract for services

Before holding a 'pitch' to determine which agency you would like to work with, whether this is a new arrangement or whether you are looking to re-tender the marketing agency account, it's prudent to carry out a company or bankruptcy search on the agencies you are considering to ensure that they are financially sound.

The description of the supply of services or deliverables sits at the heart of the marketing agency agreement. The agreement needs to explicitly state exactly what the client wants; otherwise it won't be clear what the agency should be delivering, and this could store up problems for the relationship in the future. In a nutshell, the agency agreement needs to cover the services provided and the standard of those services and costs.

If the agreement doesn't cover this at the outset, there needs to be a clear process for defining the services or deliverables under the agency relationship.

It's unwise to rely on a clause that expects the agency to perform according to 'best practice', and it's preferable to spell this out in detail in order to describe the standard of services required.

If the marketing agency has developed the description or narrative of the service to be delivered, ensure that it's fit for purpose and meets your requirements as the client.

Ideally, the process of developing the service description should be collaborative, although this won't always be possible, for example following an EU tender.

Depending on the value of the consultancy services, it's worth considering inserting a provision by which the marketing agency agrees that it's carried out its due diligence in relation to the services it will deliver and consequently it employs a 'no surprises or hidden costs' approach regarding the fees payable for those services. You'll want to avoid a situation where the marketing agency claims that it didn't know that a particular circumstance existed and therefore wants to charge more for its services.

You should also consider continuous improvement in agency performance and how the marketing agency services can be benchmarked over the longer term. Many agencies now expect this to be the norm.

Another important factor is the location of the marketing agency and where it's expected to perform and deliver its services under the agreement and the timescales for the delivery of those services. It's useful to draft an implementation plan with the marketing agency in order to help manage expectations on both sides and maintain a workable relationship.

Although the implementation plan won't form part of the main body of the marketing agency agreement it should include a list of meaningful milestones, the components of each milestone, any particular relevant considerations and dates for completion.

The marketing agency should be under a duty to mitigate any delay in achieving a milestone, and the client should consider making time of the essence for delivery (see below).

As part of the marketing agency agreement, it's wise for the client to give itself enough flexibility to accommodate the changing demands of its employer, so the agreement needs to provide for a flexible change control procedure. As a client, it's prudent to take account of how pricing for these services will be accommodated, as well as any additional consultancy time requirements.

Other key considerations for a marketing agency agreement include:

- Consider the value of entering an exclusive agency agreement where the marketing agency can't work for one of your direct competitors balanced with a non-exclusive agency agreement.

- A mutual non-disclosure clause that protects the use of confidential information.

- Copyright in the material produced, such as photographs, art work and other creative outputs as well as other intellectual property rights (see Chapter 3).

- Attendance at weekly, monthly, half yearly and annual reviews of the performance of the agency according to the milestones and the implementation plan.

- Engagement of an independent third party consultancy to run a 360 degree review annually in the interests of getting the most out of the relationship.

- Typical warranties are expressly included, for example, all services should be performed using reasonable skill and care and in accordance with the agreement and specification, in accordance with all applicable laws and regulations and in compliance with reasonable instructions.

- Ensuring that any briefs (creative briefs should ideally be one page in length) are clear and unambiguous in order to save the time and cost of re-doing work, as well as producing better results faster and at a lower cost.

- Professional indemnity and public liability insurance cover.

- Purchase order needs to be approved prior to any work being commenced.
- Payment terms (this can vary between 30–60 days for fees and 30–60 days in arrears for expenses) and ensure that invoices are properly submitted in order to comply with invoicing and other financial control requirements as well as a penalty interest clause for late payments.
- Consider assignment and subcontracting issues.
- Consider force majeure and try to have the clause restricted to circumstances that are genuinely outside the marketing agency's control.
- Consider warranties and indemnities for goods and other third party.
- Consider duration of the marketing services agreement as well as grounds for termination of the agreement and what events would be fundamental breaches and what events wouldn't amount to fundamental breaches of contract but capable of being remedied.
- Consider jurisdictional issues, choice of law and dispute resolution. In the latter, it's typical in such marketing agency agreements to have a dispute resolution mechanism, such as escalation, and then mediation or arbitration where the costs are borne by both parties.

Digital agency agreement considerations

Creating digital media raises particular issues that aren't generally covered under a standard marketing agency agreement. It's therefore crucial for the client in these cases to use an agreement that contains terms that specifically cover such activities.

For example, two key issues for consideration in using a digital media agency to develop a corporate website are acceptance testing, and transfer and/or licensing of intellectual property (IP) rights in the website and the other digital media created by the agency contained on the website. With respect to acceptance testing, website development is similar to traditional software development in that the digital agency and the client will need to agree a technical and functional specification for a website, and then software (typically html format) is written to create a website that complies with the agreed specification.

To avoid disputes about whether the digital agency has actually delivered what the parties intended, the digital agency agreement should provide for a detailed procedure to test the website to ensure that it complies with the agreed specification. In addition, the agreement should set out the procedures for remedying any errors or defects discovered during the testing process.

With respect to IP rights, the digital agency agreement should set out in sufficient detail which elements of the website are to be licensed to the client and which elements are to be assigned. A licence works rather like a lease, and an assignment is analogous to a sale.

Digital media assets and software in general can be separated into the following:

- materials created for the client by the digital agency or commissioned from third parties during the term of the digital agency agreement (bespoke materials); or
- materials created by the agency or commissioned from third parties prior to the date that the digital agency first supplied services to the client (pre-existing materials); or
- materials owned by third parties and licensed to the agency for onward supply to the client (third-party materials).

Typically, the rights in bespoke materials are assigned to the client. In contrast, the rights in pre-existing materials and third-party materials are licensed to the client by the digital agency or, in some cases of third-party materials, directly by the relevant third-party owner.

From the digital agency's perspective, there are three options with respect to digital assets used in the client's corporate website:

- to acquire the rights to digital media from third parties under a contractual arrangement;
- to license the rights from a relevant third-party owner; and/or
- to create such digital assets within the digital agency using its own employees.

Typically, the acquisition of rights and/or creating the digital media inside the agency would provide the digital agency with all of the rights that it would require to use relevant digital media without restrictions being imposed by third parties.

However, in some cases these options may not be available, in which case the digital agency will be forced to obtain appropriate licences from relevant third-party owners. The contractual terms of such licences to use digital media can be complex and the type of uses granted by the rights owner will typically be very specific, for example that the digital media can only be hosted on a website or alternatively can only be made available to end users as a streamed file, where no permanent copy is made on the user's device, rather than as a download.

The most common form of technological control of digital media rights is known as digital rights management (DRM). This consists of a variety of technological systems that enable rights holders to specify and control how digital media are used, so preventing unauthorized use. Over the last few years, the courts have taken a stronger line against IP infringement and have strengthened the remedies available to rights owners where a user attempts to circumvent DRM systems or makes an article available to others that can be used to circumvent such systems. Such remedies now include criminal penalties (see 'Remedies available for breach of contract' below).

Distributorship agreement

The key point of difference between a distributorship and an agency–principal relationship is that there is no intermediary involved in the latter, so the agency acts on behalf of the principal and will have actual, usual and implied authority to bind the principal in law.

In a distributorship agreement, the company or organization sells its products to the distributor, who then sells the products on to its customers and will add a margin to cover its costs and make a profit. In purchasing and reselling the products, the distributor contracts both with the supplier and with the customer, and title in the products will pass to and from the distributor. In an agency relationship, the contract of sale for the products is made on behalf of the principal rather than for the benefit of the agent.

In the supplier–distributor relationship, the duties owed by the principal and agent to each other are replaced by mutual contractual rights and obligations within the distribution agreement, which is essentially a variation on a sale of goods contract. This has a disadvantage for the supplier in that it exerts less control over the distributor's activities than it would if it were an agency relationship, particularly with regard to the final pricing of the products to retailers or end users. However, in selling the products to a distributor, the seller also passes on a large degree of the risk in the products.

In reselling the products to its customers, the distributor assumes liability for the products and therefore incurs a far larger degree of risk than an agent in the course of its business. This is particularly the case if the distributor isn't fully indemnified by the supplier for any claims brought in respect of the products. The higher level of risk assumed by the distributor is typically reflected in the level of remuneration or margin as compared with the commission earned by an agent. The greater the level of risk that the supplier places on the distributor, the higher the distributor's margin will generally be.

An advantage of appointing a distributor rather than an agent is that the Council Directive (EEC) No. 86/653 on Commercial Agents (Directive) doesn't apply to distribution agreements. Within the UK, there's no requirement to pay compensation to a distributor on termination of the distribution agreement, although this may not always be the case within other countries.

However, EU and UK competition rules, which prohibit anti-competitive agreements and abuse of a dominant position, may potentially have an impact on the appointment of a distributor, whereas they generally don't apply to a genuine agency relationship.

This legislation can have a significant impact on the terms on which a supplier may be able to appoint a distributor, and it's useful to consider this issue at an early stage. In particular, if there's not a 'genuine' agency relationship for the purpose of EU competition law, then a supplier will usually be committing a breach of EU or UK competition rules if it sets the prices or other terms on which the distributor must sell the contract products.

An agency will be genuine if the agent bears no significant financial or commercial risk in relation to its agency activities. In this respect, it is immaterial whether the agent acts for one or several principals, or whether the parties or national legislation categorizes the agreement as an agency relationship.

Typically, there are four flavours of distributorship agreements:

- exclusive distributorship;
- sole distributorship;
- non-exclusive distributorship; and
- selective distributorship.

Exclusive distributorship

An exclusive distributorship is an arrangement whereby a supplier agrees to sell the contract products only to the distributor within a certain defined territory, and agrees not to appoint other distributors or to sell the products directly to other customers within the territory.

Such an arrangement is frequently used to exploit a product within a new territory. The supplier appoints a distributor with local knowledge and usually an established business within the territory. The distributor in turn agrees to take on the high risk and costs associated with promoting a new product in return for the knowledge that, as exclusive distributor, it alone will benefit from the sales and marketing efforts.

The supplier has the advantage of knowing that the distributor will be motivated to sell these products, particularly if a restriction is placed on the distributor prohibiting it from selling competing products. The supplier can use the threat of withdrawing the exclusivity if target sales aren't met by the distributor within a specified period.

Sole distributorship

The term 'sole distributorship' is generally used to describe an agreement whereby a supplier appoints a distributor as its exclusive or sole distributor within a territory, but the supplier reserves the right to supply the products directly to end users. The meaning of the term should always be clarified within the agreement.

Such an arrangement combines the advantages of an exclusive distributorship for the distributor with the advantage for the supplier that it's free to promote the products itself within the territory and to continue to deal with any customers it may have had in the territory before the appointment of the distributor. Such an agreement would contain similar provisions and restrictions to those in an exclusive arrangement, but it would afford more control by the supplier over the territory should the distributor fail to meet the required minimum purchase targets or other key performance measures.

Non-exclusive distributorship

A non-exclusive appointment gives the supplier complete freedom both to sell directly and to appoint other distributors within the territory.

The terms of the appointment will be far less onerous on the distributor than those within an exclusive or sole appointment, as it will need to compete with the supplier and other distributors in terms of both sales and marketing of the product.

Selective distributorship

A supplier, in appointing a distributor as part of a selective distribution system, agrees to appoint additional distributors only if they meet certain criteria. This effectively limits the number of additional distributors who can be appointed within the territory.

Selective distributorship arrangements are perceived as particularly suitable where the nature of the product requires an enhanced level of service or advice at the point of sale to the customer and where the supplier or manufacturer will be required to provide after-sales support. Owing to their potentially exclusionary nature, such arrangements can cause competition law problems. However, examples of products for which a selective distribution system has been held to be justified include high-value cosmetics, pharmaceutical products and electrical goods.

Usually, as part of the arrangement, distributors must also agree to sell on the products only to end users or to other approved distributors. In this way, the supplier retains tight control over the manner in which its products are marketed, and it will generally have greater influence over the marketing of the product provided that EU and UK competition laws are not breached in the process.

Website contract

At some point the organization you work for will appoint a digital agency to help create and manage the corporate website. The global digital marketing industry has developed at lightning speed, and now many marketing managers will seek external specialist help that is sometimes not available in-house.

However, there are a host of issues that are typically encountered when setting up and operating a website, and these issues need to be addressed in the website contract if external agency support is required.

A key issue is search engine optimization (SEO). For a more detailed discussion on best practice on e-marketing, refer to Guru in a Bottle® *High Impact Marketing that Gets Results*.

The objective of a website design and development agreement is to ensure that the company or organization gets the website that it requires by imposing an obligation on the digital agency to create the site according to the company's specifications. The agreement is therefore similar to a general software development agreement for an IT system. However, there are many unique features that need to be carefully considered.

A website is like a house in which every single window is also a door. Visitors may follow links from other websites or be directed by retweets from other users.

Huge amounts of money are spent every year on designing, building and maintaining e-commerce websites like Amazon. Websites for much smaller businesses are just as important for commercial and organizational success and need to be treated in exactly the same way as if they were for major businesses.

With that in mind, the contract should clearly set out the functional and performance specification. It should also set out the requirements in terms of any visible content that the digital agency is to provide. These should include any legal requirements to which the company is subject and which may need to be taken into account in the design of the site content or its performance, for example usability requirements, cookies and privacy issues.

Given that the amount of money that can be spent on such a project is potentially limitless, it's advisable that a budget is agreed upfront before work commences.

As with any IT programme, costs vary depending on the complexity and functionality of the proposed website. It's also useful to ask the digital agency about its SEO process and what will happen at various stages over the length of the project.

Terms and conditions in a typical website agreement

The following is a non-exhaustive list of terms and conditions typically found in most website contracts.

Timetable

The client in this relationship must ensure that the digital agency is contractually bound to meet key milestones, in particular the date for the launch of the site. All too often a site remains partially complete, and it can be a bind to get the digital agency to finish off the job, so holding back the final payment until the job has been delivered satisfactorily ought to be considered.

Provision should also be sought for review of the quality and speed of progress, giving contractual remedies, such as liquidated damages – a pre-determined amount to be paid in respect of failure or delay (see 'Liquidated and unliquidated damages' below).

Payment mechanisms

Typically, payment terms for the web contract can be on a fixed-fee or time-and-materials basis or a combination of both.

From the client's perspective, it's preferable to negotiate a fixed fee for the design work, which will be payable by instalments on successful completion of agreed milestones. As with any other software development contract, a fee calculated on a time-and-materials basis may quickly spiral out of control!

For the digital agency, payment on a time-and-materials basis is often preferable, as this eliminates the need to anticipate all the costs of a particular project in advance. In any event, the web digital agency should always request a substantial proportion of the fees to be payable on signature of the agreement in order to cover initial outlays.

Acceptance tests

It's prudent to test that the website works properly in terms of functionality as well as being able to cope with anticipated usage levels. In addition, it may be necessary to provide for acceptance tests that assess users' reactions to the pilot website in order to carry out any modifications that are necessary.

Whilst it's reasonable for the client to require the website to pass certain specified acceptance tests, the digital agency should give careful consideration to the extent and nature of the tests and should try to retain as much control over the acceptance testing procedure as possible.

Ownership of what is developed

From the client's perspective, it's useful to possess all rights in the design of the web pages and the underlying software of the site.

Under UK law, the digital agency rather than the client owns copyright and other IP rights unless there's an agreement to the contrary that transfers such rights to the client.

A design and development agreement will need to include the transfer of all IP rights in the site or at the very least provide for an exclusive licence of such rights for the client. By ensuring that it owns or has the right to exploit the copyright and related IP rights in all aspects of the web pages, the client can transfer the whole website to another digital agency to complete the project where, for example, the current digital agency has failed to meet its obligations and the client has lost all confidence that the website will be delivered according to specification and on time.

In most cases, the digital agency will agree to transfer ownership of the IP rights developed specifically for the client or to license such rights where it isn't in a position to grant an outright transfer. However, the digital agency should ensure that it doesn't transfer to the client ownership of any IP rights in any underlying software not specifically developed for the client but needed to operate the website. In such a case, the digital agency may grant a licence on a non-exclusive basis permitting the client to use the relevant works in the operation of the website. The client should ensure that any such licence is as wide as possible; for example, the licence should be perpetual and not subject to any territorial restrictions, and there should be an obligation to put appropriate source code escrow arrangements in place.

IP rights infringement

It's common practice for the digital agency to provide the client with some protection against claims that any content or software produced by the digital agency in the course of the development of the website infringes the IP rights of third parties. These could arise either because the digital agency inadvertently uses material it's developed for and assigned to other clients or where it seeks to incorporate third-party works in the design such as photographs, video clips or music for which no permissions have been obtained. Although this is such a basic error that it's unlikely to arise, the client should nonetheless seek an indemnity from the digital agency to cover any liabilities that might arise in the future.

Conversely, the issue of IP rights infringement is also relevant to the digital agency where, as is often the case, the client provides content for inclusion in the website, and the digital agency ought to seek an appropriate indemnity. The reason is that the digital agency won't always assume responsibility for obtaining permissions to use third-party material on the website.

Termination

The client should ensure that all consequences of the termination of the digital agency agreement are adequately provided for and that any outstanding issues, such as whether the digital agency is permitted to place a credit on the site, are agreed.

Policing content

In the situation where the web digital agency is also hosting the website and particularly if the site has a message board or chat room, it will be necessary to apportion responsibility between the client and the digital agency for ensuring that content posted by visitors doesn't contain material that is illegal, defamatory or in conflict with the Committee on Advertising Practice

(CAP) Code, which now extends to content on websites. For further guidance on compliance with the CAP Code, see Chapter 4.

In order to avoid or limit liability, it will be important to ensure that there are obligations in the agreement for the removal of infringing material from the site as quickly as possible.

Maintenance and support

It's important to consider how the website will be maintained and updated after it's been launched. The digital agency may be engaged to do this, in which case it will be necessary to ensure that it's provided with fresh content. Alternatively, the client may want to take over this role itself or appoint a third party to do so, in which case it may be necessary to spell this out in the agreement. Conversely, where the digital agency agrees to provide ongoing and maintenance support it should ensure that the fees payable under the agreement reflect the cost of this additional work.

Website content licences

During the process of designing and developing a website, it will be necessary to consider what different types of content will be required for the website, such as text, photographs, audiovisual media and e-commerce content.

The client may own all the rights in the relevant content, but the more complex the design of the website, the more likely that third-party rights will be involved. In some situations, software applications may be owned by the digital agency, in which case the client will want a transfer or licensing of the necessary rights to it under the website design and development agreement. Where the rights of other third parties are involved, the client will need a licence to use the relevant content in order to avoid infringing those parties' IP rights.

Unlike website design or hosting agreements, which provide for the performance of certain services, an agreement for the provision of website content is a licence of IP rights and as such is quite different in nature.

The following key issues should be addressed in a website content licence:

- *Content to be licensed.* The nature and scope of the content to be licensed should be carefully considered, and if the description is particularly detailed it may be necessary to set it out in a schedule to the website agreement. The content may, for example, constitute the actual substance of the website, or it could be more incidental content. The agreement should also address whether there is any obligation on the licensor to provide content updates.

- *Where the content is to be placed.* The parties to the agreement may be concerned about the placement of the content, for example that it should be placed 'above the fold', that is, the part of a web page that can be viewed without the need for the user to scroll horizontally or vertically through the page, in which case it will be necessary to incorporate appropriate obligations to deal with this. This issue could arise, in particular, where payment under the agreement is dependent on the website's advertising or transaction revenue, in which case the licensor may wish to impose an obligation on the website owner as to the position of the content.

- *Nature of the licence granted.* Both parties should consider carefully the nature of the licence to be granted, for example whether the client requires the licence to be exclusive so that the licensor can't itself use the same content or license it to third parties.

- *Delivery of the website.* Dates should be specified for original content and any updates. Provision should also be made for the way in which the content is to be delivered to the client, for example by delivery of physical materials or providing the client with online access to the relevant materials.

- *Payment mechanisms.* Payment may be made by way of a fixed licence fee payable, for example, at monthly intervals or by means of more complicated revenue share or royalty structures according to which the client agrees to pay the licensor a percentage of all its revenues generated from advertising on the site. Whatever the basis for calculation, the parties should ensure that it's in fact possible to measure and audit the intended multiplier, and the licensor should always request a substantial proportion of the fees to be payable on signature of the agreement to cover its initial outlay.

- *Liability for licensed content.* The client should ensure that the licensor undertakes responsibility for the accuracy and completeness of the licensed content, although the licensor may reasonably expect the client to be responsible for any derivative works created by it. In addition, the client should seek appropriate warranties and indemnities to protect itself against any losses that it might incur for content that is illegal (for example, because it infringes third-party IP rights). For its own protection, the licensor should resist warranting the legality of the content on a worldwide basis and should in any event ensure that, if any allegations or claims are made that any content it supplies is illegal or harmful, it has the right to require the website owner to remove such content from the site so as to minimize its liability.

- *Term.* This is particularly relevant where there is an obligation on the licensor to provide regular updates of the content, since it will want to ensure that it's not committed to providing these indefinitely where, for example, it no longer wishes to offer this as a service to the client.

Website hosting agreements

Once work on the design and development of the website has been completed, the website will need to be hosted on a server. The type of server required will depend on the size and complexity of the website and the number of anticipated users. Owners of large, high-volume websites with a lot of video content that isn't hosted on YouTube, for example, may decide to carry out this hosting function themselves.

In the vast majority of cases, it's preferable to enter into a third-party managed service agreement to host the website. In those cases, typically the website is hosted on the third party's server. The host will provide the link for all traffic between the internet and the web server.

The capacity (size of the 'pipe') will depend on what network services the host itself has access to, the number of other websites that it hosts and the number of users that connect to the host.

The following key issues should be addressed in a website hosting agreement:

- *Scope of services.* In addition to the obligation to make the website available on the web from the designated server, the host might also have obligations to provide certain specified security features, maintenance and support of the website such as updating content or help-desk support, back-up and disaster recovery or statistics relating to usage of the site.

- *Server.* Where the website owner doesn't intend to use its own server, either it will have to rent space on an existing server provided by the host, or the host may be required to supply a suitably configured server. A website hosting agreement should contain a technical specification that will include the specification for the server on which the site is to be hosted.

- *Response times.* The host must provide sufficient bandwidth to ensure that, even during peak access times, the website will be accessible to all users. As with the server, the capacity of the host's connection to the internet should also be addressed in the technical specification that forms part of the hosting agreement.

- *Uptime requirements.* There may be times when the host's server crashes, making the website unavailable to visitors. Equally, even routine maintenance of the equipment will require the server to be unavailable at certain times. The website owner may therefore wish to impose availability (or uptime) requirements, often expressed as a percentage (say 99 per cent) during a specified period, such as a week, a month or a year. This needs careful drafting, and suitably qualified legal advice should be sought.

- *Timetable.* Depending on the complexity of the website and/or the hosting services, it may be necessary to draw up a detailed project timetable in order to ensure that the host is contractually bound to meet important milestones, which might include setting up the site, acceptance testing and commencement of the services. This could also be important where the host will itself be using a third-party supplier in order to provide the hosting services. The host should ensure that any deadlines proposed by the website owner are reasonable.

- *Acceptance tests.* As discussed earlier, acceptance of the hosted site or equipment should also be considered by the website owner. For example, the hosting agreement should enable the website owner to be satisfied that the website performs on the designated servers in accordance with an agreed performance specification, and can deal with anticipated usage levels. In particular, the website owner may wish to provide for the conduct of pilot tests to assess the availability and impact of usage levels on the site before commercial launch. While it's reasonable for the website owner to require the hosting services to pass certain specified acceptance tests, the host should give careful consideration to the extent and nature of the tests, and should try to retain as much control over the acceptance testing procedure as possible.

- *Liability for website content.* The most contentious issue is likely to be that of the potential liability of the host for material on the hosted website. The host will be keen to ensure that its exposure is limited to the task of hosting, and it should generally seek an assurance that the website owner will not include material on the website that infringes anyone else's rights or is defamatory, together with an indemnity to cover any liabilities that may arise. Recent government concerns raised over the way in which riots were organized over social networking websites in August 2011 have led to greater calls for those hosting websites or social networks to be more tightly regulated. The website owner should carefully review such provisions, and it should also ensure that it's not hampered in its ability to manage its legal and moral obligations in removing material that could lead to legal sanctions.

- *Hosting fees.* Typically, these are calculated by reference to the space required to run the website on the host's server and are often charged on a monthly, quarterly and half-yearly basis. The host should request a substantial upfront payment for setting up the site, to be payable on signature of the agreement. The website owner may wish to link payments to the achievement of milestones as set out in the agreement and/or to link some of the ongoing payments to usage of the site. This is more contentious and will generally apply to very large e-commerce websites.

- *Termination.* If it becomes necessary for a website owner to terminate its contract with the host, the website owner will want to ensure that the contract contains provisions that will facilitate a smooth handover to another host. This is where the trouble can really start.

- *Data collected.* The host may collate statistics on the number of unique visitors to the site, as well as other visitor and web analytics. Where the website owner is obliged to pay royalties under a content licence, the hosting contract should impose an obligation on the host to provide statistical reports to the website owner and should address the form, content frequency and timeliness of those reports. The agreement should also allow the website owner to audit the host's records. It's likely the website owner will be required by law to impose specific restrictions on the host as to the processing of personal data under the EU Privacy and Electronic Communications Regulations (see Chapter 7).

Effect of exclusion clauses found in website design, hosting and content licence agreements

As with other types of commercial agreements, the parties to agreements for the creation and management of websites will want to limit their respective liabilities to the other party. Typically, the digital agency, host or content licensor will seek to limit its liability to the client in various ways: exclude all liability for loss of profits and other types of financial loss, and for any consequential losses; and limit liability for other types of losses to an amount equivalent to the fees payable by the website owner in the relevant calendar year, subject to the Unfair Contract Terms Act 1977 (UCTA 1977).

Restrictions on exclusion of liability for breach of contract under section 3 of UCTA 1977 will only apply to a B2B agreement where the client is dealing on the 'written standard terms of business' of the supplier, so they won't apply where the contract is freely negotiated between the supplier and the customer (see earlier discussion on this point on page 17).

The issue for the client is whether to agree to these exclusions and limitations of the supplier's liability.

If the client is contracting on the supplier's standard terms, then one option is not to seek to negotiate clauses excluding or limiting liability, and to proceed on the basis that it can, if necessary, challenge the clause later on the ground that it is contrary to UCTA 1977 and therefore ineffective.

However, unless the client really has no realistic option other than to accept the supplier's terms, it will be somewhat unsatisfactory to proceed with the express intention of challenging a clause at a later date, and so it's preferable to presume the effectiveness of such a clause when undertaking a risk assessment in respect of the agreement in question.

Where, as is often the case, the website design, hosting or content licence agreement is negotiable, the client should seek to widen the scope of the supplier's potential liability as much as possible by, for example:

- deleting the supplier's exclusion of liability for financial and consequential losses or at least making it subject to the overall cap on liability, or specifying in the agreement the types of loss that the client is entitled to recover in the event of a breach, such as the additional costs of having the site designed or hosted, or the content provided, by another supplier, the cost of reconstituting lost data and the costs of lost management time; and

- increasing the overall cap on liability to a higher figure than that proposed by the supplier. The client should always consider making the exclusions and limitations reciprocal, so as to benefit the client as well, although in practice it is of course the supplier who is much more likely to need to rely on them!

Remedies available for breach of contract

The principal judicial remedy in English law is an award of damages. In contractual claims, damages may be claimed as of right whenever a contract has been breached, even where there is no actual loss. However, damages in such a case would be nominal.

Damages are payable in both contract and tort (action against the person) claims. The principal function of damages for both contract and tort is compensation, with damages being assessed according to the claimant's loss, although the method of assessment differs. The concepts of causation, remoteness, contributory negligence and mitigation apply in most cases to limit damages claims, although there are specific rules for contract and tort claims.

In this section, the discussion will be about contractual damages for breach of a legally enforceable agreement.

Types of damages

There are four key types of damages that are relevant in the situation where there's breach of contract:

- compensatory;
- nominal;
- derisory; and
- restitution.

Compensatory damages

These are awarded in respect of the actual losses suffered by the claimant, and the purpose is to compensate the claimant. Where the actual losses are small, then damages will be commensurate.

'Loss' means any harm to the person or property of the claimant and any amount by which the claimant's wealth is diminished as a consequence of the breach. This is the basis on which damages are most usually awarded for breach of contract.

Nominal damages

As its name suggests, nominal damages are small, token sums awarded for breach of contract where the claimant has suffered no loss.

In certain contractual circumstances, it may be possible to establish a breach of contract even though no loss has been caused, for example where a photographer fails to turn up to photograph an event for the client. Nominal damages are useful because they are the peg on which to hang a claim for legal costs.

The general principle in litigation is that costs are awarded in favour of the successful party. It should be remembered, however, that costs are always at the discretion of the court, and there's no guarantee that a successful party will be awarded costs at all.

Nominal damages are rare, and an action for a declaration is often viewed as a more appropriate remedy in circumstances where no loss has been incurred.

Derisory damages

These damages are awarded to indicate the court's disapproval of the reasons why, or the way in which, the claim was brought. The court may acknowledge a technical breach of contract, finding in favour of the claimant on issues of liability, but may not wish to award a sum of any significance.

Restitution damages

These damages aim to remove any gain made by the party in breach of contract. This is an exceptional remedy in the context of contractual claims.

In the Hendrix case (2003), restitution damages were ordered, but subsequent case law indicates that the courts will award these damages only in exceptional circumstances, preferring to award compensatory damages.

Liquidated and unliquidated damages

Where the parties agree by contract that a particular sum is payable on the default of one of the parties, provided that the sum doesn't constitute a penalty it will constitute liquidated damages. Liquidated damages also describe sums expressly payable as liquidated damages under statute.

In all other cases, whether pecuniary or non-pecuniary, where the court quantifies or assesses damages or loss, the damages are known as unliquidated damages.

In English law, the purpose of an award of damages for breach of contract is to compensate the injured party rather than to punish the wrong-doer. There are, however, different tests for measuring damages in contract and tort.

The principal measure of damage in contract is expectation loss but, in some circumstances, reliance loss or restitution damages may be awarded.

Damages in contract seek to put the injured party in the position it would have been in had the contract been performed satisfactorily. In other words, the innocent party may seek to recover profits expected to be received had the contract been performed. This is known as 'expectation loss'. Expectation-based damages will yield substantial recovery where the innocent party has made a good bargain. For example, where X agrees to sell goods to Y for £1,000 and fails to deliver those goods on the delivery date, if at the date of delivery the goods are in fact worth £1,500 Y's damages will be based on the value of the goods that could have achieved this.

Expectation loss is the usual measure for assessing damages for breach of contract. However, provided the innocent party has good reason not to pursue damages for expectation loss, it may be able to recover damages to put it in the position it would have been in if the contract had never been performed (reliance loss). This would compensate the innocent party for expenses incurred and losses suffered in reliance on the contract. The aim is to put the claimant in the same position it would have occupied had the contract never been made, that is, to prevent unjust impoverishment.

A claimant may prefer to claim reliance loss if it made a bad bargain and expectation-based damages wouldn't give rise to substantial recovery. But note that the courts won't permit the claimant to use the reliance measure to escape the consequences of a bad bargain.

An example of where reliance loss would be the appropriate measure is when the claimant may not be able to establish what profits it would have made if the contract had been performed or, indeed, if it would have made any profits at all.

For example, in the Anglia TV case (1971) the Norwich-based TV company entered into a contract with actor Oliver Reed to take part in a film. Reed broke the contract and the film couldn't be made. The claimant was unable to say what the profit would have been had the actor performed the contract. However, the claimant had incurred expenditure and this was recoverable.

Similarly, the cost of wasted management or staff time is recoverable as a head of damage if a claimant can establish that employees had been significantly diverted from their usual activities.

Expectation and reliance loss are mutually exclusive to prevent double recovery. The claimant must choose one or the other and can't claim both.

Damages for breach of contract should usually be recovered on the basis of either loss of profits or wasted expenditure and, where damages are awarded for loss of profits, the sum awarded will be net of any expenses that the claimant would have had to incur in order to earn the profits in question.

In that sense, the claimant may not recover for both lost profits and wasted expenditure. By and large, the reliance measure will be preferable where it's difficult to demonstrate what the claimant would have recovered using the expectation measure.

Legal costs incurred as a result of breach of contract can generally be recovered as damages.

Table 1.2 Remedies for misrepresentation

Possible cause of action	Legal remedy for the buyer
Breach of contract	Damages in contract
Fraudulent misrepresentation	Damages in tort
Negligent misrepresentation under the Misrepresentation Act 1967	Damages in tort
Innocent misrepresentation	Rescission of the contract
Negligent misstatement	Damages in tort

Misrepresentation

In the lead-up to a signed agreement, many representations may be made to the client over a period of time. In some cases those representations are simply 'advertising' the benefits of a particular product or service and won't be intended to form part of the contract with the buyer. On the other hand, there are representations such as statements made by the seller that have an intention to influence the behaviour of the buyer directly. Such representations will carry far more serious and far-reaching consequences for the party making them, particularly if they turn out to be false, untrue or misleading.

Representations in sales literature

Companies and organizations may incur liabilities for statements or representations made in sales and marketing brochures or catalogues that they hadn't intended should form part of the contract.

Liability may arise in several ways:

- Although the general rule is that statements not forming part of a written contract aren't to be regarded as part of that contract, it's only a rule of presumed intention. A court may, on the particular facts of a case, decide that the parties to a contract intended to incorporate statements from sales literature as terms of the contract.

- A statement made in sales literature may be held by a court to be binding on the seller as a term of a collateral contract.

- Such statements by the seller may lead to liability for misrepresentation under the Misrepresentation Act 1967 or at common law. The court in the Indigo case (2003) confirms two points frequently overlooked by sellers of goods and services – for a buyer to claim damages for misrepresentation, the misrepresentation doesn't have to be the only factor that induced the buyer to enter into the contract; and it doesn't necessarily have to be reasonable for the buyer to rely on the misrepresentation, as long as the buyer can prove it did rely on it and the seller ought to have known the buyer was likely to.

The remedies on the part of the buyer to which this may give rise are as follows:

- In the case of a breach of contract or collateral contract, the buyer will be entitled to damages for breach of contract. Such damages are intended to put the buyer in the same position as it would have been in had the contract been performed, so that the buyer is, in effect, compensated for the loss of bargain; and the buyer may also be entitled to terminate the contract and in a sale of goods situation the buyer can reject the goods if there's a breach of a condition of the contract or if there is a breach of an intermediate term of the contract that has particularly serious or damaging consequences.

- In the case of a misrepresentation, the buyer's remedies depend on the nature of the misrepresentation. In fraudulent misrepresentation, the buyer is entitled to rescind the contract and claim damages; in negligent misrepresentation, the buyer can rescind the contract and claim damages, subject in the case of rescission to the discretion of the court; or, in innocent misrepresentation, the buyer can either rescind the contract subject to the discretion of the court or claim damages.

Damages for misrepresentation are intended to put the buyer in the same position as it would have been had the representation not been made: unlike contractual damages, the buyer isn't compensated for his or her loss of bargain. If the misrepresentation is negligent, the buyer may be entitled to damages in negligence on the basis of the House of Lords' ruling in the Hedley Byrne *v* Heller case (1964).

It's not possible to incorporate provisions in a contract that can be guaranteed to prevent a court from giving legal effect to statements or representations in sales literature.

However, a seller should include:

- An exclusion clause that refers expressly to liability for misrepresentation as well as for breach of contract. However, a term that excludes or restricts liability for misrepresentation will be subject to the test of reasonableness, and a term that purports to exclude or limit liability for fraudulent misrepresentation will be void.

- An 'entire agreement' clause, stating that the written contract contains all the terms of the agreement between the parties. This will deter a buyer from seeking to raise the argument that a particular representation has legal effect in the first instance. However, in light of the recent judgment of the Court of Appeal in the AXA Sun Life Services case (2011), such a statement won't exclude the seller's liability in misrepresentation. In order to get round this, sellers generally include a statement in the entire agreement clause saying that neither party has relied on statements or representations made by the other, or a complete exclusion of non-contractual remedies for pre-contractual representations. It should be noted that such an exclusion clause is subject to the reasonableness test.

A buyer's standard purchase terms may make it an express term that the buyer is placing reliance on pre-contractual representations of the seller.

In contracts with consumers, public statements about a product made by the seller, the manufacturer or the manufacturer's representative – particularly in advertising or labelling – will be used in determining whether the product is of satisfactory quality.

Oral representations

A company or organization may incur liabilities in circumstances where sales and marketing employees have made inaccurate or unsustainable statements about products. The courts may, as in the case of statements made in sales literature, find that such statements are contractually binding on the company, either as an additional term of the parties' contract or as a collateral contract. Alternatively, the company may be liable in misrepresentation for such statements.

A seller may attempt to exclude or restrict liability in these circumstances by including the following clauses in its standard terms:

- a clause that restricts the authority of sales staff to make statements binding on the seller and which has the same effect as an exclusion clause; or
- an exclusion clause that refers expressly to liability for misrepresentation; or
- an entire agreement clause.

The distinction between representations and terms is important because each gives rise to different remedies for breach. The intention of the parties determines whether a statement is a term or a representation. Factors that will be considered in examining their intention are the timing and importance of the statement and the relative knowledge of the parties. For a detailed discussion on misrepresentation, see Chapter 2.

References

Cases and judgments

Anglia Television *v* Reed [1971] 3 All ER 690
AXA Sun Life Services plc *v* Campbell Martin Ltd and others [2011] EWCA Civ 133

Barbudev *v* Eurocom Cable Management Bulgaria [2011] EWHC 1560 (Comm)
BSkyB Limited and another *v* HP Enterprise Services UK Limited (formerly Electronic Data Systems Limited) and another [2010] EWHC 86 (TCC)
Clegg *v* Olle Andersson (T/A Nordic Marine) [2003] EWCA Civ 320
Experience Hendrix *v* PPX Enterprises Inc [2003] EWCA Civ 323
Hedley Byrne & Co *v* Heller & Partners [1964] AC 465
Indigo International Holdings Ltd and another *v* The Owners and/or Demise Charterers of the vessel 'Brave Challenger'; Ronastone Ltd and another *v* Indigo International Holdings Ltd and another [2003] EWHC 3154
McMeekin and another *v* Long and another [2003] 29 EG 120
Petromec Inc *v* Petroleo Brasileiro SA Petrobas [2005] EWCA Civ 891
Raiffeisen Zentralbank Osterreich AG *v* Royal Bank of Scotland plc [2010] EWHC 1392 (Comm)
Regus (UK) Ltd *v* Epcot Solutions Ltd [2007] EWHC 938 (Comm)
Thomas Witter Ltd *v* TBP Industries Ltd [1996] 2 AII ER 573

Websites

A survey of IT providers and clients by Vanson Bourne [accessed 26 August 2011] http://www.vansonbourne.com
Cloud Industry Forum website [accessed 26 August 2011] http://www.cloudindustryforum.org

Books

Kolah, A (2013) *High Impact Marketing that Gets Results*, Kogan Page, London
Kolah, A (2013) *The Art of Influencing and Selling*, Kogan Page, London

"Guaranteed to drive women wild or your money back"

Making statements in sales and marketing

In this chapter

- Definitions of tortious liability
- Distinction between contract and tort
- Remedies in contract not available in tort
- Negligent misstatements
- Misrepresentation made in sales and marketing contracts
- Fraudulent misrepresentation
- Negligent misrepresentation
- Innocent misrepresentation
- Remedies for misrepresentation
- Defamation
- Remedies for defamation
- Tort of malicious falsehood

Introduction

The temptation to push the boundaries in sales and marketing is great given that differentiation between products and services has become so blurred that customers are screening out rather than screening in brand messages.

One of the biggest marketing challenges today is to be able to win the trust and confidence of purchasers whether in a business-to-business (B2B) or business-to-consumer (B2C) context as a prerequisite for selling to them.

When making statements to potential customers or clients, sales and marketing professionals must ensure that such statements are true and that the standards expected of them must be adhered to in order to avoid an action in tort.

Definitions of tortious liability

Liability in tort arises where the brand owner breaches a duty imposed by law as opposed to obligations set out in a contract. Such a breach entitles anyone who has suffered as a result of the breach to bring an action for damages to compensate for the loss and/or injury suffered.

Under UK law, tortious liability includes actions for:

- deceit;
- negligence (including misstatements and misrepresentations);
- defamation (slander and libel);
- trade libel;
- malicious falsehood; and
- a breach of statutory duty (for example, breach of the brand owner's obligations under the Consumer Protection Act 1987).

These different heads of tort are all relevant to the brand owner's obligations and potential liabilities to both the customer and the client.

Although there may be some overlap in potential actions that can be pursued by a claimant, for example in defamation and malicious falsehood, it's essential that a brand owner has a clear grasp of the evidential hurdles that need to be overcome in order for any such action to be successful against it.

In the examples given in this chapter, the term 'brand owner' is taken to include the manufacturer or supplier and not just the retailer or marketer.

Distinction between contract and tort

A contractual claim is based upon the rights and obligations determined by reference to the express or implied terms of the contract (see Chapter 1).

On the other hand, a claim in tort relies upon duties placed upon the brand owner by law.

Where the claimant has entered into a contract with a brand owner, it may have the right to pursue a remedy in both contract and tort.

Importance of distinguishing between how damages are measured

Where liability arises in both contract and tort, the claimant is entitled to elect to pursue an action under both or select one of the two. The choice will often depend upon the damages recoverable.

This is a hypothetical example based on a real case.

A young woman seeking breast enhancement reads an advertisement: 'Boob job – have you had yours done yet?' The advertisement prominently features an expensive-looking container for 'breast enhancement' cream Boob Job Gel and also claims that a leading Hollywood actress uses this stuff, priced at £130 for a small tub.

The customer sends off for more information and receives a sales pack and order form, both of which repeat the claims prominently that Boob Job Gel will enlarge breasts by 2.5 centimetres simply by massaging it into the skin every day for several weeks.

The customer then sends off for the product, but after she has used it for several weeks there's no evidence that it has significantly increased the volume and firmness of her breasts. In fact, it has made her sore, and she's forced to take a week off from running her flower market stall and loses takings as a result.

In this example, if the claimant is successful, damages will be awarded to compensate her for the loss suffered as a result of the brand owner failing to perform, or failing to perform properly, an obligation under the contract. Therefore, damages in contract put the claimant in the position that she would have been in had the contract been performed in accordance with its terms.

Damages in tort, however, seek to place the claimant in the position that she would have been in had she never suffered the wrongful conduct of the brand owner. In this example, compensation could be payable for the pain and suffering endured as a consequence of applying Boob Job Gel and the loss of earnings as a result of being off sick for a week.

The example may be far-fetched, but in fact this type of claim is very common, particularly in the United States and Canada.

As discussed later in this chapter, public authorities are quick to clamp down on brand owners that try to make statements or claims that are not defendable and are deceptive.

Remedies in contract not available in tort

The claimant may wish to seek a remedy other than damages, and this can include:

- *specific performance* – the brand owner must deliver the product or service as promised;
- *rescission* – the contract is deemed never to have been entered into, each party returns what it has received from the contract and therefore no claims can be made against the claimant by the brand owner for non-payment of goods or services; or
- *restitution* – the claimant is put in exactly the same position it was in before it entered the contract (similar to the usual remedy in tort).

These remedies are available only in contract, and before commencing a legal action the claimant should consider whether there are any financial benefits of pursuing one form of relief above another.

Scope of liability

In choosing whether to commence an action in tort or contract against a brand owner, the claimant will need to assess the scope of the brand owner's liability under each head. A claimant may find that a claim in tort will allow it to recover for loss outside of what is recoverable according to the brand owner's obligations under the contract.

Contributory negligence

In a claim for breach of an absolute obligation under a contract, the brand owner can't rely on the principle of 'contributory negligence' to reduce the quantum of damages awarded.

Where the claimant pursues an action in tort, however (or contract where the claimant could have brought a separate action in tort), it's open to the brand owner to allege that the claimant has contributed to its own loss, thereby reducing the level of damages payable.

Negligent misstatements

A negligent misstatement action is brought at common law where the brand owner owes a duty of care to the claimant and carelessly makes a false statement that is then relied on and as a result of which the claimant suffers loss.

A claim for negligent misstatement may arise whether or not a contractual relationship exists between the parties, although if there's a contractual relationship it's more likely that a claim would be brought for negligent misrepresentation (see 'Negligent misrepresentation' below).

In a claim for negligent misstatement, the claimant must prove the following three requirements on a balance of probabilities:

- *Duty of care.* The brand owner owed the claimant a duty of care to not carelessly cause the type of harm suffered. This is potentially the most difficult requirement to satisfy.

- *Breach.* The brand owner breached the duty owed. The standard of care owed is a question of law. The question of whether the brand owner fell below the required standard is a question of fact in each case.

- *Causation.* The claimant has suffered loss that was caused by the brand owner's breach of duty.

Where there's a contractual relationship between the brand owner and the claimant, the brand owner may owe a duty in contract as well as in tort. This means that an action could be brought for negligent misrepresentation under the Misrepresentation Act 1967.

In such cases it's likely that a claimant would prefer to bring an action for misrepresentation rather than an action for negligent misstatement, for the following reasons:

- *Evidential burden.* For negligent misstatement, the burden of proof is on the claimant to establish that a duty of care existed. There's no such requirement in an action for negligent misrepresentation under the Misrepresentation Act 1967. Provided the claimant establishes that the statement was false, the burden of proof is then on the brand owner to prove that it had reasonably believed that the statement was true (section 2(1), Misrepresentation Act 1967).

- *Calculation of damages.* The normal remoteness test applies in a negligent misstatement claim, so damages will be awarded only in respect of those losses that were reasonably foreseeable. For negligent misrepresentation under the Misrepresentation Act 1967, damages are awarded on the same basis as for fraud, so the rule of remoteness in this context extends to all direct losses.

- *Rescission.* In a claim for negligent misrepresentation, the remedy of rescission may be available in addition to damages. This means that the court may order that the contract be set aside and the parties be put in the position in which they were before the contract was entered into.

Test for establishing a duty of care

There's no single comprehensive test for determining whether a duty of care exists in any particular case. Over the years, the courts have used a number of different tests to establish whether a duty of care is owed in tort by one party to another.

Caparo Industries *v* Dickman (1990)

The House of Lords judgment in this case established the principal test to be applied in cases of economic loss:

- *Foreseeability.* Was it reasonably foreseeable that the conduct of the brand owner would cause loss to the claimant? This incorporates two elements: whether the loss is of a type that was reasonably foreseeable; and whether the claimant is one of a class of person that could reasonably be foreseen to suffer such loss.
- *Proximity.* This concerns the relationship between the claimant and the brand owner. Was there a sufficient degree of proximity? This is sometimes referred to as the existence of a 'special relationship'.
- *Fairness.* Would it be fair, just and reasonable to impose a duty of care in such a situation?

Each one of these criteria must be satisfied to establish that the brand owner owed the claimant a duty of care.

A duty to take care when making a statement may arise, broadly, where:

- the information and advice contained in the statement were required for a purpose and the brand owner knew, or should have known, the purpose for which its advice might be used;
- the claimant is a person (or a member of an ascertained class) whom the brand owner knew, or should have known, might use the information and advice for that purpose;
- the brand owner knew, or should have known, that the claimant was likely to act on the information and advice for that purpose without independent inquiry; and
- the claimant so acted on the information and advice to its detriment.

The principle of 'assumed responsibility' in many cases involving negligence and negligent misstatement is decided as a question of fact and is dependent on a number of factors:

- The precise relationship between the brand owner giving the information and advice and the recipient.
- The precise circumstances in which the advice or statement or other information came into existence. Any contract or other relationship with a third party will be relevant.
- The precise circumstances in which the advice or other information was communicated to the recipient, and for what purpose(s) and whether the communication was made by the brand owner or by a third party. It will be necessary to examine: the purpose of the communication as seen by both the brand owner and the recipient; the degree of reliance that the brand owner intended or should reasonably have anticipated would be placed on its accuracy by the recipient; and the reliance in fact placed on it.
- The presence or absence of other advisers on whom the recipient relied or could have relied.
- The opportunity, if any, given to the brand owner to issue a disclaimer.

Causation

To bring a successful claim in tort, it's necessary for the claimant to prove that it suffered loss that was caused by the brand owner's breach of duty. This includes two legal principles:

- *Factual causation.* The so-called 'but for' test is the starting point. The court asks itself whether, but for the brand owner's actions, the claimant would have suffered loss.
- *Remoteness or legal causation.* The claimant is able to recover only loss that the court considers was reasonably foreseeable.

Exclusion of liability

No duty of care is owed where the terms on which someone is prepared to give advice or make a statement excludes any assumption of responsibility, if permitted under law.

As a matter of common law, a brand owner may seek to exclude or limit any potential tortious liability for negligent misstatement by:

- entering into an express contractual provision excluding or limiting liability; or
- giving notice that the statement is made on the basis that the recipient agrees to exempt the brand owner from liability; or

- issuing a disclaimer that the brand owner undertakes no responsibility for the information or advice provided.

The Unfair Contract Terms Act 1977 (UCTA 1977) could restrict the brand owner's ability to limit or exclude liability in any of these ways (see Chapter 1).

Use of disclaimers

Disclaimers may not be effective in relation to negligent misstatements for a number of reasons; for example:

- They may be too narrowly worded and omit persons to whom a duty of care may be owed.
- Where they are contractual, they may be outlawed by UCTA 1977. Section 2(2) of UCTA 1977 provides that a person can contractually exclude or restrict liability for negligence only to the extent that this satisfies the requirement of reasonableness. The reasonableness test is set out in section 11(1) of UCTA 1977 that the term must be 'fair and reasonable' having regard to the circumstances which or should have been known or in the contemplation of the parties when the contract was made. (Under section 2(1) of UCTA 1977, it's not possible to exclude liability for death or personal injury arising from negligence.)
- They may be overridden by the actual behaviour of the person seeking to deny liability.

The most effective element of a disclaimer may be that part that denies reliance and breaks the 'special relationship'.

The absence of a disclaimer may be a relevant circumstance that the court will take into account when considering whether there has been an assumption of responsibility in respect of advice given.

Damages

Damages will be awarded using a similar approach as for other tortious liabilities: putting the claimant in the position that it would have been in had the tort never occurred.

The client or third party is entitled to recover for any financial loss suffered as a result of the reliance on the misstatement, which may be the only loss suffered.

The loss sustained must be both a reasonably foreseeable consequence of the brand owner's breach of duty and a loss that the brand owner had a duty to prevent the claimant from incurring.

The damages suffered may be reduced by a proportion to take account of contributory negligence in cases where the negligence of the claimant has been a factor in causing the loss. Where it's been found that there was an assumption of responsibility, it's unlikely that contributory negligence will be relevant in all cases.

Limitation

Even the best claim will fail if it's not commenced within the relevant limitation period. Limitation is a specific defence that a brand owner must plead and prove, on the balance of probabilities, if it's to succeed.

The general rule is that a claimant has six years to bring a claim in tort from the time it suffers damage as a result of a brand owner's negligence (section 2, Limitation Act 1980). This can be contrasted with the general rule that a claimant has six years to bring a claim in contract from the time when the contract was breached (section 5, Limitation Act 1980).

Misrepresentation made in sales and marketing contracts

This chapter deals with misrepresentation in the context of a statement made in sales and marketing contracts.

As discussed in this section, the law of contract provides relief for misrepresentation, but it can also be an actionable tort as a negligent misrepresentation.

During the negotiations leading to the formation of a contract, many things are said by the brand owner. Some will be mere 'sales puffs', which have no legal effect; other statements made will amount to representations that are actionable in law.

A representation can take three forms:

- a statement of opinion that doesn't become a term of the contract;
- a statement that may induce the purchaser to enter into the contract; and
- a statement that becomes a term of the contract.

Such statements can be made orally, for example on the telephone, or in writing, for example by e-mail.

The distinction between a representation and a term in a sales and marketing contract is important, because each gives rise to different remedies for breach.

The intention of the parties determines whether a statement is a term or a representation. Factors that will be considered in examining the intention are the timing and importance of the statement and the relative knowledge of the parties at the time the agreement was made.

Representations

Representations are typically statements about existing facts. They may also be statements about the belief, opinion or intention of the maker, where what was said amounts to a statement of fact about the belief, opinion or intention held by the maker.

For example, an advertising account director says to a client that she believes if the client places its Christmas advertising promotion with the agency it will be done on time. As a result and in reliance on this statement, the client places an order for Christmas products for its store, which it pays for in advance with its supplier, who arranges a special delivery in time for the Christmas promotion. The account director in fact didn't know whether the promotion could be completed or not when she said she believed it could.

The contract is entered into by the client, and five days later the client telephones the advertising agency to see the artwork for the promotion. The account director tells the client that the artwork has been done for the advertising when in fact it's still waiting to be done. The client asks to see this within the hour, and the account director goes 'missing'.

Another fours hour later, the client speaks to the managing director of the advertising agency and discovers that there was never any hope of the work being done before Christmas. The client misses the deadline for running the Christmas sales promotion and loses business as a result.

In such an example, there is a clear-cut case of misrepresentation, and the losses flowing from that misrepresentation are fully recoverable.

Where misrepresentation is implied

The court may find that a representation has been implied by an express statement. In a claim based on an implied representation, the court must consider what a reasonable person would have inferred was being implicitly represented by the brand owner's words and conduct in its context.

As a result, it's necessary to consider the context in which an alleged misrepresentation was made, including the characteristics of the party to whom the representation is being made. It must be shown that such a party understood the statement in the sense that the court ascribes to it and that it relied on such representation.

Zentralbank Osterreich AG v Royal Bank of Scotland plc (2010)

In this case, the High Court considered it was a material fact that each of the parties had sophisticated commercial experience. In addition, the way in which one of the implied representations was pleaded was unclear, the 'elasticity of possible meaning' militated against the possibility of misrepresentation having been made, and the claim against the Royal Bank of Scotland was dismissed.

In any claim that seeks to establish an implied misrepresentation, it's important to draft pleadings very carefully to ensure the alleged representation is clear and specific. A misrepresentation can be implied or be a 'representation by conduct' if there's representation that there exists some state of facts different from the truth.

Spice Girls Limited *v* Aprilia World Service (2002)

In this case, the Court of Appeal held that the Spice Girls (SGL) had made an implied misrepresentation when they continued with arrangements to publicize the defendant's products despite knowing that band member Geri Halliwell intended to leave the group shortly, which would prevent the contract being carried out.

In 1998, the band entered into a contract with Aprilia World Service (AWS) whereby AWS would sponsor the Spice Girls' European Tour in exchange for royalties and endorsement rights in relation to a motor scooter named 'Spice Sonic'. It was envisaged that such rights would be of value until March 1999. The Spice Girls were described as 'currently comprising' five members.

Negotiations took place prior to the agreement, and the parties commenced performance of the contract under non-binding heads of agreement before the formal agreement was made. In that period all five Spice Girls took part in photo shoots and a commercial shoot knowing that AWS intended to market the Spice Sonic bearing images of all them. In correspondence, the Spice Girls' agent also underlined the band's commitment to making the sponsorship deal work.

Before the commercial was made (and before the parties entered into the formal contract), Geri Halliwell informed the other members and management of her intention to leave the group at the end of September 1999. The band's company SGL didn't inform AWS.

Following the split, SGL made a claim for unpaid royalties, and AWS counterclaimed for the loss arising from the misrepresentation that none of the group had an existing intention to leave.

In January 2002, the Court of Appeal held that SGL had represented expressly and implied by its conduct that none of the group had an existing intention to leave. It was clear that AWS wouldn't have entered into the contract had it known that Geri Halliwell had other plans, and it had suffered loss as a result.

It was accepted, however, that AWS couldn't recover costs incurred before the formal contract was made, and the claim was limited to the cost of providing certain motorcycles to the Spice Girls under the contract.

Reliance

For a misrepresentation to be actionable, it must have induced the buyer to enter into the contract. If the buyer knew the statement was a misrepresentation but didn't rely on it, it can't claim that the misrepresentation induced it to enter into the contract.

Reliance on a misrepresentation is a question of fact. The burden of proof lies on the defendant to the misrepresentation action; in other words, it needs to prove that there wasn't a misrepresentation that was relied on by the claimant.

The question as to whether a statement amounts to a representation capable of founding a claim in misrepresentation has to depend on the words involved in the context in which they were used. Until the conclusion is reached that there's an actionable representation, no question of liability for misrepresentation should arise.

If the buyer has the opportunity to discover the truth, this doesn't prevent the statement from being a misrepresentation. The appropriate test is whether there's actual and reasonable reliance on the misrepresentation.

According to recent case law on this issue, the courts have held that, to defend a claim in misrepresentation successfully, it's not necessary to show that any representation was entirely correct; establishing that it was 'substantially correct' may be sufficient. The courts will consider whether the difference between what was represented and what was actually correct is likely to have induced a reasonable person in the position of the claimant to enter into the contract.

Zentralbank Osterreich AG v Royal Bank of Scotland plc (2010)

In this case, the High Court ruled that, when considering the test of falsity, the claimant had to show that the 'difference between what was represented and the truth would have been likely to induce a reasonable person in its position to enter into the contract'. The claimant failed in its action against RBS as it was unable to show that any of the statements made by RBS had been false.

Materiality

The misrepresentation need not be the only matter that induces the other party to enter into the contract, but other than in cases of fraudulent misrepresentation or breach of warranty the buyer must be materially influenced by the misrepresentation. This means that the misrepresentation must be such that it would affect the judgment of a reasonable person in deciding whether to enter into the contract and on what terms; or the misrepresentation must be such that it would induce the buyer to enter into the contract without making inquiries that it would otherwise make.

This requirement of materiality doesn't have to be shown in cases of fraud or where the contract warrants the truth of the pre-contractual statement.

Silence

In a sales and marketing context, silence doesn't usually amount to a misrepresentation, as there's generally no duty to disclose facts that if known would affect the other party's decision to enter the contract.

Exceptions to this general rule are:

- misrepresentation by conduct by the brand owner;
- where the brand owner makes a statement that is a half-truth – a statement that may be true as to what's said but that becomes a misrepresentation by virtue of what's left unsaid;
- where the brand owner makes a statement that's true when it's made but before the contract is made the circumstances change so that the statement is no longer true. In this situation, the party that made the statement has a duty to tell the other party about the change, and failure to do so will amount to a misrepresentation.

Intention to induce the purchaser

It's common practice to argue that the brand owner made the representation with the intention of inducing the claimant to enter into a contract or with the intention that the claimant should rely on it. Some lawyers argue that this is essential only where deceit is alleged (see below). However, it's good practice for the claimant to allege the intention to induce, and it's particularly relevant when intention is a live issue, for example where it's said that the representation wasn't addressed to the claimant or to a class of persons of whom the claimant was one, or that it wasn't intended to be acted on for the purposes of the transaction into which the claimant entered. However, the courts accept that the requirement of inducement is less easy to apply in respect of implied rather than express statements, because the brand owner may not at the time appreciate what a court later holds to be the implications of those statements. However, if the brand owner intended what it said to be relied on by the claimant in deciding whether to contract, then the court must regard the brand owner as having intended that the claimant should rely on the objective meaning of the statement.

Types of misrepresentation

There are three types of misrepresentation:

- fraudulent (deceit);
- negligent; and
- innocent.

Fraudulent misrepresentation

An action for fraudulent misrepresentation is founded in the tort of deceit. It occurs where a false representation has been made knowingly or without belief in its truth or recklessly as to its truth.

There is no fraud if the brand owner honestly believes its statement to be true. Mere negligence in making a false statement doesn't amount to fraud.

The claimant must prove absence of honest belief to succeed in an action for fraudulent misrepresentation. It's enough to show that the brand owner suspected that its statement might be inaccurate, or that it neglected to make enquiries, without proving that it actually knew that it was false.

It's not necessary to establish any dishonest motive.

If the statement is ambiguous, the claimant must first prove that it understood the statement in a false sense. If the brand owner intended the statement to have that effect, then it will be guilty of fraud.

Note that sellers of residential property should take great care to avoid making fraudulent misrepresentations on the Seller's Property Information Form (SPIF).

A successful claim for fraudulent misrepresentation arose where the sellers had fraudulently indicated on the SPIF that there were no neighbour disputes and had stated orally that 'the neighbours were good and friendly', when in fact this wasn't the case. The claimants relied on these representations and wouldn't have bought the property if they had known the true position.

The simplicity of the questions on the SPIF and the obviousness of the disputes with neighbours will lead a court to conclude that the answers to the questions weren't given merely recklessly or carelessly, and the sellers would be held liable in damages for fraudulent misrepresentation.

Renault UK v Fleetpro and others (2007)

In this case, car company Renault (the claimant) alleged fraudulent misrepresentation/deceit by the defendants Fleetpro and others in that they had sold Renault cars at a discount to parties outside a marketing affinity scheme, having represented that they would sell the cars only to members of the scheme.

The High Court found that from a certain point in time the claimant's agents had knowledge of the deceit or 'turned a blind eye' to it, but held that such knowledge couldn't be attributed to the claimant. This was notwithstanding the fact that the claimant had at no stage pleaded that its agent had been deceiving it.

On this basis, defendants alleging knowledge of agents in fraudulent misrepresentation cases need to consider additional claims against such agents for a contribution or indemnity from the outset, regardless of the pleading of a claimant. The Renault case also clarifies that it's possible in principle in law to find a person liable in deceit if the fraudulent misrepresentation was made to a machine rather than to a human being.

BSkyB *v* HP Enterprise Services (2010)

In this case the High Court found that the IT supplier EDS (now Hewlett-Packard) made fraudulent misrepresentations about its ability to deliver a project within the stipulated timescale when it pitched for a US$76 million contract to build, design and implement a customer relationship management (CRM) system for BSkyB.

As a result of this case, lawyers advise clients to allege deceit and/or fraud against service providers in the hope that the action could be successful. Conversely, service providers of all kinds now scrutinize the terms and conditions when tendering for contracts in order to ensure they can justify and provide supporting evidence for statements and claims made in sales and marketing. This may mean that large tendering exercises in the future will become much more cumbersome and lengthy, and suppliers may need to increase their fees in order to reflect an increased perception of risk attached to such tenders.

Defences to allegation of fraudulent misrepresentation

There may be a defence under section 6 of the Statute of Frauds (Amendment) Act 1828, which provides:

> *Action not maintainable on representations of character etc,*
> *unless they be in writing signed by the Party chargeable. No action*
> *shall be brought whereby to charge any person upon or by reason*
> *of any representation or assurance made or given concerning or*
> *relating to the character, conduct, credit, ability, trade, or dealings*
> *of any other person to the intent or purpose that such other person*
> *may obtain credit, money, or goods upon, unless such representation*
> *or assurance be made in writing, signed by the Party to be charged*
> *therewith.*

The mischief that this section was designed to address was that, at the time the 1828 Act was passed, potential claimants were seeking to bring actions for misrepresentation against defendants who had made casual statements about other people's financial standing or probity in conversation or otherwise orally.

The 1828 Act is still in force today, and a modern interpretation indicates that the courts are concerned with proving by evidence the existence of a representation and not with excusing fraudulent behaviour. Section 16 will clearly be satisfied if the representation is contained in an e-mail provided that the e-mail includes a written indication of who is sending the e-mail and that it has been 'signed' in some way.

Where a director of a company makes a fraudulent misrepresentation intending another person to rely upon it and that party does so, the director will be personally liable irrespective of the fact that he or she is director of a company.

More problematic are statements about the future or promising to do something in the future.

Tudor Grange Holdings Ltd *v* Citibank NA (1992)

In this case, the court held that a representation as to future conduct has no effect unless it constitutes a contract. That said, the court also recognized that a statement as to the future may involve an implied representation as to the present (most commonly, as to the defendant's belief in the truth of its prediction).

Furthermore, where a statement is true when it's made but ceases to be true to the knowledge of the defendant before the contract is entered into, a failure to inform the claimant of the change in circumstances will amount to a representation, subject to certain circumstances.

This was the inference drawn in the Spice Girls case (discussed above).

In a more recent case, the High Court dismissed a claim by the tenants of a motorway services facility for damages for fraudulent misrepresentation.

FoodCo UK LLP and others *v* Henry Boot Developments Ltd (2010)

In this case, the claimants alleged that they were induced to enter into their respective leases by various fraudulent misrepresentations made by the defendant relating to the features of the planned development.

The judge concluded that the defendant had an honest belief in the predictions it had made and that, therefore, none of the key representations were false when made. The judge further held that a duty to correct would arise only if the defendant knew that previous representations it had made had become false, or didn't care whether previous representations had become false.

In most cases, a prediction about the future, particularly in the context of contractual negotiations, would be understood as implicitly representing that the maker of the prediction had an honest belief in it. If the maker of the prediction doesn't have an honest belief in the prediction at the time it makes it, then it will have made a false representation of fact.

In other cases, further implications may be appropriate. For example, it may be that the representation would necessarily be understood as meaning that the prediction is based on reasonable grounds, or that the maker of the prediction has the present intention to do what it can do to make it come true.

In the judgment of Lewison J, in order for the claimant to show fraudulent misrepresentation, the burden of proof will be much higher: 'It is not enough that objectively viewed a prediction would be understood by the representee (claimant) as implicitly representing that the maker of the prediction (defendant) had reasonable grounds for making the prediction. It is also necessary to show that the representor understood that representation in that sense.'

Lewison J didn't accept that the Court of Appeal decision in the Spice Girls judgment provided authority for the proposition that a person who makes a statement about the future necessarily implies that it doesn't know of 'any matter' that 'might' falsify the statement.

Since that case, the courts appear to take the view that, in order to find negligent misrepresentation, the statement made by the defendant needs to be viewed from the perspective of what a reasonable person in the position of the claimant would understand by the words used in their particular context.

Negligent misrepresentation

Negligent misrepresentation is often confused with negligent misstatement (see 'Negligent misstatements' above), but the key point of difference to remember is that negligent misrepresentation as defined by section 2(1) of the Misrepresentation Act 1967 applies to any form of misrepresentation between contracting parties, whereas an action for negligent misstatement may apply whether or not a contractual relationship exists and can be brought at common law or tort.

It's possible that a concurrent duty may be owed in contract and in tort, and therefore a claimant party could choose to bring an action for negligent misstatement in the law of tort instead of an action for misrepresentation under the Misrepresentation Act 1967.

A negligent misrepresentation under the Misrepresentation Act 1967 occurs where a statement is made by one contracting party to another carelessly or without reasonable grounds for believing its truth. The test is an objective one, and there's no requirement to establish fraud. Once the claimant proves that the statement was in fact false, it is for the brand owner of the statement made to establish that it reasonably believed in the truth of the statement. The burden of proof is reversed in an action for negligent misrepresentation compared to the position of fraudulent misrepresentation, where the burden on proof is on the claimant.

Section 2(1) of the Misrepresentation Act 1967 creates a right to damages where a person has entered into a contract as a result of a misrepresentation made by another party and suffers loss as a result, in circumstances where the claimant would have been entitled to recovery if the misrepresentation hadn't been fraudulent, unless the brand owner can prove that it had reasonable grounds to believe, and did believe, up to the time the contract was made that the representation was true.

This burden of proof may be difficult for the claimant to satisfy, and therefore an action for negligent misrepresentation may be a better option for the claimant to pursue, as it needs only to show that it entered into a contract with the brand owner after the misrepresentation had been made, and the claimant doesn't need to establish a special relationship giving rise to a duty of care, which it would need to do if the action was a negligent misstatement claim.

Note that section 2(1) of the Misrepresentation Act 1967 doesn't apply where the brand owner isn't the other party to the contract or its agent.

Innocent misrepresentation

Innocent misrepresentation describes only a situation where a misrepresentation has been made entirely without fault. In such circumstances, the brand owner will need to show that it had reasonable grounds to believe its statement was true. If this can't be shown then the misrepresentation may be fraudulent or negligent (see above).

Remedies for misrepresentation

There are five potential causes of action open to a claimant against a brand owner in the instance where a misrepresentation has been made (Table 2.1).

Table 2.1   Possible remedies available for an action in misrepresentation

Possible cause of action	Remedy
Breach of contract	Damages in contract
Fraudulent misrepresentation	Damages in tort with no remoteness limit and rescission
Negligent misrepresentation under the Misrepresentation Act 1967	Damages in tort with no remoteness limit and rescission (unless the court awards damages in lieu of rescission)
Innocent misrepresentation	Rescission (unless the court awards damages in lieu of rescission)
Negligent misstatement	Damages in tort

For fraudulent and negligent misrepresentation, the claimant may claim rescission (see 'Rescission' below) and damages. For innocent misrepresentation, the court has discretion to award damages in lieu of rescission or rescission but can't award both.

A misrepresentation makes a contract voidable by the claimant. As the equitable remedy of rescission is available for all types of misrepresentation, the claimant has a choice to rescind the contract or to affirm it.

Rescission

Rescission means that the contract is set aside and the parties are put back into the position in which they were before the contract was made.

Rescission may be contrasted with termination of a contract for breach of a material term that goes to the root of the agreement.

Where the brand owner breaches a condition, the claimant may elect to terminate the contract; such an election means that the future obligations of both parties under the contract are terminated, but they aren't released from obligations already accrued at the time of termination, because that wouldn't be equitable or fair.

The right to rescind the contract may be lost as a result of one of the following:

- *Affirmation of the contract.* As soon as the misrepresentation is discovered, the party to whom it's made can elect either to rescind or to affirm the contract. Once it is affirmed, the right to rescind is lost and the claimant is bound by the act of this affirmation. Affirmation may be implied by an act inconsistent with the decision to rescind the agreement. However, affirmation does require knowledge, and acts done by the claimant in ignorance of the facts won't amount to affirmation and won't bar the right to rescind the agreement with the brand owner.

- *Lapse of time.* This can prevent the claimant from bringing an action where there's been undue delay in bringing the claim. With fraudulent misrepresentation, delay won't of itself bar rescission provided that the claimant, without any fault of its own, remains in ignorance of the fraud. However, once the claimant discovers the fraud, time begins to run from the discovery of the truth. Where the misrepresentation is innocent or negligent, time begins to run from conclusion of the contract and not from the date of discovery of the misrepresentation.

- *Inability to restore the situation.* This is where it's no longer possible for the parties to be restored to their pre-contractual position. No precise rule has been formulated for the point at which the principle of equity will regard restoration as no longer possible.

- *Where a bona fide third party has acquired rights under the contract.*
  Section 1(a) of the Misrepresentation Act 1967 provides that a person isn't to be deprived of the right to rescind for misrepresentation merely because the representation has become a term of the contract.

Partial rescission of a contract isn't permissible, and the claimant may rescind only the whole contract.

The ability to rescind the whole agreement may be effected by legal proceedings or by the claimant giving notice to the other party before any bar to rescission arises.

Rescission is a remedy only against the other contracting party. Where the claimant seeks rescission for fraudulent misrepresentation, the court will dispense with certain usual requirements. For example, there is no requirement that the fraudulent misrepresentation should be material, that is, one on which a reasonable person in the claimant's position would have relied.

Where a misrepresentation induces a settlement of litigation and the proceedings are compromised by consent order, the court may set aside the consent order if it's shown to have been based on the agreement induced by misrepresentation.

Where the effect of rescission for fraudulent misrepresentation inducing a compromise agreement would put the parties back into a contractual relationship that they had previously agreed to terminate, the High Court is likely to make orders for damages or other financial relief rather than rescission.

Defamation

The law of defamation is about an individual, firm or company's right to have its reputation or goodwill protected, which is balanced against the right to freedom of speech.

In the UK, the law recognizes that every adult has a reputation and the right to have that reputation protected against false statements and imputations. There's a presumption of a favourable reputation until proved otherwise. See also Chapter 5 for a discussion on strategies for using the law for competitive advantage.

Defamatory statement

If the statement is written or is in any other permanent form, such as a picture or on television or the internet, then it's libel. If the defamatory statement is spoken, it's slander.

A statement about a person is defamatory if it tends to:

- lower the standing or damage the reputation of the aggrieved person in the estimation of right-thinking people generally, for example an advertisement that makes a derogatory statement about an individual or a competitor brand owner may give rise to a defamatory action; or

- disparage the aggrieved person or organization in its business, trade, office or profession, for example by suggesting that a company carries on its business in an incompetent, improper or dishonest way.

Many statements are capable of having more than one meaning. In defamation cases, the jury or a judge must decide on the meaning of the publication to the average reasonable person. The 'natural and ordinary' meaning of the words used on the face of the publication, excluding extraneous matters outside of the publication itself, is what is examined to determine whether a claimant has been defamed.

An apparently harmless statement may carry an inference or innuendo that's defamatory.

Right of action for defamation

Not everyone can bring an action for defamation. Those who can are:

- living individuals;
- a company for damage to its trading reputation and goodwill;
- non-trading organizations such as voluntary bodies or charities where supporters can be discouraged or the statements made impair the organization's ability to fulfil its duties and obligations to its stakeholders;
- individual members of unincorporated associations such as a sports club; and
- members of central and local government, such as MPS and councillors.

Those who can't bring an action for defamation include:

- deceased individuals or their estate or relatives of the deceased;
- unincorporated associations such as a sports club; and
- central or local government (collectively, rather than as individuals who can sue for defamation in a personal capacity).

What must be proved to succeed in an action for defamation

The following are required in order for the action to have some chance of being successful:

- publication to a third party;
- defamatory words or actions;

- such words or actions being reasonably understood to refer directly or indirectly to the claimant.

A claimant doesn't have to prove the statement is false, but it does have to prove the words are defamatory.

If a statement is defamatory it's assumed that it's false until proved otherwise. The claimant doesn't have to prove any damage – it only needs to show that the statement is defamatory.

The claimant can sue for defamation even though the people to whom the statement was published knew it was untrue.

Publication to a third party is the communication of a defamatory statement other than to the person or company claiming to be defamed. Each time a defamatory statement is published it amounts to a 'publication', giving rise to a fresh complaint.

The 'publisher' can be any party that assists in the publication and includes:

- a journalist;
- a sub-editor;
- an editor;
- a publisher;
- an advertiser;
- a marketing and PR agency; and
- a media owner.

Magazine printers, distributors and broadcasters are 'publishers', but they can avail themselves of the defence of innocent dissemination by proving they were not the author or editor of the statement complained about, took reasonable care in relation to its publication and didn't know that their actions contributed to publication (section 1, Defamation Act 1996).

'Natural meaning' of the defamatory statement

The meaning attributed to the defamatory statement is that which a reasonable person who's not unduly suspicious but who's willing to read between the lines. This is generally known as the 'natural and ordinary meaning'.

The defamatory statement will be read as a whole, together with words and pictures, rather than only a few lines taken out of context. In addition to the 'natural and ordinary meaning', an apparently harmless statement can carry an inference that's defamatory where those with special knowledge of particular facts or circumstances understand the defamatory meaning, known as 'innuendo meaning'.

It's also important that the claimant can show that the defamatory statement is about him or her rather than someone else and that he or she can be identified as the subject of the statement.

'Identification doesn't mean there has to be a name. It can be made in other ways. These include identification by name or picture, by description, by direct reference or by reference to small groups. It can also be done by jigsaw identification,' explains Jonathan Coad, partner at leading libel lawyers Lewis Silkin.

Defamation of a business

The distinction between defamation and comparative advertising is important (see Chapter 5).

The statement will need to disparage business methods, competence, judgment, honesty and other matters that strike at the heart of the reputation and goodwill of the claimant.

In some cases, such remarks and statements can have a significant impact on the share price of a quoted company.

The publication of salacious and unsubstantiated rumour is extremely dangerous because of the obvious risk it may be false.

The suggestion that a business is in trouble, making people redundant or about to go bust may make a great headline but equally can pose a potential legal risk to those making such statements. Likewise, an exposé on the use of child labour or sweatshops or dirty tactics will be subject to the same risk of the threat of proceedings unless it can fall within the grounds of defence to libel (see page 78).

'The fact that you're not the author and are merely repeating what you've heard is irrelevant,' observes Jonathan Coad.

It's important to remember that companies, like individuals, are entitled to recover damages, and they don't have to prove loss, as it's presumed, though evidence usually has to be provided.

A company's goodwill and reputation are regarded as being as important as the reputation of an individual.

Defamation on the internet

The law of defamation also applies to the internet, where the incidence of defamation is perhaps greatest. The parties involved in publication, apart from the author, can be the internet service provider (ISP) and the website owner.

Given the use of social networking sites, which unwittingly helped to fuel the riots and civil disturbances in the UK in November 2011, the government and law enforcement bodies have been forceful in ensuring that ISPs comply with legal, ethical and moral obligations for the content that travels on their networks rather than wash their hands of any responsibility for it.

Given the almost limitless reach of the internet to millions of people around the world, defamation on the internet throws up additional issues, including the jurisdiction for taking legal action against the defendant.

Through chat rooms, bulletin boards and social networking sites, rumours can spread swiftly like a computer virus, and as soon as a story disappears from one website it can pop up on another! Each time the offending web page is accessed it constitutes a fresh 'publication'.

ISPs have always been sensitive to defamation actions despite the protection traditionally afforded to them under English and EU legislation, although the tide is turning, making them much more exposed to the threat of legal action than had been possible in the past. For further discussion on the regulation of the internet, refer to Chapter 4.

Defences to a claim for defamation

The main defences to an action for defamation are:

- justification;
- fair comment;
- privilege;
- offer of amends;
- limitation (expiry of time); and
- consent.

Justification

Justification is a defence of truth. It can be successfully relied upon if a statement made, or at least the essential elements of it (the 'sting'), can be proved to be true. Intention is irrelevant. If what's alleged is true then the claimant has no reputation to defend, but may be able to establish a breach of privacy.

Fair comment

It's a defence to a defamation action for the defendant to establish that the words complained of were comment on a matter of public interest. The burden of proof is therefore on the defendant.

A defence of fair comment requires the author to prove that what he or she said was:

- comment as opposed to a statement of fact;
- on true facts, which an honest person could make;
- a matter of public interest; and
- made without any malice.

Privilege

There are situations where the public interest requires an ability to speak fully and frankly about matters without raising the risk of legal proceedings for defamation. Such situations are treated as privileged.

The defence of privilege can be absolute privilege or qualified privilege.

With respect to absolute privilege, this is a complete defence and protects statements made in judicial proceedings or similar, such as evidence given in court and statements made for the police. It's effective regardless of whether the defamatory statement was made maliciously. It also protects fair and accurate contemporaneous reports of court proceedings and decisions. It provides complete immunity from any legal action. The law extends to tribunals with quasi-judicial functions such as select committees.

With respect to qualified privilege, this is a defence available in circumstances where it's considered important that facts should be freely known and publication is in the public interest and for 'the general interest of society'. The purpose of the defence at common law is to allow a person with a duty or obligation to publish information where there's a corresponding interest in receiving it without risk of being successfully sued for defamation, where the publication is untrue. A reference given by an employer is an obvious example. The media qualified privilege defence is available if it can be shown to have behaved responsibly and complied with some, if not all, of the guidelines laid down by the courts.

Offer of amends

This is a statutory defence that requires the offer of an apology and payment of compensation, which can be decided by the court. It's not a defence in the true sense of the word but can halt legal proceedings, as, if not accepted, it's a complete defence unless the claimant can show it was made in the knowledge that it was false. It must be an offer in writing and served before service of the defence to the proceedings.

Tit-for-tat response

This is where the defamed party turns the tables on those making the statements that are defamatory. Such a response may also include the accuser and other third parties. However, this is a high-risk strategy, as the defamed party will need to make sure the response is relevant to the attack made on its reputation and goodwill and also that the circulation of its response to such an attack is measured and appropriate. The defence can also extend to statements made by close family or associates of the individual who has been defamed. This is part of a qualified privilege defence.

Consent

The complaint can't launch an action in defamation about a statement made in a publication to which it has given its express or implied consent.

Abuse of process

A defamation claim can't be brought if the cost of the complaint is out of all proportion to the damage or likely vindication of the complainant. Equally, a claim can't be brought in revenge. The purpose of the proceedings must be to protect the claimant's reputation.

Limitation period of 12 months

Given that the application of the law is to protect reputation and goodwill close to the point when the act occurred, proceedings must generally be commenced within 12 months of the year of publication of the statement. Each new publication will give rise to a fresh one-year limitation period. This is particularly an issue with regard to the internet and archives on the internet where republication can occur many years later as a result of an archive search by a user.

Remedies for defamation

Typically, there are three remedies most commonly provided by the courts to the injured party in cases of defamation:

- damages;
- injunction; and
- apologies and statements in open court.

Damages

In libel, damage is presumed, and in slander there are certain categories where damage is also presumed. Damages are 'at large'. That means that a jury will award what they think is appropriate, though tariffs are now applied and judges provide directions in most cases.

Injunction

This is a restraint preventing publication by order of the court, and any breach of such an order will be deemed to be contempt of court, which is an arrestable offence. If a matter goes to trial and the action is successful, the claimant will usually be granted a permanent injunction against the defendant in order to prevent any further acts of defamation. If an injunction is applied for at an early stage it's called an interim injunction.

Where a defendant intends to justify the alleged defamation, an application for an injunction won't succeed. The same applies if, in the absence of malice, a qualified privilege defence is pleaded.

Apologies and statements in open court

This may appear to be a pyrrhic victory, but for many claimants the rectification of libellous statements made about them is more important than financial compensation. These statements of apology are often reported where such a claimant is a high-profile individual. In such cases, the claimant is seeking a statement in court by the defendants that is very public. It is usually achieved through mutual agreement and is made to a judge.

Tort of malicious falsehood

It's possible that a false statement made about an individual or business, although not defamatory, may still be damaging. For example, in a comparative advertisement, a false statement about a competitor's products, prices or attributes is unlikely to be defamatory, but if false it may give rise to an action for malicious falsehood.

For malicious falsehood, the claimant must prove that the statement was untrue and published maliciously.

It's important to note that this is different from the position in defamation, where the claimant doesn't have to prove that the statement is false or malicious.

Unlike the case in an action for defamation, a claimant has to prove that it suffered actual damage or loss in order to be able to bring an action for malicious falsehood, subject to certain exceptions. For example, it's not necessary to prove actual damage or loss if the words in dispute are:

- calculated to cause pecuniary damage to the claimant and are published in writing or other permanent form; or
- calculated to cause pecuniary damage to the claimant in respect of its office, professional calling, trade or business (whether published in writing, orally or otherwise).

The time limit for bringing an action is the same as for defamation.

References

Cases and judgments

ADT *v* Binder Hamlyn [1996] BCC 808

Arkwright *v* Newbold (1881) 17 Ch D 301

Avon Insurance plc and others *v* Swire Fraser Ltd [2000] EWHC 230 (Comm)

BSkyB Limited and another *v* HP Enterprise Services UK Limited (formerly Electronic Data Systems Limited) and another [2010] EWHC 86 (TCC)

Caparo Industries *v* Dickman [1990] 2 WLR 358

Crystal Palace FC (2000) Limited *v* Dowie [2007] EWHC 1392 (QB)

Derry *v* Peek (1889) App Case 337

FoodCo UK LLP and others *v* Henry Boot Developments Ltd [2010] EWHC 358 (Ch)

Hedley Byrne *v* Heller [1964] AC 465

IFE Fund SA *v* Goldman Sachs International [2006] EWHC 2887 (Comm)

Jaffray *v* Society of Lloyds [2002] EWCA Civ 1101

Kyle Bay Limited t/a Astons Nightclub *v* Underwriters Subscribing under Policy
No. 019057/08/01 [2007] EWCA Civ 57

McMeekin and another *v* Long and another [2003] 29 EG 120

Redgrave *v* Hurd (1881) 20 Ch. D. 1

Renault UK Limited *v* (1) Fleetpro Technical Services Limited (2) Russell Thoms
[2007] EWHC 2541(QB)

Royal Bank of Scotland plc *v* Bannerman Johnstone Maclay [2005] CSIH 39

Smith *v* Chadwick (1884) 9 App Cas 187

Spice Girls Limited *v* Aprilia World Service [2002] BV EWCA Civ 15

Zentralbank Osterreich AG *v* Royal Bank of Scotland plc [2010] EWHC 1392

"I'm afraid that's it, all the domain names
in the world have been taken!"

Legal barriers to market entry

In this chapter

- Design rights as a barrier to market entry
- Trademark as a barrier to market entry
- Passing-off action as a barrier to market entry
- Copyright as a barrier to market entry
- Generic top-level domains (gTLDs) as a barrier to market entry

Introduction

This chapter explores legitimate barriers to market entry that prevent an unfair advantage being taken by a competitor brand owner. These laws and regulations act as a barrier to illegitimate competition and are therefore justified in the consumer and public interest. Before exploring what those barriers to market entry look like, it's useful to have in mind wider UK and EU perspectives on competition law.

UK competition perspective

In the UK, the Competition Act 1998 prohibits agreements, concerted practices and decisions between undertakings that have as their objective or effect the prevention, restriction of distortion of competition. This is the key principle that applies irrespective of whether it's competition in business-to-business (B2B) or business-to-consumer (B2C) market segments.

For an agreement to be prohibited, it must have an appreciable effect on competition and fail to qualify for an exemption under the Competition Act 1998.

For an agreement that has a whiff of a barrier to market entry about it, in order not to fall foul of the 1998 Act it must satisfy certain conditions:

- It must provide for efficiency gains.
- It must allow consumers a fair share of the resultant benefits flowing from the deal.
- It must not impose restrictions beyond those indispensable to achieving those objectives.
- It must not eliminate competition.

UK law also applies to those brand owners that enjoy a 40 per cent or above market share and are capable of acting largely independently from their competitors. The above prohibitions are enforced by the Office of Fair Trading (OFT) and market regulators.

The Enterprise Act 2002 introduced criminal sanctions against individuals for dishonest agreements that:

- fix prices;
- share markets;
- limit production; and
- rig bids.

In addition, there are EU competition rules that are equivalent to those described above, and these also apply in the UK. These are set out in Articles 101 and 102 of the Treaty on the Functioning of the European Union 2010 and enforced by the OFT and the European Commission.

Most recently, the Court of Justice of the European Union (CJEU) handed down a judgment that made it clear that luxury brands can't prevent retailers selling their products online. The judgment made clear that a clause in a selective distribution agreement that operates as an absolute ban on internet sales has as its object the restriction of competition and is unlawful (see page 99).

European Union competition perspective

A key competition issue that concerns European legislators is the barriers to market entry that prevent brand owners from engaging in cross-border sales and marketing activities across all 27 EU member states. Currently, those companies wishing to carry out cross-border transactions must adapt to up to 26 different national contract laws, translate them and hire lawyers at an average cost of €10,000 for each additional export market, according to research by the European Commission.

One argument advanced by the reformers is that 500 million consumers in Europe are losing out on having greater choice because competition within the single market is adversely affected by the lack of harmonization of laws and regulations.

In 2011, the European Commission published its proposed directive, and if adopted it will insert into the national laws of the 27 EU member states an optional set of contract law rules that contracting parties could choose as the governing law for their cross-border transactions. Support for such a move has been signalled by the European Parliament, and this could have consequences for the existing framework of barriers to market entry that exist in the UK, although the current stance of the government is to reject the need for such wide-sweeping reforms.

The new EU directive wouldn't replace existing national laws but would try to complement existing national frameworks in the hope of creating a single market, argue its proponents. The intention is to take a step closer to having a single, integrated European contract regime for all cross-border sales to consumers. If brand owners offer their products on the basis of the Common European Sales Law, then consumers would be free to choose a user-friendly European contract with a high level of consumer protection with just one click of a mouse, say its advocates.

The regulation would cover the whole life cycle of a contract, dealing with matters such as pre-contractual information duties, conclusion of a contract, right of withdrawal, rights and obligations of the parties, and remedies for non-performance.

The proposed EU directive would apply only to contracts for the sale of goods, including digital content contracts such as music, movies, software or smart phone applications, where both parties agree to be bound by the EU directive and at least one party is established in an EU member state. It would be available for both B2B and B2C transactions.

The existing competition regime in the UK does create a degree of legal uncertainty for many businesses, but the UK government is adamant that further EU legislation isn't the answer. It points to the extra costs that would inevitably result from its introduction, the remaining uncertainty given the differences of interpretation by courts in different member states, its impact on the current commercial position of English law, and the risk that it would in fact be rarely used.

Support for this view has been expressed by consumer groups in the UK, such as the Consumers' Association, which has called on the European Commission to focus on other issues, such as an EU-wide alternative disputes resolution procedure.

According to the OFT, any changes in the legal framework should foster competition, address individual infringements and provide incentives for compliance.

An independent review of intellectual property and growth published in 2011 recognized that innovation is crucial to the UK maintaining a competitive edge in global markets and that intellectual property (IP) policy is an increasingly important tool for stimulating economic growth. For example, for the past decade investment in intangible assets has outstripped investment in tangible assets, and the global trade in IP licences is worth in excess of £600 billion a year, equivalent to 5 per cent of all trade worldwide.

Professor Ian Hargreaves, who led the review, said:

We've found that the UK's intellectual property framework is falling behind what's needed. Copying has become basic to numerous industrial processes as well as to a burgeoning service economy based upon the internet. This doesn't mean that we must put our hugely important creative industries at risk. Indeed, these businesses too need change in the form of more open, contestable and effective global markets in digital content.

Whilst most brand owners will broadly agree with the principles of competition, openness and fairness, nevertheless they also expect the law to provide protection against unfair competition where considerable investment has been made in creating IP rights.

This chapter explores how some of those IP rights are protected, which in turn act as a legitimate barrier to market entry.

Design rights as a barrier to market entry

Design is a wide-ranging concept covering a diversity of sectors – from fashion and entertainment, communications and consumer products all the way to manufacturing and industrial designs. According to research by Imperial College London, design represents the largest contribution to overall intangible investment in the UK economy, and in 2008 investment in design alone amounted to 1.6 per cent of the UK's gross domestic product (GDP).

Design rights date back to the 18th century and registered design rights to the 19th century. Since 2003, the EU-wide Registered Community Design has been an alternative source of registered design protection in the UK.

Both registered and unregistered design rights are covered by a patchwork of EU and UK legal protections.

There are four different and to some extent overlapping forms of design right in the UK:

- a registered right covering the UK available from the Intellectual Property Office (IPO);
- a registered right covering the EU available from the Office for Harmonization in the Internal Market (OHIM);
- an unregistered right covering the UK;
- an unregistered EU right.

There are circumstances in which copyright and trademark protection can also be relevant. Within this patchwork are differences as to what forms of design are covered, how long the rights last, what's required to prove infringement, and the penalties for infringement.

Registered designs

To qualify for registration, a design must:

- be new;
- have individual character; and
- relate to the appearance of all or part of a product resulting from certain features of that product or its ornamentation.

The holder of a UK registered design can:

- enjoy the exclusive right in the UK to make, import, export, use or stock any product to which the design has been applied or in which it's incorporated;
- prevent others from using the design; and
- assign or license the right to other parties.

Applications for registration must be made to the UK Patent Office. The Registered Designs Act 1949 (as amended) sets out rules on protection. A Community Design Right (for which qualifications are slightly different) can also be applied for through the OHIM.

Enforcement is usually through the UK courts, and this will apply to European patents. The main remedies the courts grant are:

- permanent or interim injunctions;
- delivery-up;
- damages; and
- an account of profits.

The length of protection lasts for a maximum of 25 years, subject to renewal fees every five years.

Dyson *v* Vax (2011)

In December 1994, Dyson applied for a UK registered design relating to the dual cyclone cleaner. In 2009, competitor brand owner Vax launched its Mach Zen vacuum cleaner, which was also a multi-stage cyclone vacuum cleaner. Dyson issued proceedings against Vax, claiming that the importing and marketing of the Mach Zen infringed its registered design rights.

Dyson lost at the first hearing of the matter and then appealed to the Court of Appeal, only to lose again.

The key question on appeal was whether the Mach Zen produced on the informed user a different overall impression from that of Dyson's registered design. In the judgment of the Court of Appeal, there was no dispute that Dyson's registered design was 'a great departure' from what had gone before. Further, there was no dispute as to the characteristics of the informed user, who importantly was reasonably discriminatory and not the same person as the 'average consumer' for the purposes of determining infringement in trademark law.

As to the degree of design freedom, this was found to refer plainly to the degree of freedom of the designer of the registered design, not the degree of freedom of the designer of the alleged infringement.

However, the Court of Appeal found that there will seldom be any difference unless there's been a significant advance in technology between the date of creation of the registered design and the date of creation of the alleged infringement.

Given that there were substantial differences between the designs, the Vax cleaner produced on the informed user a different overall impression.

This judgment emphasizes the high threshold that designers must meet in order to bring a successful action for design right infringement and even higher costs of litigation when they fall short of that threshold. Despite obvious visual similarities that may exist between products, the courts have been reluctant to find design right infringement on that basis alone.

Unregistered designs

The design must:

- relate to an aspect of shape or configuration of the whole or part of an article;
- be original and not commonplace;
- be recorded in a design document or be the subject of an article made to the design; and
- be created by a qualifying person (a person or company/entity in the UK, EU, Channel Islands, Isle of Man, any UK colony or any country designated as qualifying for reciprocal protection).

The holder of a UK unregistered design can:

- enjoy the exclusive right to reproduce the design for commercial purposes by making articles to that design or by making a design document recording the design for the purpose of enabling the articles to be made;
- prevent others from infringing its right; and
- assign or license the right to other third parties.

An unregistered design is automatically protected provided that it's recorded in a tangible form such as a drawing or diagram. It's also possible to have automatic protection as a Community Unregistered Design (for which the qualifications are slightly different). The enforcement procedure and the main remedies available are similar to those for registered designs.

Protection lasts for the lesser of: 15 years from the end of the calendar year when the design was first recorded in a design document (alternatively from when an article was first made to the design); and 10 years from the end of the calendar year when articles made to the design were first made available for sale or hire.

Reform of the law required

Many brand owners that create and use designs find this patchwork of legal protection very unsatisfactory given the complexity of legal enforcement issues, and there's a discrepancy in the levels of protection between design right (technical design) and copyright (protecting artistic designs such as illustrations). In short, many designers argue that the barriers to market entry where there's an existing design right should be much higher than they are at present.

As a result, levels of registration of design rights are comparatively low in the UK given the size of the design industries and their commercial success. Around 8,000–9,000 UK designs are registered each year, with an equal number applying for IPO and OHIM registrations.

One reason is that brand owners prefer to add their designs to an electronic database – the Anti Copying in Design (ACID) register – which holds in excess of 30,000 designs and provides an audit trail to substantiate design ownership should the designer's rights be infringed. Many designers tender for contracts with designs that they have limited chance of being able to protect and frequently find that their best ideas are stolen without any compensation. In many cases, designers have invested considerable time and money in developing these designs, but either can't afford to take enforcement action or find the law inadequate to do so. ACID in particular is concerned that small to medium-sized designers' products are routinely copied by major high street retailers, and unlike the case with copyright, which is supported by criminal sanctions and law enforcement and trading standards to enforce transgressions, designers have the civil law to rely on to help defend their IP rights.

Trademark as a barrier to market entry

This is one IP right that potentially has the firepower to stop a 'lookalike' or 'me too' competitor in its tracks. The courts vigorously uphold the sanctity of a registered trademark, and it remains one of the biggest barriers to market entry for a competitor that's trying to use an unfair advantage in order to steal customers, clients and market share from an existing provider of goods and services.

It's also one area of law where litigation is most common and where the courts' interpretation of the Trade Marks Act 1994 and voluminous case law can make the difference in terms of permitted competition in the same or similar classes of goods and services.

In a commercial context, a trademark registration is capable of protecting a business, brand or product name or a logo, slogan, device or other mark in connection with that enterprise. Outside of commercial practice, public and non-governmental organizations are also able to protect their marks with respect to these IP rights.

Fundamentally, a registered trademark provides a brand owner with an effective form of protection against a competitor making improper use of its mark. Whilst a mark might be capable of being protected through other areas of the law, such as passing off, copyright or design right, registering a trademark has a number of distinctive benefits for the rights holder.

Given the vast amount of sales and marketing activity on the web, many marketers may assume that registering a brand as a company name or domain name will automatically secure protection for the brand and act 'like a trademark registration'. It won't. Registering your brand as a company or domain name is separate in law from a trademark registration and won't provide you with any protection against a third party using a trademark that is the same as or similar to that of your brand.

Another assumption commonly made by marketers is that there's no need to go through the expense of registering a trademark because the mark or device will be protected by the law of copyright – free of charge. This isn't correct. Slogans, phrases, names and titles aren't protected by copyright. Although a logo or device may be an artistic work protected by copyright, the protections offered by copyright aren't directed at dealing with the issues associated with using a logo or device in a trademark sense. In addition, copyright in a work will eventually expire, whereas a trademark can be renewed indefinitely.

Importance of a registered trademark

Registration acts as prima facie proof of the rights holder's entitlement to the mark. If a third party believes that it has a better right to a mark than the registered proprietor, it will have to apply to the UK Trademark Registry to have it declared invalid and will have a number of procedural and evidential hurdles to overcome.

The registered trademark device ® indicates to the world at large that the mark has achieved registration and is protected under the Trade Marks Act 1994.

If a mark hasn't been registered, it's a criminal offence to use the ® device. Importantly, registration for a trademark can be obtained for a mark before it's used, provided that there's an actual intention to use the mark, which protects the rights holder from any infringement prior to actual use.

An action for trademark infringement can be brought without proof that the rights holder has suffered any damage to the reputation in its mark. Filing a trademark application means that the details of the mark are kept on a central register. Most businesses when assessing whether to adopt a new mark conduct a trademark search to ensure that no trademark complications are likely to arise. Consequently, it's likely that any third parties that might otherwise unwittingly make use of the registered mark will be alerted to its existence.

Surprisingly, many competitor brand owners are blasé about checking the register and assume that, even if a trademark registration exists in the class of goods and services they want to compete in, the trademark holder won't have the appetite or financial muscle to pursue enforcement proceedings actively, so in a sense they'll 'get away with this'.

This is a high-risk strategy and a dangerous (if not stupid) assumption to make. Many law firms now act for a proprietor of a registered trademark on a contingency fee arrangement (CFA) or 'no win, no fee' basis, removing the fear of commencing a trademark infringement action if the merits of the case are overwhelmingly in favour of the claimant. In addition, 'after the event' (ATE) insurance is available to law firms, and the premium of this insurance will become part of the costs that can be claimed against the infringing party in any settlement or order made by the court.

The remedies against infringers can be particularly onerous and include:

- getting them to cease and desist;
- blocking all future use of their mark;
- withdrawing all existing products from the market;
- redesigning all packaging;
- dropping new sales and marketing campaigns;
- paying damages for the impairment made to a registered trademark and/or buying a licence from the registered proprietor.

Unlike other forms of IP protection, registered trademark protection can last indefinitely provided renewal fees are paid.

Importance of searches and enquiries before using a mark

It's prudent to carry out a number of searches and enquiries before adopting a new mark, as the existence of a registered mark will be a legal barrier to market entry that may not be capable of being removed.

The purpose of a trademark search is to ensure that there are no identical or similar marks already on the trademark register covering identical or similar classes of goods or services. In the event that there are such marks in existence, the proprietor(s) of any such earlier mark may be able to bring proceedings for trademark infringement and/or passing off.

Searches should also be conducted for company names and domain names and in journals and trade directories in the relevant business sector to be on the safe side.

If the trademark search identifies a risk, then an assessment needs to be made as to whether such a risk constitutes a serious commercial threat. If this is the case, then it's prudent to consider an alternative mark, and the search and enquiry process will need to begin over again.

What's capable of being registered as a trademark

Under the Trade Marks Act 1994 a trademark is any sign capable of being represented graphically that is capable of distinguishing the goods or services of one undertaking from those of other undertakings. This includes:

- business and product names;
- words and slogans;
- logos;
- domain names;
- the shape of goods or their packaging;
- 3D shapes;
- sounds and jingles;
- colours;
- images; and
- smells.

Trademark registrations give the registrant the exclusive right to use that mark only in connection with the goods and services for which it's registered. It's only possible to register a trademark in relation to the goods and services that you offer or genuinely intend to offer in the future.

Goods and services are classified into 45 different use classes for registration purposes, and it's necessary as part of your application for registration to list the goods and services for which you're registering your mark and identify the classes that these goods and services fall into. This can be found on the IPO website at http://ipo.gov.uk.

A registered trademark won't work as a barrier to market entry where the competitor mark isn't for the same or a similar class of goods and services. In such cases, the competitor mark is capable of being registered even if an identical or similar pre-existing mark is registered. Even where a pre-existing trademark has been registered in relation to similar goods and services, if the rights holder of the pre-existing mark decides not to raise opposition proceedings or gives consent then the trademark may still be registered.

Geographical protection

Depending on the extent to which IP rights need to be protected, it may be prudent to seek registrations across a number of jurisdictions. This process has been streamlined by the application process for a Community Trade Mark (CTM) – a single trademark application that covers the entire EU as well as international applications under the Madrid Protocol.

Also, if an application is filed in the UK, then you'll usually have a period of six months to assess whether to file applications in other countries too. If you do so, then your foreign applications could benefit from the same application date as the UK application.

Process for obtaining a UK trademark

An application has to be filed with the Intellectual Property Office (IPO), or alternatively an application can be made for a Community Trade Mark, as this will also cover the UK. For trademark purposes, all possible goods and services are subdivided into 45 'classes'. When an application is made for a trademark, the applicant must state which of these classes the mark is actually being used in and/or those classes in which there is a bona fide intention to use the mark. The higher the number of classes applied for, the greater the scope of protection afforded by trademark registration.

It should be borne in mind that, as there's an additional fee for each class applied for, the cost of application is proportionate to the registrations sought. That said, a greater number of classes increases the likelihood of encountering problems with earlier marks that may be registered, which could object to the application in their class of goods and services. So a sensible balance needs to be struck.

Once the application has been filed, the applicant will be allocated an application number and date. The application date is of particular importance, as this will act as the registration date once the mark achieves registration. Whilst the mark can't be used in infringement proceedings until the mark is registered, the act of applying for a trademark will be a barrier for any applications filed by third parties after the application date that are identical or sufficiently similar to the mark.

The IPO will then issue an examination report stating whether the application is acceptable or not. There are a number of grounds upon which the Registry won't accept an application, the main grounds being that the mark isn't considered distinctive enough to be capable of being registered or is merely descriptive of the goods and services or that the mark conflicts with an earlier mark belonging to another brand owner.

If the IPO doesn't raise any objections in the examination report or if the objections are capable of being overcome, then the proposed trademark will be advertised in the *Trade Marks Journal*. Once it has been advertised, third parties have an opportunity to object to the application. If there's no opposition filed, or if any such opposition is overcome (usually by an undertaking not to compete in a class of goods or services, for example), then the mark will proceed to registration.

Time needed to make a trademark application

Provided there aren't objections at the application stage, then registration can be achieved within a little over six months in the UK. If objections are raised, then it can take 12 months or longer. Whilst the process can be lengthy, the important date is often the date on which the application was made, not when registration is obtained, as registration is backdated to the application date.

Current costs for making a trademark application

The IPO (http://www.ipo.gov.uk) currently offers two services for registrants:

- *Standard examination service.* It costs £200 to apply to register your trademark for goods or services that fall into one class. It costs £50 for each additional class. If you file online and include the full payment at the time of filing, you'll receive a discount of £30 off the total cost. The IPO will send you an examination report by post or e-mail in around 10 business days if you file online. This report will explain whether the IPO considers the mark is capable of registration and informs you of any confusingly similar trademarks already on the register (earlier marks). If the IPO thinks that your mark is capable of being registered, it will publish it in the *Trade Marks Journal* so that third parties have an opportunity to oppose your application. If there is no opposition, it will be registered.

- *Right Start examination service.* This online service also costs £200 plus £50 for each additional class of goods or services. But with Right Start you pay an initial fee of £100 plus £25 for each additional class. Examination takes the same time as for the standard examination service, but the IPO will e-mail the examination report to you and if there are any problems you can discuss them with the examiner. If you decide to proceed with your application you must pay the IPO the outstanding balance of the application and any additional class fees. If you decide not to go ahead, you can let your application lapse and don't pay any further fees. No discount applies to this service.

Length of trademark protection

A trademark is initially valid for a period of 10 years. However, provided renewal fees are paid every 10 years, then a trademark can provide protection for the registered mark in perpetuity.

Trademark 'watch' services

A trademark 'watch' service is provided by trademark agents and specialist law firms that monitor the trademark registers in territories where the trademark is being used and will send a notification to the rights holder whenever a trademark application is filed that's identical or similar to the word, device, image, logo or design that's the subject of the 'watch'.

Leading trademark attorney Steven Jennings of law firm Lewis Silkin explains:

> *This advance notification then gives the proprietor an opportunity to warn the business concerned that they may be engaged in potentially infringing activities and if necessary to file an opposition against their trademark application in order to prevent it from achieving registration. It's often far easier to resolve disputes at this early stage than when the third party may have put more spend behind their mark or have actually launched it in the marketplace – in which case exit costs may be substantially higher.*

Should a competitor brand owner register a similar trademark then this not only may give it a defence to any infringement claim but could correspondingly narrow the scope of the proprietor's rights. It's vital that the brand owner protects the rights conferred by a registered trademark to prevent others from using and/or registering confusingly similar marks. The possible consequences of failing to take appropriate action include customers mistakenly purchasing competitors' goods and services, the dilution of the brand's integrity and erosion of brand value.

Recent trademark issues considered by the UK and EU courts

Specsavers v Asda (2012)

The well-known UK supermarket chain Asda has had opticians in its stores for many years. In mid-2008 it relaunched its optical business with an extensive marketing campaign. The campaign used a device mark with the words 'Asda Opticians' inside two adjacent white ovals on a green background. It also used the straplines 'Be a real spec saver at Asda' and 'Spec savings at Asda'.

Specsavers, a large chain of high street opticians, is the proprietor of several trademarks, including one for the word 'Specsavers' inside two overlapping oval devices, and one for the same mark without words, in black and white.

Specsavers sued Asda for infringement of several of its marks. At the same time, Asda applied to invalidate Specsavers' device mark, which hadn't been used for five years prior to the action in question.

During the proceedings, documents were disclosed that left little doubt that the Asda branding was intended to reference Specsavers, one of its main competitors. In 2010, the UK High Court found that the strapline 'Be a real spec saver at Asda' infringed the Specsavers trademarks, but dismissed the rest of the Specsavers case. Specsavers appealed against the dismissal.

The Court of Appeal (2012) found that both straplines infringed the Specsavers registrations. It further decided that Asda intentionally derived a commercial advantage by referencing the Specsavers trademark in its marketing campaign. Asda's reference to the Specsavers trademark was not held to be typical comparative advertising, but rather the core intention was to exploit Specsavers' marketing efforts. The Court of Appeal also held that Asda's logo infringed several of the Specsavers trademark registrations.

The question of the validity of the device registration proved more contentious and was referred to the CJEU for adjudication.

There are several important points for marketers that choose to 'sail close to the wind' in the way that Asda had done in this case:

● There are dangers where a marketing campaign is designed to call to mind the offering of a competitor in attempting to secure an unfair advantage.

● When targeting brand owners in this way, the 'challenger brand' must take care not to use a competitor's trademarks or signs that are similar to them without due course and in a way that takes unfair advantage of them or is detrimental to their distinctive character or reputation.

● Marketers who choose to 'sail close to the wind' should remember that early internal drafts and e-mails may become disclosed in litigation.

● The maxim 'Register what you use and use what you register' is highly relevant in light of Specsavers' non-use of a device mark that Asda now seeks to get struck out on the basis of non-use for the five years prior to the commencement of the legal action by Specsavers.

For a discussion of the rules on comparative advertising, refer to Chapter 5.

Nestlé v Cadbury (2011)

In 2008, Cadbury was successful in registering the exclusive use of the colour purple Pantone 2865c for use with chocolate bars and other chocolate products. Competitor brand Nestlé objected to the registration to the Intellectual Property Office (IPO).

The IPO Registrar, Allan James, ruled that the Cadbury goods demonstrated the necessary 'distinctive character' to qualify for the protection of a trademark in relation to chocolate in bar and tablet form, eating chocolate, drinking chocolate and preparations for making drinking chocolate, but not for cakes, boxed chocolates and other Cadbury confectionery, as the association of such products with the purple Pantone 2865c wasn't as well established in the minds of consumers.

In this respect, both sides achieved a measure of success, Cadbury more so than Nestlé.

A trademark registration for colours is notoriously difficult to pull off, as it relates to consumers seeing the colour as being tantamount to the brand. In this case, Cadbury was able to show the distinctiveness of the purple colour in connection with its brand through its consistent use of the colour in its wrappers and advertising. Despite the fact that there's a public interest argument in preventing the creation of a 'monopoly' over the particular colour in question, the IPO Registrar considered that Cadbury's reputation was so strongly associated with the shade to merit registration.

L'Oréal v eBay (2009)

The action was commenced by global cosmetic and perfumery brand owner L'Oréal against online marketplace eBay, which enabled its users to advertise for sale a vast range of L'Oréal products. Some of these products were counterfeit as well as 'parallel imports' that distorted L'Oréal's sales in various territories and in fact amounted to an illegal activity.

L'Oréal sought to place the legal burden of trademark enforcement squarely on the shoulders of eBay and to make it jointly liable for its involvement in the trademark infringements being committed by individual sellers through its online marketplace.

The CJEU began its landmark ruling by reminding trademark proprietors that they may rely on their rights only in the context of commercial activities. It wasn't open to a rights holder to pursue an individual reselling a few unwanted birthday presents on eBay. Only if the sales went beyond the realms of private activity (as seen in the volume and frequency of such transactions) could the rights holder take action for trademark infringement. This let innocent users of eBay off the hook.

With respect to parallel imports, the CJEU confirmed that EU trademark laws applied to offers for sale relating to trademark goods located in third states (non-EU/EEA states) as soon as it was clear that those offers for sale were targeted at consumers within the EU. On that basis, an advertisement placed on eBay containing L'Oréal trademarks and advertising genuine L'Oréal products that the seller (who held those goods in China, for example) was willing to have delivered to the UK would infringe the relevant L'Oréal trademarks because the seller had no permission from L'Oréal to do so and those same products hadn't as yet been placed on the market in the EU/EEA by L'Oréal.

The CJEU noted that it's for national courts to assess on a case-by-case basis whether an offer for sale is targeted at consumers in the EU by taking account of factors including shipping destinations, language and billing currencies. In addition, the CJEU confirmed that merely supplying sample products doesn't amount to the proprietor of the trademark having put those goods on the market within the meaning of the Community Trade Mark (CTM) Regulation.

With respect to unboxed and unpackaged branded products, where a reseller has removed these prior to resale, it was held by the CJEU that this could harm the image of the product and the reputation of the trademark. Indirectly, essential information required as a matter of law, such as the identity of the manufacturer under the EU Cosmetics Directive, would no longer be on the product, creating further damage to the reputation of the mark.

The CJEU reaffirmed that keywords on internet services such as eBay need to ensure that their online advertisements make it clear that the goods being resold on the marketplace are being sold by persons other than the actual brand owners. In this respect, the CJEU followed its own decision in the previous Google France case.

The CJEU also considered that online operators may benefit from an exemption from liability for trademark infringement committed by their users as a result of the E-Commerce Directive (Directive 2000/31), which exempts an 'information society service' provider such as an online marketplace operator from liability for information or data stored by it on behalf of the recipient of its services.

The court confirmed that, if a seller uploads an offer for sale that contains a sign similar or identical to a registered trademark, such that it would amount to trademark infringement, the marketplace operator may escape liability through the E-Commerce exemption, except where: it has provided the seller with some sort of 'active' assistance, such as optimizing the presentation of the offer for sale or promoting the offer for the seller; or the operator was aware of factors or circumstances on the basis of which it should have realized that the offer for sale in question was unlawful and on becoming aware it failed to act expeditiously to remove or prevent access to the offer for sale.

The issue of 'active' assistance is a question of fact for national courts to decide, but it's unlikely to require online marketplace providers like eBay actively to monitor all the data of each of its customers in order to prevent any future infringement of IP rights.

Finally, the CJEU ruled that, in issuing an injunction against a marketplace operator that has committed trademark infringement, national courts must ensure that the injunction doesn't create barriers to legitimate trade. This means that the injunction can't have as its object or effect a general and permanent prohibition on the sale of goods bearing the relevant trademark on that marketplace. Any injunction granted must be proportionate and dissuasive, requiring the online marketplace operator to prevent specific sellers whose infringing activities are known from continuing their activities on the website both now and in the future, for example by deleting an infringing seller's account.

The judgment is reflective of many other rulings where brand owners legitimately seek protection against online sellers of counterfeit goods or 'parallel imports' that look to circumvent established principles of trademark law through the use of the internet.

As a result of this decision, online providers now have a higher degree of responsibility for ensuring that appropriate mechanisms are in place in order to prevent IP infringement by their users.

The case led to a memorandum of understanding being signed in 2011 by Amazon, Nokia, eBay, Lacoste, Nike, Richemont, Unilever and many other brand owners under which they agreed a number of principles regarding notice and take-down procedures, as well as commitments to take commercially reasonable proactive and preventative measures to fight counterfeiting and improve cooperation and information exchange on a voluntary basis.

Interflora v Marks & Spencer (2011)

Google operates a system called AdWords that allows advertisements to be displayed alongside natural search results in response to keywords being entered into the Google search engine. Advertisers select those keywords and pay Google on a cost-per-click (CPC) basis. These sponsored links typically constitute a short commercial message with a link to the advertiser's website and are distinguishable from the natural search results by their format and placement.

Interflora, the flower delivery network, objected to Marks & Spencer buying the word 'Interflora' as a Google AdWord so that M&S's flower delivery site would show up prominently in the sponsored links when a user searched for the term 'Interflora'. Interflora brought an action for trademark infringement against M&S, and the High Court referred the matter to the CJEU for adjudication.

Referring to previous decisions involving Google AdWords, the CJEU held that a rights holder was entitled to prevent a competitor from using a keyword identical to a trademark to advertise goods or services that were identical to those for which the trademark was registered in the absence of consent and where it would have an adverse effect on one of the functions of the trademark.

Following the significant previous decisions in LVMH *v* Google France and L'Oréal *v* eBay, the CJEU has clarified the position that use of a trademark as a keyword amounts to trademark infringement if done by a competitor brand owner, advertiser, search engine provider or online marketplace operator.

Advertisers can bid on keywords corresponding to registered trademarks to enable advertisements to appear as a sponsored link, but it will amount to a trademark infringement if the use adversely affects one of the functions of a trademark.

There are numerous functions of a trademark, but the main ones for consideration in this context are the origin and investment functions.

The CJEU has given some guidance on when the functions will be adversely affected. For example, the origin function will be adversely affected where a consumer would be unable to determine or could determine only with difficulty whether or not the advertiser is linked to the trademark proprietor. The investment function will be adversely affected where the trademark proprietor's use of its trademark to acquire or preserve its goods' attractive reputation is interfered with. Where the registered trademark has a reputation, advertisers need to take additional care in order to avoid trademark infringement. Keyword use of a trademark with reputation will infringe if there's 'dilution' in the trademark – in other words, the trademark loses its distinctiveness or becomes generic – or there's 'free-riding' by the advertiser, where the advertiser is using the trademark to offer for sale imitations (rather than alternatives) of the trademark proprietor's goods.

A search engine provider such as Google or an online marketplace operator such as eBay that merely allows advertisers to bid on a trademark as a keyword doesn't infringe the trademark. Thus a trademark proprietor can't bring an action against these operators to prevent them from letting advertisers use their trademark. However, the operator may in some cases be liable for the actions of its customers if it knows they are infringing a trademark and it has played an active role in the selection and use of the trademark.

Online marketplaces that use trademarks as keywords in search engines to trigger sponsored links to listings on their online marketplace will be treated in the same way as an advertiser (above).

This current ruling provides scope for advertisers to continue their practices of purchasing keywords corresponding to registered trademarks to bring up their own advertisements. However, they must make sure that their advertisement makes it clear to the informed internet user that their advertisement doesn't originate from the trademark owner. For further discussion on e-marketing practices, refer to Guru in a Bottle® *High Impact Marketing that Gets Results*.

Lady Gaga *v* Lady Goo Goo (2011)

Ate My Heart Inc is a company owned and controlled by US avant-garde pop diva Lady Gaga. It has CTM registrations for LADY GAGA covering sound, video and audiovisual recordings, entertainment services and the streaming of audio and video material on the internet. Mind Candy operates the successful online children's game called Moshi Monsters, and its subsidiary Moshi Music exploits sound recordings and songs associated with the game. From 2009 the game featured a character called Lady Goo Goo, reminiscent of Lady Gaga. Moshi Monsters features a number of other parody characters (such as Broccoli Spears and Avril Le Scream). Important characters can achieve moshling status in the game.

Ate My Heart became aware of the Lady Goo Goo character only in April 2011 when the defendants applied to register LADY GOO GOO as a trade mark. They then also learnt that the defendants intended to release as a single a song called 'The Moshi Dance', sung by Lady Goo Goo, with a scheduled launch date of 18 September 2011 on iTunes. The song had been released on YouTube in June 2011 and was alleged to resemble Lady Gaga's song 'Bad Romance'.

Lady Gaga sought an interim injunction to stop the release of the song on iTunes and also requiring its removal from YouTube.

The claim for trade mark infringement was made under Articles 9(1)(b) and 9(1)(c) of the Community Trade Mark (CTM) Regulation. It was accepted that the use of the Lady Goo Goo character in the game could continue.

The judge took the view that there was a strongly arguable case that both players of the game and older people exposed to the song would think there was a commercial connection between Lady Gaga and Lady Goo Goo, perhaps because they would think Lady Gaga had adopted the Lady Goo Goo moshling. Mr Justice Voss appeared to have been influenced by the similarity in names and that 'goo goo ga ga' is a known baby phrase, and by Lady Gaga having made her name in the music field and using the term 'Little Monsters' in her tweets, as well as the fact that the YouTube tag for the song actually included a reference to Lady Gaga. There was also some evidence of confusion in blogs, but it was not unequivocal.

The judge also took the view that the LADY GAGA trade mark had the necessary reputation to found a claim and that there was the necessary link between LADY GOO GOO and the registered mark. In addition, he thought there was a good, arguable case that the use of LADY GOO GOO damaged the distinctive character of the LADY GAGA mark.

Referring to the judgment of the CJEU in the Interflora *v* Marks & Spencer case (above), the judge was of the opinion that consumers might not be able to tell that the song didn't emanate from Lady Gaga. As the YouTube release used the Lady Gaga tag and the Lady Goo Goo moshling looks a bit like Lady Gaga, consumers might also think the song was 'approved' by Lady Gaga.

In addition, there was a real risk of impairment of the LADY GAGA trademark, relying heavily on the fact that consumers would think the origin to be Lady Gaga. The use of LADY GOO GOO in the context of the song – as opposed simply to being the name of the character in the game – amounted to taking unfair advantage of the LADY GAGA trademark.

There was an arguable case of 'free-riding' outside of the game when considering the distribution of popular music under the name LADY GOO GOO, particularly as no other characters in the game had released songs under their names.

The judge pointed out that there's no defence of parody to trademark infringement. Nonetheless, it may be possible to argue that pure parodic use of a trademark is use 'with due cause' and doesn't technically amount to an infringement. However, the Lady Goo Goo character had morphed beyond parody into something else and was being used to enhance the commercial success of Moshi Monsters and to sell music downloads. Accordingly, the parody argument didn't run.

The judge allowed the defendants to continue to use LADY GOO GOO as the name of a character in the game, but not for the release of the song in iTunes or its presence on YouTube. The song release was a new departure and a commercial venture, and the YouTube release was the wrong side of the line between game character and 'Lady Goo Goo becoming a musical star in her own right'.

Lady Gaga got her injunction against Lady Goo Goo.

This case is extremely interesting, as it's one of the few cases in which a parody 'defence' has been raised to an action for trademark infringement. It appears that the court will have some sympathy with the parodic use of a trademark, but not once it strays into the realms of having a commercial purpose that competes with a brand owner's IP rights.

However, the line between commercial and non-commercial parodies isn't always clear, and it's interesting to note that Lady Gaga accepted that the Lady Goo Goo character was unobjectionable in the game, despite the fact that the game is a commercial venture generating revenues through subscriptions and merchandising.

As yet, the government hasn't given any indication that it will want to extend parody as a defence to trademark infringement despite recommendations for reform of copyright laws to allow parody in certain circumstances contained in the independent review of intellectual property and growth by Professor Ian Hargreaves, published in 2011.

Passing-off action as a barrier to market entry

The tort of passing off is intended to prevent consumers being misled into believing that goods, services or indeed whole businesses are those of someone else.

Passing off is a historical barrier to market entry that can stop phoney 'lookalike' or 'me too' products, services and businesses from entering the market where an existing brand owner is already established and clearly will face unfair competition if its rival is permitted to trade or continue to trade.

Unlike an action for the infringement of a trademark, a passing-off action protects the goodwill of a business as a whole, so it's much wider as a legal protection. But in order to succeed the claimant must satisfy a high burden of proof.

Taking legal action under passing off can also be more costly than taking enforcement proceedings for infringement of a registered trademark and tends to be used where there's a dispute around an unregistered mark.

Pursuing a claim under the tort of passing off can be a high-risk strategy, as the claimant will need to establish to the satisfaction of the court that the reputation and status of the unregistered mark actually exist, and the status of the unregistered mark that it is claimed is infringed needs to be proved. For example, advertisements that falsely suggest that one brand owner's goods or services have a connection or association with another's business may give rise to a passing-off action if this could cause damage to the innocent brand owner. As with actions for an infringement of a registered trademark, innocence isn't a defence to an action for passing off.

Common field of activity

A competitor brand owner must make the misrepresentation in the course of trade. It's not necessary that the defendant operates in direct competition with the claimant, although the further removed the businesses are from each other, the less likely the public are to be confused into thinking there's a connection.

In the case of Stringfellows (1984), a well-known nightclub in central London named after its founder Peter Stringfellow, the absence of a common field of activity was taken into account by the Court of Appeal in deciding whether the use of the word 'Stringfellows' on the packaging of McCain's frozen chips was likely to lead the public to believe that the product was in some way associated with the claimant or his club. The Court of Appeal held that, even if viewers of TV commercials for frozen McCain chips associated the product with the nightclub, the nightclub would suffer no substantial damage, and the action for passing off failed.

If the claimant's mark has become a household name, the degree of overlap between the fields of activity becomes less important, since the public are more likely to be confused as to the origin of any goods bearing the mark in question that don't emanate from the claimant.

Although generally the claimant and defendant will share a common pool of customers and potential customers, this may not be the case where the parties don't operate in a common field of activity.

Where the parties don't share a common pool of customers or potential customers, it's unclear whether the misrepresentation must be made to the claimant's customers and potential customers, or to the customers and potential customers of the defendant. Much will depend on the circumstances of each individual case.

Although the most common form of damage complained of will be loss of sales where these are unfairly diverted to the defendant, it's no defence to an action in passing off that the misrepresentation was made to customers who don't pay for the goods or services.

Evidential burden

To bring a successful action in passing off, the claimant must show that the defendant has behaved in a way calculated to deceive a proportion of the public. The courts have interpreted this to mean that the actions of the competitor brand owner are calculated to deceive and amount to a misrepresentation.

Although evidence of actual deception is helpful, it's not conclusive, and the courts tend to apply the following guidelines:

- There's no absolute bar on admitting evidence of actual deception.
- Evidence of the likelihood of deception is admissible from those accustomed to dealing in the market where the goods are of a kind sold in a specialist market and not to the general public for consumption or domestic use.
- Where the goods are of a kind sold to the general public for consumption or domestic use, evidence of the likelihood of deception from those accustomed to deal in that market may be admissible unless the experience that a judge must be taken to possess as an ordinary shopper or consumer will enable him or her, just as well as any other, to assess the likelihood of confusion.
- Evidence is always admissible to prove the circumstances and places the goods are sold in, the kind of people who buy them and the manner in which the public are accustomed to ask for those goods.

Evidence that consumers have actually been deceived is admissible. Conversely, the absence of evidence of actual deception of consumers may lend strength to the argument that no deception has occurred and that an action in passing off should fail.

The courts tend to distinguish between 'confusion', which is unlikely to damage goodwill, and 'deception', which is likely to divert trade from the claimant and/or damage goodwill in some other way.

Survey evidence

Survey evidence is often adduced in passing-off cases but is frequently discredited on the grounds that the sample size wasn't representative of the likely consumers of the product or service or leading questions skewed the respondents' answers, reducing the survey's evidential value.

In assessing surveys as evidence of passing off, the courts tend to apply the following principles:

- Respondents must be selected to represent a relevant cross-section of the public.
- Sample size must be statistically relevant.
- Survey must be conducted fairly and in accordance with best practice.
- All the surveys carried out must be disclosed, including the number carried out, how they were conducted, and the totality of the persons involved.
- The totality of the answers given and the other requisite details must be disclosed and made available to the defendant.
- Questions used mustn't be leading or should not lead the person answering into a field of speculation he or she would never have embarked on had the question not been put.
- The exact answers and not some abbreviated form must be recorded.
- The instructions to the interviewers as to how to carry out the survey must be disclosed.
- Where the answers are coded for computer input, the coding instructions must also be disclosed.

Interim injunction

The availability of interim relief is crucial to a passing-off action, since a claimant who acts quickly may obtain an interim injunction to restrain further trade by the defendant pending a full trial and mitigate further damage to goodwill during the intervening period. In practice, the outcome of the interim injunction application is often decisive to the entire action.

In the American Cyanamid (1975) case, the House of Lords set out the principles that govern whether an interim injunction for passing off should be granted:

- Is there a serious issue to be tried?
- If the claimant is ultimately successful at trial, would damages be an adequate remedy for any loss suffered by the claimant in the intervening period until trial if no interim injunction is granted?
- If the claimant is ultimately unsuccessful at trial, would damages be an adequate remedy for any loss suffered by the defendant in the intervening period until trial if an interim injunction is granted?

The 'serious issue to be tried' hurdle is not a high one, and most interim injunction applications turn on the issue of whether damages would be an adequate remedy for either or both parties. If the claimant is to obtain an interim injunction it's essential that it makes its application as soon as possible after becoming aware of the defendant's activities, since any unexplained or unreasonable delay may well be fatal to its prospects of obtaining interim relief.

Whether or not an interim injunction is granted, the court may, on the hearing of the application, order a speedy trial, meaning that the action will be 'fast-tracked' towards a full trial inside a few weeks or months, rather than the more typical 12-month time frame.

Search and seizure orders

A search and seizure order compels the defendant to allow the claimant's representatives to take possession of infringing articles that the defendant is expected to have concealed, or to obtain evidence and documents that the defendant is expected to suppress. Typically, the defendant is ordered to allow the claimant to enter its premises and take away evidence. Such orders are granted without notice to the defendant, and the jurisdiction is used sparingly.

Damages

Although an injunction is normally the most valuable remedy for a claimant in a passing-off action, if the matter goes to full trial and the claimant is successful it will normally be entitled to an award of damages or (less attractive) an account of profits.

Damages in passing-off cases can be extremely difficult to quantify. Typically, there are two heads of claims most frequently used: loss of sales; and damage to goodwill and reputation.

With respect to loss of sales, the issue for the court to determine is what proportion of sales made by the defendant would otherwise have been made by the claimant but for the defendant's act of passing off.

Damage to goodwill and/or reputation is normally more difficult to quantify, and the courts tend to take a fairly broad-brush approach.

Eddie Irvine *v* Talksport (2003)

In the passing-off action taken by F1 driver Eddie Irvine against radio station Talksport, the Court of Appeal awarded Eddie Irvine £25,000 in respect of the misrepresentation by Talksport that the driver had endorsed the radio station by using his image listening to a radio in a cheeky poster campaign.

The court assessed the damages on the basis of the sum that would have been agreed for the use of Eddie Irvine's endorsement, taking account of the level of other endorsement deals at the time.

Account of profits

A successful claimant will normally have the option of seeking an account of the defendant's profits, rather than an award of damages (although the court does have discretion to refuse to order an account of profits, since it's an equitable remedy).

Orders for an account of profits are commonly limited to dealings from the date of the letter before action or commencement of proceedings, on the grounds that an account of profits isn't available in respect of innocent passing off.

In practice, it's rare for an account of profits to be pursued, owing to the difficulty of proving what proportion of the defendant's profits was attributable to the passing off, and because of the scope for defendants to argue that they, in fact, made little or no profit from their unlawful activities, which weakens the attractiveness of such a remedy for the claimant.

Delivery-up or destruction

If an injunction is granted, or if the defendant voluntarily undertakes to cease dealing in the infringing goods, it's common to order or get an undertaking that the infringing goods be delivered up to the claimants or their lawyers or that they be destroyed by the defendant, with the destruction verified on oath. This ensures that the defendant is no longer in possession of items, dealings in which would breach the injunction or such an undertaking.

Copyright as a barrier to market entry

The stark conclusion of the Hargreaves Report (2011) was that 'the UK's intellectual property framework, especially with regard to copyright, is falling behind what is needed'. Professor Ian Hargreaves was concerned that existing copyright law had started to act as a regulatory barrier to the creation of new kinds of internet-based businesses that rely on routine copying of text, images and data.

The government signalled its acceptance of these findings and is currently exploring ways in which the IP framework needs to be adapted in order to encourage innovation and growth, although it has ruled out any significant change in the immediate short term.

One approach that's gaining support is the establishment of the world's first Digital Copyright Exchange, which will make it easier for rights holders to sell licences in their work and for others to buy them, speeding up market transactions by automating the process as well as driving down transactional costs. 'The result will be a UK market in digital copyright which is better informed and more readily capable of resolving disputes without costly litigation,' claims Professor Hargreaves.

Other reforms of the existing copyright framework include cross-border licensing within the EU market, the licensing of 'orphan works' where the owner of the copyright can't be traced, and reform of copyright collecting societies.

Copyright, Designs and Patents Act 1988 (CDPA 1988)

Copyright seeks to protect the form of expression of an idea (for example, in writing) and not the actual idea itself, which will need to be protected by the duty of confidentiality, for example. The primary purpose of copyright law is to reward authors for the creation of original works where the author has expended independent effort to create the work.

Copyright law is intended to prevent copying but doesn't provide a monopoly; it doesn't matter if a similar or identical work already exists provided it hasn't been copied. This is a major distinction with the application of trademark law and protection.

Copyright lasts for a set period, most often the life of the author plus 70 years from the end of the calendar year of death.

No formalities need to be executed in the UK for a work to receive copyright protection – protection automatically applies to all works recorded in any form provided they meet specific requirements as provided by the CDPA 1988.

In order for copyright to subsist under UK law:

- a work must fall into one of the categories of work protected by copyright;
- a work must qualify for protection under UK law (this usually depends on the nationality of the author or place of first publication); and
- the term of copyright mustn't have expired.

The following categories of works are protected under UK copyright law:

- original literary (including software), dramatic, musical or artistic works;
- sound recordings, films or broadcasts;
- the typographical arrangements of published editions.

A literary work can include, amongst many things, a marketing plan!

Length of copyright protection

With respect to written, theatrical, musical, artistic and film works, copyright lasts for the life of the creator plus 70 years from the end of the year in which he or she died.

Similarly, copyright in a film runs out 70 years after the end of the year in which the death occurs of the last to survive of the principal director, the authors of the screenplay and dialogue, and the composer of any music specially created for the film.

Both software (computer programs) and databases are capable of being protected as literary works. Where two or more people have created a single work protected by copyright and where the contribution of each author isn't distinct from that of the other(s), those people are generally joint authors and joint first owners. The term of copyright protection in such a work is calculated with reference to the date of the death of the last surviving author. Any sound recording made of a song will be protected for a different period of time from the underlying music or lyrics.

You should also note that, for copyright works originating outside the UK or another country of the European Economic Area (EEA), the term of protection may be shorter if it's shorter in the country of origin. There may also be variations in the term where a work was created before 1 January 1996.

With respect to sound recordings, there will usually be more than one copyright associated with a work such as a song. The composer of the music will be the author of the musical work and has copyright in that music. The lyrics of the song are protected separately by copyright as a literary work and will usually be owned by the person who wrote them. The term of protection for an original musical and literary work is the creator's life plus 70 years from the end of the year in which he or she dies. In September 2011, the European Union approved a directive that includes measures to align the term of protection for the music and lyrics in a musical composition. Currently, if a work is recorded then copyright in this sound recording lasts for 50 years from the end of the year in which it was made or, if published in this time, 50 years from the end of the year of publication. If the recording isn't published during that 50-year period, but it's played in public or communicated to the public during that period, then copyright will last for 50 years from when this happens.

In September 2011 the European Union approved a directive that will extend that period for sound recordings and performers' rights in sound recordings to 70 years. Sound recordings don't have to be original, but they will not be new copyright works if they've been merely copied from existing sound recordings. Sound recordings may also contain performers' rights.

With respect to broadcasts, copyright in a broadcast expires 50 years from the end of the year of the making of the broadcast. A broadcast doesn't have to be original, but there will be no copyright if, or to the extent that, it infringes copyright in another broadcast.

With respect to published editions, copyright in the typographical arrangement of a published edition expires 25 years from the end of the year in which the edition was first published. Published editions don't have to be original, but they won't be new copyright works if the typographical arrangement has been copied from existing published editions.

Use of the copyright symbol ©

Best practice in the marketing profession is to use the standard copyright notice '© [name of copyright owner] [year of first publication]'. This is helpful, as it creates a legal presumption that the named individual or company is the copyright owner and notifies the public that a work is protected by copyright. However, in the UK it's not essential to include the © symbol, as copyright arises automatically.

Marketers shouldn't assume that placing a © symbol on their work affords any greater degree of protection. This symbol has no impact on the subsistence of copyright in a work, but merely gives rise to a presumption that the name corresponds to the owner of the copyright in that work, until the contrary is proved.

The rights holder of the copyright in a work has the exclusive right to do the following:

- copy the work;
- issue copies of the work to the public;
- perform, show or play the work in public;
- communicate the work to the public;
- make an adaptation of the work or do any of the above in relation to an adaptation.

The rights holder has also the right to:

- be identified as the author or director of the work;
- object to derogatory treatment of the work;
- not have work falsely attributed to him or her;
- prevent others from infringing any of his or her rights;
- assign or license the rights to third parties.

Protection of a copyright work subsists automatically when the work is created.

Where a work is made by an employee in the course of the employment, the employer will be the first owner of copyright in the work, subject to any agreement to the contrary.

A common assumption often made by marketers is to think that ownership of the image in a photograph taken by a photographer belongs to them if they've paid the photographer for the shoot. This isn't the case. The terms and conditions under which the photographer has been engaged are critical in determining whether copyright in the material passes to the client given that copyright in the image automatically vests with the photographer unless there's agreement to the contrary and the client has bought the copyright to the image taken.

For a discussion on making agreements in marketing, refer to Chapter 1.

Infringement of copyright

It's a question of fact in each case whether there's been an infringement of copyright. If someone copies the whole of a copyright work, clearly there will be infringement. However, the position isn't always clear cut. Under the CDPA 1988, the key test is whether a substantial part of the work concerned has been copied (section 16(3), CDPA 1988).

In establishing whether there's been copying of a substantial part, the part to be considered is the part of the copyright work that has been copied, not part of the copy, and in determining substantiality the test is qualitative not quantitative.

Prohibited acts infringe copyright if they are done in relation to the work or a substantial part of it. Much of copyright litigation is spent arguing whether or not a piece of a work that's been taken constitutes a substantial part of the copyright work.

A common mistake made is to think that 'substantial' relates to the proportion of the work that's been copied. It doesn't. It's not about quantity but rather about the circumstances under which a copy has been made.

Just because only one page out of a book of several thousand pages has been copied it doesn't mean that a 'substantial part' in this sense hasn't been taken. Neither does it have anything to do with the quantity taken. For example, a tiny fragment of a painting that's less than a few centimetres square may constitute a 'substantial part'.

More pertinent is what skill and labour were needed or utilized in the creation of the work. If a work or a part of it is copied verbatim or exactly, the test will normally be fulfilled.

The principal difficulties arise in situations where the copy is similar but not identical to the work alleged to have been copied. An example might be a table of information (a compilation, so attracting literary copyright), which is reproduced with the same information but in a completely different order (ignoring any database rights that might subsist for the purpose of the example). The issue of whether or not a substantial part of the table has been copied depends on the nature of the information. If the skill and labour were in collecting the information, then a substantial part has been taken. If, however, the information was freely available but the value of the table and the difficulty in its compilation were in ordering that information in a given way, a substantial part of it wouldn't have been taken, since that order is not present in the copy.

Direct or indirect copying

It's irrelevant for the purposes of the CDPA 1988 whether the act of copying is done directly or indirectly, or whether any intervening copy infringes. In other words, a photograph of a copyright painting is an infringement of the copyright in the painting, but a photograph of the photograph is also an infringement of the painting. The fact that the first photograph was taken by the artist and copyright owner, and so didn't constitute an infringement, doesn't prevent the subsequent photograph being an infringement of the painting itself.

Fair dealing defences

The CDPA 1988 permits 'fair dealing' with certain types of copyright work for the purposes of:

- research and private study;
- criticism or review;
- reporting current events.

With respect to research and private study, 'fair dealing' with a literary, dramatic, musical or artistic work or typographical arrangement is permitted for the purpose of: research for a non-commercial purpose, provided it's accompanied by a sufficient acknowledgement unless impractical to do so; and private study.

Outside of these uses, the courts in assessing 'fair dealing' tend to have regard to whether a fair-minded and honest person would have dealt with the copyright work as the defendant did. It's clear from a number of cases regarding fair dealing that the courts will take into account the extent to which the use made of the copyright material was necessary for the relevant purpose in determining whether there's been a breach of copyright.

Interim relief remedy for copyright infringement

This is where the copyright owner suffers serious ongoing damage and an injunction preventing the acts complained of is sought. For example, where a marketer has obviously copied the 'get-up', colours and design of a soft drink that infringes the copyright of a competitor brand, then an interim injunction could be obtained to get the supermarket to remove the offending item from its shelves. In this example, there would also probably be an action in respect of infringement of trademark and passing off.

In order to obtain an interim injunction, the marketer must first show that there's a serious case to answer. On the assumption that there is, the court will then consider whether or not the damage that the marketer is suffering or is likely to suffer (if the acts are merely threatened) before the trial could be compensated by damages paid by the defendant at trial.

If money would adequately compensate for the damage, no interim injunction will be granted. The court will then consider whether or not, should the action continue to trial and the marketer then lost, the marketer would be able to recompense the defendant for any damage suffered as a result of the grant of the injunction. If the marketer could do so, the court will finally consider the balance of convenience – in other words, which side is the likelier to suffer the least injustice by the potential grant of the injunction. If the balance of convenience is decided in favour of the claimant, an interim injunction will be granted before full trial.

Other orders, such as an order allowing the search and seizure of infringing articles and/or evidence of infringement, or an order freezing an infringer's assets, may also be granted under particular circumstances at the discretion of the court. For example, this frequently occurs when a marketer fears that there has been a breach of its copyright and other IP rights and calls in the trading standards officers to make an inspection of a factory producing counterfeit merchandise and other products.

All such remedies are costly for the marketer in the short term, and potentially for the infringing defendant in the long term.

Remedies at trial for copyright infringement

At trial, should copyright infringement be proven, the claimant may obtain a number of remedies for any damage suffered as a result of the infringement:

- Injunctive relief, preventing the acts complained of being done by the defendant, can be ordered, the breaching of which constitutes a contempt of court, with very serious consequences for the defendant.

- Damages can be obtained in two ways: the claimant deciding whether to seek compensation for the damage actually suffered or whether to seek account of profits (but not both).

- 'Aggravated' or 'restitutionary' damages may be awarded by the court if, knowing that the acts concerned were copyright infringements, the defendant nonetheless carried out those acts.

- Delivery-up of any infringing articles that the defendant has in its possession may be ordered by the court. This is particularly useful in cases of stopping illegal merchandise from flooding the market and affecting the legitimate sales of branded merchandise as well as affecting the market value for this product.

Criminal sanctions for copyright infringement

In certain cases, copyright infringement may constitute a criminal offence that carries a custodial sentence, such as acts of copyright infringement carried out with the requisite knowledge for commercial purposes.

A number of the criminal offences are set out in terms that are identical to various acts of secondary infringement, for example the act of importing infringing copies into the UK with knowledge or reason to believe that they are infringing copies, which is a criminal offence under section 107(1) of the CDPA 1998.

Digital Economy Act 2010

This recent controversial piece of legislation hasn't been fully enacted, and parts still remain to be brought into force by statutory instrument. Uniquely for a primary piece of legislation, the Digital Economy Act (DEA) 2010 has been subject to judicial, parliamentary and regulatory review since coming into force, given that some sections are now deemed to be unworkable.

The DEA 2010 introduces a system for tracking and taking action against offenders who habitually infringe the copyright of rights holders by peer-to-peer file sharing on the internet.

The Act imposes certain legal obligations on internet service providers (ISPs), which include serving copyright infringement notices on subscribers where such file sharing takes place.

An anonymous copyright infringement list can be requested, and provided that a certain level of infringement has taken place the rights holder can apply to the court to gain an order to identify some or all of the subscribers on that list in order to commence proceedings.

Most operational details of the copyright infringement provisions aren't defined in the DEA 2010 but left to a series of regulatory codes produced by Ofcom, which has engaged in a detailed consultation process regarding the workability of the DEA 2010.

Sanctions in the DEA 2010 include limiting internet access as well as suspending it entirely. There's an independent appeals process covering the grounds upon which infringement reports can be made.

The 2010 Act states that 'an appeal on any grounds must be determined in favour of the subscriber unless the copyright owner or internet service provider shows that...

- the apparent infringement was an infringement of copyright; and
- the report relates to the subscriber's IP address at the time of that infringement.'

An appeal will also succeed if the subscriber can show that the rights holder or ISP broke Ofcom's regulatory code in any way.

Ofcom has the responsibility of enforcing the ISPs' obligations in any such infringement action and can impose a fine of up to £250,000 for contravention of the DEA 2010.

In deciding whether to grant an injunction against an ISP, the court is required to consider:

- steps taken by the ISP of the location to prevent copyright infringement;
- steps taken by the copyright owner to facilitate lawful access to the material;
- any representations made by a minister of the Crown;
- whether the injunction would be likely to have a disproportionate effect on any person's legitimate interests;
- the importance of freedom of expression.

The Secretary of State must be satisfied before making the request that the location is 'having a serious adverse effect on businesses or consumers', that the injunction 'is a proportionate way to address that effect' and that 'making the regulations would not prejudice national security or the prevention or detection of crime'.

Other provisions in the DEA 2010 include an amendment to the Copyright, Designs and Patents Act 1988 to increase the criminal liability for 'making or dealing with infringing articles' and 'making, dealing with or using illicit recordings' to a maximum of £50,000, so long as it is done during the course of a business.

In 2011, BT and TalkTalk challenged provisions of the DEA 2010 that forced them to send copyright infringement notices to subscribers and to provide information about subscribers in certain circumstances. The case against the government was heard by the Court of Appeal, where both ISPs argued that the DEA 2010 was incompatible with EU law. This argument was rejected, and the Court of Appeal affirmed that the DEA 2010 was fully consistent with European law.

The decision was welcomed by rights holders, who reportedly lose on average £400 million a year in revenues as a result of peer-to-peer file-sharing activities. However, the judgment has also been fiercely criticized by other groups, which argued that the sanctions imposed by the DEA 2010 impinge on an individual's privacy and freedom of speech, which is incompatible with the European Convention on Human Rights.

The decision of the Court of Appeal confirms that larger ISPs will be required to take a role in policing the rights of copyright owners in respect of infringements committed by those ISPs' customers, and in some cases this will involve bearing a proportion of the costs.

Both BT and TalkTalk must now undertake the relevant investment and expenditure to ensure compliance with the DEA 2010.

International protection of copyright

UK copyright works are protected overseas by virtue of the UK being a signatory to the four principal copyright conventions:

- the Berne Convention (Berne);
- the Universal Copyright Convention (the UCC);

- the Rome Convention;
- the World Intellectual Property Office Copyright Treaty (the WCT).

Berne and the UCC cover literary, scientific and artistic works, and the WCT covers computer programs and databases. The Rome Convention relates to musical works and rights in performances. The object of the treaties is to provide harmonization and a level playing field for the protection of copyright.

Berne Convention

Berne sets guidelines for the minimum protection that must be provided under the laws of the contracting states. Nationals of one contracting state can enjoy the same level of protection in another contracting state as can nationals of the home state. However, a state can decrease the level of protection to that of the state of origin.

For example, the UK has typographical rights, but the United States doesn't. The UK can therefore refuse to give typographical rights protection to a US author, as a UK author can't gain this protection in the United States. Currently, a total of 164 countries are signatories to Berne, and there are special provisions for developing countries. The minimum term of protection of the relevant works is 50 years.

Universal Copyright Convention

Administered by the United Nations Educational, Scientific and Cultural Organization (UNESCO), the UCC can be seen as a step on the way to Berne for developing countries, and currently has 100 signatories.

The UCC sets two minimum terms of protection for copyright: life of the author plus 25 years; and, for rights arising on publication, a minimum term of 25 years from the date of first publication.

Each contracting state undertakes to provide adequate protection for the rights of authors in respect of literary, scientific and artistic works. More specifically, the UCC provides that, if the domestic law of any contracting state requires as a condition of copyright compliance with formalities such as the use of a copyright notice, that state shall regard those requirements as satisfied in relation to all works published outside its territory in respect of an author who is not one of its nationals if, from the time of the first publication, all copies of the work published with the authority of the author or other copyright proprietor display the copyright symbol © together with the name of the owner of the copyright, and the year of publication is affixed to all material that requires protection.

As the United States is a signatory to the UCC, non-US copyright holders don't need to register with the US Copyright Office in order to obtain US copyright protection.

However, registration of copyright with the US Copyright Office in the Library of Congress is prima facie evidence of the validity of the copyright and of the existence of the work and the author.

This can assist in enforcing the copyright in a US court. Registration also allows the rights holder to claim 'statutory' (or fixed) damages where actual damages are hard to quantify.

The United States has been a signatory to the Berne Convention since 1 March 1989. From this date, foreign copyright holders are no longer required to mark their work with a copyright notice in order to benefit from copyright protection.

However, the use of a copyright notice is still advisable as a warning or reminder. In an action for copyright infringement in a US court, the use of a proper copyright notice on a work will prevent the defendant from claiming 'innocent infringement', which if successful could result in a reduction in the damages that the rights holder would otherwise receive.

Rome Convention

The Rome Convention, which is administered by the World Intellectual Property Office (WIPO), provides for certain minimum protection of copyright for:

- performers in relation to their performances;
- producers of sound recordings in relation to those recordings;
- broadcasting organizations in respect of their broadcasts.

With respect to sound recordings and broadcasts, the Convention provides, among other things, that producers of sound recordings have the right to authorize or prohibit the direct or indirect reproduction of their recordings, and that broadcasting organizations have the right to authorize or prohibit the re-broadcasting of their broadcasts, the unauthorized recording of their broadcasts or the reproduction of such recordings.

The Convention allows contracting states to provide for various exceptions to these rights, such as in relation to copyright material for private use.

Protection lasts for at least 20 years from the end of the year in which the performance or broadcast took place, or from the end of the year in which the sound recording was made. Currently, 91 countries have signed the Rome Convention.

World Intellectual Property Office (WIPO) Copyright Treaty

WIPO, whose mandate it is to administer Berne, also created the WIPO Copyright Treaty (WCT) to complement and operate in conjunction with Berne.

The WCT concerns computer programs and databases and grants the authors of such works the right to authorize:

- distribution to the public of the original and/or copies of a work through sale or other transfer of ownership;
- commercial rental to the public of the original and/or copies of a work;
- any communication of a work to the public by wire or wireless means (including on-demand, interactive communication through the internet).

Currently, 89 countries are signatories to the WCT. The period of protection offered by the WCT in respect of the relevant works is 50 years, except in those countries that have adopted a 70-year protection period.

The WCT was signed by the UK in 1997, and the UK has complied with the requirements of the WCT by means of the Copyright and Related Rights Regulations 2003 (SI 2003/2498), which amended the CDPA 1988.

In 2009, the EU member states ratified the WIPO Copyright Treaty and the WIPO Performances and Phonograms Treaty – the so-called 'internet treaties'.

In 2001, the EU adopted the Copyright Directive, which incorporates most of the provisions of the treaties. All 27 EU member states have now implemented the Copyright Directive.

Recent copyright issues considered by the UK and EU courts

Lucasfilm v Ainsworth (2011)

The Empire strikes back (!) in a copyright war over the design of the *Star Wars* storm trooper helmet, which became the subject of a multimillion-pound legal dispute. Judges in the UK Supreme Court unanimously found in favour of Lucasfilm and George Lucas, who created the science fiction phenomenon, in a dispute over reproductions of a helmet design. The court had to decide whether the helmets were sculptures and whether a claim that US copyright law had been infringed was 'justiciable in England' – in other words, could be pursued in the UK courts.

In previous legal actions the *Star Wars* Empire had failed to stop British prop designer Andrew Ainsworth, who helped to create the helmets and suits used in the 1977 film, from selling replicas.

In a landmark ruling, the UK Supreme Court held that the helmet wasn't a sculpture, and paved the way for proceedings to be brought in England over claims of breaches of US copyright. The judgment said 'there are no issues of policy which militate against the enforcement of foreign copyright. States have an interest in the international recognition and enforcement of their copyrights as the Berne Convention shows.'

This case could have significant implications in so far as the UK Supreme Court found that English courts have jurisdiction to decide allegations of foreign copyright infringement claims provided that the defendant is based in the UK. The ruling may have opened the door to allegations of world-wide infringement claims against UK businesses for unregistered IP rights in English courts, whereas previously IP rights holders would have had to bring separate claims in each jurisdiction where their rights had been infringed.

Temple Island Collections v New English Teas (2012)

The case deals with the tricky area of copyright law – the scope of protection for images manipulated by post-production software.

The rights holder, Temple Island Collections (TIC), claimed to be the owner of copyright subsisting in a black and white photograph of a red bus travelling across Westminster Bridge. Once the photograph had been taken, it was manipulated on a computer using Adobe® Photoshop software, where the red colour was strengthened, the sky was removed, the rest of the image was changed to monochrome except for the bus, and the image was stretched. The whole endeavour, including taking the original photograph, took around 80 hours.

The image was published in February 2006 and was used by the claimant on various souvenir products. The image became famous, and a number of other organizations licensed it from TIC, including the Historic Royal Palaces.

The defendants, New English Teas (NET), were aware of the famous image and in the past had settled a previous copyright infringement dispute with TIC. In this case, the defendants took four photographs – three of different aspects of the Houses of Parliament and one of a classic red Routemaster bus – which were then combined and manipulated to produce a new image.

TIC brought proceedings against NET for copyright infringement. NET denied infringement, arguing that TIC couldn't use copyright law to give itself, effectively, a monopoly right over monochrome images of the Houses of Parliament and a red bus.

The UK Patents County Court found that copyright plainly subsisted in TIC's photograph, as it was indeed the author's own 'intellectual creation' and had involved skill and labour, both in terms of the choices relating to the basic photograph itself (the motif, angle of shot, light and shade, illumination and exposure) and in terms of the post-production work. The judge also found that NET had indeed copied TIC's photograph – it had access to TIC's work and there were obvious similarities between the images. However, in order for it to be an infringement of copyright, the court had to determine whether a substantial part of TIC's work had been reproduced.

The issue turned on a qualitative assessment of the reproduced elements. In terms of composition, the reproduced elements amounting to a substantial part included the classic Routemaster red bus on the right of Westminster Bridge, the riverside façade of the Houses of Parliament, the substantial amount of sky, and the top of the bus at roughly the same height as the façade of the Houses of Parliament within the image frame. As for visual contrast features, the reproduced elements consisted of the bright red bus against a monochrome background and the element of the blank white sky, which created a strong skyline.

Two factors that influenced the judge's decision were: the nature of TIC's image; and the collection of other similar works relied on by NET.

With respect to the nature of TIC's image, the nature of the image was not 'a mere photograph'. Its appearance was the product of deliberate choices and deliberate manipulations by the photographer. With respect to the collection of other similar works, this worked against NET, as it emphasized how ostensibly independent expressions of the same idea can turn out differently.

Taken together, the court found that NET's image infringed TIC's original photographic work.

The case is a warning to marketers to think carefully before manipulating an image for which they don't own the copyright, as this case appears to widen the scope of copyright protection in the composition of visual images.

Meltwater *v* Newspaper Licensing Agency (2012)

In 2009 the Newspaper Licensing Agency (NLA) introduced a licensing scheme for media monitoring agencies wishing to link to content from its members' websites, as well as a licence for the clients of these monitoring agencies. Meltwater is a monitoring agency that provides these services to clients and public relations agencies, and it reluctantly agreed to pay NLA a license fee.

The legality for levying such a licence payment for end users was then jointly challenged by Meltwater and the Public Relations Consultants Association (PRCA) with reference to the Copyright Tribunal on the grounds it was unreasonable and unfair.

The matter reached the Court of Appeal, where the judges ruled that copying and sharing of such media coverage amount to copyright infringement unless they are licensed by the content owner. This also applied to receiving or sending an e-mail with a headline or tweeting a news hyperlink within a commercial environment.

Based on the verdict from the Court of Appeal, the Copyright Tribunal adjourned to rule on the NLA licensing scheme raised by Meltwater and the PRCA. In 2012, the Copyright Tribunal ruled that changes needed to be made to the terms of the NLA licence, which had the effect of reducing price increases by 90 per cent, allowed Meltwater to retain its index of media coverage on its servers and removed the limitation on search access to 100 days.

The NLA copyright licence fee is now calculated on the basis of the number of employees within the retrieving organization as well as the number of users for the service.

During the Copyright Tribunal, the NLA revealed that it is going to require all commercial UK users of Google News or Google Alerts to obtain an NLA licence, and this too is likely to be contested in the courts.

Francis Ingham, Chief Executive of the PRCA, observes:

> *What that means is that all non-private browsing of news content made freely available on the internet will infringe copyright if it's done without a rights holder licence. We believe that browsing content made available on the internet shouldn't infringe copyright. And simply using headlines of an article for bibliographic reference could infringe copyright too. We advocate common-sense licensing that helps publishers run profitably and allows UK citizens to use the internet without fear of unintentional infringement. For example, if publishers want to charge for content, they can put it behind a pay wall. If it's freely available, publishers should allow search engines to find the content so readers can easily access it. The everyday act of sharing hyperlinks to content should not require a licence. The sharing of links in e-mail and social media increases readership of news stories and the revenue for publishers.*

The Copyright Tribunal verdict means that all end users of media monitoring services will need to have an NLA licence.

The definition of whether the mere act of browsing the internet amounts to copyright infringement is likely to be decided by the UK Supreme Court in 2013, and the NLA's scheme will remain in place until that point.

'Technology is evolving much faster than copyright law and as it stands, UK copyright legislation restricts the ability of UK internet users from enjoying the full benefits of the internet, putting UK plc at a disadvantage relative to other countries. We will continue to lobby for changes to legislation until this situation is resolved,' concludes Francis Ingham.

Future plans by the government in the wake of the Hargreaves Report

The government has fully endorsed the proposal for a Digital Copyright Exchange (DCE) that would go beyond the role played by collecting societies and create a more efficient marketplace for the rights holders and licensees to do business.

According to Professor Ian Hargreaves, the establishment of a DCE will be a world first and could generate in excess of £2.2 billion annually to the UK economy.

Licences and royalties would be negotiated by the licensor and the licensee via the DCE, but would be subject to controls on unfair competition. The DCE itself would be funded by deriving revenue from charges on licensing transactions, rather than for searches of the database or uploads of ownership information for copyrighted works.

A subsidiary role of the DCE would be to provide a public register of title to copyright, as a means of reducing the problem of 'orphan works' where the owner of a copyright can't be identified or located, but it would also be a powerful tool against copyright infringement.

The suggestion appears to be that those who infringe copyright in works that are on the DCE's register might be treated differently from other infringers, for example by having constructive knowledge of the existence and ownership of the copyright (as they would have 'no excuse for not checking').

The DCE would need to attract a 'critical mass' of material that's available and capable of being licensed in order to be operational.

The government has pledged to support the initiative by ensuring that Crown copyright materials would be available on the DCE from the outset and by encouraging other public bodies to do the same.

With respect to private copying and other copying that doesn't damage the underlying aims of copyright, the government aims to introduce exemptions for limited private copying, text and data mining, and library archiving. Such exemptions would override any contradicting terms in licence agreements. However, the government recognizes that any new exemptions would need to work within the framework of existing EU laws and should be implemented in a way that doesn't prejudice the incentives for rights owners to create the works in the first place.

The government also appears to recognize that humour should have a part to play in the creative process and plans to introduce an exception for copyright infringement to enable a work to be parodied for comedic effect without requiring prior consent of the rights holder. For a discussion on comparative advertising, refer to Chapter 5.

Generic top-level domains (gTLDs) as a barrier to market entry

A registered domain name is an effective barrier to market entry for any competitor brand owner thinking about using the same domain to promote its own goods and services on the web.

However, in June 2011 the Internet Corporation for Assigned Names and Numbers (ICANN) took a historic step to allow the radical liberalization of internet domain name endings – technically known as generic top-level domains (gTLDs) – which may result in the removal of these barriers as a result of liberalizing the options available for brand owners.

According to many commentators, this may have far-reaching implications for the protection of IP rights as well as online sales and marketing strategies.

Under the new rules, brand owners, organizations and institutions 'in good standing' can apply for the right to slap anything they like – and in any script – on the other side of the all-important dot.

At the time of writing there are currently only 22 gTLDs in addition to about 250 country code top-level domains, such as dot eu (European Union), dot ca (Canada) and dot jp (Japan).

At this time, if an organization wants to create a website, it contacts a domain name registrar to acquire ownership of a second-level domain (the string to the left of the dot) in connection with one of the existing top-level domains (for example, http://www.koganpage.com).

Under the newly adopted plan, any established public or private entity can apply for its own gTLD, which will allow it to control a gTLD for its trademark, such as dot coca-cola or dot Microsoft. Equally, it could be for particular goods and services, such as dot shoes or dot lawyers, or a topic of particular interest, such as dot fishing. The new gTLD can also include diacritical (accent) marks and non-Western script, such as Chinese and Arabic characters.

The decision to liberalize the web address market comes in the wake of much debate, as well as ICANN dragging its feet over the move to open up this valuable piece of 'internet real estate'.

Brand owners now have infinitely more options available to them than simply the traditional dot com, dot net or dot uk suffixes to play with.

But before there's a stampede for grabbing these new suffixes, evidence of user behaviour on the internet suggests that there's been a marked decrease in the importance of the web address in recent years, largely owing to the power of search engines driving the majority of activities on the web.

There are considerable costs and time involved in making such an application. For example, the process for creating a dot brand includes an application of more than 200 pages and includes an administrative check, among other things. Significantly, ICANN is charging a US$185,000 fee for each registered dot brand address. And for each, ICANN will also charge a fee of US$25,000 annually over the course of a 10-year licence.

Other indirect costs include the establishment and maintenance of an infrastructure and the maintenance of original domains through a transitional period, along with related legal fees, likely to top US$1 million to US$2 million even before the website is operational.

Going down this route then isn't for the faint-hearted or those without deep pockets! As a result, many commentators believe that these caveats, costs and restrictions will mean that most brand owners will decide that an individualized domain name isn't worth the hassle.

A priority system established by ICANN also gives preference to public bodies filing gTLDs over consumer brand owners.

If your application for a gTLD is accepted, then you'll run the registry for your gTLD and will be able to control the registration of all future second-level domains for that gTLD – a useful barrier to market entry. As an operator of a registry, you can sell second-level domains to the public at any price, or choose not to sell them at all, or perhaps make them available only to persons within your own organization.

Some of the main aspects of the application review process are:

- whether the proposed gTLD string is likely to result in user confusion deriving from similarity with any reserved name, any existing gTLD or any new gTLD string applied for in the current application round;

- whether the proposed gTLD represents a geographic name, in which case the applicant must be the relevant governmental or public authority;

- whether the applicant is technically, operationally and financially capable of operating a gTLD registry.

You may want to consider owning your own gTLD to protect your brand better. If internet users become aware of the new gTLDs, they may put more trust in websites with a brand name as the gTLD (for example, dot selfridges).

Cybersquatters and counterfeiters using second-level domains in connection with gTLDs other than the dot brand gTLD may not be as effective if customers know to look for the dot brand websites.

Alternatively, owning a more general gTLD can be an effective way to control the dialogue on a broad topic. For example, a hotel owner may want to own dot hotels and then limit the sale of second-level domains using that gTLD to its strategic partners, maintaining a barrier of market entry for its competitors.

If the new gTLDs are widely accepted by internet users – and that's a moot point – and attract high levels of internet traffic, owning a gTLD may increase an organization's credibility and legitimacy.

Given the expense of applying for a gTLD and running a registry, web users may feel that organizations that own a gTLD are more reliable. Owners of a gTLD may also be seen as technical leaders in their industries.

On the other hand, there's a risk that the new gTLDs won't be widely adopted and, whilst there are currently 22 gTLDs in use today, dot com is by far the most popular, and many of the gTLDs, such as dot coop and dot pro, attract comparatively little web traffic.

Even if a brand owner has no intention of owning its own gTLD it should still monitor the gTLD process. During the application phase in 2012, ICANN published a list of the proposed new gTLDs, providing third parties with the opportunity to file objections to proposed gTLD strings based on the following grounds:

- The string is confusingly similar to another proposed gTLD applied for by the third party.

- The string infringes the existing rights of the third party (such as trademark rights).
- The string is unacceptable to the community affected by it.

Developments in use of gTLDs may also have an impact on online sales and marketing strategies. A brand owner may want to monitor whether any of its competitors have applied for a gTLD with its brand.

If a competitor brand owner applies for a gTLD incorporating a frequently used term in a market segment, then it may be worth considering an application for a second-level domain under that gTLD.

In the future, brand owners may also need to monitor the new gTLDs for cybersquatters and counterfeiters, who may apply for second-level domains confusingly similar to the brand owner's company name, trademarks or brands.

The future of websites will effectively change post-January 2013 when this free-for-all becomes a reality and brand owners attempt to embed a marketing message as an integral part of their web address.

While it's expected that only a few hundred organizations will apply for their own gTLD, adoption of the new gTLDs may affect trademark and sales and marketing strategies for many years to come.

References and further reading

Cases and judgments

American Cyanamid *v* Ethicon Ltd [1975] AC 396
Ate My Heart Inc *v* Mind Candy Ltd [2011] EWHC 2741 (Ch)
Dalgety Spillers Foods *v* Food Brokers Ltd ([1994] FSR 504)
Designers Guild Limited *v* Russell Williams (Textiles) Limited (1999) 22(7) IPD 22067, CA, [2000] 1 WLR 2416, HL
Dyson *v* Vax Ltd [2011] EWCA Civ 1206
Google France and Google Joined Cases C-236/08 to C-238/08 [2010] ECR I-2417
Interflora *v* Marks & Spencer and others, Case C-323/09 (2011), Court of Justice of the European Union
Irvine *v* Talksport Ltd [2003] EWCA Civ 423
L'Oréal *v* eBay [2009] EWHC 1094 (Ch)
Lucasfilm *v* Ainsworth [2011] UKSC 39
Nestlé *v* Cadbury [2011], adjudication by the IPO
Pierre Fabre Dermo-Cosmétique SAS *v* Président de l'Autorité de la concurrence, Case C-439/09 (2011), Court of Justice of the European Union
Specsavers *v* Asda [2010] EWHC 2035 (Ch)
Stringfellow *v* McCain Foods (GB) Ltd [1984] RPC 501
Temple Island Collections Ltd *v* New English Teas Ltd [2012] EWPCC 1

Websites

Anti Copying in Design [accessed 17 March 2012] http://acid.eu.com

Association of Corporate Counsel provides excellent analysis on domestic and international intellectual property issues [accessed 13 March 2012] http://www.lexology.com

Berne Convention: contracting parties [accessed 19 March 2012] http://www.wipo.int

Intellectual Property Office: classes of goods and services that are protectable by a registered trademark can be viewed on the Intellectual Property Office website [accessed 19 March 2012] http://www.ipo.gov.uk

Internet Corporation for Assigned Names and Numbers (ICANN) [accessed 10 March 2012] http://www.icann.org

Lewis Silkin provides excellent insight in the area of trademark and other intellectual property rights [accessed 13 March 2012] http://www.lewissilkin.com

Memorandum of understanding between online marketplace operators and rights holders [accessed 20 March 2012] http://ec.europa.eu

Osborne Clarke provides excellent analysis on marketing case law [accessed 13 March 2012] http://www.marketinglaw.co.uk

Rome Convention: contracting parties [accessed 19 March 2012] http://www.wipo.int

Universal Copyright Convention: Declaration [accessed 19 March 2012] http://www.unesco.org

World Intellectual Property Office: contracting parties [accessed 19 March 2012] http://www.wipo.int

Reports and articles

Collins, Philip (Chairman, Office of Fair Trading) (2011) Transcript of a speech on the topic of competition law, King's College London, June

Hargreaves, Ian (2011) *Digital Opportunity: A Review of Intellectual Property and Growth*, May

Imperial College London (2010) *The Role of IPRs in UK Intangible Investment*, published by Imperial College London and commissioned by the IPO

Book

Kolah, A (2013) *High Impact Marketing that Gets Results*, Kogan Page, London

"Selling fireworks to kids on Facebook
wasn't your best marketing idea, was it?"

Legal requirements for sales and marketing activities

Introduction

Outlining the dos and don'ts for responsible sales and marketing and consumer protection is a mammoth task that could easily fill several volumes of Guru in a Bottle® *Essential Law for Marketers*! Many of the chapters in this book provide an examination of UK and EU laws and regulations through the lens of a particular sales and marketing activity, for example comparative advertising (Chapter 5), direct marketing (Chapter 6) and sales promotions (Chapter 8).

In this chapter, we examine the International Chamber of Commerce (ICC) Consolidated Code, which was revised in 2011. Uniquely, the ICC Code is core to many national country regulations that underpin marketing communications practice around the world and is therefore incredibly powerful.

In addition, the patchwork of UK and EU legal requirements and regulations that are common to a much wider range of sales and marketing activities than covered elsewhere in the book are also discussed here.

Closer to home, the ASA's regulations contained in the Committee on Advertising Practice (CAP) and Broadcast Committee on Advertising Practice (BCAP) Codes are also covered in this chapter.

Given the importance of protecting children and young people from sales and marketing exploitation, this warrants a whole section at the end of this chapter.

Taken together, the laws and regulations discussed here represent the cumulative 'hygiene factors' that all sales and marketing professionals must comply with in order to be legal, decent, honest and truthful.

ICC Consolidated Code for Advertising and Marketing Communications Practice (2011)

Background to the Consolidated ICC Code (2011)

The ICC Code sets the ethical standards and guidelines for brand owners. Developed by experts from a wide range of market and customer segments around the world, the ICC Code (2011) is a globally applicable framework that harmonizes best practice from the Americas, Africa, Europe, the Middle East and Asia Pacific.

The ICC Code applies to marketing communications in their entirety, including all words and numbers (spoken and written), visual treatments, music and sound effects, and material originating from other sources.

The Code is voluntary but has been incorporated by industry regulators across the world, including the ASA, and from that perspective is an excellent starting point in understanding principles behind the use of press, television, radio, other broadcast media, outdoor advertising, movies, digital interactive media, direct mail, electronic messaging, telephone and other media channels.

The ICC Code is also often referred to in legal arguments, as well as by the courts, where prevailing best practices and standards in the global sales and marketing industry need to be referred to in order to settle disputes.

The ICC Code is particularly relevant from a business to consumer (B2C) perspective and takes account of social, cultural and linguistic factors. For example, when judging communications addressed to children, the ICC Code provides that their natural credulity and inexperience should always be taken into account in any determination as to the appropriateness of those communications.

Assumptions made by the ICC Code

The ICC Code makes a number of assumptions that it is important to understand as you read the Codes: from a B2C perspective, individual customers and prospects are assumed to have a reasonable degree of experience, knowledge and sound judgement and to be reasonably observant and prudent when making purchasing decisions; and from a B2B perspective, companies and professional organizations are assumed to have an appropriate level of specialized knowledge and expertise in their field of operations. These same assumptions are applied in the CAP, BCAP and Direct Marketing Association Codes of Practice.

The ICC Code is structured in two main parts: general provisions on advertising and marketing communication practice that contain fundamental principles; and then a series of detailed sections that cover particular activities such as direct marketing, sponsorship and sales promotion. For a discussion on sponsorship law and practice, refer to Chapter 10.

General provisions of the ICC Code

Basic principles
All marketing communications should be legal, decent, honest and truthful, should be prepared with a due sense of social and professional responsibility and should conform to the principles of fair competition as generally accepted in business (Article 1).

The ICC Code adds that no communication should be such as to impair public confidence in marketing. These are the foundation principles upon which the rest of the ICC Code is based.

Decency
Marketing communications shouldn't contain statements or audio or visual treatments that offend standards of decency currently prevailing in the country and culture concerned (Article 2).

Honesty

Marketing communications should be framed so as not to abuse the trust of consumers or exploit their lack of experience or knowledge. Relevant factors likely to affect consumers' purchasing decisions should be communicated in such a way and at such a time that consumers can take them into account (Article 3).

Social responsibility

Marketing communications should respect human dignity and shouldn't incite or condone any form of discrimination, including that based upon race, national origin, religion, gender, age, disability or sexual orientation.

In addition, such activities shouldn't without justifiable reason play on fear or exploit misfortune or suffering, or appear to condone or incite violent, unlawful or anti-social behaviour or play on superstitious beliefs (Article 4).

Truthfulness

Perhaps the most important principle in the ICC Code and one that goes to the root of all marketing communications is that all such activities must be truthful and not misleading (Article 5).

Marketing communications shouldn't contain any statement, claim or audio or visual treatment that directly or by implication, omission, ambiguity or exaggeration is likely to mislead the consumer.

The ICC Code spells this out in some detail, and although not exhaustive the following is a useful checklist as to what 'truthfulness' means in practice:

- Characteristics of the product that are material in influencing the consumer to make a purchase, for example the nature, composition, method and date of manufacture, range of use, efficiency and performance, quantity, commercial or geographical origin or environmental impact, must be clear.
- The value of the product and the total price to be paid by the consumer must be clear.
- The terms for delivery, exchange, return, repair and maintenance of the product must be clear.
- Other information, including terms of guarantee, intellectual property (IP) rights and trade names, compliance with international and national standards, and awards and the extent of benefits for charitable causes as a result of making a purchase, must be truthful.

Use of technical or scientific data and terminology

In much the same way that Article 5 provides for 'truthfulness', this principle (Article 6) captures situations where marketers may 'sail close to the wind' without actually being dishonest and may be tempted to be economical with the truth.

In practice, marketers shouldn't engage in the following activities:

- misuse technical data such as research results or quotations from technical and scientific publications;
- present statistics in such a way as to exaggerate the validity of a product claim; or
- use scientific terminology or vocabulary in such a way as to suggest falsely that a product claim has scientific validity.

Use of 'free' and 'guarantee'

This is perhaps unusual, as it's a specific rather than a basic point of principle, but it addresses marketers' liberal use of the words 'free' and 'guarantee' within a sales and marketing context, as this has been open to much abuse. For further guidance in this area, refer to the CAP and BCAP Codes.

In order to stem underhanded and oblique sales and marketing activities, the ICC Code provides that the use of the term 'free', such as in 'free gift' or 'free offer', should be used only in very limited circumstances (Article 7):

- where the 'free offer' involves no contractual obligation whatsoever; or
- where the 'free offer' involves only the obligation to pay shipping and handling charges, which shouldn't exceed the cost estimated to be incurred by the marketer itself; or
- where the 'free offer' is in conjunction with the purchase of another product, but provided that the price of that product hasn't been inflated to cover all or part of the cost of the 'free offer'.

Such a provision closes the door to many 'sharp practices' where the consumer is led to believe that there's a value-added benefit (for example, a significant financial saving) when in fact there's nothing of the kind and instead the marketer is treating the consumer as gullible to such a tactic.

The provision also states that marketing communications shouldn't state or imply that a 'guarantee', 'warranty' or any such expression gives the impression that the consumer will enjoy additional rights over and above those provided by national laws. The terms of any guarantee or warranty, including the name and address of the guarantor, should be easily available to the consumer, and any exclusion clauses or limitations on consumer rights or remedies must be clear, conspicuous and in accordance with national and international laws.

Substantiation

Sales and marketing often includes claims, descriptions or illustrations that are communicated to consumers in order to influence them in making an informed choice – what's commonly known as 'evidence-based marketing'. The ICC Code provides that such claims, descriptions and illustrations should be capable of both verification and substantiation (Article 8).

In the UK, the CAP and BCAP Codes are consistent with the ICC Code, which provides that such substantiation should be available so that evidence can be produced without delay and on request when required.

Identification

About a decade ago or even longer it was the fashion to place 'advertorials', which were paid-for advertising but made to look like editorial with the veneer of 'independence' about the content in the advertisement. Thankfully, this type of marketing is losing its appeal, as there should be clear water between advertising copy and what's genuine editorial content. The ICC Code specifically states that such activity should be clearly distinguishable as such, whatever the form or medium used.

When an advertisement appears in a medium containing news or editorial matter, it should be readily recognizable as an advertisement, and the identity of the advertiser should be immediately apparent (Article 9).

Marketing communications shouldn't misrepresent the true commercial purpose and, as a result, copy that's promoting the sale of a product, for example, shouldn't be disguised as 'market research', 'consumer surveys', 'user-generated content', 'independent blogs' or 'independent reviews' where in fact these are far from being unsolicited or independent points of view.

Identity

This is linked to Article 9, and the ICC Code provides that the identity of the marketer should be apparent in marketing communications and where appropriate should include contact information to enable the consumer to get in touch without difficulty (Article 10).

The above doesn't apply to 'teaser promotions', which will be followed up with other communications activities that will reveal the identity of the brand owner. For example, this happened in 2012 with a Snickers campaign on Twitter where celebrities Rio Ferdinand and Katie Price tweeted out-of-character posts about their interests in knitting and China's GDP respectively.

Comparisons

As discussed in Chapter 5, comparison advertising can be a lethal marketing weapon! The ICC Code provides that any comparison advertising mustn't mislead and must comply with the principles of fair competition (Article 11).

Points of comparison should be based on facts that can be substantiated and shouldn't be unfairly selected.

Denigration

Marketing communications shouldn't denigrate any person or group of persons, firm, organization, industrial or commercial activity, profession or product or seek to bring it or them into public contempt or ridicule (Article 12).

Testimonials

Testimonials and case studies are some of the most powerful ways of getting a message across to a desired market and customer segment, as they have a quality of independence about them. For further guidance in this area, refer to Guru in a Bottle® *High Impact Marketing that Gets Results*.

The ICC Code recognizes the potency of such communications and provides that marketers shouldn't use or refer to any testimonial, endorsement or supportive documentation unless it's genuine, verifiable and relevant, as to do otherwise would be dishonest (Article 13).

The ICC Code adds that testimonials or endorsements that have become obsolete or out of date and therefore misleading through passage of time should be removed from all marketing communications.

Portrayal or imitation of persons and references to personal property

The roots for this principle are directly from the need to protect the personal privacy of citizens (see Chapter 7), and the ICC Code provides that marketing communications shouldn't portray or refer to any persons, whether in a private or a public capacity, unless prior permission has been obtained; nor should marketing communications without prior permission depict or refer to any person's property in a way likely to convey the impression of a personal endorsement of the product or organization involved (Article 14).

Exploitation of goodwill

In the same way that Article 14 is a principle about respect for privacy, the ICC Code on exploitation of goodwill spells out that marketers shouldn't make an unjustifiable use of a name, initials, logo or trademarks of another firm, company or institution (Article 15).

Imitation

Marketing communications shouldn't in any way take an unfair advantage of a brand owner's IP rights or goodwill in the absence of consent (Article 16). This principle effectively forbids a marketer from unfairly riding on the coat-tails of another brand in its market sector – a principle upheld by the courts in recent cases (see Chapter 5).

Marketing communications shouldn't imitate those of another brand owner in any way likely to mislead or confuse the consumer, for example through the general layout, text, slogan, visual treatment, music or sound effects.

Where a marketer has established a distinctive marketing communications campaign in one or more countries, other marketers shouldn't imitate that campaign in other countries where the marketer that originated the campaign may operate, thereby preventing the extension of the campaign to those countries within a reasonable period of time.

However, should the UK government relax the restriction on the right of parody in trademark law (as discussed in Chapter 3), then this principle may need to be modified should other EU jurisdictions also follow suit.

Safety and health

Marketing communications shouldn't without justification on educational or social grounds contain any visual portrayal or any description of potentially dangerous practices or situations that show a disregard for safety or health as defined by national laws and standards (Article 17).

Instructions for use of products destined for consumers should include appropriate safety warnings and, where necessary, legal disclaimers over liability for misuse of the product.

Within the context of advertising, children should be shown to be under adult supervision whenever a product or an activity involves a safety risk, such as a climbing frame for the garden, which could potentially pose a hazard for children if not supervised by an adult.

Information provided with the product should include proper directions for use and full instructions covering health and safety aspects whenever necessary. Such health and safety warnings should be made clear by the use of pictures, text or a combination of both.

Children and young people

The principle applicable here (Article 18) is discussed in detail in the section 'Protection of children and young people from sales and marketing exploitation' at the end of this chapter.

Privacy policy

This principle is in alignment with data protection principles as discussed in Chapter 6. The ICC Code provides that those who collect data in connection with marketing communication activities ('data controllers') should have a privacy policy, and the terms of this should be readily available to consumers (Article 19).

The data protection policy should provide a clear statement if any collection or processing of data is to take place, whether this in itself is evident or not.

Appropriate measures should be taken to ensure that consumers understand and exercise their rights to opt out of marketing lists (including the right to sign on to general preference services), to require that their data aren't made available to third parties for their marketing purposes and to rectify data that are held and are inaccurate.

Where a consumer has expressed a wish not to receive marketing communications using a specific medium, whether via a preference service or by other means, this wish should be respected.

Particular care should be taken to maintain the data protection rights of the consumer when personal data are transferred from the country in which they are collected to another country. When data processing is conducted in another country, all reasonable steps should be taken to ensure that adequate security measures are in place and that the data protection principles set out in the ICC Code are respected. For a discussion on the Safe Harbor principles, see Chapter 6.

Transparency on cost of communication

Where the cost to consumers of accessing a message or communicating with the marketer is higher than the standard cost of postage or telecommunications, in other words there is a premium rate for sending or receiving such a message, then this cost should be made clear (Article 20). The ICC Code provides that this can be expressed either as a 'cost per minute' or as a 'cost per message'. When this information is provided online, consumers should be clearly informed at the time they're about to access the message or online service and be allowed a reasonable period of time to disconnect the communication without incurring any charge.

Where a communication involves a premium cost, the consumer shouldn't be kept waiting for an unreasonably long time in order to achieve the purpose of the communication, and calls shouldn't be charged until the consumer can begin to fulfil that purpose.

Unsolicited products and undisclosed costs

Marketing communications associated with the practice of sending unsolicited products to consumers who are then asked for payment ('inertia selling'), including statements or suggestions that recipients are required to accept and pay for such products, should be avoided (Article 21).

Marketing communications that solicit a response constituting an order for which payment will be required, such as for an entry in a business directory, should make this unambiguously clear in order for the offer to be rejected.

The ICC Code also states that orders shouldn't be presented in a form that might be mistaken for an invoice or otherwise falsely suggest that payment is due – a common 'scam' perpetrated by those seeking to extort money from companies that need to renew the registration of their domain names.

Environmental behaviour

This principle is similar to Article 17 in that marketing communications shouldn't appear to condone or encourage actions that contravene the law, self-regulatory codes or generally accepted standards of environmentally responsible behaviour (Article 22). For further guidance in this area, see the environmental provisions under the CAP Code.

Responsibility

Observance of the rules of conduct laid down in the ICC Code is the primary responsibility of the brand owner. Other parties also required to observe the

ICC Code include advertising and marketing agencies, publishers, media owners, and other subcontractors to the brand owner (Article 23).

Agencies and other practitioners should exercise due care and diligence in the preparation of marketing communications and should operate in such a way as to enable the brand owner to fulfil its responsibilities.

Publishers, media owners and subcontractors who publish, transmit, deliver or distribute marketing communications should also exercise due care in the acceptance of them and their presentation to the public.

Employees of any of the above who take part in the planning, creation, publication or transmission of a marketing communication are also responsible – commensurate with their pay grade – for ensuring that the rules of the ICC Code are observed and should act in the spirit and letter of the ICC Code.

The ICC Code applies to the marketing communication in its entire content and form, including testimonials and statements and audio or visual material originating from other sources. The fact that the content or form of a marketing communication may originate wholly or in part from other sources doesn't justify non-observance of the ICC Code rules.

Effect of subsequent redress for contravention

Subsequent correction and appropriate redress for a contravention of the ICC Code by the party responsible is desirable but doesn't excuse the contravention of the ICC Code (Article 24).

Implementation

The ICC Code and the principles enshrined in it should be adopted and implemented nationally and internationally by the relevant local, national or regional self-regulatory bodies (Article 25).

Respect for self-regulatory decisions

No marketer, communications practitioner or advertising agency, publisher, media owner or subcontractor should be party to the publication or distribution of an advertisement or other marketing communication that has been found unacceptable by the relevant self-regulatory body (Article 26).

Specific principles under the ICC Code (2011)

Digital interactive media

The ICC Code has integrated rules that apply to marketing communications using digital interactive media throughout the guidelines. There's also a section dealing with issues specific to digital interactive media techniques and platforms.

The use of digital interactive media needs to comply with the following standards:

- Clear and transparent mechanisms to enable consumers to choose not to have their data collected for advertising and marketing purposes should be available.
- Clear indication that a social network site is commercial and is under the control or influence of a brand owner should be made apparent to the user.
- Limits must be set so marketers work on an 'opt-in' or 'permission' basis for communication with consumers.
- There needs to be respect for the rules and standards of acceptable commercial behaviour in social networks, and the posting of marketing messages should occur only when the forum or site has clearly indicated its willingness to receive such messages.
- Special principles apply when dealing with children and young people (see 'Protection of children and young people from sales and marketing exploitation' below).

Online behavioural advertising (OBA)

The ICC Code addresses responsibility in the use of online behavioural targeting in the delivery of advertising that involves collecting information about a user's online activity over time on a particular device and across different unrelated websites in order to serve advertisements tailored to that user's interests and preferences.

The following rules apply to website operators and third parties on non-affiliated websites:

- There needs to be a clear and conspicuous notice regarding if and how OBA data collection is to be used. Such a notice should include the type of data collected and the purpose for collecting the data.
- The website should have an easy-to-use mechanism to let consumers decide about the collection and use of their data for OBA purposes.
- A brand owner must have received explicit consumer consent for OBA in all cases of collecting and using data via technologies or practices intended to harvest the data from all or almost all websites visited by a particular computer or device across multiple web domains.
- A brand owner must obtain explicit consumer consent for creation and use of OBA segments relying on sensitive data.
- A brand owner must maintain appropriate physical, electronic and administrative security and data protection safeguards in conducting OBA activities.

Environmental claims

Given the increased importance of environmental issues within marketing, the ICC Code was updated in line with international standards, and its companion resource, the ICC Framework for Responsible Environmental Marketing Communications, can be accessed at http://www.iccwbo.org. Taken together, these tools help marketers and their agencies evaluate claims to ensure their messages hold up to the basic principles of truthful, honest and socially responsible communications and avoid misleading consumers. For further guidance in this important area, refer to the CAP Code.

Whilst the principles in the ICC Code appear simple, applying them to make new environmental claims, often based on terms that aren't universally understood, is much more complicated. ICC guidance maps that process for companies and provides a standard for brand owners to evaluate such claims should they be challenged under national and international laws and regulations.

An environmental claim refers to any claim in which explicit or implicit reference is made to environmental or ecological aspects relating to the production, packaging, distribution, use or disposal of products.

The ICC Code guidance on use of environmental claims includes:

- ensuring that all statements and visual treatments don't mislead, overstate or exploit consumers' concern for the environment;
- avoidance of general claims like 'environmentally friendly', 'green', 'sustainable' and 'carbon friendly' unless there's validation of such claims against a very high standard of proof;
- presenting qualifications in a way that is clear, prominent, understandable and accessible to consumers;
- presenting improvement claims separately so it's clear whether each claim relates to the product, an ingredient of the product, the packaging or an ingredient of the packaging; and
- avoiding emphasizing a marginal improvement as a major environmental gain, highlighting the absence of a component that's never been associated with the product category or making a comparison with a competitor's product (unless a significant environmental advantage can be verified).

Sales promotion

As discussed in Chapter 8, fairness, transparency and a clear explanation are key factors in a responsible sales promotion. Among the areas covered by the ICC Code are:

- presentation and administration of promotions;
- safety and suitability;
- information requirements; and
- particular obligations of promoters and intermediaries.

Sponsorship

This section of the ICC Code applies to all forms of sponsorship relating to corporate image, brands, products, activities or events of any kind run by commercial and voluntary organizations. It includes sponsorship elements forming part of other marketing activities, such as sales promotion and direct marketing, or in conjunction with a corporate social responsibility (CSR) programme.

A consistent theme of this section is respect for the rights holder, sponsorship property, sponsor, supporters or fans, participants and spectators.

Direct marketing

As discussed in Chapter 6, standards for the ethical conduct of direct marketing in all its forms should include the clear presentation of terms and fulfilment requirements and procedures of each offer along with a clear presentation of the consumer's rights in relation to each offer.

This section in the ICC Code includes requirements when using electronic media for direct marketing and when using telemarketing.

For telemarketers, there are precise guidelines about responsible behaviour in:

- making outbound calls;
- reaching a sales agreement or agreement for further contact;
- monitoring and recording conversations; and
- the use of automatic dialling equipment.

For further discussion on best practice in direct marketing, refer to Guru in a Bottle® *High Impact Marketing that Gets Results*.

EU Consumer Rights Directive 2011

Background to the EU Consumer Rights Directive 2011/83/EU

The EU Consumer Rights Directive, published in November 2011, requires all 27 EU member states to introduce new consumer protection laws by December 2013.

In the UK, the government has signalled its intention to create a new Consumer Bill of Rights that aims to streamline confusing and overlapping legislation and regulation in this area as well as strengthen consumer protection that will implement the EU Consumer Rights Directive. The proposed Consumer Bill of Rights will update and clarify the law for:

- goods and services;
- digital content;

- unfair contract terms; and
- consumer rights (in particular, misleading sales practices).

As a result, the Consumer Bill of Rights will repeal and replace a number of pieces of legislation, including the Consumer Protection (Distance Selling) Regulations 2000 and the Unfair Terms in Consumer Contracts Regulations 1999. It will also repeal or substantially amend the consumer law aspects of the following statutes, leaving intact those parts that apply to B2B transactions:

- Misrepresentation Act 1967;
- Sale of Goods Act 1979;
- Sale and Supply of Goods and Services Act 1994;
- Supply of Goods (Implied Terms) Act 1973;
- Unfair Contract Terms Act 1977.

For a discussion on the current statutory provisions covering these areas as they affect B2C and B2B transactions, refer to Chapter 1.

Scope of the EU Consumer Rights Directive

The EU Consumer Rights Directive aims to simplify elements of the existing EU consumer rights directives into one set of rules and create greater consistency in consumer law across the EU. It applies to B2C sales contracts and is particularly significant for online shopping. See also 'Consumer Protection from Unfair Trading Regulations (CPRs) 2008' below.

The key features of the EU Consumer Rights Directive

Elimination of hidden charges and costs on the internet

Consumers will be protected against 'cost traps' on the internet. This happens when fraudsters try to trick people into paying for 'free' services, such as horoscopes or recipes. From now on, consumers must explicitly confirm that they understand that they have to pay a price.

Increased price transparency

Traders have to disclose the total cost of the product or service, as well as any extra fees. Online shoppers won't have to pay charges or other costs if they're not properly informed before they place an order.

Banning pre-ticked boxes on websites

When shopping online – for example, when buying an airline ticket – a consumer may be offered additional options during the purchase process, such as travel insurance or car rental. These additional services may be offered through so-called 'pre-ticked' boxes. Consumers are currently often forced to uncheck those boxes if they don't want these extra services. Under the directive, pre-ticked boxes are banned across the EU.

Fourteen days for consumers to change their mind on a purchase

The period under which a consumer can withdraw from a sales contract is extended to 14 calendar days (previously seven days). This means that consumers can return the goods for whatever reason if they change their mind. This is a fundamental change in consumer protection when purchasing goods on the internet, and other new measures include:

- Additional protection for consumers when faced with lack of information where a seller hasn't clearly informed them about the withdrawal right. In such cases the return period will be extended to a year.

- Consumers will also be protected and enjoy a right of withdrawal for solicited visits, such as when a trader called beforehand and pressed a consumer to agree to a visit. In addition, a distinction no longer needs to be made between solicited and unsolicited visits – any circumvention of the rules is not permitted.

- The right of withdrawal is extended to online auctions, such as eBay, though goods bought in auctions can be returned only when bought from a professional seller rather than through a private sale.

- The withdrawal period will start from the moment the consumer receives the goods, rather than at the time of conclusion of the contract, which was the case. The rules apply to internet, phone and mail order sales, as well as to sales outside shops, for example on the consumer's doorstep, in the street, at a Tupperware party or during an excursion organized by the trader, for example a wine-buying trip on the ferry to Calais.

Better refund rights

Traders must refund the consumer for the product within 14 days of the withdrawal. This includes the costs of delivery. In general, the trader will bear the risk for any damage to goods during transportation until the consumer takes possession of the goods.

Introduction of an EU-wide model withdrawal form

Consumers will be provided with a model withdrawal form that they can use if they change their mind and wish to withdraw from a contract concluded at a distance or on the doorstep. This will make it easier and faster to withdraw from any such contract entered within the EU, although the use of such a form isn't obligatory.

For further guidance on distance selling regulations, refer to the CAP and BCAP Codes.

Eliminating surcharges for the use of credit cards and telephone hotlines

Traders won't be able to charge a consumer more for paying by credit card or other means of payment than what it actually costs the trader to offer such means of payment. Traders that operate telephone hotlines allowing the consumer to contact them in relation to the contract won't be able to charge more than the basic telephone rate for such calls.

Clearer information on who pays for returning goods

If traders want consumers to bear the cost of returning goods after the consumers change their mind, traders have to inform consumers clearly about that beforehand; otherwise traders will have to pay for the returns themselves. Traders must clearly give at least an estimate of the maximum costs of returning bulky goods bought by internet or mail order, such as a sofa, before the purchase, so consumers can make an informed choice before deciding from whom to buy.

Better consumer protection in relation to digital products

Information on digital content will also have to be clearer, including about its compatibility with hardware and software and the application of any technical protection measures, for example limiting the right for the consumer to make copies of the content.

Consumers will have a right to withdraw from purchases of digital content, such as music or video downloads, but only up until the moment the actual downloading process begins.

Common rules for brand owners, making it easier for them to trade all over Europe

These include:

- a single set of core rules for distance contracts (sales by phone, post or internet) and off-premises contracts (sales away from a company's premises, such as in the street or on the doorstep) in the EU, creating a level playing field and reducing transaction costs for cross-border traders, especially for sales by internet; and

- standard forms, which will make life easier for businesses: a form to comply with the information requirements on the right of withdrawal.

Most lawyers have welcomed the new EU directive as a major step forward for the European consumer online retail market, as harmonization of rules across all 27 member states will make it much easier for consumers to purchase in another EU country via the internet. The intention is that consumers won't be deterred by the different rules of different countries and that this will stimulate more online retail sales within the EU.

On the other hand, the EU Consumer Rights Directive could have a negative impact on some traders, particularly those that don't ordinarily ship products internationally, given that there's now an obligation to ship anywhere within the EU, and this may require traders to enter into an international courier contract. This may affect businesses like eBay, which may be forced to change its terms and conditions, as it could no longer specify countries within Europe that it won't ship to, and onerous shipping and returns provisions may still apply.

Consumer Protection from Unfair Trading Regulations (CPRs) 2008

The CPRs apply to B2C transactions and apply to conduct before, during and after the contract is made. In particular, the CPRs introduce a general prohibition against unfair commercial practices, specific prohibitions against misleading and aggressive practices, and a blacklist of 31 practices that will be deemed unfair in all circumstances.

All B2C advertising must comply with the CPRs, which forbid brand owners from using misleading, aggressive or unfair sales techniques, and the CPRs implement the EU Unfair Commercial Practices Directive 2005/29/EC.

As discussed earlier in this chapter, the government is currently reviewing consumer protection legislation, and a new Consumer Bill of Rights is likely to replace the CPRs no later than December 2013.

The CPRs also affect B2B practices closely connected to consumers. For example, a trader supplying food products to a supermarket will need to ensure its labelling complies with the CPRs.

In some circumstances, the CPRs may also apply to a consumer-to-business (C2B) transaction, for example if a consumer sells a car to a second-hand car dealer then that business would have to observe the CPRs.

Unfair commercial practices

The general prohibition simply states that unfair commercial practices are prohibited. The wording is deliberately wide to catch any unfair practices that may be developed in the future.

A practice is 'unfair' if it fails to meet the standard of 'professional diligence' (the standard of skill and care that would reasonably be expected of a trader in its field of activity) and it materially impairs an average consumer's ability to make an informed decision, causing him or her to make a purchase decision he or she wouldn't have otherwise made.

In most cases, the average consumer will be taken to be reasonably well informed, reasonably observant and circumspect.

However, where a trading practice is specifically targeted at a particular consumer group, the average consumer will be the average member of that group.

In addition, if a clearly identifiable group of consumers is particularly vulnerable to a trading practice (because of age, infirmity or credulity) in a way a trader could reasonably be expected to foresee, and the practice is likely materially to distort decisions made only by that group, the benchmark will be the average member of that group. For example, the hard of hearing might be particularly vulnerable to a trader's advertisement claiming that a telephone is 'hearing aid compatible'.

Misleading actions and omissions

Misleading acts and omissions are unfair commercial practices. In each case, the action or omission must cause or be likely to cause the average consumer to take a different decision. A misleading action contains false information or in some way deceives or is likely to deceive the average customer.

Examples include:

- providing misleading information about the main characteristics, availability or origin of a product or false information about the trader itself (such as industry awards);
- marketing a product in such a way that it creates confusion with a competitor's products (for example, by using a similar brand name or logo, which could give rise to passing off as well as trademark infringement); and
- agreeing to be bound by a code of practice that contains a firm commitment (for example, that its members will use only wood from sustainable sources), displaying the code logo, but breaching that commitment.

Misleading omissions are made when a trader omits or hides material information, provides it in an unclear, unintelligible, ambiguous or untimely manner, or fails to make clear it has a commercial intent.

What's 'material' will depend on the circumstances, but it's generally defined as information the average consumer needs to make an informed purchase decision.

Limitations of space or time and whether the trader has taken other steps to convey the information, such as stating that terms and conditions apply and where they can be found, will be taken into account as part of the context.

When a trader makes an 'invitation to purchase', for example by including an order form in a press advertisement or a page on a website enabling consumers to place an order, the regulations specify the material information that must be included unless that information is apparent from the context.

Aggressive practices

A commercial practice is aggressive if it significantly impairs or is likely significantly to impair the average consumer's freedom of choice by the use of harassment, coercion (including physical force) or undue influence and so causes or is likely to cause the consumer to take a different decision.

'Undue influence' results from a trader exploiting a position of power, even without using or threatening physical force.

The blacklist

Thirty-one practices are deemed to be unfair in all circumstances. A trader carrying out any one of these will have breached the CPRs, whether or not it had any effect on the average consumer.

In addition to pyramid promotion schemes, bogus sales and 'door-stepping' consumers at home, the blacklist includes:

- 'bait advertising' – advertising products at a specified price without disclosing that the trader has reasonable grounds to believe it may not be able to supply them or their equivalent at that price for a reasonable period or in reasonable quantities;
- 'bait and switch' – inviting consumers to buy one product but then trying to persuade them to buy a different one, for example by refusing to show them the original item or to take orders or make delivery arrangements or by showing a defective sample;
- falsely stating a product will be available (or available on certain terms) only for a very limited time to persuade the consumer to make an immediate decision;
- using 'advertorials' without making it clear that the brand owner has paid for the promotion;
- passing on materially inaccurate market information to persuade the consumer to buy on less favourable terms than prevailing market conditions;
- claiming to offer a competition or prize promotion without awarding the prizes described or a reasonable equivalent;
- describing a product as 'free', 'without charge' or similar if the consumer has to pay anything other than the unavoidable cost of responding, collecting or paying for delivery of the item (it doesn't apply to any offer that is 'buy one, get one free', known as 'BOGOF');
- making persistent and unwanted solicitations by telephone, fax, e-mail or similar, except in certain circumstances and as justified to enforce a contractual obligation (for example, legitimate debt collection);
- requiring policyholders claiming on an insurance policy to produce irrelevant documents or deliberately failing to respond to correspondence to dissuade consumers from pursuing their contractual rights; and
- including in an advertisement a direct encouragement to children to buy advertised products or persuade their parents or other adults to buy such products for them ('pester power').

Enforcement

This is typically carried out by the Office of Fair Trading (OFT) and Trading Standards Services (TSS). There's no right of action for consumers or competitors in respect of a breach of the CPRs.

Enforcement bodies have a duty to enforce the CPRs using the 'most appropriate means', and these can range from informal regulatory or self-regulatory procedures to a civil action for an enforcement order and in severe cases criminal proceedings.

At the lower end of the scale, a complaint made by an authorized body could be dealt with under its own codes of practice. An obvious example would be the ASA, which regulates the content of advertisements, sales promotions and direct marketing in the UK. At the upper end of the scale, a criminal prosecution can be brought by the OFT.

Breaches of the general prohibition of the CPRs require proof that the trader acted knowingly or recklessly, whereas other breaches are strict liability and don't require any proof of a specific state of mind.

Defence

A defence to criminal charges include that the offence was caused by something or someone beyond the trader's control, provided the trader can show it took all reasonable precautions and exercised due diligence. For example, in the case of an advertisement, if the defendant can prove that its business is the publishing of advertisements and that it received the advertisement in the ordinary course of business and didn't know that publication would be an offence, this would amount to a reasonable defence.

Penalties

A company found guilty of an offence under the CPRs could face on summary conviction a fine not exceeding £5,000. An officer or manager of the company who consents to or acts negligently in relation to the offence can be found personally liable and fined or sentenced for up to two years in prison. Any prosecution would need to be brought within three years from the date of the offence or one year from the discovery of the offence by the prosecutor.

Business Protection from Misleading Marketing Regulations (BPRs) 2008

The Business Protection from Misleading Marketing Regulations 2008 came into force in May 2008 alongside the Consumer Protection from Unfair Trading Regulations 2008.

The BPRs implement the EU Misleading and Comparative Advertising Directive 2006/114/EC (MCAD 2006) and deal with misleading and comparative advertising. For further guidance on comparative advertising, refer to Chapter 5.

Business-to-business marketing and comparative advertising must comply with the BPRs, which prohibit advertising that's misleading to the traders to whom it's addressed or that injures or is likely to injure a competitor.

For the BPRs, 'advertising' is defined broadly to mean 'any form of representation which is made in connection with a trade, business, craft or profession in order to promote the supply or transfer of a product'. This includes face-to-face oral statements, telemarketing and descriptions on and accompanying goods, including claims on packaging as well as advertising in the traditional sense of the word.

'Comparative advertising' is advertising that identifies a competitor or a product of a competitor. In order to be allowed, it has to meet all the conditions in the BPRs that relate mainly to aspects of the fairness of the comparison to a competitor or its product(s).

Advertising Standards Authority (ASA) CAP and BCAP Codes

As discussed in Chapter 5, there are a variety of options to consider when thinking about challenging the sales and marketing activities of competitors, and these include:

- litigation (with the attendant risks of the likelihood of success and legal costs that litigation entails);
- a complaint to the ASA for a breach of the CAP and BCAP Codes (where relevant and more likely);
- a complaint to a specific regulatory body, such as the Financial Services Authority (FSA), OFT or TSS (which is rare);
- using public relations, advertising or a viral campaign to bite back in response (likely to be more effective and less expensive); and
- a direct approach to a media owner where, for example, there's a risk of copyright and trademark infringement as a result of a comparative advertising campaign (such an approach can be very effective in stopping the offending article going to press).

Benefit of self-regulation

The CAP Code (non-broadcast) and BCAP Code (broadcast, television and radio) are administered by the ASA and are a free service, although a complainant can apply to use a paid-for fast-track service, which could speed things up even if the rival brand owner has other ideas and wants to slow things down!

The CAP and BCAP Codes tend to mirror each other, and as a result the relevant Codes have been grouped together for ease of discussion purposes in this chapter. There's some overlap with the ICC Code, which should also be referred to when assessing whether proposed sales and marketing activities comply with accepted industry practices.

Compliance with the CAP and BCAP Codes

(CAP Code 1, 4, BCAP Code 1, 4)
The core principle for all marketing communications is that they should be legal, decent, honest and truthful. With respect to broadcast advertisements, they shouldn't mislead or cause serious widespread harm or offence, especially to children and vulnerable people.

The fact that a marketing communication complies with the CAP Code doesn't guarantee that every publisher will accept it. Media owners can refuse space to marketing communications that break the CAP Code and aren't obliged to publish every marketing communication offered to them.

Both the CAP and the BCAP Codes are recognized by the government, OFT and courts as among the established means of consumer protection in non-broadcast and broadcast marketing communications. Any matter that principally concerns a legal dispute will normally need to be resolved through law enforcement agencies or the courts.

The ASA and CAP will treat in confidence any genuinely private or secret material supplied unless the courts or officials acting within their statutory powers compel its disclosure.

Broadcast rules

Special rules apply within broadcast communications in so far as broadcasters must ensure that all advertisements are cleared before broadcast and are scheduled suitably and in accordance with BCAP's rules on scheduling of advertisements. BCAP strongly advises broadcasters to follow relevant Clearcast (for television advertising) or Radio Advertising Clearance Centre (RACC) (for radio advertising) scheduling warnings, although compliance doesn't guarantee compliance with the BCAP Code should a complaint be made against the advertiser to the ASA or Ofcom.

Broadcasters must ensure that previously approved copy is not rerun for subsequent campaigns without periodic checks to ensure that all claims made in such advertisements are still accurate.

For radio, copy originally cleared by the RACC that's over six months old will need to be re-submitted for consideration by the RACC and assigned a new clearance number. Broadcasters or their respective clearance body must independently assess evidence submitted in support of an advertisement and any advice they have commissioned. Substantiation of factual claims made by advertisers and other supporting evidence must be held by the broadcaster or the relevant clearance body.

'Special category' radio advertisements, whether broadcast locally, regionally or nationally, must be centrally cleared by the RACC, and broadcasters or their advertising sales houses must keep a record of centrally cleared radio commercials.

The 'special categories' are:

- consumer credit, investment and complex financial products and services;
- gambling products and services;
- alcohol products;
- medical and health and beauty products and treatments;
- food, nutrition and food supplements;
- slimming products, treatments and establishments;
- adult shops, 'strip-o-grams', escort agencies and premium-rate sexual entertainment services;
- dating and introduction services;
- commercial services offering individual personal and consumer advice;
- environmental claims;
- matters of public controversy, including matters of a political or industrial nature;
- religious organizations;
- charitable causes; and
- films, DVDs, video, computer and console games that have an 18 certificate or rating.

Radio commercials that don't fall into the 'special category' list and are broadcast only by one station or in one locality must be cleared for broadcast by the station concerned.

Typically, most radio commercials are centrally cleared by the RACC, as many national radio campaigns are sold and broadcast across the UK commercial radio network.

There are several requirements that need to be complied with:

- Broadcast advertisements must reflect the spirit, not merely the letter, of the BCAP Code.
- Broadcast advertisements must be prepared with a sense of responsibility to the audience and to society.
- All broadcast advertisements must comply with the law, and broadcasters must make that compliance a condition of acceptance.

With respect to non-broadcast advertisement rules, there are more detailed requirements for brand owners to comply with the following:

- Marketing communications must reflect the spirit, not merely the letter, of the CAP Code.

- Marketing communications must be prepared with a sense of responsibility to consumers and to society.

- Marketers must comply with all general rules and with relevant sector-specific rules.

- No marketing communication should bring advertising into disrepute.

- Marketing communications must respect the principles of fair competition generally accepted in business.

- Any unreasonable delay in responding to the ASA's enquiries will normally be considered a breach of the CAP Code.

- Full name and geographical business address of the marketer must be given to the ASA or CAP without delay if requested.

- Marketing communications must comply with the CAP Code. Primary responsibility for observing the CAP Code falls on marketers. Others involved in preparing or publishing marketing communications, such as agencies, publishers and other service suppliers, also accept an obligation to abide by the CAP Code.

- Marketers should deal fairly with consumers.

- Marketers have primary responsibility for ensuring that their marketing communications are legal and shouldn't incite anyone to break it.

TripAdvisor LLC (2012)

The TripAdvisor website has become incredibly powerful in building as well as destroying the reputation of hoteliers and restaurateurs across the UK and globally and was the subject of a Channel 4 documentary 'Attack of the TripAdvisors', which explored the commercial impact that negative comments can have and the frustration many business owners felt in being powerless to fight back.

KwikChex.com, an online service that helps such businesses manage their online reputations, sought an adjudication by the ASA after having reportedly received over 2,000 complaints from hoteliers and restaurateurs about negative comments posted on the TripAdvisor website.

On its website, TripAdvisor made a series of claims: 'Read reviews from real travellers', 'TripAdvisor offers trusted advice from real travellers and a wide variety of travel choices and planning features' and 'More than 50 million honest travel reviews and opinions from real travellers around the world'.

KwikChex and two hotels challenged whether these claims were misleading and could be substantiated, because they understood that TripAdvisor didn't verify the reviews on its website and as a result couldn't prove that the reviews were genuine or from real travellers rather than from competitors.

The ASA agreed and upheld the complaints against TripAdvisor, forcing it to remove such claims about its service.

Although the ASA noted that prior to posting a review TripAdvisor correspondents were asked to declare that their review was a genuine opinion of the hotel and that they had no personal or business affiliation with the hotel or had not been offered an incentive to write a review for it, the ASA noted that correspondents were not similarly asked to confirm that they didn't harbour a competitive interest in the place they were reviewing or that they were not posting a review on behalf of a competitor or other interested third party.

The ASA didn't consider that the existing declaration would necessarily prevent non-genuine reviews from being posted on the site and considered that, whilst TripAdvisor took steps to monitor and deal with suspicious activity, it wasn't possible to prevent all non-genuine content appearing on the website undetected.

The ASA also considered that a 'right of reply' on the site was provided, but that consumers wouldn't necessarily be able to detect and distinguish non-genuine reviews from genuine content, which was fundamentally unfair to hoteliers.

The main reason for the ASA upholding the complaints that TripAdvisor had been misleading in its statements on its site was less to do with the adequacy of the screening mechanisms it employed but rather that it had implied that all consumers could be confident that all reviews on the site were genuine, which couldn't be substantiated or indeed verified.

As a result of the ASA adjudication, TripAdvisor now states on its website: 'You'll find millions of hotel reviews and opinions at TripAdvisor so make sure you read these reviews and choose the perfect hotel for your next stay. Millions of travellers like you have shared their reviews of hotels, B&Bs, inns, and more. Add your own travel reviews and help travellers around the world plan and have a great trip.'

Transparency of marketing communications

(CAP Code 3, BCAP Code 2, 3)
The overriding principle that applies, whether in print or broadcast media, is that there needs to be a distinction from the consumer's point of view between editorial and advertising and marketing.

Editorial content in broadcast media also extends beyond radio and television channels to text and interactive services. A television trailer of a forthcoming programme isn't subject to television advertising regulations, as it's treated as a 'programme promotion' rather than advertising. Television commercials must be obviously distinguishable from editorial content, particularly if they use a situation, performance or style reminiscent of editorial content, to prevent the audience being confused between the two. However, as audiences become much more sophisticated in screening out messages, marketers will undoubtedly turn up the dial in terms of creative narrative to the point where the advertisements will be as entertaining as the content around them! For best practice in marketing communications, refer to Guru in a Bottle® *High Impact Marketing that Gets Results*.

The sensitivities around presenters involved in news and current affairs appearing in television or radio commercials continue to exist given the trusted position such journalists have in the minds of viewers, so a blanket ban to safeguard the 'impartiality' of their news and current affairs personae remains in place.

Transparency on both online and offline environments is also an important principle, whether that be an unsolicited marketing e-mail, an 'advertorial' or a marketing flier – they all must be clear that the sender isn't an impartial commentator or consumer but that a brand owner is behind the communication.

Misleading consumer advertising

(CAP Code 3, BCAP Code 3)
As discussed above, this whole area is already subject to the EU Consumer Rights Directive 2011/83/EU, which needs to be implemented by all 27 EU member states by no later than December 2013, and so the current detailed provisions of the CAP Code and BCAP Code may change as a result.

Currently, the ASA may have regard to the Consumer Protection from Unfair Trading Regulations (2008), as discussed above, when adjudicating on complaints about advertisements that are alleged to be misleading. The ASA will take into account the impression created by advertisements as well as specific claims made in them and will adjudicate on the basis of the likely effect on consumers rather than the brand owner's intentions.

Marketing communications mustn't materially mislead or be likely to do so. Obvious exaggerations ('puffery') and claims that the average consumer who sees the marketing communication is unlikely to take it literally are allowed provided they don't materially mislead. For example, 'Red Bull Gives You Wings' is allowable. Comedy and parody (where this is permitted) are acceptable.

The CAP and BCAP Codes warn about omitting and disguising material information or presenting it in an unclear, unintelligible, ambiguous or untimely manner.

The test of whether something is 'material' is from the perspective of the consumer who needs to make an informed purchase decision. There are other provisions that deal with the use of quoted prices for advertised products, the name and address of the brand owner for getting in touch, the use of 'free', and other provisions that mirror the Consumer Protection from Unfair Trading Regulations (2008) as well as the EU Consumer Rights Directive 2011/83/EU.

L'Oréal (UK) Ltd t/a L'Oréal Paris (2012)

In 2012, L'Oréal faced three ASA adjudications in relation to its advertising of its skin care products. The first was a television commercial for a mascara product that featured close-ups of a model wearing the mascara and a voiceover: 'The secret? Our collagen enriched formula and claw brush flick out and extend the look of lashes at the corners, for up to seven times more volume.'

The second was a press advertisement for a moisturizer that featured a photograph of actor Jane Fonda with the caption: 'Your experience. Our expertise. Age Re-perfect Pro-Calcium + SPF15 Trust Science for skin that feels toned, smoother, more resilient.'

The third was a two-page 'advertorial' that featured an anti-wrinkle cream and close-up black and white shots of actress Rachel Weisz with the accompanying copy: 'New Revitalift Repair 10, Our 1st multi-tasking anti-ageing moisturiser targets 10 signs of ageing in one' and 'Wrinkles appear reduced; skin looks smoother; skin feels firmer; skin is hydrated; skin feels more toned; skin feels more supple; complexion looks more even; skin is luminous; skin texture feels refined; skin looks plumper; it's not a facelift, it's Revitalift.'

All three advertisements were challenged on the grounds that the images misleadingly exaggerated the effects that could be achieved by the products.

The complaints made in relation to the Age Re-perfect cream and the mascara adverts weren't upheld, although the complaint made in relation to the Revitalift advert was upheld by the ASA.

When adjudicating on the mascara advert, the ASA considered that, although post-production techniques had been used in the production of the advertisement, the length and volume of the lashes shown in the advertisement didn't go beyond what a consumer would expect to be able to achieve when using the product.

This was verified by the photographs provided by L'Oréal of consumers wearing the product that showed lashes comparable to those shown in the advertisement, despite not having been subject to post-production techniques.

Clearcast provided testimony that it had been assured by the advertising agency and L'Oréal that the advert had been created in line with the 'CAP Help Note' on production techniques in cosmetics advertising. As a result, the ASA considered that the illustrated effect shown was in line with the effects shown in the consumer photos and held that the advert was not misleading.

With respect to the advertisements featuring Jane Fonda and Rachel Weisz, the ASA considered that consumers were likely to expect a degree of glamour in images for beauty products and would expect the models to have been professionally styled and made up for the photo shoot and to have been photographed professionally.

The ASA also acknowledged that brand owners were keen to present products in their most positive light, using techniques such as post-production enhancement and the retouching of images. Such an approach was considered acceptable by the ASA, with the important caveat that the resulting effect mustn't be one that misleadingly exaggerates the effect the product is capable of achieving.

In relation to the advertisement featuring Jane Fonda, the ASA accepted that the overall appearance of the actress hadn't been significantly modified and concluded that the image didn't exaggerate the effect that could be achieved by the product.

This wasn't the case with the magazine advertisement featuring Rachel Weisz, which made a large number of claims. In particular, those claims that the product made skin feel firmer, toned, supple and refined were classified as being 'tactile' rather than 'visible' effects, and on this basis the ASA held that these effects wouldn't be represented in the image.

The ASA did consider that the claims that skin appeared plumper and hydrated were acceptable claims for a moisturizing product.

However, with regard to the remaining claims, that 'skin looks smoother' and 'complexion looks more even', the ASA found that, despite the image not misrepresenting the luminosity or wrinkling of Rachel Weisz's face, the image had been altered in a way that substantially changed her complexion to make it appear smoother and more even and this was therefore misleading.

What these adjudications indicate is that the ASA takes a balanced approach to the use of post-production techniques provided that these don't distort what's being portrayed to the consumer.

Comparative advertising

(CAP Code 3, BCAP Code 3)
The ASA will consider 'unqualified superlative claims' as comparative claims against all competing products.

'Superiority claims' must be supported by evidence unless they're obvious 'puffery' where the consumer is unlikely to take the claim literally, such as the claim 'probably the best lager in the world'.

Objective superiority claims must make clear the aspect of the product or the brand owner's performance that's claimed to be superior to its rival(s).

The EU Misleading and Comparative Advertising Directive 2006/114/EC is discussed in detail in Chapter 5.

Under the CAP Code, marketing communications that include a comparison with an identifiable competitor mustn't mislead or be likely to mislead the consumer about either the advertised product or the competing product. They must compare products meeting the same need or intended for the same purpose and objectively compare one or more material, relevant, verifiable and representative features of those products.

There are a large number of comparative advertising cases where confusion has been alleged by rivals and where the arguments centre on similarities between products and other distinguishing marks and also allege trademark infringement.

Virgin Media (2012)

For several years, Virgin and Sky have been at loggerheads and at one point Sky refused to allow Virgin to broadcast Sky News as part of the satellite/cable package for Virgin customers. There's also been an ongoing battle in relation to their advertisements, and the ASA was asked to adjudicate over three national press advertisements for Virgin's TiVo set-top box service.

The first advertisement had the caption 'This new box leaves Sky+ looking like a relic from a bygone era' attributed to a reviewer writing for *Stuff* magazine.

The second advertisement copy stated: 'Only Virgin Media gives you the freedom to record two shows while watching a third. Or record three shows while you watch something you've recorded earlier.'

And the third advertisement was headlined 'A truly next generation PVR that should have Sky shaking in its boots', with supporting copy: 'Virgin Media TiVo Service. *Stuff* thinks it's the best way to watch television. Ever. What do you think?'

BSkyB challenged whether the claim referring to Sky was misleading because its HD 1TB set-top box was the product most comparable to Virgin's, not Sky+. It also challenged the second Virgin advertisement on the basis that the Sky+ HD box also allowed viewers to record two shows while watching a recorded programme. In the third advertisement, BSkyB challenged the claim that *Stuff* magazine had ranked TiVo ahead of the Sky+ HD 1TB box on the basis that it was misleading.

The ASA noted that competitors' products should generally be compared with the most directly comparable product, but considered that the claim in the overall context of the first advertisement was clearly the reviewer's opinion and would be interpreted as a general comparison with Sky+ (as opposed to with a specific set-top box). The claim wasn't therefore misleading.

On the issue of the second advertisement, the ASA held that the claim also wasn't misleading, because it would be interpreted in the context of the additional sentence as referring to the fact that consumers would be able to record two shows whilst watching a third live programme. As this couldn't be done with other set-top boxes, the claim was considered to be accurate and not misleading.

The ASA examined the reviews of both Virgin and BSkyB set-top boxes in *Stuff* magazine. It considered that the claim made by Virgin didn't give a true reflection of all the reviews combined, and Virgin shouldn't have implied that its set-top box was ranked above its rival.

The ASA also noted that claims in testimonials, likely to be interpreted as factual by consumers, must not be misleading.

Under the CAP Code, special protection is afforded to products that come from a unique geographical area and method of production; for example, champagne is given special protection by being registered as having a 'designation of origin' and as a result products with a 'designation of origin' must be compared only with other products with the same designation.

Marketing communications that include a comparison with an unidentifiable competitor mustn't mislead or be likely to mislead the consumer. The elements of the comparison mustn't be selected to give the brand owner an unrepresentative advantage.

LG Electronics (2012)

This adjudication concerned an LG press advertisement, website and sales promotion for its new range of 3D televisions.

The press advertisement headline read: 'It's 3D TV (But not as we know it)', with further copy: 'Unlike other 3D TVs, with LG Cinema TV, everyone will feel the full effect of the 3D experience. That's because the ultra wide viewing angles allow you and your family and friends to sit where you want in comfort.' The website copy stated: 'LG Cinema gives you wider viewing angles so you don't have to rearrange your living room. You can sit where you want, how you want, and you'll still get the same immersive 3D experience... the LG Cinema 3D TV produces a brighter and clearer picture in stunning FULL HD 3D picture quality.' The sales promotion for LG 3D Cinema included the text 'FULL HD 1080P'.

ASA received complaints from rival Samsung, which challenged whether the claims 'FULL HD 3D picture' and 'FULL HD 1080P' and 'HD 1080P' were misleading, because it believed the technology used passive 3D technology, which had a lower line resolution than that used by full HD.

In addition, Samsung challenged whether the claims 'You can sit where you want, how you want, and you'll still get the same immersive experience' and 'That's because the ultra wide viewing angles allow you and your family and friends to sit where you want in comfort' could be substantiated, on the grounds that passive 3D televisions have a very small viewing angle for 3D content.

The ASA agreed with Samsung and ruled against LG with respect to the HD claims.

Samsung and LG each provided arguments in relation to the definition of full HD and the supporting technology involved. The ASA noted that there was no official standard definition of full HD but agreed with Samsung that it was commonly understood by both the industry and consumers to have a particular meaning (a screen with a line resolution of 1920×1080). However, because this effect could be achieved only by using the advertised product with additional passive technology such as 3D glasses and the advertisements didn't make this clear to the consumer, the ASA considered the claims in the absence of clarification to be misleading. The ASA held that it was inaccurate and misleading to assert that the 3D picture was 1080p when, by its use of passive 3D technology that interlaces right- and left-eye images, the 3D view is at best 1080i.

In respect of the claims relating to viewing position, the ASA considered that it would be interpreted as meaning that viewers would be able to view the content in 3D provided that they were seated in such a way that they could comfortably view the entire screen and that consumers would be aware that the 3D image would be distorted if viewed outside the optimum angle.

The ASA considered that the viewing angles were within the expectation of the average consumer who had an interest in 3D televisions, and therefore considered that these claims weren't misleading.

The ASA makes clear in this adjudication that the distinction between passive and active 3D is important and that brand owners should make clear to consumers which system is being used as well as any additional requirements needed to achieve the 3D effect.

Price comparisons

(CAP Code 3, BCAP Code 3)
Marketing communications that include a price comparison must state the basis of the comparison. Comparisons with a competitor price must be with the price for an identical or substantially equivalent product and must explain significant differences between the products.

If the competitor offers more than one similar product, the brand owner should compare its price with the price for the competitor's product that's most similar to the advertised product. Price comparisons mustn't mislead by falsely claiming a price advantage, and comparisons with recommended retail prices (RRPs) are likely to mislead if the RRP differs significantly from the price at which the product or service is generally sold.

Direct Wines Ltd t/a Laithwaites Wine (2012)

A television advertisement for Direct Wines featured a voiceover:

> *The extraordinary wines in this Discovery Dozen normally sell for under £7 a bottle. Today, as an introduction, they're half-price at just over £3 a bottle. That's only £39.99 for the entire case' and 'Call now on 0845 XXX XXXX to order your first Discovery Dozen. Continue your journey of discovery with exciting new wine selections delivered conveniently to your door every 12 weeks and because you are always in control you simply enjoy the wines you want as often as you want.*

On-screen text stated 'Each case £79.99 (plus £7.99 delivery)', 'Future wine delivered every 12 weeks' and 'There's no obligation, you can delay or stop your deliveries at any time – just let us know.'

The complainant challenged whether the television advertisement was misleading, because it believed the advertisement failed to make clear that customers would receive additional full-price cases of wine every three months unless they opted out.

The ASA recognized that Direct Wines had worked closely with Clearcast when preparing the television commercial and that it aimed to make the offer clear. The ASA took account of the television advertisement script and web pages, and these demonstrated that customers contacting Direct Wines to take up the offer were unlikely to be misled, as the script and web pages made the terms of the offer clear.

However, the ASA ruled that consumers might interpret the delivery of future wine as separate to the half-price wine offer and believe that if they wanted to receive further cases of wine this was something they could opt in to receive.

According to the ASA, the television advertisement didn't make it sufficiently clear to consumers that by taking up the offer they'd be joining a wine club, which they'd actively have to opt out of if they didn't wish to receive further cases of wine. On that basis, the ASA felt the television advertisement was misleading.

Imitation and denigration

(CAP Code 3)
Marketing communications mustn't mislead the consumer about who manufactures the product or discredit or denigrate another product, brand owner, trademark, trade name or other distinguishing mark. In addition, marketing communications mustn't take unfair advantage of the reputation of a competitor's trademark, trade name or other distinguishing mark or of the 'designation of origin' of a competing product. Specifically, the CAP Code provides that any imitation or replica of a product with a protected trademark or trade name is prohibited. For further guidance in this area, refer to Chapter 3.

Prohibited categories

(BCAP Code 10)
Broadcast advertisements for some products or services aren't permitted because the products or services can't be legally advertised, are hazardous or run the risk of causing serious or widespread offence.

The list of prohibited products and services includes:

- breath-testing devices and products intended to mask the effects of drinking alcohol;

- betting systems and products intended to facilitate winning games of chance;
- all tobacco products and non-tobacco products and services that share a name, emblem or other feature with a tobacco product, as well as rolling papers and filters;
- firearms, including replica guns, gun clubs and offensive weapons;
- prostitution, sexual massage services and escort agencies;
- any material that offends the Obscene Publications Act 1959 (as amended); and
- pyramid sales schemes.

Endorsements and testimonials

(CAP Code 3)
Marketers must hold documentary evidence that a testimonial or endorsement used in a marketing communication is genuine, unless it's obviously fictitious, and hold contact details for the party that provides this testimonial. Testimonials must relate to the advertised product, and any claims made mustn't mislead the consumer, as they're likely to be interpreted as being factual in nature.

No testimonial should be used without permission, although limited exceptions exist, for example using accurate statements taken from a published source, quotations from a publication or references to a test, trial, professional endorsement, research facility or professional journal, which may be acceptable without express permission.

Independent third-party, customer or client endorsements and testimonials are some of the most powerful marketing communications tools that can help support the reputation of the brand owner given the independence of the statements being used.

Pricing

(CAP Code 3, BCAP Code 3, 22)
The CAP and BCAP Codes specifically refer to the *Pricing Practices Guide* published by the Department for Business, Innovation and Skills (BIS), which takes account of the Consumer Protection from Unfair Trading Regulations 2008 (CPRs).

The general principle is that price statements mustn't mislead the consumer by omission, undue emphasis or distortion and must relate to the product featured in the marketing communication. The price given must also include statements about the manner in which the price will be calculated, as well as definite prices. Quoted prices must include the non-optional taxes, duties, fees and charges that apply to all or most buyers. VAT-exclusive prices may be given only if all or most consumers pay no VAT or can recover VAT; marketing communications that quote VAT-exclusive prices must prominently state the amount or rate of VAT payable if some consumers are likely to pay VAT.

If a tax, duty, fee or charge can't be calculated in advance, for example because it depends on the consumer's circumstances, the marketing communication must make clear that it's excluded from the advertised price and explain how it's to be calculated.

Marketing communications that state prices must also state applicable delivery, freight or postal charges. If these can't reasonably be calculated in advance, then the marketing must state that such charges will be payable.

There's also a requirement for marketers to be explicit about the charges that will be incurred if consumers need to call a premium-rate telephone number, and the use of premium-rate telephone numbers is also subject to the PhonepayPlus Code of Practice.

If the price of one product depends on another, then the marketing communications must make clear the extent of the commitment the consumer must make to obtain the advertised price.

Price claims such as 'up to 50 per cent off' mustn't exaggerate the availability or amount of benefits likely to be obtained by the consumer.

General notices saying, for example, 'half-price sale' or 'up to 50 per cent off' shouldn't be used unless the maximum reduction quoted applies to at least 10 per cent of the range of products on offer at the commencement of the sale.

'Free' or 'gratis' claims used in marketing communications

(CAP Code 3, 7, 32, BCAP Code 3)
Marketing communications mustn't describe a product as 'free', 'gratis', 'without charge' or similar if the consumer has to pay anything other than the unavoidable cost of responding and collecting or paying for delivery of the item. Marketing communications must make clear the extent of the commitment the consumer must make to take advantage of a 'free' offer.

The CAP and BCAP Codes expressly forbid use of the term 'free' if:

- the consumer has to pay packing, packaging, handling or administration charges for the 'free' product;
- the cost of response, including the price of a product that the consumer must buy to take advantage of the offer, has been increased, except where the increase results from factors that are unrelated to the cost of the promotion; or
- the quality of the product that the consumer must buy has been reduced.

Marketers mustn't describe an element of a package as 'free' if that element is included in the package price unless consumers are likely to regard it as an additional benefit because it has recently been added to the package without increasing its price.

The CAP and BCAP Codes also prevent marketers using the term 'free trial' to describe 'satisfaction guaranteed or your money back' offers or offers for which a non-refundable purchase is required.

Virgin Media (2011)

A flyer for Virgin Media stated: 'Free BlackBerry for just £15 a month. BlackBerry Curve 8520 smartphone with unlimited email & web 500 texts + 100 mins BlackBerry Messenger Built in Wi-Fi.' The ASA was asked to adjudicate as to whether the use of the claim 'free' was misleading as the BlackBerry phone was dependent on the package at a cost of £15 per month to the consumer.

Virgin Media considered the offer to be a conditional purchase transaction and therefore the phone, BlackBerry device or mobile broadband dongle that it provided to customers on Pay Monthly contract tariffs were provided 'free', with customers paying a monthly price for their chosen allowance of minutes, texts, web access or other services. Virgin Media also backed this up with statistical data that showed the number of customers who paid for the tariff but chose not to take the 'free' phone.

A critical part of the consideration to be made in assessing whether the BlackBerry was 'free' was the need to show that the calls and web and e-mail access were sold separately without the BlackBerry phone.

The evidence presented by Virgin Media showed that a significant proportion of its customers bought calls and web and e-mail but didn't take the phone, and on that basis the ASA ruled that the BlackBerry was genuinely 'free' and the flyer wasn't misleading.

Availability of advertised products

(CAP Code 3, BCAP Code 3)
A clear way to damage reputation for a brand owner is to advertise products and then not be able to fulfil demand, leaving consumers disappointed and feeling let down. The CAP and BCAP Codes specifically provide that advertisers must have made a reasonable estimate of demand and, should estimated demand be likely to outstrip supply, then the advertisement needs to make clear that stocks are limited and are likely to sell out.

Other provisions contained in the CAP and BCAP Codes can be summarized under the general heading of 'fair dealing', and there's an expectation that marketers will at all times act in the best interests of consumers. For example, if a marketer uses the word 'new', then the product shouldn't have been available on the market for more than 6–12 months previously in order for that claim to have been made honestly.

Environmental claims

(CAP Code 3, 7, 9, 19, 49, BCAP Code 9)
This is an increasingly important area of marketing communications as brand owners attempt to position themselves as responsible citizens that care about the planet and the sustainability of their products and services. Both the CAP and the BCAP Codes insist on such claims being clear and capable of being substantiated, and any environmental claims made mustn't mislead the consumer and should be accurate.

It's a particularly sensitive topic given the strength of feeling many consumers have about purchasing only products that are environmentally sustainable, and if a product has never had a demonstrably adverse effect on the environment it's not open to marketers to cynically claim it's 'good' for the environment!

Warning bells should ring if any marketing communications contain claims such as 'environmentally friendly', 'kinder to the planet', 'greener', 'carbon neutral' or 'zero carbon'.

The Department for Environment, Food and Rural Affairs (Defra) has produced a useful guide, *How to Make a Good Environmental Claim*, for businesses interested in making environmental claims within their sales and marketing activities.

Finnair (2010)

A poster for the Finnish airline Finnair featured an image of its Airbus flying over the Finnish coastline with the caption: 'Be eco-smart. Choose Finnair's brand new fleet.' The ASA was asked to adjudicate on whether the claim 'Be eco-smart' misleadingly implied that flying was environmentally friendly and whether Finnair could substantiate that its new fleet was 'eco-smart' in comparison with older aircraft.

In its defence, Finnair argued it didn't intend to claim that flying was 'environmentally friendly' and accepted that flying wouldn't always be the best form of transport from an environmental perspective.

In a search for 'environmental credentials' the airline sought to convey its belief that it was 'eco-smart' to choose its airline over others because it took environmental concerns into consideration. It also argued that it was preferable to fly Finnair because its flights via Helsinki were more direct to Asian destinations, which meant its aircraft could carry less fuel and travel for shorter distances. It also pleaded that Helsinki had an advantage as a hub airport because it had fewer passengers but more runways in contrast to other comparable airports, such as London Heathrow. As a result, the local airspace was less congested and there was a reduction in unnecessary time flying whilst planes waited to land.

Finnair's rationale behind the advertisement was that it wanted to highlight the fact that consumers should be eco-conscious about how they flew and believed people would be 'eco-smart' by choosing to fly Finnair.

With respect to the age of its aircraft, Finnair produced evidence that the average age of its fleet was less than five years, making it one of the most efficient fleets in the world, which theoretically required 16.5–18.7 per cent less fuel on the long-haul flights between Helsinki and Asian destinations.

The ASA accepted that Finnair wasn't attempting to convey the message that flying was environmentally friendly per se but rather that it would be eco-smart to choose an airline like Finnair. However, the ASA considered that readers of the advertisement were likely to interpret the claim 'eco-smart' without qualification as a claim analogous to 'environmentally friendly' that conveyed the impression that flying with Finnair would have little or no detrimental effect on the environment, and as a result the 'eco-smart' reference was likely to mislead consumers.

The ASA also rejected the claim that flying with Finnair was better for the environment compared with its rivals, as it was unclear whether passengers would be transported in older or newer aircraft to their destinations and there wasn't sufficient evidence that shorter routes were better for the environment, as claimed.

In addition, lack of robust comparative data for emissions for actual flights as opposed to theoretical emissions data resulted in a breach of the CAP Code.

Distance selling
(CAP Code 9, BCAP Code 8)
As discussed in Chapter 6, the Consumer Protection (Distance Selling) Regulations 2000 (SI 2000/2334), which implemented the Distance Selling Directive (97/7/EC), came into force in October 2000 and apply certain rules to contracts formed at a distance. These regulations are also the basis for the CAP and BCAP Codes, which regulate the use of direct response mechanisms in marketing communications.

In addition, the Direct Marketing Association (DMA) requires its members to observe the DM Code of Practice (2012), which covers some direct marketing procedures that aren't covered by the CAP and BCAP Codes.

UK law distinguishes between B2B and B2C distance selling, and as of March 2012 the BCAP Code applies only to B2C distance selling advertisements.

The change in the BCAP Code on distance selling was done to avoid imposing unnecessary restrictions on brand owners conducting B2B advertising. However, other provisions in the BCAP Code provide protection for B2B customers from misleading advertising practices.

Both the CAP and the BCAP Codes apply to consumers within a B2C context, and distance selling marketing communications must make clear the marketer's identity and geographic address in a form that can be retained by consumers.

Distance selling marketing communications must include:

● The main characteristics of the product and the price, including any VAT or other taxes payable.

- The amount of any delivery charge.

- The estimated delivery or performance time and arrangements.

- A statement that, unless inapplicable, consumers have the right to cancel orders for products. Suppliers of services must explain how the right to cancel may be affected if the consumer agrees to services beginning less than seven working days after the contract was concluded. The trader must however make it clear when the services will commence.

- Any telephone, postal or other communication charge calculated at higher than the standard rate (for example, if a premium-rate call is required).

- Any other limitation on the offer (for example, period of availability) and any other condition that affects its validity.

- A statement on whether the trader intends to provide substitute products of equivalent quality and price if those ordered are unavailable and one that it will meet the cost of returning substitute products on cancellation.

- If goods are supplied or services performed permanently or recurrently, the minimum duration of such open-ended contracts.

The latest time that goods are delivered or services begin, the trader must give the consumer written information on:

- How to exercise his or her right to cancel (subject to certain exceptions – see page 169). Traders must allow at least seven clear working days after delivery or after the conclusion of a service contract unless the consumer agrees to an earlier start date for the consumer to cancel.

- In the case of goods, whether the consumer has to return the goods to the trader on cancellation and if so who's to bear the cost of return or recovery of the goods.

- Any other guarantees and after-sales services.

- The full geographical address of the trader for any consumer complaint to be received.

- The conditions that apply to the cancellation of any open-ended contract.

A trader must fulfil orders within 30 days from the day a consumer sends his or her order unless:

- the nature of the product or service makes it reasonable to specify a longer period in the marketing communications, for example made-to-measure products, plants that are out of season, or products or services that are supplied on an instalment basis may reasonably specify a longer period; or

- a longer performance period has been agreed with the consumer.

A trader must refund money promptly and at the latest within 30 days of notice of cancellation being given if:

- The consumer hasn't received the products within the specified period. If the consumer prefers to wait, he or she must be given a firm dispatch date or fortnightly progress report by the trader. Alternatively a trader may if asked or if it is stated before purchase provide a substitute of equivalent quality and price.
- Products are returned because they're damaged when received, are faulty or aren't as described. If this is the case, the trader must bear the cost of transit in both directions.
- The consumer cancels within seven clear working days after delivery subject to the conditions (see below). Consumers can assume that they may try out products, except for audio or video recordings or computer software, but should take reasonable care of them before they are returned. A consumer must return the product and, unless the product is a substitute product sent instead of the ordered product, the trader may require the consumer to pay the costs of doing so providing the trader made that clear at the latest time the product was delivered.
- An unconditional money-back guarantee is given and the products are returned within a reasonable period.
- Products that have been returned are not received back, provided that the consumer can produce proof of posting.

If all contractual obligations to a consumer are met, the trader doesn't have to provide a refund on:

- services that have already begun with the consumer's agreement (subject to the right to cancel);
- products the price of which depends on financial market fluctuations that are outside the control of the trader;
- perishable, personalized or made-to-measure products;
- audio or video recordings or computer software if unsealed by the consumer;
- newspapers, periodicals or magazines; and
- betting, gaming or lottery services.

Traders should take particular care when packaging products that might fall into the hands of children and not falsely imply that consumers have already ordered the marketed product by including in marketing material an invoice or similar document that seeks payment.

In addition, the CAP and BCAP Codes provide that a trader shouldn't ask a consumer to pay for or return unsolicited products, except for substitute products supplied in conformity with provisions in the CAP and BCAP Codes.

ASA regulation of marketing activities on websites

Pre-March 2011

Prior to March 2011, many marketers wouldn't have considered messages on a company's blog or Facebook page to be 'advertising', but all that changed from 1 March 2011 as the CAP Code remit extended to websites and in particular marketing messages online, including the rules relating to misleading advertising, social responsibility and the protection of children.

Historically, the ASA had only the power to regulate adverts in e-mails or text messages and online advertisements where they were contained within paid-for advertising space on third-party websites, such as banner ads, pop-ups or keyword advertising on search engines.

Post-March 2011

From 1 March 2011, the ASA has regulated advertisements and other marketing communications placed by a business on its own website and in other non-paid online space under its control. According to the ASA, the extension has 'the protection of consumers and children at its heart' and is intended to fill an online gap, because in recent years the ASA had received an increasing number of complaints about online adverts but had no power to take action to regulate them.

ASA remit

The ASA's remit covers the online marketing communications of all organizations operating from the UK.

It's important to note that the ASA's powers aren't limited just to advertisements and marketing materials contained on a dot co dot uk website.

The CAP Code now applies to all online marketing communications, including marketing on a company's or sole trader's own UK-based website and in other 'non-paid' space it controls (including its official Facebook and Twitter pages) where the communications are intended to sell something.

If a brand owner 'adopts and incorporates' user-generated content (UGC) within its own marketing communications, such as retweeting customers' comments on Twitter, that communication now falls within the ASA's remit and can be regulated.

Excluded communications

The following types of information that may appear on a brand owner's website are specifically excluded from the scope of the CAP Code:

- statutory reports;
- news releases and other public relations material;
- editorial content;
- natural listings on a search engine or a price comparison site;
- customer charters and codes of practice;
- investor relations material; and
- 'heritage advertising', provided it's not part of the company's current promotional strategy and is placed in an appropriate context.

Foreign media

The CAP Code also doesn't apply to marketing communications in 'foreign media'.

If a marketing communication appears in media based in a country that has a self-regulatory organization (SRO) that's a member of the European Advertising Standards Alliance (EASA), the EASA will coordinate any cross-border complaints so that the SRO in the country of origin of the communication will have jurisdiction, but consumers need complain only to their local SRO.

In the online context, the origin of a marketing communication may not be clear, such as a tweet to the world at large by a global company.

The ASA has indicated that whether or not it will refer a complaint to a foreign SRO or consider the complaint to fall within its own remit will depend upon the circumstances of the marketing communication that's the subject of the complaint, including whether the relevant company has operations in the UK and whether the communication was directed, in whole or in part, to customers in the UK.

Implications for marketers

If your organization has an online presence, you'll need to ensure that your online advertising and marketing materials comply with the CAP Code on an ongoing basis. Given the potential complexity of your online advertising strategy, this may not be a straightforward task.

Some of the steps you should consider include the following:

- Identify and audit all online advertising and marketing channels.
- Review procedures to check that all advertising and marketing content is compliant with the CAP Code, whether contained on your company website, non-paid-for space under your control such as a dedicated space on a social networking site like Facebook, or paid-for space provided by a third party such as Amazon or Lastminute.com.
- Don't just check traditional advertisements and sales promotions but also consider banners, pop-ups, paid searches, e-mails, viral marketing and 'advergames'.

- Consider whether you use customer testimonials and comments in your marketing communications. In addition, do you moderate comments posted to message boards on your websites or social media space? If so, ensure that any UGC that's been incorporated into your marketing communications is compliant with the CAP Code.
- Ensure that all employees responsible for advertising and marketing and managing websites and social media interaction, as well as those who blog, are aware of the implications of the new rules.
- If traditional marketing and e-marketing teams are in separate functional areas, consider making them more integrated if possible.
- Consult with affiliates and other third parties to ensure compliance with the CAP Code.
- Review carefully all relevant third-party contracts to ensure that any relevant issues are addressed, for example that there are terms and conditions providing you with control over the content that's posted in the name of the company, that third parties are required to cooperate in relation to any complaints received in relation to advertising and marketing content, and that there are other checks and balances in place.
- Ensure that internal guidelines are in place for all website, e-mail and social media advertising and marketing content and that these guidelines are adhered to.
- Ensure that the CAP Code is integrated into in-house marketing policy guidelines in order to ensure compliance with best practice, and update these guidelines to take account of the review of the CAP Code.
- Seek professional advice and guidance and ensure all employees are up to date in their education and training on these issues.
- React appropriately to any complaints raised by the ASA and seek to resolve these as fast as possible.
- Monitor any rulings, guidance and pronouncements made by the ASA on an ongoing basis so that you remain up to date with the approach the ASA is taking to its new online powers, and any consequences for your online marketing activities, by signing up for its free newsletter at http://www.asa.org.uk.

As discussed in Chapter 5, consider how to use the CAP Code as a weapon for competitive sales and marketing advantage by bringing a complaint to the ASA in respect of any online advertising by a competitor that you consider to be misleading or otherwise in breach of the CAP and BCAP Codes. However, note that competitors may be thinking along the same lines, so be extra mindful when including in your online marketing communications any comparative advertising or other content that could drive them to bring a complaint about you to the ASA. See also Chapter 7 for the discussion on the EU Privacy and Electronic Communications Regulations, which are also relevant for marketers.

Protection of children and young people from sales and marketing exploitation

Consumer Protection from Unfair Trading Regulations 2008

Sales and marketing to children (those under 18 years old) is governed by the same legislation and codes of practice that relate to advertising generally in the UK, such as the Consumer Protection from Unfair Trading Regulations 2008, as discussed earlier in this chapter.

For example, the CPRs make it an offence knowingly or recklessly to engage in an unfair commercial practice. A commercial practice is unfair if it contravenes the requirements of professional diligence and it materially distorts or is likely materially to distort the economic behaviour of the average consumer with regard to the product. Schedule 1 to the CPRs sets out a list of 31 commercial practices that will be considered to be unfair in all circumstances, and this includes any advertisement that's a direct exhortation to children to buy advertised products or persuade their parents or other adults to buy advertised products for them.

This provision is also incorporated into the ICC Code and CAP Code.

ICC Code (2011)

As discussed earlier in the chapter, the ICC Code (2011) lays down a number of key marketing principles that have become adopted or incorporated into various national bodies' codes, including the CAP and BCAP Codes.

Article 18 of the ICC Code, on children and young people, is one of the most detailed and provides that special care should be taken in marketing communications directed to or featuring children and young people.

The following provisions of Article 18 apply to marketing communications addressed to children and young people as defined in national laws and regulations relevant to such communications:

- Such communications shouldn't undermine positive social behaviour, lifestyles and attitudes.
- Products unsuitable for children and young people shouldn't be advertised in media targeted to them, and advertisements directed to children and young people shouldn't be inserted in media where the editorial matter is unsuitable for them.
- Material unsuitable for children should be clearly identified as such.

Marketing communications shouldn't exploit the inexperience or credulity of children and young people.

When demonstrating a product's performance and use, marketing communications to children and young people should not:

- minimize the degree of skill or understate the age level generally required to assemble or operate the product;
- exaggerate the true size, value, nature, durability and performance of the product; and
- fail to disclose information about the need for additional purchases, such as accessories or individual items in a collection or series, required to produce the result shown or described.

Whilst the use of fantasy in marketing communications is appropriate for young as well as older children, it shouldn't make it difficult for them to identify the distinction between reality and fiction.

Marketing communications directed to children should be clearly distinguishable to them as such.

Marketing communications shouldn't contain any statement or visual treatment that could have the effect of harming children and young people mentally, morally or physically. Children and young people shouldn't be portrayed in unsafe situations or engaging in actions harmful to themselves or others or be encouraged to engage in potentially hazardous activities or behaviour.

Marketing communications shouldn't suggest that possession or use of the marketed product will give a child or young person physical, psychological or social advantages over other children and young people or that not possessing the product will have the opposite effect.

The ICC Code also raises a number of other ethical and moral points that marketers need to observe when constructing communications with children and young people:

- Such activities shouldn't undermine the authority, responsibility, judgement or tastes of parents, having regard to relevant social and cultural values.

- Such activities shouldn't include any direct appeal to children and young people to persuade their parents or other adults to buy products for them ('pester power' is expressly forbidden).

- Prices shouldn't be presented in such a way as to lead children and young people to an unrealistic perception of the cost or value of the product, for example by reducing the size of the recommended retail price relative to other sales and marketing information. In other words, such an advertisement shouldn't imply that the product is immediately within the reach of every family budget.

- Communications inviting children and young people to contact the brand owner should encourage them to obtain the permission of a parent or other appropriate adult if any cost, including that of a communication, is involved.

ASA regulations on sales and marketing to children

(CAP Code 5, BCAP Code 5)

The CAP and BCAP Codes on sales and marketing to children are similar to those set out in both the ICC Code (2011) and the DMA Code of Practice (2012) and include special sections on advertising to children.

The CAP and BCAP Codes define a child as anyone under the age of 16 years and provide that advertisements and promotions addressed to or likely to appeal to children should contain nothing that's likely to result in their physical, mental or moral harm. For example, advertisements shouldn't include the following:

- children entering into strange places or talking to strangers;
- children being shown in hazardous situations or behaving dangerously or using or being in close proximity to dangerous substances or equipment, without direct adult supervision; and
- encouragement to children to copy any practice that might be unsafe for a child.

Levi Strauss (2012)

A magazine advertisement pictured three young people holding lit fireworks, with the copy:

> *When all is said and done, have you done or said enough? Have you just gone along for the ride, or have you steered destiny's hot rod? When you leave this world, did you make it any better than it was when you arrived? All you need is all you've got; your wits and the clothes on your back. Your epitaph is yours to earn; your legacy is yours to make. Go forth.*

The ASA was asked to adjudicate on the advertisement as to whether it was harmful and irresponsible because it encouraged young people to play with lit fireworks.

Despite a number of safety precautions, such as use of models 19 years of age and older positioned standing a certain distance apart and in an open space, the ASA considered that the overall impression would be of young people holding lit fireworks.

Although the advert was placed in a magazine with 93 per cent of its readers being over the age of 18 years, the ASA considered that it wouldn't be possible to prevent some younger people from viewing the advertisement. In addition, the placement was timed to appear in late autumn, when fireworks would be more widely available because of Guy Fawkes Night and the festival of Diwali, where fireworks are typically part of the celebrations. The ASA considered that this would increase the likelihood of emulation by children exposed to the magazine advertisement and also that the caption would encourage risk taking and daring. On that basis, the ASA held that the advertisement as a whole breached the CAP Code in relation to social responsibility and harm and offence provisions.

The risk of children emulating a dangerous activity is something that the ASA takes very seriously. This adjudication accords with a previous adjudication where a catalogue advert for a 'fire station' play tent that featured images of young children pretending to extinguish a real fire was also held to have breached the CAP Code, as the advertisement would appeal to children because it featured children in a realistic situation and children would have an interest in the product being advertised; hence it was likely to encourage children to emulate the dangerous activity shown.

Under the provisions of the CAP and BCAP Codes, advertisements addressed to or likely to appeal to children shouldn't exploit their credulity, loyalty, vulnerability or lack of experience, in much the same way as provided under the ICC Code. Parental permission should be obtained before children are committed to purchasing complex and costly goods and services.

Advertisements aimed at children shouldn't:

- actively encourage children to make a nuisance of themselves to parents, teachers or others;
- make a direct appeal to purchase;
- exaggerate what's attainable by an ordinary child using the product being advertised or promoted;
- exploit their susceptibility to charitable appeals;
- make children feel that they're lacking in courage, duty or loyalty if they don't buy or don't encourage others to buy a particular advertised product;
- make children feel inferior or unpopular for not buying the advertised product; and
- make it difficult for children to judge the size, characteristics and performance of any product advertised and to distinguish between real-life situations and fantasy.

Promotions addressed to or targeted directly at children:

- must make clear that adult permission is required if a prize or an incentive might cause conflict between a child's desire and a parent's or other adult's authority;
- must contain a prominent closing date if applicable; and
- mustn't exaggerate the value of a prize or the chances of winning it.

Promotions that require a purchase to participate and include a direct exhortation to make a purchase mustn't be addressed to or targeted at children.

The CAP and BCAP Codes also include scheduling rules around advertising age-restricted computer and console games to prevent television commercials appearing around programmes made for or likely to appeal particularly to children. In addition, the BCAP Code prevents television commercials from exploiting the trust that children and young people place in parents, teachers or other people.

Direct Marketing Association Code of Practice (2012)

All DMA members must comply with the general rules regarding children and young people when using all online and offline media.

Basic principles

When collecting data in both online and offline environments from children under 12 years of age, verifiable and explicit consent from a parent or guardian is required.

Parent or guardian consent

No unsolicited commercial communications to children under 12 years of age can be sent without first obtaining the verifiable and explicit consent of the parent or guardian. Legislation regarding consent for the sending of commercial communications must be complied with. Commercial communications addressed or likely to appeal to children and young people shouldn't contain anything likely to result in their physical, mental or moral harm.

Participation activities

Children and young people shouldn't be encouraged to enter strange places or talk to strangers. Particular care is needed where they are asked to make collections, enter schemes or gather labels, wrappers, coupons and other similar items.

Hazardous situations

Children and young people shouldn't be shown in hazardous situations or behaving dangerously in the home or outside, except to promote safety. They shouldn't be shown unattended in street scenes unless they are old enough to take responsibility for their own safety. They shouldn't be shown using or in close proximity to dangerous substances or equipment without direct adult supervision.

Examples include petrol and certain medicines and household substances, as well as electrical appliances and machinery, including agricultural machinery.

Inexperience, vulnerability and credulity

Advertisements or promotions addressed or likely to appeal to children and young people shouldn't exploit their inexperience, vulnerability, credulity or natural loyalty. Children and young people shouldn't be made to feel inferior or unpopular for not buying the advertised product or not undertaking a particular activity, and they shouldn't be made to feel they're lacking in courage, duty or loyalty if they don't buy or don't encourage others to buy a particular product or undertake a particular activity.

Distinguishing between fact and fiction

It should be made easy for children and young people to judge the size and characteristics of any product advertised and to distinguish between real-life situations and fantasy.

Adult permission must be obtained before children and young people are committed to purchasing costly products, and advertisements and promotions addressed to them shouldn't encourage them to make a nuisance of themselves to parents, teachers or others.

Direct appeal to children and young people

Advertisements and promotions shouldn't make a direct appeal to children and young people to buy the advertised products or persuade their parents or other adults to buy the advertised products for them. Such advertisements and promotions shouldn't exaggerate what's attainable to an ordinary child using the product being advertised or promoted.

Healthy lifestyle

Advertisements and promotions shouldn't actively encourage children and young people to eat or drink at or near bedtime, to eat frequently throughout the day or to replace main meals with confectionery or a snack food.

Charitable appeals

Charitable appeals shouldn't exploit the susceptibility of children and young people to charitable appeals and should explain the extent to which their participation will help any charity-linked promotion.

Adult content

Brand owners should take care not to send material to or otherwise target advertising at children and young people that's suitable only for adults and must exercise care when packaging products for dispatch to adults that may fall into the hands of children and young people.

Consumer credit

DMA members must comply with the Consumer Credit Act 1974 and not make offers of credit to those under 18 years, as well as provide a prominent statement in any advertising and marketing that credit terms aren't available to those under 18 years of age.

Promotions aimed at children

Promotions addressed to children and young people mustn't encourage excessive purchases in order to participate, must require adult permission if prizes or incentives are likely to cause conflict between a parent or guardian and the child, such as holidays or pets, must clearly explain any proof of purchase required and mustn't exaggerate the chance of winning or the value of a particular prize.

Gambling and alcohol

DMA members mustn't make offers for or in any way promote gaming schemes or alcoholic drinks to children and young people, taking care not to produce any commercial communication for these products that might appeal to children and young people.

Data protection

DMA members mustn't rent lists known to contain children under 12 years of age without first obtaining a parent or guardian's verifiable and explicit consent. Furthermore, DMA members mustn't attempt to obtain information from children and young people about other persons, such as parents and other family members, for the purposes of marketing. For further guidance on data protection issues, refer to Chapter 6.

References and further reading

Cases and judgments

Direct Wines Ltd t/a Laithwaites Wine (2012), ASA adjudication
Finnair (2010), ASA adjudication
Levi Strauss & Co t/a Levi's (2012), ASA adjudication
LG Electronics (2012), ASA adjudication
L'Oréal (UK) Ltd t/a L'Oréal Paris (2012), ASA adjudication
TripAdvisor (2012), ASA adjudication
Virgin Media (2011), ASA adjudication
Virgin Media (2012), ASA adjudication

Websites

Advertising Standards Authority (ASA) has an excellent website that is updated daily and contains the full CAP and BCAP Codes as well as other useful resources [accessed 6 April 2012] http://www.asa.org.uk
Department for Business, Innovation and Skills (BIS), *Pricing Practices Guide* [accessed 17 April 2012] http://www.bis.gov.uk
Department for Environment, Food and Rural Affairs (Defra), *How to Make a Good Environmental Claim* [accessed 17 April 2012] http://www.defra.gov.uk

Direct Marketing Association (DMA) requires its members to observe the DM Code of Practice (2012), which covers some direct marketing procedures that aren't covered by the CAP and BCAP Codes [accessed 17 April 2012] http://www.dma.org.uk

International Chamber of Commerce (ICC) has developed a Codes Centre website [accessed 12 April 2012] http://www.codescentre.com, which is a one-stop shop resource that features a searchable and user-friendly online version of the Consolidated ICC Code of Advertising and Marketing Communications Practice (2011). In addition there are links to other self-regulatory codes from around the world

KwikChex.com: online service provider providing a right-of-reply service for brand owners who feel powerless to respond to negative blogs [accessed 18 April 2012] http://www.kwikclix.com

Lexology: a highly reliable resource for the latest case law in this area [accessed 6 April 2012] http://www.lexology.com

PhonepayPlus Code of Practice [accessed 18.4.2012] http://code.phoneplayplus.org.uk

TripAdvisor website [accessed 18 April 2012] http://www.tripadvisor.co.uk

Book

Kolah, A (2013) *High Impact Marketing that Gets Results*, Kogan Page, London

*" Product placement, merchandise tie-ins,
celebrity endorsement...and...action!"*

5

Law as a weapon for competitive sales and marketing advantage

In this chapter

- The UK and EU advertising regime
- Comparative advertising as a weapon for achieving sales and marketing advantage
- Product placement on television as a weapon for achieving sales and marketing advantage

Introduction

Marketers may be forgiven for assuming that the professional practice of law is all about what you can't do. Let's face it, most lawyers are hard-wired to say what you can't or shouldn't do any sales and marketing campaign that 'sails close to the wind', such as an aggressive price comparison or ambush marketing campaign or extending the hand of corporate hospitality to a government official. For a discussion on ambush marketing and providing corporate hospitality to customers and others, see Chapter 10.

What few marketers appreciate is that, in the right hands, the law can be a powerful weapon for achieving sales and marketing advantage. Rather than being a drag on marketing creativity, understanding how the law can be used to support such activities can lift your thinking to a new level and achieve surprising results. In essence, this chapter is about doing just that.

Top-flight sales and marketing professionals are the most creative and competitive bunch of people you're likely to meet in your career. And that's no surprise. They've studied the 'art of war'!

You need to travel back to the Zhou Dynasty in 544 *bc* to discover the ancient secrets of combat as told by one of the greatest warriors who ever lived – Sun Tzu – in *The Art of War*. This celebrated ancient warrior unlocked the secrets of how to achieve a desired outcome and defeat the competition all at the same time – and he has inspired generations of war generals, business leaders, politicians, sports stars and marketers to do the same.

Sun Tzu believed that warriors should aim to become invulnerable by understanding themselves and what they planned to do rather than by dreaming of defeating the enemy. The key was to seek to exploit the enemy's vulnerabilities. Victory should be an inevitable outcome, and that means there need to be no slip-ups on the way. Swift movement to confuse the enemy is as important as keeping the enemy unaware of your plans. Speed is the essence of attack, and a good warrior always makes sure the rearguard is covered.

Sun Tzu believed passionately in exploiting every piece of information in order to turn the battle his way. You should aim to scare your enemies by making yourself appear larger or more powerful than you are, timing your attacks for when your enemy is at its most vulnerable and not attacking when you can't win. Treat the enemy with great respect, even after you've won, as this could stymie any appetite it may have for revenge.

Sun Tzu added that victory isn't the same as doing battle. In war, victory is certain only after measurement, estimation, calculation and comparison have been achieved.

In a modern context, almost every sales-and-marketing-led organization will apply some or all of Sun Tzu's concepts, whether consciously or not. There are even specific training companies that have been used by global brand owners to train their sales and marketing teams in doing business according to *The Art of War*.

There are many instances of when a company has gone to war and won, such as Microsoft's battle with Netscape. Equally, there are plenty of instances when a brand owner has gone to war and lost, such as Ryanair's epic battle with British Airways. These and other examples in this chapter confirm Sun Tzu's view that one battle doesn't make a victory.

In the context of comparative advertising and product placement, undermining the competition without resorting to war is a tenable offensive and cost-effective strategy. For example, supermarket chains frequently use television advertising to show how their products are cheaper and fresher than their rivals' products in order to drive incremental sales.

Ensuring that you remain the first among equals in your chosen market segment, such as Apple, Google or Facebook, is a strategy that Sun Tzu would have endorsed. The future belongs to the bold, and this chapter will expose how the law can be turned into a weapon for competitive advantage for those brand owners brave enough to engage in 'brand combat'.

Before dissecting how certain competitive sales and marketing activities can achieve the outcomes you're looking for, you should survey the existing regulatory landscape to ensure that you don't fall down the legal potholes that you're certain to encounter along the way.

It's highly probable that any type of comparative advertising or product placement will require expert legal advice before such plans reach an advanced stage. Ultimately whether to proceed should be a commercial decision that's made based on sound legal advice that weighs both the benefits and the risks for engaging in such high-stakes activities. And don't assume that there aren't risks even after the legal advice provides the 'green light' to proceed. Being bold necessitates making a judgement call, and this can have far-reaching implications for the reputation of the brand, the products and the services as well as your own career if you get it wrong.

The UK and EU advertising regime

Regulatory framework

The regulatory framework for advertising in the UK is a patchwork of legislative controls including the Communications Act 2003, the Consumer Protection from Unfair Trading Regulations 2008, which implements the EU Unfair Commercial Practices Directive 2005/29/EC, and the Business Protection from Misleading Marketing Regulations 2008, which implements the EU Misleading and Comparative Advertising Directive 2006/114/EC (MCAD 2006).

By far the greatest impact on this area of sales and marketing practice is from the self-regulatory Codes overseen by the Advertising Standards Authority (ASA).

The Communications Act 2003

This sets out provisions for the regulation of broadcast, television and radio services, including provisions aimed at securing standards for broadcast advertising. Within the context of comparative advertising and product placement discussed in this chapter, the standards' objectives – incorporated into the Broadcast Code on Advertising Practice (BCAP) – are that the inclusion of advertising that may be misleading, harmful or offensive in television and radio services is prevented. In addition there's a requirement that broadcasters don't use techniques that exploit the possibility of conveying a message to viewers or listeners or unduly influencing them without making them fully aware of what has occurred.

Consumer Protection from Unfair Trading Regulations (CPRs) 2008

All business-to-consumer (B2C) advertising must comply with the CPRs, which forbid brand owners from using misleading, aggressive or unfair sales techniques, and the CPRs implement EU Unfair Commercial Practices Directive 2005/29/EC.

Business Protection from Misleading Marketing Regulations (BPRs) 2008

Business-to-business (B2B) marketing and comparative advertising must comply with the BPRs, which prohibit advertising that's misleading to the traders to whom it's addressed or that injures or is likely to injure a competitor, and the BPRs implement EU Misleading and Comparative Advertising Directive 2006/114/EC.

Self-regulatory framework

The ASA enforces two main self-regulatory Codes for broadcast and non-broadcast advertising in the UK.

The ASA's wide remit includes:

- advertisements in newspapers, magazines, brochures, leaflets, circulars, mailings, fax transmissions, catalogues, follow-up literature and other electronic and printed material;
- posters and other promotional media in public places;
- cinema and video commercials;
- advertisements in non-broadcast electronic media;
- view-data services;
- marketing databases containing consumers' personal information;
- sales promotions;
- advertisement promotions; and
- online advertising, including content on websites (since March 2011).

Research shows that consumers view advertising as an integral part of their daily culture and as a source of information and entertainment. However, the acceptance of advertising by consumers relies not just on its entertainment value but also on its trustworthiness, which is what the Codes are designed to protect.

Overall, the advertising system in the UK works well – a balance of self-regulation for non-broadcast advertising, such as newspaper, print and web advertising, with co-regulation for broadcast advertising for television and radio. For further discussion on the CAP and BCAP Codes that are the 'hygiene requirements' for sales and marketing activities, refer to Chapter 4.

Non-broadcast media

The current non-broadcast code is the 12th edition of the UK Code of Non-Broadcast Advertising, Sales Promotion and Direct Marketing (the CAP Code) and came into force from 1 September 2010. The CAP Code is written by the advertising industry through the Committee on Advertising Practice (CAP) and is based on the revised International Chamber of Commerce Consolidated Code for Advertising and Marketing Communication Practice (2011).

All the main trade and professional bodies representing advertisers, agencies, service suppliers and media owners are members of CAP and have signed up in principle not to accept any advertising that contravenes the CAP Code.

The CAP Code sets out a number of important principles that are relevant in the context of comparative advertising, including that advertising should:

- be legal, decent, honest and truthful;
- be prepared with a sense of responsibility to consumers and society; and
- respect the principles of fair competition generally accepted in business.

In addition, advertisements shouldn't mislead by inaccuracy, ambiguity, exaggeration or otherwise. Advertisers must hold documentary evidence to prove that they can objectively substantiate all claims before submitting an advertisement for publication. The CAP Code is applied by the ASA in spirit as well as to the letter of the law.

An advertiser isn't required to obtain clearance from the ASA that a campaign complies with the CAP Code. However, CAP does provide a copy advice service. This can be useful, but advertisers and their legal advisers should be aware that the ASA is not bound by the advice given by CAP. As a result the ASA may uphold complaints about advertising that CAP has considered complies with the CAP Code. The ASA takes account of prevailing standards and practices when making its decisions, which is one reason why the ASA isn't bound by its own previous decisions. However, previous decisions can provide a means of guidance to the industry on how the CAP Code should be interpreted and also act as a record of ASA policy for consumers, media, government and all parts of the advertising business.

There are more than 30 million press advertisements and 100 million pieces of direct marketing produced every year in the UK, so it would be impossible to pre-clear every one of them. To assist marketers, the CAP copy advice team provides free pre-publication advice to help them create advertisements, promotions and direct marketing that meets the CAP Code. As well as providing bespoke advice on individual campaigns, the team also updates a searchable online database that the advertisers, agencies and media can check to read the latest positions on hundreds of different advertising issues. For further information on direct marketing best practice, refer to Chapter 6.

Following the extension of the ASA's digital remit to cover marketing communications on brand owners' websites, the CAP copy advice team has recently introduced a new premium bespoke website audit service for advertisers. The audits offer a tailored and expert assessment of companies' websites against the CAP Code with a view to giving their marketing communications a clean bill of health and providing compliance guidance. CAP also produces a free quarterly e-mail newsletter that can help you keep up to date with all the latest developments, which is available at http://www.cap.org.uk.

Despite a print advertisement being cleared, the ASA can act on just one complaint against that advertisement if its feels that the Codes have been breached. The higher the number of complaints received by the ASA, the higher the chance that the advertisement may have broken the Codes, particularly with respect to matters of taste and decency.

Once the ASA receives a complaint, the complaints team will assess the marketing communication and the nature of the objection and decide how best to resolve the complaint.

The ASA also proactively monitors advertisements to keep advertising standards high and maintain a level playing field for business and regularly conducts surveys into specific media or industry sectors to ensure the Codes are being followed in those areas. The vast majority of brand owners comply with the ASA's rulings and act quickly to amend or withdraw an advertisement that breaks the Codes.

The ASA has a range of sanctions at its disposal to act against the few miscreants that don't comply with the Codes, and it relies on the cooperation of media owners to help enforce these rulings.

The first sanction – and one of the most powerful – is the weekly publication of the ASA's adjudications, which generates a great amount of media attention in the UK and frequently internationally. For a discussion on how best to manage public relations, refer to Guru in a Bottle® *High Impact Marketing that Gets Results.*

Negative media coverage can significantly damage a brand owner's reputation, particularly if it's seen to be flouting the rules designed to protect consumers and fair competition. The ASA's rulings are available on its website (http://asa.org.uk) for a period of five years, and in some cases adjudications may be available for longer if used as a reference in Advice Online and Help Notes produced by CAP to help advertisers interpret the Codes.

The second sanction is the refusal by media owners to feature advertisements that break the Codes. This means the ASA can ask media owners not to print problematic advertisements.

Other sanctions exist to prevent direct mail that breaches the Code from being distributed and to reduce the likelihood of posters appearing that breach the Codes on grounds of taste, decency and social responsibility.

With the extension of the ASA's digital remit to cover marketing communications on companies' own websites, CAP's member bodies have agreed new sanctions to strengthen CAP's ability to secure compliance with the rules. These include an enhanced 'name and shame' section on the ASA's website, the removal of paid-for search advertising linking to offending advertisements, and the placement of ASA paid-for search advertisements highlighting an advertiser's non-compliance.

Ultimately, the ASA can refer non-broadcast advertisers that persistently break the Codes to the Office of Fair Trading (OFT) for legal action under the Consumer Protection from Unfair Trading Regulations 2008 and Business Protection from Misleading Marketing Regulations 2008.

Broadcast media

Broadcast advertising covers television, including interactive television and radio advertising. The UK is subject to EU broadcasting legislation, which has been implemented largely by the Communications Act 2003 and was updated as part of the implementation of the Audiovisual Media Services Directive (2007/65/EC) in 2009.

The Office of Communications (Ofcom) is responsible for the control of the content of all broadcasting including advertising through its Broadcasting Code covering radio and television, but it outsourced broadcast advertising regulation to the ASA. Under the current regime, the ASA operates and enforces the Broadcast Advertising Code (BCAP Code), produced by the Broadcast Committee of Advertising Practice (BCAP).

The BCAP Code

The BCAP Code sets out the rules that govern advertisements on any television channel or radio station licensed by Ofcom.

The rules are framed to ensure that advertisements are 'legal, decent, honest and truthful' and don't mislead or cause harm or serious or widespread offence.

A new code and advice were published by BCAP in 2010 and include a requirement for broadcast advertising to be socially responsible.

Pre-clearance

The Advertising Codes require that all claims must be substantiated before being published or aired, and the vast majority of television and radio advertisements are pre-cleared before they are broadcast.

Under the terms of the Ofcom licence, all broadcasters must take reasonable steps to ensure that the advertisements broadcast comply with the Television and Radio Advertising Codes. To help them do this, the broadcasters have established and funded two pre-clearance centres: Clearcast for television commercials; and the Radio Advertising Clearance Centre (RACC) for radio advertisements.

Clearcast pre-vets all UK broadcast advertising on behalf of the commercial television networks, which are jointly responsible with advertisers and agencies for ensuring that the advertising shown on their networks is BCAP

Code compliant. The RACC pre-vets advertising for radio. Both organizations provide advice on what's likely to be acceptable advertising content.

It's important that advertisers and their legal advisers are willing to take the time to explain to Clearcast the market segment in which they operate. However, there's no guarantee that amendments made to any proposed broadcast advertising in accordance with Clearcast's advice will be sufficient to defend any subsequent complaint made to the ASA, which has the prerogative to uphold such a complaint if it feels there has been a breach of the Codes.

Theoretically, a broadcaster that continually transmits advertisements that break the Codes can be referred by the ASA to Ofcom, which has the power to fine it or even revoke its licence. However, such referrals are very rarely necessary, as the vast majority of advertisers and media owners respect ASA decisions and agree to comply with the Codes.

Comparative advertising as a weapon for achieving sales and marketing advantage

This is one weapon that can achieve competitive advantage that even ambush marketing can't deliver. And it's perfectly lawful!

Comparative advertising is also one of the trickiest areas of advertising law, as it deals with brand owners comparing their products and services head to head with their competitors.

But – and it's a big 'but' – you can't afford to slip up, as that'll put you in the firing line for a series of regulatory and legal challenges, including trademark and possibly copyright infringement, which can be extremely costly and damage your reputation among consumers in the market.

There are many legal pitfalls, but by following the principles in this chapter it's possible to execute an effective comparative advertising campaign. And you'll need to work closely with your legal team in order to pull this off!

EU Misleading and Comparative Advertising Directive 2006/114/EC

The MCAD 2006 effectively harmonized the law on comparative advertising across the 27 EU member states and was implemented in the UK by the Business Protection from Misleading Marketing Regulations 2008.

The MCAD 2006 contains some key concepts. 'Advertising' is defined as a form of representation that is made in connection with a trade, business, craft or profession in order to promote the supply or transfer of goods or services (Article 2(a), MCAD 2006), and a 'comparative advertisement' is one that explicitly or by implication identifies a competitor or goods or services offered by a competitor (Article 2(c), MCAD 2006).

A comparative advertisement is permitted under the MCAD 2006 as long as it fulfils the following 'golden rules':

- It mustn't mislead whether by way of act or omission.
- It must compare goods or services meeting the same needs or intended for the same purpose.
- It must objectively compare one or more material, relevant, verifiable and representative features of those goods and services, which may include price.
- It mustn't create confusion in the marketplace between the advertiser and a competitor or between the advertiser's brands and those of a competitor.
- It mustn't discredit or denigrate the brands, activities or circumstances of a competitor.
- It must relate to products with the same designation as the brands of a competitor.
- It mustn't take unfair advantage of the reputation of the brands of a competitor.
- It mustn't present products as imitations or replicas of products bearing a protected trademark.

The above 'golden rules' have been the subject of much legal argument, and ultimately the Court of Justice of the European Union (CJEU) has had to provide guidance in its interpretation through a number of high-profile cases discussed in this chapter.

The above is a useful legal checklist, but it's also worth bearing in mind some practical marketing considerations before proceeding with any comparative advertising campaign:

- Are the data that have been collected that sit behind the comparative advertising campaign absolutely watertight?
- How bullish or confident are the lawyers in their advice to press ahead with the comparative advertising campaign no matter how eager you may be?
- How will consumers receive the comparative advertising campaign (favourably or not)?
- How will other brand owners and third parties that have an existing contractual relationship with you react (favourably or not)?
- How is the comparative advertising likely to be viewed by the ASA and Ofcom?
- How will the comparative advertising be viewed by your peer group within your market segment?

- What implied claims are being made by the comparative advertising, and will this make a competitor or competitors angry?

- Will complainants have a strong case, and what sort of action are they likely to take?

- In light of potential legal action against you, what are the associated risks and costs for the litigants in pursuing you?

- What's the rough likelihood of success for a legal action against you?

- What are the downsides of running the comparative advertising campaign even if the lawyers give it a 'green light'?

- What are the public relations and reputational issues that could arise as a result of the comparative advertising campaign?

- If an objection was upheld by the ASA, what would be the wasted media and production costs and would this be counterbalanced by media coverage about your campaign to justify running the risk of the advertisement?

If a comparative advertisement doesn't fall within the conditions as defined under the MCAD 2006, it could expose the marketer to an action for trademark infringement as well as an action for trade libel, malicious falsehood, infringement of copyright and even the tort of passing off.

Ajinomoto Sweeteners v Asda Stores (2010)

The claimant is a manufacturer and retailer of the artificial sweetener aspartame to the food and beverage industry. It commenced an action in malicious falsehood against supermarket chain Asda in relation to the marketing of Asda's own-label range 'Good For You', which made a reference to 'no hidden nasties, colours or flavours, no aspartame and no hydrogenated fat'.

Ajinomoto argued that, in their natural and ordinary meaning, the words used by Asda meant that aspartame:

- was especially harmful or unhealthy; or

- was potentially harmful or unhealthy; and

- is a sweetener that consumers concerned for their own health and that of their families should avoid.

By advertising its own products as not containing aspartame, Asda was impliedly making a statement that was derogatory of products that did contain aspartame and by extension of aspartame itself, and this was derogatory and false and amounted to malicious falsehood.

In a unanimous verdict, the Court of Appeal held that, if comparative advertisements make direct or indirect comparisons with competitors or their products and contain statements that are capable of being interpreted as damaging by a reasonable consumer, then that meaning will be relevant for the purposes of a malicious damage claim no matter how many other innocent and reasonable interpretations of the statement there may be.

If malice can be proved in relation to the damaging meaning, then a claim for malicious falsehood is likely to succeed.

What this decision vividly illustrates is the paramount importance of rigorous analysis of any statements made in comparative advertisements. Marketers should aim to include only those statements that are defensible as being factually accurate and not misleading, as any ambiguity, however clever and sophisticated, could give rise to substantial claims.

Kimberly-Clark v Fort Sterling (1997)

In this case a successful passing-off action was brought by Kimberly-Clark, the maker of Andrex, the UK's leading brand of toilet paper, in respect of the use of its trademark by another toilet paper manufacturer, Fort Sterling.

In 1996, a promotional pack of Fort Sterling's Nouvelle brand toilet paper contained a strip that stated that, if any customer was dissatisfied with the Nouvelle paper, the customer could claim an equivalent-sized pack of the Andrex paper. However, the packaging also included a 'disclaimer' notice in small print that Andrex was the registered trademark of Kimberly-Clark.

An injunction to prevent the passing off was granted by the court. The judge emphasized that it was important to assess how the product and packaging would appear to normal busy customers. The judge held that the display of the product and the size and style of the Andrex trademark would be likely to lead a substantial number of customers to believe that Nouvelle was a product of or associated with Kimberly-Clark. Fort Sterling wasn't saved by a disclaimer contained in the small print on the packaging.

As discussed in Chapter 3, an infringement also occurs if the use of a trademark affects its function, for example in guaranteeing quality or in communication, investment or advertising.

Specsavers v Asda Stores (2010)

In this case the High Court held that the strapline 'Be a real spec saver at Asda' amounted to a trademark infringement and took unfair advantage of Specsavers' marks, but the court didn't uphold the objection to the over lapping logo or the strapline 'Spec savings at Asda'.

Identification of a 'competitor' in a comparative advertisement

An advertisement might fall within the scope of the MCAD 2006 even if it doesn't mention any specific competitor, product or service by name. For example, if an advertisement implicitly refers to a competitor or its products and services, then it's comparative advertising even if several competitors could claim to have been identified in this way.

If a business can be identified in a particular advertisement, this doesn't mean that it should be regarded as a competitor regardless of the type of goods or services it offers. The nature of the goods and the needs that they meet are fundamental to their 'competitiveness'.

The criterion for determining whether a 'competitor' is expressly or impliedly referred to in the comparative advertisement has also been the subject of legal jurisprudence.

Article 2(c) of the MCAD 2006 requires only a relatively loose assessment of whether somebody is a competitor and whether its goods or services could be substituted to a certain degree for those of the advertiser.

However, Article 4(b) of the MCAD 2006 requires specific assessment of the goods or services that have been comparatively advertised to determine whether there's a real possibility of substitution.

Advertising that refers only to a type of goods and doesn't identify any competitor either expressly or impliedly may be lawful and wouldn't be classified as 'comparative advertising'. Instead, other provisions of the CAP and BCAP Codes may apply to that advertisement.

For a discussion of the CAP and BCAP Codes, refer to Chapter 4.

The CJEU has held that the purpose of the conditions in the MCAD 2006 is to achieve a balance between the different interests that may be affected by comparative advertising.

The aim of the MCAD 2006 is seen as being to stimulate competition between brand owners for the benefit of the consumer by permitting rivals to highlight in an objective way the merits of comparable products and services. The other objective of the MCAD 2006 is to prohibit commercial practices that distort fair competition, are detrimental to competitors and have an adverse effect on consumer choice. Specifically, a comparative advertisement that complies with MCAD 2006 won't amount to trademark infringement.

Kingspan Group plc *v* Rockwool (2011)

Kingspan manufactures insulation materials made of plastic foam, and its competitor Rockwool manufactures non-combustible stone wool insulation materials. The case concerned Rockwool's comparative advertising in the form of a national road show (2007–08), which purported to demonstrate the relative performance of both products under test conditions before an invited audience of industry professionals. In addition to the small-scale fire demonstrations, a marketing DVD was produced of footage of large-scale fire tests carried out independently under the ISO 9705 fire test standard by SP Technical Research Institute of Sweden. All these efforts were designed to demonstrate that Rockwool's product was superior to that of Kingspan's product in order to address a misconception in the market that both products were made of the same or similar material.

Kingspan issued proceedings for malicious falsehood and trademark infringement, alleging that the road shows and DVDs falsely represented that its products were dangerous. It also sought a number of declarations that the road shows and DVDs didn't comply with the MCAD 2006 as implemented in the UK by the Business Protection Regulations 2008.

Rockwool denied the allegations, arguing that SP's tests were objective, compared like for like and formed the basis of legitimate comparative advertisements. It argued that the use of Kingspan's trademarks was thus permissible under MCAD 2006 and therefore lawful.

With respect to the malicious falsehood claim that Rockwool's DVDs published words about Kingspan that were false, that these were published maliciously and that special damage occurred as a result, the court rejected this argument on the basis that Rockwool hadn't acted out of malice, although it did find as fact that the DVDs contained false representations. This was despite Rockwool having enlisted an independent research institute to carry out the comparative product tests.

Judge Kitchin observed: 'I believe that the videos each give a misleading impression as to the contribution to fire that Kingspan's products will make when properly installed.' This would appear to have negated the value of the 'independent' tests paid for by Rockwool.

With respect to the trademark infringement action, the judge found in favour of Kingspan as a result of its trademark being used in the context of the road shows and the DVDs.

The judge held that 'when considered through the eyes of persons who specify or influence the specification of the building materials to be used in a project they are each misleading and fail objectively to compare one or more material, relevant, verifiable and representative features of Rockwool's and Kingspan's products.'

As a result, there was trademark infringement because Rockwool had without due cause taken unfair advantage of and caused detriment to the reputation of the Kingspan trademarks and had discredited and denigrated Kingspan's products.

This case shows that any comparisons made in such advertisements must be objective, and simply enlisting an independent research organization to make such comparisons won't necessarily persuade the court on this point. Had both parties agreed to appoint SP Technical Research Institute of Sweden and agreed to share the cost of the research, this would've been more compelling as evidence although possibly still open to legal challenge if it hadn't been conducted in accordance with the provisions of Article 4(c) of the MCAD 2006.

The comparative advertisement must compare material, relevant, verifiable and representative features of goods or services (Article 4(c), MCAD 2006), which follows the reasoning of the CJEU in applying the MCAD 2006 in two cases involving German-owned discount supermarket chain Lidl.

Lidl Belgium *v* Colruyt NV (2006)

Supermarket chain Colruyt had sent direct mail to customers that compared its prices with those of its rival Lidl Belgium. Lidl brought proceedings claiming that the advertising was misleading and was neither objective nor verifiable as required under the MCAD 2006.

Colruyt had used two comparative advertising strategies: comparing the general level of prices charged by it and its competitors for their ranges of comparable produce and inferring the amounts customers could save; and asserting that all of its products bearing a red label with the word 'basic' were sold by its stores at the lowest price in Belgium.

The Belgian court asked the European Court of Justice (ECJ) to rule on the extent to which comparisons of 'baskets' of goods had to be transparent, for example whether the comparative advertisement had to list all the goods and whether the goods in each basket had to be identical in terms of size, branding and other features in order to be fairly compared.

The ECJ said that it had to interpret the conditions required of comparative advertising in terms of being most favourable to such advertising – in other words, a presumption of allowing it. The ECJ's main point was that a brand owner can't suggest from a selection of products that its whole range is cheaper, as that would be fundamentally unfair.

Whilst general comparisons between baskets of goods were permissible under Article 4(c) of the MCAD 2006 without the advertiser having to list exhaustively all products that might have been compared, consumers had to be able to identify the products if necessary to verify the claims promptly. Therefore seeing comparison through the lens of the typical busy shopper was critical in determining whether the comparative advertising complied with Article 4(c) of the MCAD 2006.

The ECJ also held that, as long as individual pairings were of comparable products, a comparative advertisement relating to a 'basket' of disparate goods would not contravene Article 4(b) of the MCAD 2006 relating to 'substitutability'.

The ECJ also ruled that comparative advertising that uses a sample of goods to claim that the brand owner's general price level is lower than that of its main competitor might be misleading and contrary to Article 4(a) of MCAD 2006 where:

- a range of savings is advertised against a collective group of competitors instead of matching the difference to each individual competitor;

- the advertising doesn't identify the details of the comparison made or inform the persons to whom it's addressed of where they can verify the claims; and

- the advertising doesn't reveal that the comparison relates only to a sample and not to all of the brand owner's products.

In a separate dispute, this time in France, Lidl brought an action against its rival Vierzon in relation to a price comparison advertisement reproduced from till receipts listing 34 products bought from both supermarkets.

Lidl *v* Vierzon (2010)

The comparative advertisement by Vierzon used general descriptions of the products, accompanied by their weight or volume. Lidl objected that the products weren't comparable because their qualitative and quantitative differences meant they didn't meet the same needs as required by Article 4(b) of the MCAD 2006.

Lidl argued that because the products were merely listed on till receipts there wasn't enough information for consumers to understand the differences between the products or to understand the reasons for the price differences (contrary to Article 4(c) of the MCAD 2006) and therefore the advertisement was misleading (contrary to Article 4(a) of the MCAD 2006).

The French national court referred to the ECJ the question of whether the foodstuffs could be said to be sufficiently interchangeable given that the extent to which consumers would like to eat those products and the degree of pleasure experienced when consuming them would vary according to the conditions and the place of production, the ingredients used and the level of experience of the producer. With this level of variation between products, could a comparison be fair?

As in the previous Lidl case (2006), the ECJ interpreted this question with the presumption that where possible the courts should allow a fair comparison, as it's in the interests of consumers to do so.

The ECJ said that Article 4(b) of MCAD 2006 didn't in any way deal with or prejudge the angle from which a comparison might be lawfully made or the characteristics of the products to which comparative advertising might refer. The court added that, if it were to be decided that foodstuffs could never be comparable under Article 4(b) of MCAD 2006, then that would effectively rule out any real possibility of comparative advertising of an important category of consumer goods.

However, it was for national courts to carry out an individual and specific assessment of the products in the comparative advertisement and not a matter for the ECJ, and so it referred this finding of fact back to the French court. Nevertheless, the ECJ did provide guidance where national courts had to make a determination as to whether the comparative advertisement was misleading and in breach of the MCAD 2006. This would apply when:

- information contained in a comparative advertisement gives the mistaken impression that the selection of goods shown in it is representative of the general level of the rival competitor's prices in comparison with those of the advertiser (in other words, it falsely suggests that consumers would make savings of the kind claimed by the advertisement by regularly buying their everyday goods from the advertiser rather than from the rival competitor); or

- the comparative advertisement falsely suggests that all of the advertiser's products are cheaper than those of its rival competitor; or

- the comparison in the advertisement is based solely on price but is also based on food products that have different features capable of significantly affecting the average consumer's choice, without such differences being apparent from the comparative advertisement concerned.

With respect to the objectivity requirements of Article 4(c) of the MCAD 2006, the ECJ ruled that, to comply with the verifiability condition, a comparative advertisement must identify the compared products sufficiently to enable the consumer to check the accuracy of the prices shown. For example, such a condition wouldn't be satisfied if the stores named in the advertisement sold a number of different food products that matched the descriptions given in the comparative advertisement.

With price comparisons in this sector, clearly well-known branded items such as a Mars bar could be price-compared very easily, making it possible for the busy consumer to come to a view on a fair basis.

These and subsequent cases illustrate that the courts are currently minded to rule on the lawfulness of comparative advertising solely under the provisions of the MCAD 2006. So long as the comparative advertisement is a fair and objective price comparison that doesn't take unfair advantage of or denigrate the competitor's trademark(s) or brand(s) then it's perfectly legal.

That said, the Trade Marks Directive (89/104/EEC) does provide additional scope of protection for the use of a trademark where permission hasn't been sought from the intellectual property (IP) rights holder.

Historically, the 1997 Trade Marks Directive (89/104/EEC) was the EU's first attempt to regulate comparative advertising per se before the MCAD 2006 and confined itself to the infringement of IP rights as opposed to specific consumer protection considerations.

As can be seen from the previous cases, comparative advertising often uses trademarks belonging to an IP rights holder without consent, so there were obvious areas of uncertainty about how the new sui generis comparative advertising law should be reconciled with the older-established principles of trademark infringement under the 1997 Trade Marks Directive and how this should be applied consistently across the EU.

For further discussion on the application of trademark laws, see Chapter 3.

The EU Trade Marks Directive 1997 sets out a comprehensive scheme of legislation covering all matters relating to registered trademarks, including the grounds of infringement that are relevant from a comparative advertising perspective: a registered trademark is infringed when a third party uses in the course of trade a sign that is identical with that mark in relation to goods or services identical with those for which that mark is registered (Article 5(1)(a), Trade Marks Directive 1997); and a registered trademark is infringed when a third party uses in the course of trade a sign where because of its identity with or similarity to that mark and the identity or similarity of the goods or services covered by the trademark and the sign there's a likelihood of confusion on the part of the public, which includes the likelihood of association between the sign and the trademark (Article 5(1)(b), Trade Marks Directive 1997).

These provisions were tested in the following case involving mobile operator O2 and Hutchison 3G over a television commercial promoting 3G's rival mobile phone services.

O2 v Hutchison 3G (2006)

Part of the brand identity of mobile operator O2 is the use of various registered trademarks consisting of images of bubbles, and it took action under Article 5(1)(b) of the Trade Marks Directive 1997 as a result of rival mobile operator Hutchison 3G running a television commercial in which the term 'O2' and moving pictures of bubbles were used in a comparative advertisement. The implication of the television commercial was that the 3G service was cheaper than the similar service provided by O2.

The Court of Appeal referred several questions of interpretation of the MCAD 2006 to the ECJ. However, the main point of law referred to the ECJ was whether use of a third-party registered trademark in a comparative advertisement fell within Article 5(1) of the Trade Marks Directive 1997 and therefore constituted an infringement even if it didn't cause confusion or jeopardize the essential function of the trademark in any way.

The ECJ ruled that use of a third-party registered trademark in these circumstances didn't fall within Article 5(1) of the Trade Marks Directive 1997 because of the absence of confusion among those watching the television commercial.

The essence of the ECJ's guidance is that third-party trademarks can be used freely for comparative purposes as long as it's clear who owns that mark. The moment the public mistakes one mark or proprietor for another or receives a false impression that there's a trade connection between the two brands compared then there are grounds for bringing an action for trademark infringement under Article 5(1)(b) of the Trade Marks Directive 1997.

However, from a marketing perspective, something would have gone seriously wrong if a comparative advertisement gave an impression of collaboration rather than comparison, as it would defeat the objective of the marketing campaign in the first place!

Cases where the 'challenger' brand owner sought to ride on the coattails of the established brand leader have also been the subject of much debate.

For example, in 2009 the high street chain Dixons ran a cheeky comparison advertisement that on balance it wouldn't have got away with had it been challenged under the MCAD 2006. The 96-sheet billboard poster said: 'Get off at Knightsbridge, visit the discerning shopper's fave department store, ascend the exotic staircase and let Piers in the pinstripe suit demonstrate the magic of the latest high-definition flat screen, then go to dixons.co.uk and buy it.'

Harrods appeared to prefer not to chase the marketing suits at Dixons through the courts, and they seemed to have kissed and made up, as Dixons now operates an upscale electrical concession within Harrods, which is now under new ownership.

But not all brand owners take the attitude of 'turning the other cheek' when an upstart looks for a free ride on its coat-tails.

L'Oréal v Bellure (2009)

The case concerned cheap perfumes manufactured by Bellure that were designed to smell like L'Oréal's luxury fragrances and which were sold in packaging similar to various registrations for shape marks owned by L'Oréal. In effect, these were 'me too' products of much more expensive luxury products of a well-known brand owner but stopped just short of being 'rip-offs'.

Price and smell comparison lists were provided to distributors of these 'me too' products indicating what well-known perfume corresponded in fragrance to each cheap imitation perfume.

Unusually, it was accepted by both parties that neither traders nor consumers would be likely to be misled as to the origin of the products, but in any event L'Oréal took action against Bellure for trademark infringement.

Although the case may appear to be a straight trademark infringement matter, the interpretation of the MCAD 2006 became the cause for appeal and a difference in interpretation between the UK and the EU courts.

At the Court of Appeal, English judges referred certain questions relating to the use of the L'Oréal trademarks in the comparison price lists to the ECJ. At the same time the Court of Appeal had expressed scepticism as to whether the law should protect brand owners in these circumstances given the absence of confusion or detriment to the registered trademarks.

However, the ECJ took a completely different approach and found strongly in favour of protecting the trademarks of the brand owner to prevent any free-riding on its coat-tails.

The ECJ ruled:

- Unfair advantage could be taken of the repute of a mark under Article 5(2) of MCAD 2006 without the need to show either a likelihood of confusion or detriment to the registered mark.

- Use of L'Oréal's registered trademarks in price and smell comparison lists could constitute infringement under Article 5(1)(a) of MCAD 2006 even though the essential function of a trademark wasn't harmed, provided that such use could affect one of the other functions of the mark, such as guaranteeing quality, communication, investment or advertising.

● Article 4(g) of MCAD 2006 prevented an advertiser from stating explicitly or implicitly in comparative advertising that its product or service was an imitation or replica of a product bearing a well-known trademark. The advantage gained by the advertiser as a result of such unlawful comparative advertising also had to be considered as taking unfair advantage of the reputation of that mark within the meaning of Article 4(f) of MCAD 2006.

The Court of Appeal reluctantly applied the ECJ's ruling so as to find in favour of L'Oréal, but Lord Justice Jacob made it very clear that he disagreed with the principle that 'free-riding' by merely telling the truth about comparisons, where no consumers were being deceived and there was no impairment of the claimant's brands, should be prohibited. His point of view was that if there was clear exploitation it would need intrinsically to take an 'unfair advantage', which in the present circumstances was a moot point.

The ECJ hadn't chosen to split hairs on such a distinction but approached all 'free-riding' as illegal and unfair.

Arguably, had the ECJ applied Lord Justice Jacob's reasoning, it might have come to the very different conclusion that there was no breach of Article 5(2) of MCAD 2006.

The ECJ had held that, if an advertiser states explicitly or implicitly in comparative advertising that its products are 'imitations or replicas' of a product bearing a well-known trademark, then the resulting advantage will amount to an unfair one.

Lord Justice Jacob dissented with this reasoning: 'If a man trades in lawful replicas or in lawful copies, why should he not be able to inform the public what they are? And why should the truth be kept from the public?'

Most marketers will agree that, although interesting, Lord Justice Jacob's view would have created anomalies in the law that would have led to more rather than less legal uncertainty!

A trademark is infringed by unauthorized use in the course of trade of an identical or similar sign in relation to similar goods or services, where the trademark has a reputation and where use of that sign without due cause takes unfair advantage of or is detrimental to the distinctive character or the repute of the trademark.

The ECJ had held that the taking of unfair advantage doesn't require that there be a likelihood of confusion or a likelihood of detriment.

There will be an unfair advantage where the advertiser using a rival's mark seeks to ride on its coat-tails in order to benefit from the power of attraction, the reputation and the prestige of that mark and to exploit it without paying any financial compensation to the IP rights holder.

Overall, the European and UK courts have taken the view that comparative advertising is permissible and simply having a trademark doesn't insulate the brand owner from the chill wind of competition. There's even an argument that the right of a brand owner to use comparative advertising is an exercise of its freedom of expression provided for by Article 10 of the European Convention on Human Rights.

In the UK, the ASA also has authority to adjudicate on comparative advertising complaints, as both the CAP and the BCAP Codes substantively incorporate the MCAD 2006. Although complaints to the ASA are relatively inexpensive, they're often viewed by lawyers as lacking real authority, since the ASA can't grant injunctions, levy fines or award compensation in such cases, although it does have the power to refer offenders of the Codes to the OFT and Ofcom in extreme cases.

All the comparative advertising cases discussed in this chapter affirm the robust approach that's currently taken in the UK and EU and that the courts will look favourably at a claimant for trademark infringement only where the comparative advertisement gives rise to a likelihood of confusion between competing goods and services.

However, it's important to remember that the matter to be decided will be done through the lens of the consumer rather than the injured IP rights holder. The courts will make a presumption in favour of allowing comparative advertising provided it's lawful.

Product placement on television as a weapon for achieving sales and marketing advantage

It's hard to estimate with any accuracy the economic value of having a product or brand trademark in camera shot on ITV1's 'Coronation Street', and it's even harder to determine the effect this has on driving incremental sales of products and services for the advertiser. But the fact that since February 2011 product placement can be used by British television production companies on commercial television has created a new battleground for savvy marketers eager to grab audience attention as traditional forms of above-the-line advertising struggle to be noticed (Table 5.1).

Table 5.1 Early pioneers of product placement on British television (2011–12)

Brand owner	Product placement	Television show	Channel
Kärcher	Kärcher vacuum cleaner	Tommy's Fix It Yourself	Discovery Real Time Channel
Microsoft	Xbox shown in the title sequence of the sports panel show	A League of Their Own	Sky1 HD and Sky Living
Mission Foods	Mission Foods products feature in the cooking programme, which it also helps to fund	Mexican Food Made Simple	Channel 5
Nationwide	Nationwide logo on top of an ATM in a shop	Coronation Street	ITV1
Nescafé	Dolce Gusto coffee machine in the kitchen area on set*	This Morning	ITV1
New Look	New Look's branded clothes appeared on-screen on this reality TV talent contest to find a new stylist	Style the Nation	Channel 4
Pedigree	Dentastix dog chews posters and billboards digitally transposed into some of the scenes of the documentary series	A Different Breed	Sky1 HD
TRESemmé	TRESemmé hair care products in shot	Britain and Ireland's Next Top Model	Sky Living HD

Source: Various published announcements in the marketing media (2011/12).

*This is the first instance of British product placement allowable under the new Ofcom Broadcasting Code (2011).

However, in the UK product placement, or 'embedded advertising' as it's sometimes referred to, is still in its infancy but could grow rapidly as television producers of top shows look to brand owners to help underwrite production budgets, as they do routinely in the United States, where product placement generates billions of dollars in revenues for the rights holders and broadcasters (Table 5.2).

Table 5.2   Top 10 US primetime shows with product placement activity

Rank	Programme	Network	Total number of occurrences
1	American Idol	Fox	577
2	The Biggest Loser	NBC	533
3	The Celebrity Apprentice	NBC	391
4	Dancing with the Stars	ABC	390
5	The X Factor	Fox	312
6	Extreme Makeover: Home Edition	ABC	224
7	America's Got Talent	NBC	220
8	Friday Night Lights	NBC	201
9	America's Next Top Model	CW	178
10	The Amazing Race: Unfinished Business	CBS	161

Source: Nielsen (2012).

Data from 1 January to 30 November 2011. Primetime entertainment programming on five broadcast networks (ABC, CBS, CW, Fox and NBC). First-run episodes only. As a result of coding enhancements implemented in 2009, occurrence counts now reflect the total number of show segments in which a brand or product appears or is mentioned.

History of product placement

Product placement has been a fact of life for cinema goers and television viewers in most countries around the world for over 60 years.

In 1949, NBC launched the United States' first daily television news programme, the 'Camel News Caravan', featuring a newsreader smoking a Camel cigarette and a policy that banned footage of 'No smoking' signs and anyone puffing on a cigar, including Sir Winston Churchill!

Today, brand and product tie-ins are less brazen but equally effective as a weapon for achieving sales and marketing advantage over competitor brand owners' above-the-line marketing efforts.

The James Bond film franchise is credited with having started the current fashion of placing well-known branded products in the centre of the action, with brands such as Aston Martin and Omega taking high-profile roles on-screen. In the latest Bond movie, *Skyfall* (2012), actor Daniel Craig is seen drinking a Heineken beer.

Typically, this type of marketing activity is supported by heavy above-the-line advertising spend as well as online and social media interaction with fans so as to create the cut-through required.

In the United States, around US$4 billion is spent annually by brand owners in product placement activities on film and television. Some brand owners such as Apple have a special department that's responsible for 'seeding' Apple products into mainstream shows, such as smash-hit medical drama 'House' starring Hugh Laurie.

Exponents of the art of product placement prefer to remain in the shadows of their famous brands, which tends to give the appearance of something a bit surreptitious or underhanded in the way product placement works. In some cases, product placement can blur the boundaries between advertising and content for the unsuspecting viewer.

The US version of 'The Apprentice' hosted by Donald Trump has Dove Body Wash, Sony PlayStation and Visa paying up to US$2.6 million to be the product that the teams have to work on each week.

Barbara Maultsby, vice-president of UPP, one of the biggest product placement agencies in the United States, defends the practice: 'When you see a fake brand, it takes you out of the reality of the situation.'

The success of hit television show 'Mad Men' has turned product placement into an art form, given that it is devoted to telling the story of the rise and fall of the advertising industry and blatantly uses product placement across the whole series.

Critics of product placement are plentiful and various and include consumer groups frightened that editorial and creative independence has been sold to the highest bidder and church groups that worry that the corrosive effect of commercialization of television content is projected to millions of viewers in their living rooms. Even the esteemed Writers Guild of America, the union representing television scriptwriters, has jumped on product placement practices, alleging that its members are being forced to write advertising copy disguised as storylines and that 'tens of millions of viewers are sometimes being sold products without their knowledge, in opaque, subliminal ways'.

US campaign group Commercial Alert has labelled product placement an 'affront to basic honesty', but this hasn't dented the enthusiasm among successful British television producers like Peter Bazalgette of 'Big Brother' fame, who has launched his own embedded advertising company and who predicts the UK market could be worth in excess of £100 million a year in revenues.

Product placement shouldn't be confused with advertiser-funded programming (AFP), which is discussed in Chapter 10.

Product placement on British television is subject to the Audiovisual Media Services (AVMS) Directive 2007, the Ofcom Broadcasting Code (2011) and regulations that provide for standards of product placement on television, on-demand programme services (ODPS), film and video-on-demand (VOD) services.

Ofcom Broadcasting Code (2011)

UK regulations introduced on 28 February 2011 permit television channels and programme makers to receive payment in return for including references to products or services in television series, soaps, entertainment shows and sports programmes in the UK. The rules seek to modernize the UK law, not just to meet EU requirements, but also because the traditional prohibition on product placement was becoming increasingly anachronistic in the face of the hundreds of foreign (primarily US) films and programmes full of product placement that are broadcast on UK television every day.

Ofcom, the government-approved regulatory authority for the telecommunications industries, updated its Broadcasting Code to contain rules about what type of products can be placed in programmes, where product placement is allowed, and how placed products can be featured.

Broadcasters have to inform viewers of paid-for references by displaying the letter 'P' for three seconds at the start and end of a programme that contains product placement.

Evidence in 2012 suggests that viewers are confused by the 'P' logo – only 9 per cent of respondents knew its true meaning, while 11 per cent of viewers thought it referred to parking (!), but the vast majority (75 per cent) hadn't a clue. Ofcom may have to go back to the drawing board on that one.

Although these changes in UK law present a lot of exciting opportunities for marketers, some restrictions still apply:

- Broadcasters won't be allowed to run product placement in children's shows, news bulletins, UK-produced current affairs productions, consumer advice shows or religious affairs programming.
- Product placement of alcoholic drinks and foods high in salt, sugar and fat are still prohibited.
- Product placement will continue to be banned for all BBC programmes.
- Programmes shouldn't positively endorse placed products or give them too much prominence.

Editorial independence

The Ofcom Broadcasting Code (2011) requires broadcasters to retain editorial control over the programmes they transmit. The rules serve to protect viewers from both excessive commercial references in programming and surreptitious advertising by:

- limiting the extent to which references to products, services and trademarks can feature in programming;
- requiring that viewers are made aware when a reference to a product, service or trademark features in programming as a result of a commercial arrangement between the broadcaster or producer and a third-party funder; and
- helping to ensure that broadcasters do not exceed the limits placed on the amount of advertising they can transmit.

In all cases where product placement is being considered, it must be editorially justified, and the use of product placement must be incidental to the programme content, although how 'incidental' is likely to be a matter of 'creative interpretation' that is still to be tested by a complaint to Ofcom or the courts, but it's likely to be given a 'light touch'. For example, the 'Guidance notes' issued by Ofcom (2011) specifically refer to celebrities 'plugging' their autobiography, movie, album or new television series, which is considered 'editorially justifiable'.

The Ofcom Broadcasting Code (2011) specifically excludes control on the use of 'props' that are required for dressing a set, such as everyday items used in BBC1's soap 'EastEnders'. Props mustn't have any residual 'advertising' value and can't be supplied on terms that would make them a product placement, which would make them subject to regulation and of course wouldn't be permitted on the BBC.

Any breach of these restrictions contained in the Broadcasting Code (2011) is punishable by fines of up to £250,000, although it's unlikely to happen soon, as product placement take-up by brand owners has been slower than anticipated according to the commercial department at ITV.

It's envisaged that the relaxation of the prohibition on product placement will give commercial broadcasters a new source of revenue, as well as providing advertisers with a new audience. However, there's no conclusive evidence as yet as to the impact these changes are going to make.

Broadcasters and content providers need to take care when interpreting the fragmented approach to product placement for different types of programming in order to ensure they are lawfully taking full advantage of the new sales and marketing opportunities these new rules provide.

This hasn't stopped the evangelists of product placement extolling its virtues in the new television landscape. 'Viewers expect to see real brands in shows and have a positive view to such placements – as long as the brands fit with the storyline, mood and character of the show,' explains Gary Knight, commercial content director at ITV, echoing the point made by Barbara Maultsby.

However, Gary Knight concedes that brand owners and marketers are still on a learning curve when it comes to understanding how to use product placement for achieving competitive advantage. 'Further regulation education is required, as some clients believe they can get US-style overt product placement and expect brands to be written into scripts, which is way beyond the UK rules,' he concludes.

The following are the top 10 best-practice tips for product placement as recommended by the UK advertising industry body Thinkbox (2011):

- Talk to broadcasters first and early about product placement opportunities.
- Think of product placement as one tool among many available to the marketer.

- Play to the strengths of the genre such as its ability to educate viewers and normalize brands as part of a long-term strategy to shift perceptions or brand choices.
- Handle research in this young sector with care.
- Give product placements time to work.
- Ensure you have planned how placements will be activated off-screen by other activities, and how they can be integrated into a brand's other promotions and messaging efforts.
- Make sure placements appear naturally on-screen.
- Avoid the hard-sell approach.
- Complement the genre with other strategies.
- Respect the viewers.

References and further reading

Cases and judgments

Ajinomoto Sweeteners Europe SAS *v* Asda Stores Limited [2010] EWCA Civ 609

Kimberly-Clark Ltd *v* The Fort Sterling Ltd [1997] FSR 877

Kingspan Group plc *v* Rockwool Ltd [2011] EWHC 250 (Ch)

Lidl Belgium GmbH & Co KG *v* Etablissementen Franz Colruyt NV (Case C-356/04) 2006

Lidl SNc *v* Vierzon Distribution SA (Case 159/09) 2010 ECJ

L'Oréal SA and others *v* Bellure NV and others (Case C-487/07) 2009

L'Oréal SA and others *v* Bellure NV and others [2010] EWCA Civ 535

O2 Holdings Ltd *v* Hutchison 3G Ltd [2006] EWHC 2571

Specsavers *v* Asda [2010] EWHC 2035 (Ch)

Websites

Advertising Standards Authority (ASA) has an excellent website that is updated daily and contains the full CAP and BCAP Codes as well as other useful resources [accessed 6 April 2012] http://www.asa.org.uk

International Chamber of Commerce (ICC) Consolidated Code for Advertising and Marketing Communication Practice (2011) [accessed 6 April 2012] http://www.iccwbo.org

Lexology: a highly reliable resource for the latest case law in this area [accessed 6 April 2012] http://www.lexology.com

Thinkbox provides useful best-practice guidance to advertisers involved in broadcast advertising activities [accessed 12 April 2012] http://www.thinkbox.tv

Reports and articles

ASA (2012) Price comparisons and VAT claims in advertising, BCAP consultation document
Ofcom (2011) Guidance notes on commercial references in television programming
Thinkbox (2011) Key insights on the UK product placement television market

Books

Kolah, A (2013) *High Impact Marketing that Gets Results*, Kogan Page, London
Smith, S and Milligan, A (2011) *Bold: How to be brave in business and win*, Kogan Page, London
Sun Tzu (2008) *The Art of War*, Penguin Classics, London

"Will that be big enough to clean the carpet?"

Direct marketing and direct selling

Introduction

Research over the last decade shows that direct marketing and direct selling have an important role to play in achieving customer retention as well as driving customer lifetime value (CLV) and customer equity within a business.

For a detailed discussion on direct marketing and selling techniques, refer to Guru in a Bottle® *High Impact Marketing that Gets Results* and Guru in a Bottle® *The Art of Influencing and Selling*.

Personal data about customers and clients are among the most valuable assets in any business or organization. Information assets must be used effectively to achieve business goals but must also comply with regulatory requirements that are designed to protect against the exploitation of individuals who haven't consented to the use of such personal data.

In the past, direct marketing and direct selling were all about customer relationship management (CRM), where organizations equipped themselves with tools to manage their relationships with their customers and clients. It was the brand owner that called the tune. Not any more. Those days are gone. The commercial and legal relationship between the brand owner and customer must now be recalibrated. A seismic shift in the balance of bargaining power between buyers and sellers has rendered the traditional doctrine of CRM almost completely obsolete.

Today, individual customers are equipped with the tools to take charge of their relationships with suppliers – what's now being called vendor relationship management (VRM). And in the future personal information management services (PIMS) empowering individuals to take more control over their lives will become the norm.

As part of the recalibration in the relationship between buyers and sellers, the government published its consumer empowerment strategy (VRM by another name) in 2011. As part of the initiative, the government and the Information Commissioner's Office (ICO) are encouraging the release of personal data back to individuals in an open and reusable (electronic) form. A working group that includes some of the biggest brand owners in the UK, including Barclaycard, MasterCard, HSBC, the John Lewis Partnership, T-Mobile/Orange (Everything Everywhere), Centrica, Home Retail Group, Google and Scottish and Southern Energy, has been tasked to make it happen.

The 'carrot and stick' approach of enhanced consumer engagement coupled with strengthened data protection for consumers could yield significant benefits for brand owners in their direct marketing and direct selling activities if they can figure out how to seize the opportunities in front of them.

For example, in the future, individual customers are likely to enjoy enhanced powers to check that their details are up to date and correct. New data-sharing rules that allow this to happen could pave the way for a growth in volunteered personal information (VPI), which could become the most valuable source of customer data to fuel direct marketing and direct selling in the future.

'Increased information sharing with customers creates a big opportunity for brands to build on their existing relationships to become PIMS themselves: if anyone is going to help individuals manage and use their data better, why not the brand owner?' argues marketing commentator Alan Mitchell.

At the same time, the laws and regulations governing data protection in the UK and across the EU are likely to be strengthened in the wake of growing public concern about the protection of personal information, vividly illustrated by the series of arrests made in connection with the *News of the World* phone-hacking scandal in 2011 and 2012, where the personal details of people became the centre of front-page 'scoops' published by the now defunct newspaper.

EU Justice Commissioner Viviane Reding recently called for an overhaul of the 17-year-old laws on data protection to enforce safeguards on how personal information is used alongside the publication of the proposed EU Data Protection Regulation in 2012. As many companies are based in the United States or hold data on servers there, agencies watching over privacy issues in EU territories could be given enhanced powers of enforcement. Reding said:

> The protection of personal data is a fundamental right for all
> Europeans, but citizens do not always feel in full control of their personal
> data. I want to explicitly clarify that people shall have the right – and not
> only the possibility – to withdraw their consent to data processing.
> Any company operating in the EU market or any online product targeted
> at EU consumers must comply with EU rules. To enforce EU law,
> national privacy watchdogs shall be endowed with powers to investigate
> and engage in legal action against non-EU data controllers.

This tougher stance led Google to review its privacy policy in 2012, although David Smith, Deputy Information Commissioner at the ICO, remained unconvinced of its efforts. 'The requirement under the Data Protection Act (DPA) 1998 is for a company to tell people what it actually intends to do with their data, not just what it might do at some unspecified point in the future. Being vague doesn't help in giving people effective control about how their information is shared,' he said.

The concern was that personal information was to be shared across some 60 Google services, including mail, calendar, Android phone call logs and search histories.

On the other hand, Coca-Cola updated its responsible marketing code in 2012 to take account of the toughening EU privacy laws and regulations proposed in this area.

As part of the code, the company pledged only ever to ask for the minimum amount of personal data and not pass the data on to third parties for marketing purposes. 'As we increase our marketing in the digital area, our priority is to set the standard across the industry,' said Laura Misselbrook, Communications Manager at Coca-Cola.

Marketers will need to keep a close eye on legal developments in this important area of marketing practice, as these are likely to change in the next 12–24 months by placing on marketers increased responsibilities and standards for protecting the privacy of consumers in the use and transmission of their personal data.

A European Directive in 1995 required all member states to implement laws and regulations on the processing of personal data, and as a result the Data Protection Act 1998 was implemented and came into force in 2001.

Over the last decade, new ways in which individuals can be identified have evolved, and rules relating to international transfer of data no longer reflect today's reality. In this regard the development of UK data protection laws lags well behind sales and marketing practice and is a cause for growing concern amongst consumer watchdog and civil liberty groups.

The lack of harmonization across all 27 EU member states has come about partly as a result of the need to accommodate 'external factors' such as different national legal systems, social norms and regulatory traditions to the detriment of disclosure obligations that marketers must comply with. The net effect is an uneven patchwork of legal protections for UK consumers and citizens across the EU.

However, harmonization may not be the answer in order to achieve compliance across the EU. In February 2012 the ICO announced:

> *We have doubts as to whether complete harmonisation is possible or even desirable given that key concepts in the law such as 'fairness' depend on these factors which necessarily vary from one member state to another. If taken too far, the drive for harmonisation will lead to burdens on business and complexity for individuals that may achieve harmonisation on paper but will not necessarily deliver sensible and effective data protection in practice.*

Direct marketing and selling, whether conducted online or offline, consist of communications that could be invited by the customer or sent unsolicited by the brand owner in an attempt to market or sell goods and services.

In the past, such communications may have come via the post but increasingly direct marketing and selling are conducted by telephone and e-mail.

For a discussion on effective direct marketing techniques, refer to Guru in a Bottle® *The Art of Influencing and Selling*.

The Data Protection Act 1998 and the Privacy and Electronic Communications (EC Directive) Regulations 2003 (SI 2003/2426) (Privacy Regulations) as amended by the Privacy and Electronic Communications (EC Directive) (Amendment) Regulations 2011 (SI 2011/1208) from 26 May 2011, together with legal guidance on them issued by the ICO as well as various voluntary advertising and marketing codes, combine to create a complex web around direct marketing and selling activities in the UK that isn't very clear or consistent.

For a discussion on the EU Privacy Directive, which should be read in conjunction with this chapter, refer to Chapter 7.

This chapter reviews the current framework of UK data protection laws and regulations and how this applies to direct marketing and selling in a contemporary context, as well as looking over the horizon to likely legal reforms that will shape direct sales and marketing practices in the future.

Data Protection Act 1998

The DPA 1998 establishes a framework of rights and duties that is designed to safeguard personal data. This framework balances the legitimate needs of organizations to collect and use personal data for business and other purposes against the right of individuals to respect for the privacy of their personal details.

The legislation itself is complex, and in places it's hard to understand – even for lawyers! However, it's underpinned by a set of eight straightforward, common-sense principles.

If you make sure you handle personal data in line with the spirit of those principles, then it's likely your direct marketing and selling activities will be compliant! Given that the breach of the DPA 1998 is a serious offence that can result in severe fines and in some instances even criminal sanctions, it's prudent to contact the ICO for free guidance and advice (http://ico.gov.uk) or seek expert legal advice in order to ensure that your direct marketing and sales activities are compliant with current data protection laws.

Key concepts used in the DPA 1998

The disclosure requirements under the DPA 1998 are based on the definition of certain key concepts:

- *Data.* Information that is processed, or intended to be processed, automatically, or is recorded manually as part of a structured filing system, or is an 'accessible record', such as a database of customers. The important point to be aware of is that it covers both computer records and certain manual records.
- *Personal data.* Data that relate to a living individual who can be identified from the data and other information that is in the possession or is likely to come into the possession of the data controller.
- *Sensitive personal data.* A specified subset of personal data, being more personal matters, for example religious belief, sexual orientation, political affiliation, health matters, racial or ethnic origin, trade union membership, and commission or alleged commission of any criminal offence.
- *Data subject.* A living individual who is the subject of personal data (includes minors).
- *Data controller.* A person or entity who either alone or with others determines the purposes and the manner in which any personal data are to be processed.
- *Data processor.* A person or entity other than an employee of the data controller who processes personal data on behalf of the data controller.
- *Processing.* Obtaining, recording or holding personal data or carrying out any operation or set of operations on the personal data, for example organizing, retrieving, consulting, disclosing, transferring, combining or erasing (almost anything!).
- *Possession.* Defined very widely – not necessarily that the personal data are in the physical control of the data controller.

Eight data protection principles in the DPA 1998

Those involved with direct marketing and selling ('data controllers') must comply with the eight data protection principles in the DPA 1998 when processing personal data.

The first principle is by far the most important in the direct marketing and selling context, and it comprises two key elements: fair processing information and the conditions under which that processing takes place.

Principle 1: Fair processing of personal information

The marketer ('data controller') must ensure, so far as practicable, that customers and prospects ('data subjects') are provided with or have made readily available to them the following information ('fair processing information'):

- the identity of the data controller;
- the purpose for which the data are intended to be processed; and
- any further information that is necessary, taking into account the specific circumstances in which the data are or are to be processed, to enable processing in respect of the data subject to be fair (Schedule 1, Part II, DPA 1998).

In practice, this information could be provided in questionnaires, application forms, and privacy policies on websites and/or at the point of collection of personal data on a website where a user registers for that site.

In deciding whether further information is 'necessary', the ICO has indicated that data controllers should consider what processing of personal data they'll be carrying out once the data have been obtained and whether or not data subjects are likely to understand:

- the purposes for which their personal data are going to be processed;
- the likely consequences of such processing, so that the data subject is able to make a judgment as to the nature and extent of the processing; and
- whether particular disclosures can reasonably be envisaged.

The ICO 'Guide to data protection' states:

> *Fairness generally requires you to be transparent – clear and open with individuals about how their information will be used. Transparency is always important, but especially so in situations where individuals have a choice about whether they wish to enter into a relationship with you. Assessing whether information is being processed fairly depends partly on how it is obtained. In particular, if anyone is deceived or misled when the information is obtained, then this is unlikely to be fair.*

Fair processing information should also be provided or made readily available to consumers ('data subjects') if the data have been obtained from someone other than the individual concerned, such as a friend or spouse.

This should be done before or as soon as practicable after the marketer first processes the data – in other words, as soon as the marketer receives and holds the data.

The two exceptions to these disclosure requirements are where: providing the fair processing information would involve a disproportionate effort for the marketer; or it is necessary for the marketer to record the information that's going to be contained in the data or to disclose the data to comply with a legal obligation (other than an obligation imposed by contract) (Schedule 1, Part 2, DPA 1998).

There are slightly different requirements where disclosure to a third party within a reasonable period was envisaged at the time of collection of such data.

It's common practice within direct marketing to ask an existing customer to 'recommend a friend' – a favourite technique used on many social networking and e-commerce sites. Such an offer is usually accompanied by some sort of incentive such as an e-gift voucher in order to entice the customer to provide the friend's personal details. Once the marketer ('data controller') receives the information about the 'friend' it will be 'processing' the data and will be obliged to provide the fair processing information to the new contact as soon as practicable. Typically, this would be provided in the first letter to the 'friend' enclosing the marketing information, accompanied by an ability to opt out of receiving, or opt in to receive, further marketing information or offers in the future.

Processing personal data Processing needs to comply with the strict conditions provided for under Schedule 2 of the DPA 1998.

The key conditions are: the customer or prospect ('data subject') has given consent to the processing in the first place; and processing is necessary for the purposes of legitimate interests pursued by the marketer or third party to whom the data are disclosed ('data controller'), except where the processing is unwarranted in any particular case by reason of prejudice to the rights, freedoms or legitimate interests of the customer or prospect.

The EU Data Protection Directive (95/46/EC) refers to 'consent' as that which has been freely given and is a specific and informed indication of the wishes of the data subject that signifies agreement to personal data being processed.

It's not open to the marketer to claim 'implied' consent – it must be actual consent. The ICO has taken this to mean there must be some active communication between the parties. Although a customer or prospect may 'signify' agreement other than in writing, the marketer can't infer consent from non-response to a communication, for example from a customer's failure to return or respond to a leaflet.

Broadly speaking, if the marketer already holds information obtained for a specific purpose, that information can be used for a different purpose that wouldn't have been envisaged by the customer or prospect at the time of the collection of the information only if the marketer has the data subject's consent or the processing is permitted under one of the other conditions set out in Schedule 2.

However, where a company has collected data to deliver a product and then wishes to use the data for direct marketing purposes, it may be permitted to do that under the 'legitimate interests' condition. The ICO tends to take a wide view of the 'legitimate interests' condition. In determining what constitutes 'legitimate interests', marketers should bear in mind: whether the legitimacy of the interests pursued by the data controller or the third party to whom the data are to be disclosed has been established; and whether the processing is unwarranted in any particular case by reasons of prejudice to the rights and freedoms of the customer or prospect.

Where a company wants to use existing data for new direct marketing purposes, the customer or prospect will have to be provided with a new set of fair processing information relating to this new purpose as well as an opportunity to opt out of such processing.

If the data subject doesn't object, the subsequent processing is arguably not 'unwarranted'. However, special rules apply for e-marketing (see page 228), where the customer or prospect must in all cases opt in.

For direct marketers, the requirement to provide fair processing information is particularly important. For example, a company that buys or rents a customer mailing list should give the prescribed fair processing information to all individuals on that list in a timely fashion. Marketers should consider giving a clear opt-out on the first paper mailing to those on a new mailing list, perhaps accompanied by a prepaid envelope and/or a free phone number and/or an e-mail address to make opting out as easy as possible. If this first mailing is done electronically, then the opt-in provision applies.

It's prudent for the buyer of a customer mailing list to ask for a warranty that the names on the list were collected lawfully and that the data subjects haven't opted out before the purchase of the list. Industry best practice in these circumstances is to obtain customers' consent to the obviously new use and to proceed only when they've opted in, such as for e-marketing purposes.

Processing sensitive data If sensitive personal data are involved, then the key condition that must be satisfied in the case of direct marketing is that the marketer must obtain 'explicit consent' (condition 1, Schedule 3). Sensitive personal data are seldom collected for marketing purposes, but it's possible, in the context of personal grooming, skin care products, medical devices and insurance products, that customers and prospects will be required to share information of a sensitive personal nature.

The ICO guidance in this area is that communication with the customer or prospect needs to be absolutely clear and in appropriate cases should cover the specific detail of the processing, the particular type of data to be processed or even the specific information required, the purposes of the processing, and any special aspects of the processing that may affect the individual, for example disclosures that may be made of the data.

Principle 2: Processing personal data for specified purposes

Personal data shall be obtained only for one or more specified and lawful purposes and can't be further processed in any manner incompatible with the specified purpose(s).

This requirement aims to ensure that brand owners are open about their reasons for obtaining personal data, and that what they do with the information is in line with the reasonable expectations of the individuals concerned. There are clear links with other data protection principles – in particular the first principle, which requires personal data to be processed fairly and lawfully. If a marketer obtains personal data for an unlawful purpose, there will be a breach of both the first and the second data protection principles.

However, compliance with disclosure requirements for the other data protection principles will ensure that that you've complied with the second principle automatically.

In practice, the second data protection principle means that a marketer must:

- be clear from the outset about why it is collecting personal data and what it intends to do with the data;
- comply with the DPA 1998 fair processing requirements, including the duty to give privacy notices to individuals when collecting their personal data;
- comply with what the DPA 1998 says about notifying the ICO; and
- ensure that, if the marketer wishes to use or disclose the personal data for any purpose that's additional to or different from the originally specified purpose, the new use or disclosure is fair.

Principle 3: Personal data should be adequate, relevant and not excessive in relation to the purposes for which they are processed

In practice, it means the marketer should ensure that: it holds personal data about an individual that's sufficient for the purpose it is holding the data for in relation to that individual; and it does not hold more information than it needs for that purpose.

A marketer should identify the minimum amount of personal data it needs to fulfil its purpose properly. As the data controller it should hold that much information, but no more. This is part of the practice known as 'data minimization'.

Principle 4: Personal data should be accurate and, where necessary, kept up to date

Although this principle sounds straightforward, the law recognizes that it may not be practical to double-check the accuracy of every item of personal data received, so the DPA 1998 makes special provision about the accuracy of information that individuals provide about themselves or that's obtained from third parties.

To comply with these provisions, marketers should:

- take reasonable steps to ensure the accuracy of any personal data obtained;
- ensure that the source of any personal data is clear;
- carefully consider any challenges to the accuracy of information; and
- consider whether it's necessary to update the information.

Principle 5: Personal data processed for any purpose(s) should not be kept for longer than is necessary for that purpose(s)

In order to comply, the marketer will need to:

- review the length of time it keeps personal data;
- consider the purpose(s) it holds the information for in deciding whether and for how long to retain it;
- securely delete information that's no longer needed for the purpose(s); and
- update, archive or securely delete information if it goes out of date.

This principle links with the third and fourth principles, so, for example, personal data held for longer than necessary will, by definition, be excessive and may also be irrelevant. In any event, it's poor practice and inefficient to hold more information than necessary.

It's good practice regularly to review the personal data held on customers and prospects and delete anything no longer required. Information that doesn't need to be accessed regularly, but that still needs to be retained, should be safely archived or put offline.

If a marketer holds more than small amounts of personal data, it is best practice to establish standard retention periods for different categories of information. This should take account of any professional rules or regulatory requirements that also apply.

It's also best practice to have a system for ensuring that the brand owner keeps to these retention periods in practice and for documenting and reviewing the retention policy. For example, if certain personal data records aren't being used, then consideration should be given as to whether they should be retained. In certain circumstances where the brand owner is holding only a small amount of personal data, it may not need a formal data retention policy.

In a situation where only a small amount of personal data are being held, the marketer must still comply with the law, and it's best practice to conduct a regular audit and to check through the personal data records held to make sure these aren't being held for too long; conversely, personal data records shouldn't be deleted prematurely, as the customer may have a query or complaint about the product or service previously bought and this information will need to be retained for dealing with queries that may arise in the future.

Personal data will need to be retained for longer in some cases than in others. How long different categories of personal data should be kept will be determined on individual business needs. The marketer will need to make a judgment call about:

- the current and future value of that information;
- the costs, risks and liabilities associated with retaining that information; and
- the ease or difficulty of making sure that the information remains accurate and up to date.

In addition, the marketer will need to make a judgment call on what the information is used for and what the standard industry practice is in its market segment as well as the surrounding circumstances for holding the personal data.

Similarly, where a brand owner receives a notice (known as a Section 11 notice) from a former customer requiring it to stop processing personal data for direct marketing purposes (sometimes referred to as the 'right to object') it would be entirely appropriate for the company to retain enough information about that former customer in order to stop including that person in any future direct marketing activities.

Brand owners mustn't assume that because consent from the customer or prospect may have been given in the past it can't be withdrawn in the future or that customers or prospects are not able to change their minds. That said, previous personal data could be used for analysing market trends provided that this purpose has been made clear to the customer or prospect. However, because the database will have to be amended to show that the person sending the Section 11 notice is to receive 'no direct marketing', some companies find it expedient simply to delete this personal information from their database because the original reason for which the information was collected, such as a marketing promotion, no longer applies and removes the rationale for holding the personal data.

One option that avoids deletion of data is to redesign a database in light of e-marketing regulations (discussed below) in order to suppress certain marketing activities rather than impose a blanket suppression of all direct marketing. For example, new contacts who hadn't opted in to receive e-mail communication could still be sent ordinary mail if they'd been offered the chance of opting out when their data were collected for marketing purposes and hadn't done so.

Principle 6: Personal data should be processed in accordance with the rights of the individual

The reference to 'rights of individuals' is to the following:

- a right of access to a copy of the information included in their personal data;
- a right to object to processing that is likely to cause or is causing damage or distress;
- a right to prevent processing for direct marketing;
- a right to object to decisions being taken by automated means;
- a right in certain circumstances to have inaccurate personal data rectified, blocked, erased or destroyed; and
- a right to claim compensation for damages caused by a breach of the DPA 1998.

This is an important part of the DPA 1998, as it gives the so-called 'right of subject access' for a customer or prospect by virtue of section 7 of the DPA 1998. It's most often used by individuals who want to see a copy of the information an organization holds about them. However, the right goes further than this in scope. An individual who makes a written request and pays a fee (currently a £10 maximum can be levied by the brand owner) is entitled to the following information:

- whether any personal data are being processed;
- a description of the personal data, the reasons they are being processed and whether they will be given to any other organizations or persons;
- a copy of the information constituting the data, as well as details of the source of the data where these are available.

Organizations are under a duty to respond to a subject access request promptly and in any event within 40 calendar days of receiving it. As with other aspects of the DPA 1998 there are exceptions to this rule, and some types of personal data are exempt from the 'right of subject access', but these won't apply within a marketing context and so the brand owner will need to comply with the subject access request in the normal way.

For the recipient of a subject access request, it's important to determine whether the person making the request is the individual to whom the personal data relate. This is to avoid personal data about one individual being sent to another, accidentally or as a result of deception. The key point is that verification must be done reasonably. In practice, this wouldn't entail asking for lots more information if the identity of the person making the request is obvious. This is particularly the case, for example, when there's an ongoing relationship with that individual and personal information about that individual can be easily verified.

However, compare the above situation with the following: an online retailer receives a subject access request by e-mail from a customer. The customer hasn't used the site for some time and, although the e-mail address matches the company's records, the postal address given by the customer doesn't. Alarm bells should start to ring.

In this situation, it would be reasonable to gather further information, which could be as simple as asking the customer to confirm other account details, such as a customer reference number or even a password on that account before responding to the request.

There may be occasions when the subject access request requires disclosure relating to other third-party interests. In principle, this shouldn't be a bar to a response provided that it's appropriate to disclose such information. Such a decision will involve balancing the data subject's right of access against the other individual's rights in respect of his or her own personal data. If the other person consents to disclosing the personal information, then it would be unreasonable not to do so. However, if there's no such consent, then a decision whether to disclose the information anyway needs to be made.

The ICO guidance in this area is that a data controller can't refuse to provide subject access to personal data about an individual simply because the data were obtained from a third party. The rules about third-party data apply only to personal data that include information about the individual who is the subject of the request and information about someone else.

The ICO has produced separate guidance on dealing with subject access requests involving other people's information, available from its website (http://www.ico.gov.uk).

Principle 7: Personal data should be kept under adequate security precautions to prevent loss, destruction or unauthorized disclosure

In practice, it means the marketer must have appropriate security to prevent the personal data it holds being accidentally or deliberately compromised. In particular, the marketer will need to:

- design and organize its security to fit the nature of the personal data it holds and the harm that may result from a security breach;
- be clear about who in its organization is responsible for ensuring information security;
- make sure it has the right physical and technical security, backed up by robust policies and procedures and reliable, well-trained staff; and
- be ready to respond to any breach of security swiftly and effectively.

It's important to understand that the requirements of the DPA 1998 go beyond the way information is stored or transmitted. This data protection principle relates to the security of every aspect of the processing of personal data. Any security measure put in place needs to ensure that:

- only authorized people can access, alter, disclose or destroy personal data;
- those people act only within the scope of their authority; and
- if personal data are accidentally lost, altered or destroyed, they can be recovered to prevent any damage or distress to the individuals concerned.

The DPA 1998 states that security should be appropriate to: the nature of the information in question; and the harm that might result from its improper use or from its accidental loss or destruction.

The DPA 1998 doesn't define what is 'appropriate', but it does say that an assessment of the appropriate security measures in a particular case should consider technological developments and the costs involved.

The DPA 1998 doesn't require state-of-the-art security technology to protect the personal data held, but brand owners should regularly review their security arrangements as technology advances. This should take account of the nature and extent of the premises and computer systems, the number of staff employed, and the extent of their access to personal data and personal data physically held by a third party on behalf of the brand owner.

There's no 'one size fits all' solution to information security, and the level of security chosen should depend on the risks to the organization.

Principle 8: Personal data should not be transferred outside of the European Economic Area (EEA) unless that country or territory ensures adequate protection of rights and freedoms of data subjects in relation to processing of personal data

Prior to making any such transfer, the brand owner should consider whether it can achieve its aims without actually processing the personal data. For example, if personal data can be made anonymous so that it's not possible to identify individuals from the data now or at any point in the future, then the data protection principles won't apply and the transfer can take place outside of the EEA. In such cases, it would be prudent to seek appropriate legal advice before taking such a step.

A brand owner will be processing personal data in the UK and transferring it even if:

- the information relating to individuals has been collected on paper in an unstructured way; and
- this material is sent overseas with the intention that once it's there it will be processed using equipment operating automatically; or
- it will be added to a highly structured filing system relating to individuals.

Putting personal data on a website will often result in transfers to countries outside the EEA. The transfers will take place when someone outside the

EEA accesses the website. Loading information on to a server based in the UK so that it can be accessed through a website will increase the likelihood that a transfer might take place, and so the brand owner must consider whether that would be fair for the individuals concerned. If information on the website is intended to be accessed outside the EEA, then this will amount to a transfer under the DPA 1998.

There are no restrictions on the transfer of personal data to EEA countries (Table 6.1).

Table 6.1 European Economic Area (EEA) countries

Austria	Greece	Netherlands
Belgium	Hungary	Norway
Bulgaria	Iceland	Poland
Cyprus	Ireland	Portugal
Czech Republic	Italy	Romania
Denmark	Latvia	Slovakia
Estonia	Liechtenstein	Slovenia
Finland	Lithuania	Spain
France	Luxembourg	Sweden
Germany	Malta	UK

Source: ICO (2011) The guide to data protection.

Outside of these countries, the European Commission (EC) has decided that certain countries (shown in Table 6.2) have an 'adequate' level of protection for personal data (for an update on the list, visit http://www.europa.eu.int).

Table 6.2 Countries considered by the EC to have an 'adequate' level of protection for personal data

Andorra	Faroe Islands	Israel
Argentina	Guernsey	Jersey
Canada	Isle of Man	Switzerland

Source: ICO (2011) The guide to data protection.

Although the United States isn't included in the EC list, personal data sent to the United States under the Safe Harbor scheme is considered to be adequately protected. When a US company signs up to the Safe Harbor arrangement they agree to: follow the data protection principles of information handling; and be held responsible for keeping to those principles by the Federal Trade Commission (FTC) or other oversight schemes. Certain types of companies can't sign up to the Safe Harbor scheme, and an up-to-date list of those that are in the Safe Harbor scheme can be found at the US website http://export.gov.

Even if data protection law in a country hasn't been approved as adequate, it's still possible for a marketer to send personal data about customers and prospects to that country provided that:

- an assessment is made by the marketer;
- the marketer uses contracts including the EC approved model contractual clauses in any agreement where there's a transfer of personal data in order to comply with data protection principles;
- the marketer gets its binding corporate rules approved by the ICO if it's a multinational organization; or
- the marketer relies on the exemptions from the rule.

The DPA 1998 sets out the factors that need to be taken into account in making such an assessment. These relate to:

- the nature of the personal data being transferred;
- how the data will be used and for how long; and
- the laws and practices of the country you are transferring it to.

This means doing a risk assessment, and the marketer must decide whether there's enough protection for individuals in all the circumstances of the data transfer. This is known as an 'assessment of adequacy'. Again, given the technical complexities involved, it will be prudent to consult a legal expert in these matters.

To assess adequacy, the marketer should look at:

- the extent to which the country has adopted data protection standards in its law;
- whether there's a way to make sure the standards are achieved in practice; and
- whether there's an effective procedure for individuals to enforce their rights or get compensation if things go wrong.

In some cases it will be impractical to carry out a detailed analysis of adequacy involving the legal situation in a non-EEA country, and this is likely to be more relevant for a business that regularly transfers large volumes of personal data to a particular country on a regular basis, rather than a company that might only occasionally transfer personal data to any of a wide range of countries. In some cases a marketer may reasonably decide there's adequacy without carrying out a detailed test.

A common situation is where there's a transfer of personal data to a 'processor' acting on the instructions of the data controller under contract. In such a case, the marketer is still legally responsible for making sure the data are processed in line with the data protection principles. In particular, personal data can be transferred only if there's a contract requiring the processor to have appropriate security and act only on the instruction of the data controller.

Thus individuals' information should continue to be protected to the same standard as in the UK, and they'll have the same rights they can exercise in the UK. This is because the marketer remains liable for ensuring that the processing complies with the data protection principles.

For example, Company A in the UK sends its customer list to Company B outside the EEA so that Company B, acting as a processor, can send a mailing to Company A's customers. It's likely that adequate protection exists if:

- the information transferred is only names and addresses;
- there's nothing particularly sensitive about Company A's line of business;
- the names and addresses are for one-time use and must be returned or destroyed within a short timescale;
- Company A knows Company B is reliable; and
- there's a contract between Company A and Company B governing how the information will be used.

When selecting a processor, a marketer will need to satisfy itself that the processor is reliable and has appropriate security before it can legally engage in such activities.

However, the level of protection is unlikely to be adequate and could result in legal action being taken against the marketer if: the transfer is to a processor in an unstable country; and the nature of the information means that it's at particular risk.

There are several exceptions to the eighth principle where personal data can be transferred in the absence of adequate protection, and this will apply only in limited contexts. These include:

- where there is consent from the data subject;
- where the transfer is in the furtherance of contract performance between the data controller and the data subject;
- where there is substantial public interest (this would be in the case of crime detection, not marketing);
- where the transfer is vital in the interests of the data subject (again, unlikely to arise in a marketing context);
- where the transfer is of public register information, provided it complies with any restrictions on access to or use of the information in the register;
- where the transfer is necessary to make a legal claim.

Conducting an internal audit to ensure compliance with the DPA 1998

An audit is commonly undertaken by companies and organizations that wish to comply with best practice in the handling and managing of personal data in their business, and the exercise is often conducted by an external expert.

There are broadly two approaches that can be taken: a process audit, where for example only marketing activities are scrutinized, or a horizontal audit, where for example subject access requests across the whole organization are analysed. The pros and cons for each approach need to weighed carefully, taking account of the time and resources that will need to be expended.

Auditors tend to use a customized questionnaire as well as 'depth' interviews as part of the information-gathering process.

A typical approach for a horizontal DPA 1998 audit is provided in Table 6.3.

E-mail marketing

The use of personal data for sending unsolicited e-mail messages (commonly referred to as 'spam') won't pass the test of 'fair processing' under the DPA 1998 where this is done in the absence of consent of the data subject. Marketers must work on a permission-based (opt-in) approach to customer and client communications, where opt-in to receive any form of marketing communication is now the norm. This opt-in right is enshrined in the EU Privacy and Electronic Communications Directive.

For more guidance on best practice in e-marketing, refer to Guru in a Bottle® *High Impact Marketing that Gets Results*.

As discussed in Chapter 7, the EU Privacy and Electronic Communications Regulations (Privacy Regulations) apply if the recipient of an e-mail is an individual subscriber (residential subscriber, sole trader or non-limited liability partnership in England, Wales and Northern Ireland).

E-marketing includes SMS messages, mobile pictures, video messages and voicemail messages, not just e-mail messages.

The Privacy Regulations control the sending of unsolicited electronic communications via a public electronic communications network and currently don't cover those messages sent via Bluetooth technology.

Although users can avoid receiving Bluetooth messages by disabling the Bluetooth function on their mobile devices, this would affect the way they can use the technology.

Even if the Privacy Regulations don't apply in the situation of Bluetooth activity, the DPA 1998 will continue to apply and will cover an unsolicited receipt of a Bluetooth marketing message by an individual.

Table 6.3 A typical audit under the DPA 1998

Audit issue	Type of information collected
Which individual's personal data are held?	Customers, clients, employees, suppliers, others.
What type of information is collected?	Names, addresses, telephone numbers, e-mail, details of occupation.
What type of sensitive personal information is collected?	Racial or ethnic origin, political opinions, religious beliefs, trade union membership, health matters, sexual orientation.
How are the personal data collected?	Need to ascertain whether the data are obtained directly or indirectly from the data subject, as well as the medium of such data collection.
How relevant are the personal data?	Need to ascertain whether the personal data exceed what's necessary for the purposes for which they were collected.
What steps are taken to ensure that personal data are kept accurate?	Need to find out whether there are procedures in place to ensure that personal data are kept accurate for the period of retention (for example, prompting online customers to update their personal data every six months).
What security measures are in place?	Need to consider what technical and organizational measures are in place to ensure that personal data are protected against unauthorized access, damage or erasure. Regulation 5(1A) of the Privacy and Electronic Communications (EC Directive) Regulations 2003 as amended by the Privacy and Electronic Communications (EC Directive Amendment) Regulations 2011 sets out more precisely the appropriate technical and organizational measures.
To which third parties are personal data disclosed?	Need to ascertain the types of third parties to whom data may be disclosed, the purposes of disclosure, and also whether data subjects have consented to disclosure.
Are personal data disclosed to third-party data processors?	These are data processors under the control and instruction of the brand owner.
Are the personal data transferred outside of the UK?	Need to ascertain that this complies with the principles provided by the DPA 1998.
Are procedures in place to ensure compliance with individuals' rights?	Can individuals gain access to the personal data held about them, prevent the use of their personal data for direct marketing and request a deletion of inaccurate personal data?

The Privacy Regulations provide that individual subscribers must opt in to receive e-mails, subject to limited exceptions (known as the 'soft opt-in'). The soft opt-in applies where the marketer has:

- Obtained the contact details of the individual in the course of the sale or negotiations for the sale of a product or service. This tends to suggest that the soft opt-in will apply only where the marketing e-mail is sent by the same company that conducted the original negotiations or sale.

- Carried out the direct marketing in respect of its similar goods and services only. This tends to suggest that the soft opt-in won't apply where unconnected goods or services are offered at the same time as similar ones.

- Given recipients a simple means, without charge, at the time of initial collection of the data to refuse (or opt out of) the use of their contact details for direct marketing purposes.

- Included in each subsequent e-mail to customers or prospects who haven't initially refused use of their details for direct marketing purposes a right to opt out of receiving future direct marketing by e-mails.

Any legal entity that's an individual company, partnership or other corporate body that is legally distinct from its members ('corporate subscriber') isn't entitled to equivalent protection in respect of receiving unsolicited e-mails.

These opt-in provisions also don't apply to employees who are using corporate e-mail systems for personal purposes.

This means that companies and limited liability partnerships and their employees remain open to unsolicited e-mail and SMS messages, although the ICO privacy guidance on this point states that marketers must obtain the prior consent of recipients in order to send unsolicited e-mails to any e-mail address used by a non-limited liability partnership.

Combating a 'spam' attack

There are three ways in which individuals are fighting back against a spam attack:

- *Fight-back 1.* There are now many more spam filters available free of charge, as well as ISPs providing spam filtering as standard for customers.

- *Fight-back 2.* For extra protection, individuals can register with the Direct Marketing Association (DMA) E-mail Preference Service (EMPS), which maintains a list of those who have said they don't want to receive e-mail marketing, and all members of the DMA agree not to send e-mail marketing to them. This free registration service was extended a few years ago to include employees working for a 'corporate subscriber', and individuals at work can also exercise their legal right to object under section 11 of the DPA 1998 if their business e-mail address incorporates personal data, which it may well do if the individual's name is included in the e-mail address, such as ardi.kolah@guruinabottle.com.

- *Fight-back 3*. Amendments to the Consumer Protection from Unfair Trading Regulations 2008, implementing the Unfair Commercial Practices Directive 2005/29/EC, provide for legal action against a brand owner engaging in unfair business-to-consumer (B2C) practices such as unwarranted and persistent solicitations by e-mail, telephone, fax or other remote media outside of a contractual obligation.

In all cases of direct marketing by e-mail, the marketer must reveal its identity to the recipient (whether an individual or a corporate subscriber) and provide a valid address to which the recipient may send a request for the communications to cease (Regulations 23 and 24, Privacy Regulations). This may not be so easy in the case of SMS texts, given the size of mobile telephone screens, but the ICO has indicated that this isn't a valid reason for avoiding compliance with these rules.

The provisions of the Privacy Regulations relating to e-mail marketing provide for consent to be notified by 'the sender', which means that businesses engaging in direct marketing may find it hard to use mailing lists obtained from third parties. They'll not be entitled to contact individuals on the list to obtain their consent to unsolicited e-mail, even if they've an existing offline relationship with the intended customer or prospect, since it's the sender that needs to have collected the e-mail contact details in the course of a sale or negotiations for a sale.

The International Chamber of Commerce (ICC) published a Consolidated Code of Advertising and Marketing Communication Practice (2011), which provides a framework for the self-regulation of direct marketing, including e-mail marketing activities. The ICC Code isn't a substitute for the DPA 1998 or the Privacy Regulations but incorporates these in order to provide a statement of global best practice and, although it is not legally binding, it is often referred to in disputes.

The ICC Code provides that direct marketing communications sent via electronic media should include a clear and transparent mechanism enabling the consumer to express the wish not to receive future solicitations.

Unsolicited direct marketing communications sent via electronic media may be sent only where there are reasonable grounds to believe that the consumer who receives such communications will have an interest in the subject matter or offer.

Bought-in e-mail lists

Marketers should be wary of using bought-in lists, as the 'soft opt-in' criteria can't be satisfied with bought-in lists. Such lists may be used only if they have been compiled on a clear prior-consent basis – the intended recipient has actively consented to the receipt of unsolicited messages by e-mail from third parties.

It should be noted that the sale of contact lists to third parties can take place only where those on that list have opted in to receive marketing e-mails in accordance with the disclosure requirements of the DPA 1998.

Brand owners must be wary of buying e-mail marketing lists that aren't compliant with the DPA 1998. The privacy guidance issued by the ICO also states that marketers must obtain a positive indication of consent under the Privacy Regulations.

Status of using a tick box as a form of consent

Recital 17 of the E-Privacy Directive provides the example of a tick box on a website as an 'appropriate method' for giving consent.

The ICO advises brand owners that there must be some form of communication where the individual knowingly indicates consent. This may involve clicking an icon, sending an e-mail or subscribing to a service. The important thing is that individuals understand that by taking such action they signify consent.

Specifically, the ICO privacy guidance states that the fact that an individual has had the chance to object to direct marketing but has not chosen to do so, for example by failing to tick a box that states 'Tick here if you do not wish to receive further communications', doesn't amount to consent, although this may form part of a mechanism for consent if the context makes this clear.

A pre-ticked opt-in consent box is unlikely to satisfy the conditions as an 'appropriate method' for giving consent.

The 'soft opt-in' exception is sometimes hard to apply

The ICO privacy guidance also addresses a number of questions of interpretation over the 'soft opt-in' in relation to e-mail marketing. For example, it's not clear what constitutes a 'similar' product or service. The ICO privacy guidance states that this includes products or services about which the customer would reasonably expect to receive information, although the ICO has stated that it will focus on failures to comply with opt-out requests rather than on marketers' interpretation of 'similar' in this context.

The exception will apply only where there's been a sale or negotiations for the purchase of a product or service.

It's a moot point that lawyers like to argue over as to whether the same exception applies to prospects where their e-mail address has been obtained in order to send a quote or information about a product or service. This may be sufficient, as the ICO privacy guidance refers to a person actively expressing an interest in purchasing a company's products or services and therefore would naturally include a request for a quote but not the use of cookie technology to identify a person's area of interest when the person is browsing the website.

For further guidance on the use of cookies on a website, refer to Chapter 7.

Marketers should be wary of relying on the soft opt-in, as it's available only to a business that collects the contact details initially, which means that it won't apply where a business buys a marketing database containing e-mail addresses. As already mentioned above, in such cases consent will be required.

As it is often difficult to determine whether the exception applies, the safest route in most cases is to seek opt-in consent for all types of direct marketing by e-mail to individuals.

Proximity and m-marketing

Mobile device adoption is growing exponentially, and almost all industry projections for its growth in the future are stratospheric! There are approximately 5.9 billion mobile subscribers, which is equivalent to 87 per cent of the world population, and around 10 per cent of all website hits and page views now come from a handheld device.

As a result of this rapid take-up, legislators are struggling to regulate proximity and m-marketing activities before they get out of hand, given the intrusive nature of such marketing activity and the risks they pose to the infringement of personal privacy. For example, geo-location services can provide a very intimate insight into people's private lives through their physical movements via their smart phone devices. The location of a smart phone device and the address of a Wi-Fi access point can easily be linked to a natural person, who's then usually directly and indirectly identifiable from such data.

In addition, smart phone users are very often unaware they're transmitting their location to third parties or to whom they're transmitting such data. And that's scary!

For a discussion on proximity and m-marketing best practice, refer to Guru in a Bottle® *High Impact Marketing that Gets Results*.

The growth of smart phones has fuelled interest amongst responsible marketers keen to unleash the power of proximity and m-marketing to create much deeper consumer engagement. Advertising sites in shopping centres, sports and entertainment arenas, exhibition and public spaces and in fact any public place are the locations now being targeted for such sales and marketing activities. For example, the popularity of the use of QR codes and other interactive technologies on poster advertising is testament to the way in which traditional advertising is changing, allowing the user to access a web landing page without searching for it, download a trailer for a movie and watch it instantly or receive a coupon direct to a mobile device.

The 'cashless society' took another step forward in 2012 when Visa and Vodafone created the world's largest m-marketing partnership to allow customers to pay for items directly from their handsets. Old-fashioned money is so last-century! The Vodafone-branded 'mobile wallet' can be used for paying for goods and services in 30 countries spanning five continents and uses near field communications (NFC) enabled SIM cards. All customers need to do is to wave their enabled devices in front of a payment terminal in order to purchase low-value items from the balance in their Visa prepaid accounts. Customers wanting to make higher-value purchases are able to do so by combining the ease of use with the input of a secure password into the terminal at the checkout.

Many marketers have hailed these advances in geo-location technologies as the future of direct marketing and selling.

Geo-location data

Geo-location data are simply the geographic locations of customers, prospects or objects. Marketers have begun to experiment with a range of technologies that can detect the presence of a smart phone device such as 3G and next-generation 4G phones as well as the embedded GPS navigation features in such devices, particularly in closed spaces such as a shopping mall, stadium, train carriage or municipal building.

'Listening and location detection' hardware includes a GSM base station that relays data about users to mobile telecommunications operators and Wi-Fi access points that transmit a unique ID that can be detected by a smart phone device and monitor two-way data traffic flows.

Marketers have also dabbled with Bluetooth technology as part of their repertoire of proximity and m-marketing activities but with mixed results.

All of these proximity marketing technologies are able to log and retain information that can identify the device, make and model. They can also retain details about individual usage by the device user other potentially other behavioural marketing data.

Application of the DPA 1998

Given that geo-location 'personal data' are capable of identifying an individual whether as standalone data or combined with other data sets, they are subject to the provisions of the DPA 1998, the EU Data Protection Directive and the Privacy Regulations.

As with any other forms of data, 'data controllers' must ensure that when processing such geo-location data they adhere to the data protection principles as discussed in this chapter as well as in Chapter 7.

An important consideration is that an individual must have consented to the processing of such geo-location data or that the processing of such data is necessary in order to comply with a contractual obligation to that individual.

Application of the EU Data Protection Directive

Regulation 14(2) of the Privacy and Electronic Communications (EC Directive) Regulations 2003 is relevant, as it provides that location data relating to a user or subscriber of a public electronic communications network or a public electronic communications service may be processed only: where the user or subscriber can't be identified from such data; or where necessary for the provision of a value-added service with the consent of that user or subscriber.

Prior to obtaining the consent of the user or subscriber to process location data, the brand owner is also required to provide the individual with information regarding the types of location data that will be processed, the purpose for which the data will be progressed, how long the data will be processed for, and whether the data will be transmitted to any third party.

Within the current legal framework applicable to the use of geo-location data, consent is an important concept.

Privacy guidance from the ICO makes it clear that consent should be 'very clear' when given, in terms of the permitted processing, the type of information to be processed and the purposes of the processing in question. In light of this, the service provider won't be able to rely on a blanket 'catch-all' statement on a bill or website but rather will need to obtain specific informed consent for each value-added service requested and to market its own electronic communications services.

Distance selling

The Consumer Protection (Distance Selling) Regulations 2000 (SI 2000/2334), which implemented the Distance Selling Directive (97/7/EC), came into force in October 2000 and, rather like the E-Commerce Regulations (see above), they apply certain rules to contracts formed at a distance. These Regulations are also the basis for the Committee on Advertising Practice (CAP) Code, which is relevant for direct marketing activities by brand owners that use direct response mechanisms to allow readers to place orders without the need for face-to-face contact.

A 'distance contract' is any contract concerning goods or services that is concluded between a supplier and a consumer under an organized distance sales or service provision scheme. Such methods make exclusive use of one or more means of distance communication up to and including the moment at which the contract is entered into (Regulation 3, Distance Selling Regulations).

The Distance Selling Regulations require certain information to be provided, such as the supplier's identity, a description of the goods or services and certain cancellation rights.

Owing to an amendment made to these regulations in April 2005, brand owners may deliver the specified information to the consumer at any time from when the order is placed until the service concludes. If the information isn't provided until after the service commences, consumers have a right of cancellation for seven days after the information is received. If the consumer does cancel, the brand owner is entitled to charge for any services it provided prior to the point of cancellation, as the consumer is deemed to have enjoyed the benefit of these goods or services.

The Financial Services (Distance Marketing) Regulations 2004 (SI 2004/2095), which implemented the Directive on Distance Marketing of Consumer Financial Services (2002/65/EC), introduced provisions similar to those of the Consumer Protection (Distance Selling) Regulations for the distance selling of financial services from 31 October 2004.

The CAP Code of Non-Broadcast Advertising, Sales Promotion and Direct Marketing (CAP Code) is also relevant within the context of distance selling. The CAP Code provides that any form of marketing communications must include:

- The main characteristics of the product.
- The price, including any VAT or other taxes payable.
- The amount of any delivery charge.
- Estimated delivery or performance time and arrangements.
- A statement that unless inapplicable consumers have the right to cancel orders for products. Marketers of services must explain how the right to cancel may be affected if the consumer agrees to services beginning less than seven working days after the contract was concluded. They must, however, make it clear when the services will begin.
- Any telephone, postal or other communication charge calculated at higher than the standard rate (for example, if a premium-rate call is required).
- Any other limitation on the offer (for example, period of availability) and any other condition that affects its validity.
- A statement on whether the marketer intends to provide substitute products (of equivalent quality and price) if those ordered are unavailable and that it will meet the cost of returning substitute products on cancellation.
- If goods are supplied or services performed permanently or recurrently, the minimum duration of open-ended contracts.

In addition, brand owners must convey the following written information to customers at the earliest opportunity:

- How to exercise their right to cancel, unless inapplicable. Marketers must allow at least seven clear working days after delivery (or after the conclusion of service contracts unless the consumer agrees to an earlier start date) for consumers to cancel the agreement.

- In relation to the sale of goods, whether the customer has to return the goods on cancellation and who is to bear the cost of return or recovery of those goods.
- Any other guarantees and after-sales services that apply to the goods or services sold.
- A full geographical address for any complaints.
- All conditions that apply to the cancellation of any open-ended or rolling contract.

Marketers must fulfil orders within 30 days from the day a customer makes the order unless:

- the nature of the product or service makes it reasonable for the brand owner to specify a longer period, for example in its marketing communications for made-to-measure products, plants that are out of season, or products or services that are supplied on an instalment basis the brand owner may reasonably specify a longer period for fulfilment; or
- a longer fulfilment time period has been contractually agreed with the customer.

A brand owner must refund money promptly and at the latest within 30 days of notice of cancellation being given by the customer if:

- The customer hasn't received products within the specified time period. If the customer is prepared to wait, the brand owner must provide the customer with a firm dispatch date or fortnightly progress report. Alternatively a brand owner may, if requested or if stated pre-purchase, provide a substitute product of equivalent quality and price.
- Products are returned because they are damaged, faulty or not as described; in such cases the brand owner must bear the cost of transit in both directions.
- Customers cancel within seven clear working days after delivery, unless the product is perishable, personalized, or made-to-measure, audio or video recordings or computer software if opened by the customer, newspapers, periodicals or magazines, or betting, gaming or lottery services. Customers should assume they may try out products, except for audio or video recordings or computer software, but should take reasonable care of them before they are returned. Customers must return the product and, unless the product is a substitute product sent instead of the ordered product, the brand owner may require the customer to pay the costs of doing so providing it has made clear the latest time that the product can be returned without quibble.
- Products that have been returned by the customer fail to arrive and the customer can show proof of posting (such as a recorded delivery receipt).

If all contractual obligations to the customer are satisfied, then the brand owner isn't under an obligation to provide a refund on:

- products where the price depends on financial market fluctuations that are outside the control of the brand owner;
- perishable, personalized or made-to-measure products;
- audio or video recordings or computer software if unsealed by the consumer;
- newspapers, periodicals or magazines;
- betting, gaming or lottery services;
- services that have already begun to be delivered with the customer's agreement.

A brand owner mustn't falsely imply that a customer has already ordered the product by including in marketing material an invoice or similar document that seeks payment where no intention to purchase that product has been received from the prospect. In addition, a brand owner shouldn't ask a customer to pay for or return unsolicited products except in situations where it is supplying a substitute product that was requested by the customer.

Future reform of data protection regulation in the EU

In January 2012, the EC unveiled plans to overhaul EU rules governing data protection comprehensively, with far-reaching consequences for direct marketing and direct selling.

The overarching objective of the proposed changes to the 1995 EU Data Protection Directive is to bolster the privacy of the European online community and to stimulate commercial opportunities in the European digital economy.

The 1995 EU Data Protection Directive was incorporated into national laws of EU member states in a variety of different ways – and this disparity in the approach to data protection has created anomalies in the application and enforcement of the EU Directive across all 27 member states. As a result, the EC has been vocal in demanding a more consistent approach across the EU in order to restore trust and confidence with consumers who feel they've been exploited.

Activities by some brand owners such as Facebook and Google have effectively stripped back the right of consumers to remain anonymous – something that the EC has pledged to restore, known as the 'right to be forgotten'. This is likely to fetter the previous freedoms that marketers enjoyed in the manipulation of consumer data.

The proposals feature a policy of communication with an overview of the EC's plans as well as new legislation that will establish a structure for EU data protection and a directive that covers protection of personal information in relation to the prevention, detection, investigation or prosecution of criminal offences and judicial conduct.

It's likely that the key elements of a new system will include a single body of rules for all 27 EU member states, an obligation to notify the appropriate national supervisory authority (such as the ICO) of serious breaches of data security possibly within 24 hours, and the 'right to be forgotten'.

Major technology brand owners such as Facebook and Google are on tenterhooks about the proposed rules. However, it's not just large corporates that will be subject to the rules, as every organization that deals with personal data, for example in a database or in lists, will be required to take notice of the changes. Those that fail to do so are expected to face big fines, as much as 2 per cent of their worldwide turnover for non-compliance, and the proposal covers non-EU companies that operate within the EU.

The fear is that brand owners will suffer in their sales and marketing activities if they're not able to use personal data legitimately to drive their businesses.

Chris Graham, Information Commissioner, observes:

There's no doubt the EU's legal framework for data protection needs modernising in the face of increasingly sophisticated information systems, global information networks, mass information sharing, the ever growing online collection of personal data and the increasing feeling of individuals that they've lost control of their personal information. The Commission's proposal goes a long way towards satisfying many of these requirements.

While recognising that there's tension between the drive for harmonisation of data protection standards across the EU and the desire for flexibility, however in a number of areas the proposal is unnecessarily and unhelpfully over-prescriptive. This poses challenges for its practical application and risks developing a 'tick box' approach to data compliance. The proposal also fails to properly recognise the reality of international transfers of personal data in today's globalised world and misses the chance to adjust the EU regulatory approach accordingly.

The DMA is equally concerned about the potential impact of the EU Data Protection Regulation on its members' ability to market their goods and services to customers. Chris Combemale, Executive Director of the DMA, adds: 'This is just the start of a long process before the Regulation comes into law. We'll be conducting research to assess the economic impact of the Regulation on the multi-billion pound direct marketing industry so we can put a strong case to the lawmakers at every stage to ensure that there are no detrimental consequences for the industry.'

The European Parliament and the EU member states still need to ratify such a proposal, and it's anticipated that it won't be until 2014 or later that these changes come into force and are adopted across the EU.

References and further reading

Websites

Direct Marketing Association [accessed 3 April 2012] http://www.dma.org.uk

European Commission has a good website on data protection [accessed 31 March 2012] http://ec.europa.eu

Information Commissioner's Office has a very useful website that provides guidance on best practice and compliance [accessed 25 March 2012] http://www.ico.gov.uk

Stewart Room, a British lawyer, is an expert in this area and maintains his own website [accessed 25 March 2012] http://www.stewartroom.com

Reports and articles

Coca-Cola Great Britain Responsible Marketing Charter (2012)

Information Commissioner's Office (2011) The guide to data protection

Information Commissioner's Office (2011) Your personal little book about protecting your personal information

Information Commissioner's Office (2012) Initial analysis of the EC's proposals for a revised data protection legislative framework

International Chamber of Commerce (ICC) (2011) Revision of the ICC Consolidated Code of Advertising and Marketing Communication Practice

Books

Kolah, A (2013) *High Impact Marketing that Gets Results*, Kogan Page, London

Kolah, A (2013) *The Art of Influencing and Selling*, Kogan Page, London

"My mom told me never to accept
cookies from strangers!"

The EU Privacy and Electronic Communications Regulations

In this chapter

- Background to the Privacy and Electronic Communications (EC Directive) (Amendment) Regulations 2011
- Implementation of the 'Cookie Directive' in the UK
- Modification to the law of privacy as a result of the 2011 Regulations
- Online advertising and marketing

Introduction

Ever since the furore over the UK phone-hacking scandal in 2011 engulfed the owners of News International, as well as politicians of all political parties, the government and law enforcement officers, the issue of privacy and electronic communications has become a national obsession. The public revulsion that followed the disclosure of the hacking of private phone messages of murder and terrorist victims and war widows didn't just rip apart the UK's biggest selling Sunday newspaper, the *News of the World*, but also raised serious questions about the legal safeguards in place to protect an individual's right to privacy whilst at the same time protecting freedom of speech within the law.

From a marketing perspective, brand owners have come to realize just how fast they must respond in real time in order to avoid being engulfed in controversies that can have dire consequences for corporate reputation and ultimately the bottom line. To suggest that advertisers such as Ford, Mitsubishi, Vauxhall, Lloyds Banking Group, Halifax, Boots, Sainsbury's, Virgin Holidays and the Co-operative Group pulled their advertising in the *News of the World* because they were so switched on to what consumers were saying online about the phone-hacking controversy is to understate how seriously senior executives in some of the UK's biggest companies now take the impact of social media on their business and ultimately the bottom line.

Writing in the *London Evening Standard*, City Editor Anthony Hilton commented:

> *The greatest risk in business today is not of production failure or accounting fraud or even terrorist attack. The thing that keeps company bosses awake at night is reputational risk – the fear that the behaviour of even just one rogue employee in a vast organization will destroy the reputation of the whole business and make it so toxic that even its most loyal customers, suppliers and employees want nothing more to do with it, lest they too become tainted by association in the public mind.*

For further discussion on the management of public relations, see Guru in a Bottle® *High Impact Marketing that Gets Results*.

The reality is that people as consumers have more power than they have as voters, and this hasn't escaped the attention of the government, European Parliament, industry regulators and judiciary, which are under increasing pressure to be seen to be in touch with public opinion rather than removed from it.

Background to the Privacy and Electronic Communications (EC Directive) (Amendment) Regulations 2011

On 26 May 2011, the Privacy and Electronic Communications (EC Directive) (Amendment) Regulations 2011 (2011 Regulations) came into force in the UK, providing marketers with a 12-month window in order to comply by May 2012 or risk legal action by the Information Commissioner.

These regulations affect direct electronic marketing on laptops, desktops, and digital and mobile devices and the security and confidentiality of such communications. The 2011 Regulations amend the Privacy and Electronic Communications (EC Directive) Regulations 2003.

As you'll read in this chapter, the main practical change is in relation to cookies – small text files that are stored on a user's device when visiting a website. The cookie assists the web or mobile site in recognizing the user's device and delivering a more tailored and user-friendly experience.

Previously, the 2003 Regulations required that website users be given clear information on what cookies are and how they are used and that website users be given an opportunity to refuse to accept them being placed on their computers. Website owners accommodated this requirement by including the necessary information and the opportunity to opt out in a prominent privacy policy on their websites, either included in or linked to the website terms of use.

Since 2003, there have been numerous examples of 'implied consent' that continued to be an invasion of privacy and unwanted electronic communication, and effectively this resulted in amendments to the 2003 Regulations.

The 2011 Regulations now change the opt-out requirement to an opt-in requirement. What this means is that web users must give their express consent to cookies being installed on their device before the website owner can use them. The only exception to this requirement is where the cookie is 'strictly necessary' for a service, for example in an online checkout context.

Although this has led to redrafting the wording of privacy policies, as well as changing the operability of websites, it does present practical problems and severe inconvenience for website owners, which is why in the main many website owners are still in breach of the 2011 Regulations and many have been slow to adopt these requirements.

Over the next few years this is likely to change, as the Information Commissioner now has enhanced powers of investigation and enforcement, including the right to impose penalties for breach of the 2011 Regulations up to £500,000 and the right to audit the marketer's activities without the need for consent.

In 2012, Jon Woods, General Manager at Coca-Cola for the UK and Ireland, said that the 2011 Regulations around behavioural targeting presented one of the biggest regulatory challenges for the business in the future. 'We need to be transparent about what data is being taken and what cookies are being used so that consumers feel confident using our brands. The issue is that the agencies we rely on to manage digital are experts but this might mean that they learnt this yesterday and are telling us today because it moves so fast,' he said.

In 2012 Coca-Cola updated its Responsible Marketing Charter in response to the challenges that the new 2011 Regulations present. Laura Misselbrook, Communications Manager at Coca-Cola, explained:

> With digital marketing being one of the fastest-moving areas, it remains
> a key pillar within our Responsible Marketing Code. As we increase our

marketing in the digital area, our priority is to set the standard across the industry and drive best practice going forward allowing Coca-Cola Great Britain to continue to deliver creative, cutting-edge and responsible campaigns.

We have a Responsible Marketing Policy that covers all our beverages, and we do not market any products directly to children under 12. One example which is integral to our approach is our Traffic Light System. This is applied across all our brands to ensure that our online campaigns are targeting the right audience and age profile. The system allows us to evaluate the content of a site that we are integrating into our digital activity and provides an outline of the audience of any given website. Given that content can be easily shared and passed on in the digital environment, the age targeting buffer allows us as a business to gain an understanding into the suitability of any given website at any time and adapt our plans accordingly.

Implementation of the 'Cookie Directive' in the UK

Marketers increasingly need to use electronic means to market directly to customers and clients. Direct marketing consists of any advertising or marketing communication – whether trying to sell products or services or promote a company or brand – that's directed to particular individuals or customer segments.

The rules covering this apply to any message consisting of text, voice sounds or images and so cover e-mails, text, pictures and video messages and answerphone and voicemail messages. It's not clear whether the rules cover 'push' marketing techniques delivered by Bluetooth and near field communication (NFC) devices, although a user's setting to 'on' mode would seem to indicate that consent to receive such packets of data has been given.

There are restrictions on how companies collect data about customers, and how they send marketing information that hasn't been requested by a customer, known as unsolicited marketing. For a discussion on the Data Protection Act 1998, see Chapter 6.

If marketers don't comply with these rules then they run the risk of incurring significant fines, being sued for damages, losing valuable customer goodwill and suffering reputational damage that will be hard to reverse in the short term and could be fatal.

Collecting data about customers or clients ('personal data') relates to a living individual who can be identified from the data, for example the person's name, address or job title. It's generally information that will enable you to market effectively to that person. For a marketer to use personal data, for example to store the information or use it to send out marketing material, there are certain steps that need to be followed at the time of collection.

In particular, a marketer must remember to provide the following information to the website or mobile user at the point of collection of personal data:

- the name of the organization on whose behalf the marketer or agency is making contact;
- an explanation of the use of the information, particularly uses that aren't obvious, for example if third parties or group companies will use the data or if the marketer intends to send marketing out under different trading names;
- if there's other information that the marketer might hold or collect at a later date, how it will collect this, for example via marketing surveys, and the reasons why the data are being collected;
- if the website owner intends to use cookies, an explanation as to what they are and the purposes for which they are being used (see below). Marketers will be able to use cookies only if they are strictly necessary for the provision of a service requested by the customer without the customer's consent.

2011 Regulations

Under the 2011 Regulations, cookies can be placed on laptops, desktops, and digital and mobile devices only where the user or subscriber has given its consent. Regulation 6 requires:

(1) *Subject to paragraph (4), a person shall not store or gain access to information stored, in the terminal equipment of a subscriber or user unless the requirements of paragraph (2) are met.*

(2) *The requirements are that the subscriber or user of that terminal equipment*

    (a) *is provided with clear and comprehensive information about the purposes of the storage of, or access to, that information; and*

    (b) *has given his or her consent.*

(3) *Where an electronic communications network is used by the same person to store or access information in the terminal equipment of a subscriber or user on more than one occasion, it is sufficient for the purposes of this regulation that the requirements of paragraph (2) are met in respect of the initial use.*

(3A) *For the purposes of paragraph (2), consent may be signified by a subscriber who amends or sets controls on the internet browser which the subscriber uses or by using another application or programme to signify consent.*

(4) *Paragraph (1) shall not apply to the technical storage of, or access to, information*

(a) *for the sole purpose of carrying out the transmission of a communication over an electronic communications network; or*

(b) *where such storage or access is strictly necessary for the provision of an information society service requested by the subscriber or user.*

Single exception to the opt-in cookie rule

The only exception to the opt-in rule is if what the marketer is doing is 'strictly necessary' for a service requested by the website user. This exception is a narrow one but might apply, for example, to a cookie a marketer can use to ensure that, when a user of its website has chosen the goods he or she wishes to buy and clicks the 'Add to basket' or 'Proceed to checkout' button, the website 'remembers' what the user chose on a previous page.

This exception needs to be interpreted quite narrowly because the use of the phrase 'strictly necessary' means its application has to be limited to a small range of activities and because the use of the cookie must be related to the service explicitly requested by the website user.

For example, the exception wouldn't apply just because the marketer had decided that the website would be more attractive if it remembered users' preferences or the marketer was keen to harvest behavioural analytics in order to improve the user experience of the site.

Audit of cookies used on the website

Depending on the nature of the business, a marketer may decide to carry out a comprehensive audit or simply check what data files are placed on website users' devices and why.

Marketers should analyse which cookies are strictly necessary and might not need consent. This could also present an opportunity to 'clean up' web pages and to cease using any cookies that are unnecessary or that have been superseded as the site has evolved.

The 2011 Regulations are intended to add to the level of protection afforded to the privacy of website users, and therefore the more intrusive the use of cookies, the more priority a marketer will need to give to considering changing how these cookies are being used.

Some of the things done on a website won't have any impact on the privacy of a website user and could even be helpful in keeping information safe. Other technologies will simply allow the marketer to improve the website based on information such as which links are most frequently used or which pages get the lowest number of unique views. However, some uses of cookies can involve creating detailed profiles of an individual's browsing activity. In such a case, it's clear that this is intrusive and therefore requires meaningful consent.

It might be useful to think of the requirement to obtain consent as a continuum, where at one end of the scale there are neutral cookies and at the other end of the scale there is the intrusive use of technologies such as online behavioural advertising techniques. Compliance with the 2011 Regulations is therefore far from straightforward.

Reliance on the website user's own browser settings to help comply with the opt-in regime

The regulators recognized that compliance with the new regime would raise all sorts of practical problems, and one suggestion was to get the user to predetermine which cookies it would allow and which cookies it wouldn't allow and this opt-in would be built into the internet browser used by the website user to visit the site.

At present, most browser settings aren't sophisticated enough for a marketer to assume that the website user has given consent to allow the website to set a cookie, although over the next 18 months this is likely to change and the technology will be available.

The other issue is that not every website user will use a browser to access the site. For example, a user may access the site through an application on a mobile phone. So for the time being, consent to accept a cookie needs to be achieved through other means.

Pop-ups and similar techniques

Pop-ups or interstitials could be used as an opt-in device on the website. On the surface, this may appear to be an attractive option, but it's also one that might well spoil the experience of using a website if the site uses several cookies.

Many websites routinely and regularly use pop-ups or 'splash pages' to make website users aware of changes to the site or to ask for user feedback. Similar techniques could, if designed well enough, be a useful way of informing users of the techniques that are being used and the choices they have. It's important to remember though that gaining consent in this potentially frustrating way isn't the only option.

Website terms and conditions

There are already lots of examples of gaining consent online using the terms of use or terms and conditions to which website users agree when they first register or sign up.

Where users open an online account or sign in to use the services on offer, they will be providing consent to allow the marketer to operate the account and offer the service. However, it's important to note that changing the terms of use alone to include consent for cookies wouldn't be sufficient to comply with the 2011 Regulations even if the website user had previously consented to the overarching terms.

Marketers need to make website users aware of the changes and specifically that the changes refer to the use of cookies. Marketers will then need to gain a positive indication that users understand and agree to the changes. This is most commonly obtained by asking the user to tick a box to indicate consent to the new terms. The key point is the need to be transparent with website users about how the website operates. Consent can be gained only by giving website users specific information about what they are agreeing to and providing them with a way to show their acceptance.

Any attempt to gain consent that relies on users' ignorance about what they are agreeing to is unlikely to comply with the 2011 Regulations.

User-driven settings for the website

Some cookies are deployed when website users make a choice about how the site works for them. In such circumstances, the consent could be gained as part of the process by which users confirm what they want to do or how they want the site to work. For example, some websites 'remember' which version a user wants to access, such as the version of a site in a particular language.

If this feature is enabled by the storage of a cookie, then the website owner could explain this to the user, and this could alleviate the need to ask website users each time they visit a site by explaining to them that by allowing the site to remember the choice the users are in effect giving consent to set the cookie.

This would apply to any feature where the marketer tells users that it can remember certain settings they have chosen. For example, it may be the size of the text a user wants to have displayed, the colour scheme on the site or even the 'personalized greeting' users see each time they visit the site.

Feature-led consent on the website

Some objects are stored when users choose to use a particular feature of the site such as watching a video clip or when the site remembers what a user has done on previous visits in order to personalize the content served and thereby enhance the user experience. In these cases, assuming that users are taking some action to tell the web page what they want to happen – opening a link, clicking a button or agreeing to the functionality being 'switched on' – then the marketer can ask for users' consent to set a cookie at this point.

Provided the marketer makes it clear to the user that choosing to take a particular action will make certain things happen, the marketer may interpret this as the user's consent.

The more complex or intrusive the activity the more information the marketer will be expected to provide. In practice, it's likely that a website of even a minimum level of sophistication will need to employ one or more of the above means to obtain consent to use each type of cookie.

Where the feature is provided by a third party, the marketer will need to make website users aware of this and point them to information on how the third party might use cookies and similar technologies so that users are able to make an informed choice as to whether to consent or not.

Functional uses

Marketers will often collect information about how users access and use the website, and these data are often collected in the background and not at the request of the user.

An analytic cookie might not appear to be as intrusive as others that might track a user across multiple sites but the marketer still needs the consent of the user.

The marketer should consider how it currently explains its policies to users and make that information more prominent, particularly in the wake of the changes created by the 2011 Regulations. The marketer should also consider providing users with more details about what it does do – perhaps a list of cookies used with a description of how they work – so that users can make an informed choice about what they will allow.

One possible solution might be to place some text in the footer or header of the web page that is highlighted or that turns into a scrolling piece of text when the marketer wants to set a cookie on the user's device. This could prompt users to read further information (perhaps served via the privacy pages of the site) and make any appropriate choices that are available to them.

If the information collected about website use is passed to a third party the marketer should make this absolutely clear to the user. The marketer should review what this third party does with the information about website users.

The marketer may be able to alter the settings of the user's account to limit the sharing of visitor information. Similarly, any options the user has should be prominently displayed and not hidden away.

Third-party cookies

Some websites allow third parties to set cookies on a user's device. If the marketer's website displays content from a third party, for example from an advertising network or a streaming video service, then this third party may read and write its own cookies or similar technologies on to the marketer's users' devices.

The process involved in gaining consent for these cookies by third parties is more complex. There are a number of initiatives that seek to ensure that users are given more and better information about how their information might be used. These will no doubt adapt to achieve compliance with the 2011 Regulations as marketers and the industry become more familiar with these rules.

The Information Commissioner's Office (ICO) advises anyone whose website allows or uses third-party cookies to make sure that they are doing everything they can to get the right information to users and that they are allowing users to make informed choices about what is stored on their device.

This may be the most challenging area in which to achieve compliance under the 2011 Regulations, and it's likely to require an industry-wide response involving other European data protection authorities. The ICO has undertaken to issue guidance in future as possible technical solutions are evaluated and developed.

Modification to the law of privacy as a result of the 2011 Regulations

Outside of the changes introduced with respect to the protection of the use of cookies on websites, the 2011 Regulations make a number of important changes to the 2003 Regulations with respect to the safeguarding of data, spam e-mails and third-party information notices. See also Chapter 6 for a discussion on the Data Protection Act 1998, including e-marketing.

Security of services

Regulation 5 of the 2003 Regulations already stated that a provider of a public electronic communications service had to take appropriate measures to safeguard the security of its service. The regulation has been amended by the insertion of a new paragraph (1A), which specifies the minimum efforts expected of providers in relation to fulfilling this duty with respect to security of services.

An example of these particular efforts includes the obligation to implement a security policy with respect to the processing of personal data and ensuring that personal data can be accessed only by authorized persons for legally authorized purposes.

Personal data

Under Regulation 3(b) of the 2011 Regulations 'personal data breach' now has a new definition: 'a breach of security leading to the accidental or unlawful destruction, loss, alteration, unauthorised disclosure of, or access to, personal data transmitted, stored or otherwise processed in connection with the provision of a public electronic communications service'.

New Regulation 5A then puts an obligation on public electronic communications service providers such as Microsoft and BT to notify the Information Commissioner of the occurrence of a personal data breach and where the breach is likely adversely to affect the personal data or privacy of the website user or subscriber. The regulation also places a duty on the service provider to notify the breach to the website user or subscriber concerned. Service providers won't have to notify users should they be able to demonstrate that the relevant data accessed were in a form unintelligible to persons not authorized to view them. Service providers must also keep an inventory of all personal data breaches, so that the Information Commissioner may verify compliance with the notification obligations.

Regulations 5B and 5C provide that the Information Commissioner may audit service providers' compliance with Regulation 5A, and may issue a fixed monetary penalty of £1,000 if it is found that the provider is in breach of any of the notification obligations. Service providers should exercise particular care when handling personal data and should also comply with these notification obligations.

Spam

Regulation 23 of the 2003 Regulations regarding anonymous e-mails for the purpose of direct marketing has been amended to incorporate two new subsections regarding compliance with Regulation 7 of the Electronic Commerce (EC Directive) Regulations 2002.

Regulation 7 of the Electronic Commerce (EC Directive) Regulations 2002 provides that commercial communications by service providers shall be clearly identifiable as such and shall further clearly identify the person behind the communication. In addition, the service provider must give full details of any promotional offers and related conditions within that e-mail in clear and unambiguous language.

Regulation 23 states that e-mails not only must comply with Regulation 7 of the Electronic Commerce (EC Directive) Regulations 2002 but must not contain any encouragement to recipients to visit websites that contravene Regulation 7 of the Electronic Commerce (EC Directive) Regulations 2002.

The relevant provision of the 2011 Regulations on which this amendment is based (Article 13) further sets out a right of persons so affected by an infringement of this restriction to bring legal proceedings in respect of that infringement. This right is however already covered by a general right to bring proceedings in respect of non-compliance with the 2011 Regulations under Regulation 30.

Third-party notices

Under Regulation 31A, the Information Commissioner can serve notices on communications providers requesting that they provide information about other people's use of an electronic communications network or service, where that person's compliance with the 2003 Regulations is in question. It's thought that the rationale behind this provision is to make it easier for the Information Commissioner to serve notices on those who engage in cold calling or sending spam e-mails in breach of the 2011 Regulations.

For a detailed review of the rules as they apply to direct marketing, see Chapter 6.

Online advertising and marketing

Since the enactment of the 2011 Regulations, many advertising and marketing agencies have been scratching their heads over what they need to do to comply with what many regard as one of the most annoying marketing laws of the decade!

In 2011, members of the Internet Advertising Bureau (IAB) Europe and the European Advertising Standards Alliance (EASA) attempted to navigate through the requirements of the 2011 Regulations by drawing up their own code of online behavioural advertising (OBA) only to discover that this wasn't compliant with the conditions contained in the 2011 Regulations.

For example, an icon that allowed a website user a one-click option to access further information around behavioural adverts, as well as managing preferences and opt-out of receiving OBA, was deemed to be a 'highly intrusive practice' by the European Data Protection Supervisor and fell short of the 2011 Regulations requirements.

In this situation, cookies are being collected to enable marketers to send advertisements for products and services to website users in the hope that the users may be interested in these based on their online activity.

The main objection voiced to the proposed joint practice adopted by the IAB and EASA to enable website users to object to being tracked for the purposes of serving behavioural advertising was that it didn't meet the requirement to obtain actual informed consent, as the tracking and serving of adverts take place unless people object. For consent to be valid, it must be freely given, specific and informed. Absence of action can't indicate consent.

Despite a few websites featuring a cookie notice on every page and a tick box requesting opt-in consent, these are still in the minority, with the vast majority of marketers choosing to ignore these new conditions. For example, few, if any websites, will block access to other parts of the site that serve cookies when the user doesn't actually tick the box. There's been a universal allergic reaction from marketers to defacing every landing page with a notice drawing attention to the use of cookies and asking for consent to their use before the website user goes any further into the site.

The solution, as highlighted in the checklist (below), is to ensure that the website uses only cookies that are absolutely necessary for the delivery of the service, and it could signal the rapid decline of behavioural advertising techniques unless express consent for these highly effective but deeply intrusive techniques has been given. On current industry estimates, only 10 per cent of website users consent to such techniques, so the continuing practice by marketers in 2012 and beyond is likely to lead to several high-profile enforcement actions by the ICO.

In summary, the following points should be observed:

- Website operators should review and list the various cookies used on their website, such as flash cookies, browser cookies and third-party cookies, to assess which ones are strictly necessary to provide users with web-based services and which ones aren't and to remove those in the latter category. As a general rule of thumb, the less intrusive the cookie, the lower the risk and the need for obtaining specific and active consent.

- Remember that the aim of the 2011 Regulations is to improve internet users' privacy, so the more intrusive the use of cookies then the higher the priority that must be given to considering how to change that use.

- Any attempt to gain consent that relies on website users' ignorance about what they are agreeing to is unlikely to be compliant.

- Consider how intrusive the use of cookies is and discuss this with third-party cookie providers to agree a suitable approach to obtain users' consent.

- Remember that the more intrusive the activity, the more priority a marketer must give to obtaining meaningful consent from the website user. For example, using a cookie to create detailed profiles of an individual's browsing activity would be considered very intrusive and would therefore require meaningful consent.

- Website operators should decide what solution to adopt to obtain consent in the circumstances. Information about cookies needs to be provided to all users before placing a cookie for the first time. Once consent is gained at that point, there's no requirement to gain consent each time the same person uses the same cookie for the same purpose in the future.

- Requesting consent could be achieved through a variety of mechanisms, such as the use of standard terms and conditions, pop-up check boxes or general browser settings. There's no one simple solution, and it will very much depend on the user experience and the type of cookies involved as to the form of consent used.

- Begin to create and implement appropriate and tailored solutions to gain website users' consent.

- The ICO is likely to be taking enforcement action against website owners towards the end of 2012, so marketers need to have reviewed their cookie practices and to have implemented a practical and effective strategy to obtain users' consent well before then.

References

Website
Information Commissioner [accessed 29 November 2011] http://www.ico.gov.uk

Reports and articles
Coca-Cola Great Britain Responsible Marketing Charter (2012)

Book
Kolah, A (2013) *High Impact Marketing that Gets Results*, Kogan Page, London

Answer: 1909

"And for an extra 200 points, in what year
did Louis Bleriot became the first person
to fly single-handedly over the English Channel?"

Sales and price promotions

Introduction

Sales and price promotions are an accepted part of the marketing mix alongside fact-finding analysis, product planning, pricing, branding, channels of distribution, physical handling, personal selling, advertising, packaging and display. In fact, promotion has always been part of the 'DNA' of marketing (Figure 8.1).

Figure 8.1   The seven Ps of marketing

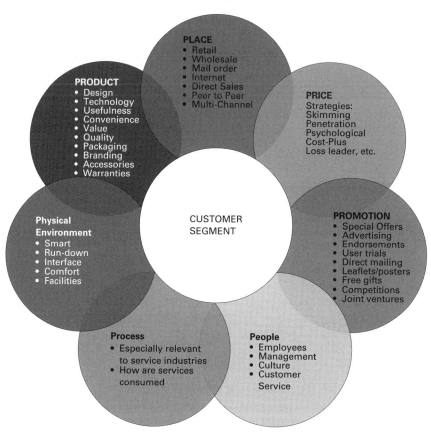

Typically, promotions can be offer coupons, refunds, premiums (goodies or giveaways to give them their technical description!), extra products free of charge, free trial-sized samples, sweepstakes, buy-one-get-one-free offers, charity-linked promotions, instant wins, competitions, prize draws and other special offers you can dream up.

If you're promoting to the trade (B2B markets) – such as wholesalers and retailers – then you can also offer things like free-goods deals, buy-back allowances, display and advertising allowances and assistance with advertising and marketing costs, which is common practice in the licensing and merchandising industry.

Sales promotions can take place across any media, from in-store, point of sale through to national newspapers, radio and television, mobile phones and the internet. The growth of sales and price promotions over the last decade has given it a strong presence within the retail and shopping experience, both online and offline. For example, discounters like Last Minute and

Groupon couldn't exist if there wasn't an insatiable appetite amongst consumers for a bargain. Given the squeeze on disposable incomes as a result of a challenging economy, the hunt for a great deal has become much more significant for millions of householders. A walk down any high street will reveal a mix of special offers, discounts and buy-one-get-one-free (BOGOF) offers in an attempt to capture our attention and share of wallet.

The Institute of Sales Promotion (ISP) defines a sales promotion as: 'A marketing initiative, the purpose of which is to create a call to action that has a direct impact on the behaviour of the brand's target audience by offering a demonstrable benefit that is not necessarily tangible.'

The nearest we get to a legal definition of sales promotion is contained in section 8 of the UK Code of Non-Broadcast Advertising, Sales Promotion and Direct Marketing:

> *A sales promotion can provide an incentive for the consumer to buy using a range of added direct or indirect benefits, usually on a temporary basis, to make the product more attractive. A non-exhaustive list of sales promotions includes 'two for the price of one' offers, money-off offers, text-to-wins, instant wins, competition and prize draws. The rules do not apply to routine, non-promotional, distribution of product or product extensions, for example one-off editorial supplements (printed or electronic form) to newspapers or magazines.*

Typically, brand owners in their sales and price promotions will look to give away free goods, sell goods at a discount or invite consumers to participate in competitions and prize draws – all with the intention of boosting sales of products or services, either in business-to-consumer (B2C) markets, such as promotional elements involved in sponsorships, or business-to-business (B2B) markets, such as trade promotions and incentives.

The skills required to run a successful sales promotion are both creative and technical given the legal complexities involved. Perhaps the most infamous sales promotion disaster of recent times was the Hoover sales promotion in 1992.

Hoover fiasco (1992)

The company had failed to keep pace with its rivals, which were manufacturing more innovative household products, with the result that it was suffering a major dent in its sales in the UK. In a desperate attempt to reverse this and get customers flocking back to the brand, Hoover launched an offer of two free flights to the United States for customers who spent £100 or more on any Hoover product. Within weeks and as if by magic retailers were reporting that Hoover products were flying out of the door! In fact, people were buying two vacuum cleaners at a time to take advantage of the 'too good to believe' offer. The travel agency handling the promotion reported 100,000 responses by the end of 1992, twice what they'd expected.

Incredibly no one at Hoover had checked the economics of the promotion, and the brand quickly went from 'hero to zero' as customers reported unexpected delays and difficulties in obtaining flights. Questions were starting to be asked publicly as to how Hoover could possibly fund two free flights to the United States off the back of a £100 sale. Given that the company was £10 million in the red prior to the sales promotion, such breathtaking recklessness was guaranteed to exacerbate the company's financial difficulties to say the least. Worse still, BBC1's 'Watchdog' uncovered dubious practices within the company in its feeble attempts to deny customers the free flights unless they had complied with the small print, which included paying for hotel accommodation, car hire and insurance worth at least £300.

It's fair to say Hoover was engulfed by the stupidity of its own sales promotion and then was pursued through the courts by its angry customers, who wanted to get their hands on free air tickets given that they had complied with the terms and conditions of the sales promotion. The company had no choice but to capitulate at a vast cost to its business and provide the tickets to its customers at enormous expense.

Hoover was eventually sold off, and its holding company had to make a £20 million provision in order to honour its contractual obligations to its customers, with a final bill for cleaning up the mess close to £50 million.

Discounts and other special offers

Special offers are temporary inducements to make customers (B2B or B2C) buy on the basis of price or price-related factors. Special offers play with price, giving customers or intermediaries a way to get the product or service for less – at least while the offer lasts.

You may wonder why marketers want to play with the price in the first place. For example, if you think the price should be lower anyway, why not just cut the price permanently? The reason often given by marketers is that a price cut is easy to do, but hard to undo. On the other hand, a special offer allows the company to discount the price temporarily whilst still maintaining the list or published price. When the offer ends the list price is the same – you haven't given anything away permanently.

It's easy to get caught up in a cat-and-mouse game of making and matching your competitor's special offers. Customers can be flooded with price-based promotions. Discounts and freebies can start to outweigh brand-building marketing activities, distracting customers' attention on price over the brand and business benefit messages. And there's evidence to suggest that special promotions increase customers' sensitivity to price. For example, special promotions attract price switchers and thereby reduce the size of the core and loyal customer base, so sales and price promotions have the potential to erode brand equity, reduce customer loyalty and cut deeply into your profits.

This is a slippery slope from both a business and a legal perspective, and you can easily lose your footing on it!

However, there may be a number of situations when maintaining your list price and offering a discount is a good marketing strategy:

- when your reason for wanting to cut the price is short-term in order to counter a competitor's special offer, for example a discounted air fare or holiday package, or respond to the launch of a new rival product;

- when you want to experiment with the price in order to gauge price elasticity for your product or service without committing to a permanent price cut until you've seen the data;

- when you want to stimulate customers to buy your product or service and offer a price discount as an inducement in that they buy the product and then reorder the product or service at full price;

- when your list price for the products and services you are selling needs to be high to indicate quality, for example if they are premium products in the luxury goods market, or they have to be consistent with other prices in your product line; or

- when your rivals offer special lower prices and you think you have no choice but to enter the price war also, as customers come to expect special offers.

Legal framework: the UK and the European Union

There are more than a hundred laws affecting the conduct of sales and retail promotions. Some types of promotion, particularly involving packaging, product safety and statements made at the point of sale, are subject to enforcement by local authority trading standards. Legislative powers of the Advertising Standards Authority (ASA) were increased over a decade ago to give its director-general the power to apply for court injunctions against any brand owner or promoter that flagrantly continues to use an advertisement or promotion that the ASA has ruled against.

Many of the laws that have an impact on sales and price promotions are to be found as aspects of wider scope legislation that's intended to regulate consumer credit, trades descriptions and other consumer affairs issues. It's therefore unsurprising that the legal framework for sales and retail promotions derive from small sections of a large number of Acts.

Marketers should at least assume that English law applies to an internet promotion if it targets residents of England and Wales. By the same token, if a promotion targets, or is available to, residents in other countries, then other national laws will also probably apply. This is a complex area, and this chapter discusses sales and price promotions under English law.

The European dimension

In 1994, the EU undertook a wide-ranging review of all marketing communications within member states, including all forms of advertising, direct marketing, sponsorship, sales promotions and public relations (PR). The result was a Green Paper, which made a number of observations:

- Cross-border commercial communications are a growing phenomenon.
- Differing national regulations create obstacles for brands wanting to run cross-border communications and also create problems for consumers seeking redress against unlawful cross-border commercial communications.
- Some of the divergences between regulatory frameworks of member states create barriers as cross-border communications proliferate across the internet.

The result of these discussions was a measure of coordination between self-regulatory systems in Europe, achieved through the European Advertising Standards Alliance (EASA), which brings together the advertising self-regulatory organizations from 23 EU member states and five non-EU countries. One of its functions is to act as a postbox, ensuring that cross-border complaints are sent to the relevant national self-regulatory body. As far as the law is concerned, the rules vary throughout the EU.

For example, Germany has the most restrictive rules on sales promotions, although some relaxation has taken place in recent years; France has limits on the value of premiums ('giveaways'), which can be no more than 7 per cent of the total product value; Portugal requires a licence to run sales promotions; and in Italy all promotions need to be notified to the authorities.

If in any doubt about how these rules apply, marketers should seek advice from the relevant profession or industry body or from a qualified lawyer who specializes in this area of marketing practice.

Irrespective of which country a sales and price promotion is run in, it is essential to evaluate it at an early stage by reference to a number of critical tests:

- Is it legal? In particular, are there any specific legal rules that apply? Failure to comply with these rules could be a criminal offence in certain circumstances.
- What are the legal commitments it imposes? Most promotions create legally binding contracts, which can't be avoided by small print.
- Does it comply with all relevant codes of practice? Even if legal, there are many codes affecting sales and price promotions that may be breached if care isn't taken. Failure to comply with these can lead to serious sanctions and PR repercussions.
- Does it make sense? The test of common sense is often forgotten in the enthusiasm generated by an idea for a new sales promotion campaign.

A useful test is to ask whether the uninformed consumer would understand the sales and price promotion. It's obvious, but marketers should ask someone who hasn't been working on the promotion to check it for sense prior to roll-out!

This chapter covers some of the key factors in making an assessment of a sales and price promotion campaign, taking account of the above criteria. For prize promotions, see Chapter 9.

The UK self-regulation framework

Sales promotion activities in the UK are governed by a mixture of statutory controls and regulations, which have been in place since as long ago as 1890, when poster companies set up a Joint Censorship Committee to prevent objectionable posters going on public display. Today, there are a number of bodies that are empowered by Parliament to oversee these types of marketing activities.

For example, the Information Commissioner's Office issues guidelines on marketing by electronic means and the use of data (see Chapters 6–7) and warns that marketers as instigators of e-mail campaigns that use data collected unfairly will be held accountable. The Gambling Act 2005 (see Chapter 9) has probably had the greatest impact on prize promotions, and the Olympic Games legislation (see Chapter 10) has imposed a draconian regime on those who aren't official sponsors or licensees of the London 2012 Olympic Games.

The balance between self-regulation and statute laws has varied over time and varies considerably between countries in the EU. For example, in Germany sales and price promotions are largely governed by statutory controls, whereas the UK employs a largely self-regulatory regime over such promotions. These laws and regulations have been developed in response to concerns over exploitation of consumers and ethical concerns.

The rule of thumb is that provided brand owners and promoters apply best marketing practice in their sales and price promotions then they shouldn't fall foul of the self-regulatory regime provided they keep within the letter and spirit of these codes.

Advertising Standards Authority

Most promotions run by marketers in the UK will be subject to regulation by the ASA, the UK's independent watchdog, which is committed to maintaining high standards in all forms of marketing and communications for the benefit of consumers, advertisers and society at large.

The ASA Council is the jury that decides if advertisements and other forms of marketing communications, including sales promotions, breach the Advertising Codes. Currently, the ASA chairman is Lord Chris Smith, and the Council is made up of two panels – broadcast and non-broadcast – with some members sitting on both.

Committee of Advertising Practice

The Committee of Advertising Practice (CAP) was set up in 1961 in order to regulate all print advertising and prevent the need for time-consuming government legislation. CAP writes and reviews the British Code of Advertising, Sales Promotion and Direct Marketing (CAP Code), which all advertisers have to adhere to.

As discussed in detail in Chapter 4, a separate Broadcast Committee of Advertising Practice (BCAP) is responsible for writing and reviewing the UK Code of Broadcast Advertising, with the aim of preventing advertisements from being misleading, causing harm or offence, and breaching boundaries of taste and decency.

Members of CAP are drawn from the main industry bodies representing advertisers, agencies and media owners:

- Advertising Association;
- Cinema Advertising Association;
- Data Publishers Association;
- Direct Marketing Association;
- Direct Selling Association;
- Incorporated Society of British Advertisers;
- Institute of Practitioners in Advertising;
- Institute of Promotional Marketing;
- Internet Advertising Bureau;
- Mobile Broadband Group;
- Mobile Marketing Association;
- Newspaper Publishers Association;
- Newspaper Society;
- Outdoor Media Centre;
- Professional Publishers Association;
- Proprietary Association of Great Britain;
- Royal Mail;
- Scottish Newspaper Society.

In addition to the CAP Committee, the Sales Promotion and Direct Response Panel (SPDRP) provides expert advice and guidance on sales promotions and direct marketing in all non-broadcast media.

Through their membership of trade bodies or through contractual agreements with media publishers and carriers, brand owners, agencies and others involved in promotions agree to comply with the CAP and BCAP Codes so that marketing communications are legal, decent, honest and truthful and consumer confidence is maintained.

Some CAP member organizations, for example the Institute of Sales Promotion (ISP), the Incorporated Society of British Advertisers (ISBA) and the Direct Marketing Association (DMA), also require their members to observe their own codes of practice in addition to the CAP Codes. Those individual trade body codes of conduct may cover some practices that aren't covered by the CAP Code.

Non-Broadcast Advertising, Sales Promotion and Direct Marketing Code (CAP Code)

In the UK, the 12th edition of the CAP Code came into force in September 2010. It's the rule book for non-broadcast advertisements, sales promotions and direct marketing communications in cinema, press, posters and online.

This Code is the industry's self-regulatory method for ensuring that advertisers meet the high level of standards the public demands, whilst keeping a level playing field amongst advertisers. The Code broadly covers marketing and communications that are likely to mislead, cause harm and offence, and be in breach of the acceptable limits of taste and decency expected.

The CAP Code is primarily concerned with the content of marketing communications and not with terms of business or products themselves. Some rules, however, go beyond content, for example those that cover the administration of sales promotions, the suitability of promotion items, the delivery of products ordered through an advertisement and the use of personal information in direct marketing.

Editorial content is specifically excluded from the CAP Code, though it might be a factor in determining the context in which marketing communications are judged.

Fundamental requirements for sales and price promotions

These are set out in the Code in relation to promotional marketing, and in essence all promotions should be:

- legal, decent, honest and truthful;
- conducted equitably, promptly and efficiently;
- seen to deal fairly and honourably with consumers;
- in line with accepted principles of fair competition; and
- in line with the spirit as well as the letter of the rules and not bringing the industry into disrepute.

The CAP Code supplements the law, fills gaps where the law doesn't reach and often provides an easier way of resolving disputes than by civil litigation or criminal prosecution. In many cases, self-regulation ensures that legislation isn't necessary.

Although advertisers, promoters and direct marketers, agencies and media may still wish to consult lawyers, compliance with the Code should go a long way to ensuring compliance with the law in areas covered by both the Code and the law.

By creating and following self-imposed rules, the marketing community produces marketing communications that are welcomed and trusted. By practising self-regulation, it ensures the integrity of advertising, promotions and direct marketing.

The value of self-regulation as an alternative to statutory control is recognized in EC directives, including those on misleading and comparative advertising (Directives 2005/29/EC and 2006/114/EC). Self-regulation is accepted by the Department for Business, Innovation and Skills and the Office of Fair Trading (OFT) as a first line of control in protecting consumers and the industry.

The vast majority of advertisers, promoters and direct marketers comply with the CAP Code. Those that don't may be subject to sanctions.

Adverse publicity may result from the rulings published by the ASA weekly on its website. The media, contractors and service providers may withhold their services or deny access to space.

Trading privileges (including direct mail discounts) and recognition may be revoked, withdrawn or temporarily withheld.

Pre-vetting may be imposed and, in some cases, non-complying parties can be referred to the OFT for action, where appropriate, under the Consumer Protection from Unfair Trading Regulations 2008 or the Business Protection from Misleading Marketing Regulations 2008.

The system is structured so that it doesn't operate in an unfair or anti-competitive manner or restrict free speech unjustifiably. ASA decisions are subject to independent review, including in exceptional cases by the Administrative Division of the High Court.

The CAP Code isn't a substitute for the legal protection of the consumer, producer or distributor against fraudulent practice or where there are breaches of contractual obligations or data protection issues (see Chapter 6), but rather complements English law.

Observance of the CAP Code is the responsibility of individual sales promoters, brand owners, companies, sales promotions agencies and their partners and agents. Ignorance of the law and the CAP and BCAP Codes of course isn't a defence for infringement, and sanctions could be enforced against those who don't abide by them, so it's important to get to grips with the key principles in this area of marketing practice.

Of 25,562 complaints in 2010, 11,037 were non-broadcast complaints, 964 of which were upheld by the ASA (Table 8.1).

Companies operating in the leisure industry tended to attract more complaints than any other (Table 8.2).

And television followed by internet and outdoor attracted the most complaints by media type to the ASA (Table 8.3).

Table 8.1 Cases and complaints resolved by outcome in 2010

	Non-broadcast		Broadcast		Overall totals	
	Complaints	Cases	Complaints	Cases	Complaints	Cases
No investigation	1,625	1,545	1,418	812	3,043	2,357
No investigation (after preliminary work)	5,650	4,783	6,133	3,444	11,783	8,227
No investigation (after Council decision)	1,118	205	2,614	222	3,732	427
Total not investigated	8,393	6,533	10,165	4,478	18,558	11,011
Informally resolved	1,329	1,191	258	176	1,587	1,367
Formal investigation	1,315	465	4,102	195	5,417	660
Of which:						
Upheld	*964*	*348*	*1,388*	*116*	*2,352*	*464*
Not upheld	*216*	*74*	*2,706*	*71*	*2,922*	*145*
Other	*135*	*43*	*8*	*8*	*143*	*51*
Total investigated	2,644	1,656	4,360	371	7,004	2,027
Totals	11,037	8,189	14,525	4,849	25,562	13,038

Source: Advertising Standards Authority (2011).

These figures are typical of any year and represent a fraction of the total number of promotions, but they involve some big names and some consistent failings. Every month, the ASA publishes a report that details the complaints it has upheld and some of those it hasn't.

For example, some of the main offenders were betting companies like William Hill and Bet365, which ran advertising promotions enticing customers with so-called 'free bets'. The ASA upheld complaints against these promotions on the grounds of their not having made the terms and conditions of their offers clear. Typical problems included not letting consumers know that in order to access the 'free bet' they had to deposit their own money in an account with the company – sometimes as much as £200. The ASA also upheld complaints that, unlike the case for other bets, if customers won the 'free stake' wouldn't be returned to them.

In difficult economic times, the importance of keeping advertisements and promotions responsible and truthful takes on greater significance. The ASA for example has been quick to take action on financial services brand owners where their advertising promotions simply don't add up.

For example, in 2010 the ASA took action against Borro.com, whose television advertisement offered short-term loans but didn't state the substantial

Table 8.2 Cases and complaints resolved by sector 2009–10

Sector	Complaints 2009	Complaints 2010	Percentage change (%)	Cases 2009	Cases 2010	Percentage change (%)
Leisure	3,774	5,287	40	2,664	2,551	–4
Non-commercial (including voluntary sector)	5,479	4,124	–25	1,049	840	–20
Food and drink	2,729	2,512	–8	881	816	–7
Retail	1,731	2,349	36	1,241	1,370	10
Health and beauty	3,053	2,080	–32	1,311	1,233	–6
Computers and telecoms	1,861	1,565	–16	1,243	1,184	–5
Financial	1,389	1,519	9	934	940	1
Households	1,898	1,172	–38	605	558	–8
Holidays and travel	1,689	1,057	–37	1015	825	–19
Motoring	1,823	1,037	–43	517	608	18
Business	1,034	951	–8	810	621	–23
Publishing	749	660	–12	651	559	–14
Utilities	557	283	–49	188	185	–2
Property	242	242	0	222	217	–2
Clothing	249	211	–15	119	123	3
Alcohol	201	203	1	140	148	6
Employment	212	120	–43	186	103	–45
Education	116	87	–25	111	76	–31
Unknown	88	40	–54	73	35	–52
Industrial and engineering	30	20	–33	24	18	–25
Agricultural	20	19	–5	20	19	–5
Tobacco	10	8	–20	10	8	–20
Electrical appliances	16	1	–94	13	1	–92

Source: Advertising Standards Authority (2011).

Table 8.3 Complaints and cases resolved, segmented by media type 2009–10

Sector	Complaints 2009	Complaints 2010	Percentage change (%)	Cases 2009	Cases 2010	Percentage change (%)
Television	13,109	14,112	7.7	4,330	4,577	5.7
Internet	3,546	2,648	−25.3	2,823	2,327	−17.6
Outdoor	2,774	1,856	−33.1	589	660	12.1
National press	1,823	1,488	−18.4	1,354	1,210	−10.6
Direct mail	964	932	−3.3	829	676	−18.5
Magazine	809	878	8.5	657	779	18.6
E-mail	730	739	1.2	612	616	0.7
Regional press	801	726	−9.4	644	644	0.0
Radio	785	625	−20.4	444	412	−7.2
Leaflet	397	356	−10.3	329	334	1.5
Point of sale	347	342	−1.4	328	303	−7.6
Other	368	320	−13.0	263	307	16.7
Circular	355	266	−25.1	241	230	−4.6
Brochure	205	232	13.2	201	231	14.9
Cinema	280	194	−30.7	75	78	4.0
Transport	1,535	179	−88.3	120	129	7.5
Insert	129	147	14.0	114	118	3.5
Text message	123	145	17.9	113	143	26.5
Catalogue	192	137	−28.6	172	130	−24.4
Press general	208	101	−51.4	143	98	−31.5
Packaging	184	86	−53.3	175	85	−51.4
Mailing	47	82	74.5	38	78	105.3
VOD	4	69	1,625.0	3	53	1,666.7
Directory	73	58	−20.5	72	57	−20.8
Mobile	39	10	−74.4	30	10	−66.7
Ambient	35	9	−74.3	26	8	−69.2
Facsimile	6	5	−16.7	5	5	0.0
In-game advertising	1	1	0.0	1	1	0.0
Voicemail	3	1	−66.7	3	1	−66.7

Source: Advertising Standards Authority (2011).

rate of interest payable. The ASA also acted on 63 complaints about a television advertisement by Wonga.com, another short-term loan company, whose light-hearted advertisement was likely to mislead vulnerable consumers about the nature and implications of its product. The ASA also ruled against AdMoney.co.uk, whose text messages were irresponsible and misleading because they implied the recipient had already been accepted for a loan.

Copy Advice provided by the CAP

A 24-hour free and confidential Copy Advice service is provided by CAP, which is designed to help you create non-broadcast marketing communications or multimedia concepts that comply with the CAP Code.

Copy Advice can guide you on the content, tone and placement of any advertisement or sales promotion that falls within the remit of the non-broadcast CAP Code. The advisers provide advice across the following marketing and communications activities:

- press and magazine advertisements;
- direct marketing;
- sales promotions;
- door drops;
- inserts;
- cinema advertising;
- outdoor and ambient media;
- online advertising, including marketing communications on a company's website, or third-party websites under the company's control;
- commercial e-mails;
- SMS and mobile marketing;
- viral marketing;
- leaflets, brochures and catalogues.

As discussed in Chapter 4, the ASA now regulates marketing communications on websites and in other non-paid-for space under the control of the brand owner.

Television and radio advertisements require pre-broadcast clearance by (formerly the Broadcast Advertising Clearance Centre, BACC) and the Radio Advertising Clearance Centre (RACC) respectively.

Advantages of pre-copy clearance for sales and price promotions

- Pre-publication vetting by Copy Advice can help you to avoid ASA scrutiny and potential action, which can be both costly and damaging to your brand reputation.

- Marketers can contact Copy Advice at any stage of the creative process – concepts, copy or artwork – but the sooner the better to get campaigns right the first time.

- The Copy Advice service can identify any contentious issues before you spend time and resources taking them forward. Users of Copy Advice are consistently delighted, with 93 per cent reporting they are satisfied with the service and 97 per cent saying they would consult it again in the future.

Express four-hour service

An express four-hour turnaround service is available at a cost of £240 (£200 plus VAT) for advertisers, agencies and other intermediaries. This rate applies if you request an invoice. If you pay online when you submit your enquiry, you will receive a 15 per cent discount, reducing the cost to £204 (£170 plus VAT). Prices are correct as of April 2012.

This isn't clearance that the sales and price promotion is legal, and such advice is not legally binding. Conformity with the advice does not prevent the ASA from later investigating and upholding any complaints about breaches of the CAP and BCAP Codes. However, it does substantially reduce the risk of such an outcome.

If the promotion appears on television or radio, the commercial will be subject to mandatory clearance by Clearcast prior to being aired. Again, this isn't legal clearance, but it reduces the risk of a brand owner or promoter being in breach of the BCAP Code.

Breaches of the CAP Code

The ASA investigates complaints under the CAP Code. If it finds that a brand owner has breached the CAP Sales Promotion Code, it will publicize the breach among media and consumer bodies, and often this publicity finds its way into the national press. The negative publicity and damage to a brand owner's reputation are the principal consequence of being held to be in breach of the CAP Sales Promotion Code or failing to challenge the decision successfully.

Because of the wide-ranging membership of the ASA, a breach can, for example, result in the media refusing to publish further similar advertising.

Persistent or serious breaches can also be actionable under the Consumer Protection from Unfair Trading Regulations 2008 and the Business Protection from Misleading Marketing Regulations 2008 (see later in this chapter).

There have been very few injunctions sought by the ASA against promoters over the last 20 years, and recidivist offenders of the CAP Code tend to be tabloid newspapers. Outside of these types of complaints, marketers must be careful to ensure that they have sufficient quantities of their promotional products in order to meet likely demand and to avoid customers suffering unnecessary disappointment (see page 274).

The Cap Code, section 8

The overriding principle is that marketers must conduct their promotions equitably, promptly and efficiently and be seen to deal fairly and honourably with participants and potential participants. This includes avoiding 'causing unnecessary disappointment'.

For this chapter, the parts of section 8 that are relevant are:

- protection of consumers, safety and suitability;
- availability;
- administration;
- significant conditions for promotions;
- trade incentives; and
- charity-linked promotions.

The part of the CAP Code, section 8 that deals with prize promotions is dealt with in Chapter 9.

Protection of consumers, safety and suitability

The CAP Code states that promoters shouldn't offer promotional products that are of a nature likely to cause offence or products that, in the context of the promotion, may reasonably be considered to be socially undesirable, such as a free phone card for a sex chat line.

In addition, marketers are required to take special care with promotional products where the distribution of such products is subject to legal restrictions, such as alcohol, condoms and cigarette rolling papers, or when promoting to children.

In the latter case, marketers shouldn't directly exhort children to buy products. In other words, marketers mustn't take advantage of the children's lack of experience or encourage them to pester their beleaguered parents! Obtaining parental consent for a child's participation is often a good idea. This is pretty common-sense stuff!

Contractual issues Although the CAP Sales Promotion Code is important, most promotions also create legally binding contractual commitments. Failure first to appreciate these and then to honour them has caused some of the most notorious sales promotions problems.

The key to this issue is the contractual relationship. As discussed in Chapter 1, a contract is an agreement that creates obligations enforceable in law. There are key elements in this, for example an offer by one party that has been accepted by another, consideration (or payment) on either side, an intention to create legal relations, and certainty in the terms of the agreement. Some promotional techniques try to avoid legal commitment on the basis of one or other of these rules, but these attempts will often fail.

Usually a promoter will be providing something of value to a participant – whether selling goods or services or offering the chance of winning a star prize. In return, the promoter may require some form of 'consideration' from participants, such as requiring them to pay a purchase price. The question of whether a participant has provided consideration is critical, because it will bind the company and the participant in a contractual relationship.

What constitutes 'consideration' isn't limited to cash payments. For example, if a participant is required to complete a questionnaire in order to enter the promotion, this may constitute consideration, particularly if the information has significant marketing value to the brand owner.

The way the consideration is made is by the participant is immaterial.

Where goods or services are sold at their normal retail price, the price paid for the goods will still amount to a 'payment', and in most cases a contract will be concluded. The fact that a promotion states that 'No purchase is necessary' doesn't mean that, when a consumer actually does make a purchase, no consideration is given.

Where a brand owner offers to supply products or services under a promotion and asks for no consideration in return, then the brand owner is offering a gift to participants.

Roddy Mullin (2010), a UK sales promotion and marketing expert, says:

The word 'free' is one of the most powerful available to promoters and its use is closely governed. If the consumer has to pay for anything other than postage, it may be a fine promotional offer but it is not 'free'. This applies to a contribution towards a mail-in item and the cost of premium-rate telephone lines as much as the requirement to make a purchase before taking up the offer.

For example, free samples of a shower gel or the invitation to a free prize draw where no purchase is necessary would amount to a gift. As a consequence, if a brand owner doesn't comply with the terms of such a promotion it's possible to argue that the participants have no right of action for breach of contract. In such a situation, the winner of a free prize draw, if it could be shown that there was genuinely no consideration, probably could not sue the brand owner for the prize if the brand owner refused to send it (see Chapter 9).

Since the promotion is likely to create a legally enforceable commitment, it's important that the terms of the promotion are clear, and that any restrictions are fair and obvious to the consumer in order to make them legally effective.

Whilst it's possible to exclude or restrict liability for failure, it's much easier to get it right first time. This means not running promotions that from the outset are clearly going to be incapable of fulfilment, and making any restrictions clear. It's not possible to get it right all the time and, as a promoter, a brand owner will naturally be concerned to protect its position against unexpected liabilities.

Marketers also prefer to avoid onerous obligations and to have flexibility in relation to those obligations. However, care must be taken in drafting the terms and conditions of a promotion, because certain terms may breach codes of practice or be prohibited or made unenforceable by legislation, which is increasingly onerous, for example the Distance Selling Regulations (see Chapter 6).

Availability

As mentioned earlier, promoters are expected to avoid situations like the Hoover fiasco and have sufficient quantities of their promotional products to meet likely demand. Phrases such as 'subject to availability' don't relieve marketers of their responsibilities. Demand needs to have been estimated in advance, and you should have plans to meet unexpected demand.

If all else fails, an item of equivalent value must be offered. If there are limitations on participation (such as age restrictions) or any costs that entrants may incur in taking part, these must be clearly stated.

In addition, arrangements must be made to dispatch the goods within 30 days.

Administration

This is perhaps the easiest area in relation to avoiding complaint, as it's not difficult to get the rules of the competition right. The CAP Code places the responsibility to ensure that the promotion is conducted under proper supervision squarely on the shoulders of the brand owner. It also goes further in that companies, agencies and intermediaries should not give consumers justifiable grounds for making a complaint.

For example, you can't change the terms of the promotional offer later if you realize you are going to run out of stocks of a promotional item. However, it is good industry practice to provide a closing date for the offer, such as 'Offer closes 31 October', which needs to be prominently displayed on the pack of the product.

Significant conditions for promotions

Any guesswork as to what to state in the terms and conditions you need to communicate to your desired customer segment has been removed, as this is helpfully spelt out in the CAP Code in a very user-friendly way.

Before purchase or, if no purchase is required, before or at the time of entry or application, marketers must communicate all applicable significant conditions. These include:

- *How to participate.* A promotion should give clear instructions as to how customers can take part. Important conditions of entry need to be spelt out, as do costs and any other major factors that are reasonably likely to affect customers' decision to participate in the promotion.
- *Free-entry route explanation.* This should be explained clearly and prominently.
- *Start date.* This should be stated where applicable.
- *Closing date.* A promotion must clearly state (if applicable) the closing date in a prominent way where there are purchases and submissions of

entries or claims that need to be made. Closing dates are not always necessary, such as in the following cases: comparisons that refer to a special offer (whether the company's previous offer or a rival's offer) if the offer is and is stated to be 'subject to availability'; promotions limited only by the availability of promotional packs (gifts with a purchase, extra-volume packs and reduced-price packs); and loyalty schemes run on an open-ended basis. Unless the promotional pack includes the promotional item or prize and the only limit is the availability of that pack, prize promotions and promotions addressed to or targeted at children always need a closing date. Promoters must be able to demonstrate that the absence of a closing date will not disadvantage consumers. Promoters must state if the deadline for responding to undated promotional material will be calculated from the date the material was received by consumers. Unless circumstances outside the reasonable control of the promoter make it unavoidable, closing dates must not be changed. If they are changed, promoters must do everything reasonable to ensure that consumers who participated within the original terms are not disadvantaged.

- *Proof of purchase.* Any proof of purchase requirements need to be clearly stated.

- *Restrictions.* A promotion should set out geographical, personal or technological restrictions such as location, age or the need to access the internet. Promoters must state any need to obtain permission to enter from an adult or employer where relevant.

- *Availability.* The availability of promotional packs should be stated if it is not obvious, for example if promotional packs could become unavailable before the stated closing date of the offer.

- *Promoter's name and address.* Unless it is obvious from the context or if entry into an advertised promotion is only through a dedicated website containing that information in an easily found format, the promoter's full name and correspondence address must be stated.

Marketing communications that include a promotion and are significantly limited by time or space must include as much information about significant conditions as practicable and must direct consumers clearly to an easily accessible alternative source where all the significant conditions of the promotion are prominently stated. Participants should be able to retain those conditions or easily access them throughout the promotion.

Kellogg's (2011)

A television advertisement, national press advertisement, and sales promotion on Kellogg's cereal packaging encouraged consumers to collect codes from cereal packets and use them to claim a free box of cereal.

The national press advertisement announced: 'we're helping you to wake up to breakfast... for FREE! For a limited time simply collect codes from promotional packs to get your FREE Kellogg's cereal from a selected range.' Packets of Kellogg's Corn Flakes, Crunchy Nut, Bran Flakes, Coco Pops, Fruit 'n Fibre, Frosties and Rice Krispies were displayed.

The top of the packets had printed '750g VALUE PACK', '600g VALUE PACK' or 'FAMILY VALUE PACK'. The small print stated '+18 years, see special packs, 3 purchases necessary, on-line applications only, free cereal from a selected range'.

The on-pack promotion read: '750g VALUE PACK Kellogg's Fruit 'n Fibre... CLAIM A FREE BOX OF CEREAL. Further purchases & internet access required. Claim by 30.09.11. See back of pack.'

The back of the packaging provided instructions on how to claim the free box of cereal. It involved collecting three unique codes from promotional packs of cereal, entering them on a website and printing a coupon.

The side of the packaging read 'Choose your FREE box from any of the following cereals' and displayed packets of Kellogg's Coco Pops Mega Munchers, Coco Pops Moons & Stars, Coco Pops Coco Rocks, Crunchy Nut Clusters Chocolate, Crunchy Nut Clusters Honey Nut, Crunchy Nut Feast Chocolate, Crunchy Nut Feast Honey Nut, Crunchy Nut Bites, Krave, Special K Fruit & Nut Clusters, Special K Bliss Strawberry & Chocolate, Special K Oats & Honey and Special K Red Berries. Terms and conditions of the promotion were detailed underneath.

The ASA criticized Kellogg's press advertisement, which featured cereals that, although they carried promotional codes, were not the cereals that could be claimed free of charge. The ASA ruled that 'consumers were likely to be equally or more interested in seeing which cereals they could obtain for free than in seeing which cereals they had to buy in order to claim a free box, and were therefore likely to expect that the advertisement was showing them the free cereals'.

Although the advertisement stated 'FREE Kelloggs cereal from a selected range', it was likely that consumers would infer that the cereals that contained promotional codes were the same cereals that could be claimed free of charge, and that the 'selected range' referred to was the range of cereals shown in the advertisement. It wasn't sufficiently clear that consumers could not choose their free cereal from those shown in the advertisement, and that the 'selected range' of free cereals was entirely separate from the range shown.

As a result, the ASA upheld the complaint that the advertisements were likely to mislead and disappoint consumers, because they didn't make clear that the range of free cereals didn't include the cereals shown in the advertisements (with the exception of Special K Fruit & Nut Clusters in the television advertisement) and was entirely separate from the range of cereals from which consumers had to collect promotional codes.

Trade incentives

For manufacturers, producers, licensors and other B2B enterprises, providing some form of trade incentive to another company that's involved in retailing its products and services can be extremely powerful for helping to boost sales. In this context, incentive schemes must be designed and implemented to take account of the interests of everyone involved and mustn't compromise the obligation of employees of a business to give honest advice to consumers.

If they intend to ask for help from, or offer incentives to, another company's employees, promoters must require those employees to obtain their employer's permission before participating. Promoters must observe any procedures established by companies for their employees, including any rules for participating in promotions.

This whole area of trade incentives also falls within the scope of the Bribery Act 2010, which requires UK businesses to have adequate procedures in place in order to prevent any 'associated person' from taking and giving bribes (see Chapter 10).

Charity-linked promotions

Most major brands and organizations now have quite well-developed corporate social responsibility (CSR) programmes, which are often linked to a well-known charity or cause. CSR has become an integral part of the marketing mix, and so it's no surprise that marketers see a place and a benefit in such relationships when communicating with customers and other stakeholder groups. In the right hands, it can be incredibly powerful.

The flip side is that charities are now much more commercial in outlook than perhaps they were in the past, largely as a result of government cuts that have turned off what was once a regular supply of contracted-out work that the charity sector was servicing, and they now have to think more creatively in order to maintain funding for their various activities.

For some charities, this has become an uncomfortable experience given that many charities have individuals who (for personal reasons) don't want to regard themselves as being involved in anything remotely 'commercial'.

On the other hand, there are some charities that have embraced the commercial opportunities of 'lending their brand' to third parties with enthusiasm. A recent publicity leaflet for the National Children's Home (NCH) boldly claimed that 'selling anything with the NCH is kidstuff'.

Before a company goes leaping into the arms of a charity keen to engage with customers and other stakeholder groups in order to keep the wheels of its fundraising activities spinning, a review of the obligations imposed on the company by the CAP Code is worth considering.

Promotions run by the company that claim a benefit for the registered charity or cause must:

- name each charity or cause that will benefit and be able to show the ASA or CAP the formal agreement with those benefiting from the promotion;

- if it's not a registered charity, define the nature and objectives of the CSR promotion to the satisfaction of the ASA;
- specify exactly what will be gained by the named charity or cause and state the basis on which the contribution will be calculated;
- state if the promoter has imposed a limit on its contributions;
- not impose a cut-off point for contributions by consumers if an amount is stated for each purchase and, if a target total is stated, extra money collected should be given to the named charity or cause on the same basis as contributions below that level;
- be able to show that targets set are realistic;
- not exaggerate the benefit to the charity or cause derived from individual purchases of the promoted product;
- if asked, make available to consumers a current or final total of contributions made; and
- not directly encourage children to buy, or exhort children to persuade an adult to buy for them, a product that promotes charitable purposes.

Where a promotion states or implies that part of the price paid for goods or services will be given to a charity or cause, state the actual amount or percentage of the price that will be paid to the charity or cause. For any other promotion linked to a charity or where a third party states or implies that donations will be given to a charity or cause, the promotion must state the total (or a reasonable estimate) of the amount the charity or cause will receive.

From a marketing perspective, such arrangements can work extremely well for all parties and should be encouraged. However, it pays to bear in mind that there needs to be a close fit between your image and values and those of the charity or cause.

There also needs to be an effective mapping of customers, supporters, audiences and other stakeholder groups that will help underpin a successful relationship with the charity or cause rather than look like some promotional gimmick, which needs to be avoided at all costs. Professional advice for commercial organizations looking to create such relationships can be sought from the Charities Aid Foundation.

Consumer Protection from Unfair Trading Regulations 2008 (CPRs)

One important piece of legislation that affects marketing communications is the Consumer Protection from Unfair Trading Regulations 2008 (the CPRs). These regulations need to be read in conjunction with the CAP Code, and apply to individuals acting outside the course of their business.

The CPRs prohibit unfair marketing to consumers, including misleading or aggressive advertising. Whenever it considers complaints that a marketing communication misleads consumers or is aggressive or unfair to consumers, the ASA will have regard to the CPRs. That means it will take factors identified in the CPRs into account when it considers whether a marketing communication breaches the CAP Code.

The likely effect of a marketing communication is generally considered from the point of view of the average consumer whom it reaches or to whom it is addressed. The average consumer is assumed to be reasonably well informed, observant and circumspect.

In some circumstances, a marketing communication may be considered from the point of view of the average member of a specific group: if it's directed to a particular audience group, the marketing communication will be considered from the point of view of the average member of that group; and if it's likely to affect the economic behaviour only of a clearly identifiable group of people who are especially vulnerable, in a way that the promoter could reasonably foresee, because of mental or physical infirmity, age or credulity, the marketing communication will be considered from the point of view of the average member of the affected group.

Within the context of CPRs, marketing communications (including promotions) are unfair if they: are contrary to the requirements of professional diligence; and are likely to materially distort the economic behaviour of consumers in relation to the advertised products or services.

'Professional diligence' is the standard of special skill and care that a promoter may reasonably be expected to exercise towards consumers, commensurate with honest market practice and the general principle of good faith in the promoter's field of activity.

Marketing communications (including promotions) are misleading if they: are likely to deceive consumers; and are likely to cause consumers to take transactional decisions that they would not otherwise have taken.

A 'transactional decision' is any decision taken by a consumer, whether it's to act or not act, about whether, how and on what terms to buy, pay in whole or in part for, retain or dispose of a product or whether, how and on what terms to exercise a contractual right in relation to a product.

Marketing communications can deceive consumers by ambiguity, through presentation or by omitting important information that consumers need to make an informed transactional decision, as well as by including false information.

Marketing communications are aggressive if, taking all circumstances into account: they are likely significantly to impair the average consumer's freedom of choice through harassment, coercion or undue influence; and they are therefore likely to cause consumers to take transactional decisions they would not otherwise have taken.

Under these regulations, the Trading Standards Service has the power to prosecute not just companies but also individuals for indulging in unfair commercial practices, which carries severe financial penalties as well as up to two years' imprisonment.

Business Protection from Misleading Marketing Regulations 2008

B2B marketing communications are subject to the Business Protection from Misleading Marketing Regulations 2008 (the BPRs), and these regulations need to be read in conjunction with the CAP Code.

B2B marketing communications that breach the CAP Code may be referred to the OFT for consideration under the BPRs. Under the BPRs, a marketing communication is misleading if it: in any way, including its presentation, deceives or is likely to deceive the traders to whom it's addressed or whom it reaches and, by reason of its deceptive nature, is likely to affect their economic behaviour; or, for those reasons, injures or is likely to injure a competitor.

The BPRs also set out the conditions under which comparative marketing communications, directed at either consumers or business, are permitted (see Chapter 5). The CAP Code incorporates those conditions.

Consumer Protection (Distance Selling) Regulations 2000

A promotion may involve selling products or services to participants without them coming into face-to-face contact with the marketer; for example, it may invite orders through the internet, text messaging, phone calls, faxing, interactive television or mail order – via catalogues or mail order advertising in newspapers or magazines.

These are all examples of distance selling. An increasing range of goods and services is available to consumers shopping in these ways.

Businesses that normally sell by distance means and have systems in place for trading in this way, for example by having standard letters or e-mails that they send to consumers they deal with at a distance, must also comply with the Consumer Protection (Distance Selling) Regulations 2000 (DSRs), which were amended in 2005 and which implement the European Council Directive 97/7.

The purpose of the DSRs is to provide customers with confidence to buy products and services where there's no face-to-face contact with the seller, for example on Amazon, and ensure that businesses meet certain basic requirements.

There are exemptions to the application of the DSRs either in whole or in part in respect of particular types of contracts, and if you're unsure whether this applies to your own circumstance you should seek appropriate legal advice.

The key features of the DSRs are as follows:

- The consumer must be given certain information in a clear manner before a purchase of products or services is made. This includes general information relating to the goods and services, the existence of a right of cancellation where applicable, and acknowledgement that, if required, the promoter reserves the right to provide substitute goods or services of an equivalent value in the event that the original goods or services are not available.

- The consumer, after making a purchase, must be sent confirmation in writing or another durable medium. The information to be included in the written confirmation is prescribed in detail by these regulations.

- The consumer (subject to certain exceptions) has a cooling-off period of seven working days in which the contract can be cancelled at no cost to the consumer.

- Where a consumer cancels a contract, all money paid must be returned within 30 days of the date notice of cancellation is given, and related credit agreements are also cancelled.

- The provision of products or services must be made within 30 days (beginning with the day after the order was placed).

For further guidance on the distance selling regulations, refer to Chapter 6.

Electronic coupons and vouchers

Coupons continue to prove popular with both consumers and promoters. They provide a tangible and instant reward that can be easily measured at the point of sale.

In 2010, the value of all coupons redeemed was estimated at £500 million a year – a 17 per cent increase over the previous year as consumers seek better value in times of increasing prices and decreasing income.

They are also excellent tools for generating product trial or securing repeat purchase.

An Institute of Promotional Marketing (IPM) survey found that 44 per cent of people who redeemed a coupon against a product that they had never tried before said that they would definitely or probably buy that product again at its full price.

The IPM survey also recognized that the internet has become a very efficient and targeted way of distributing coupons to consumers. The exceptional graphics and dynamic multimedia capabilities of the internet allow manufacturers and retailers to collaborate in reaching desired customer segments in a very direct way. Consumers can access manufacturer and retailer websites or third-party coupon distribution sites to find retailer and manufacturer-sponsored coupons. As a result, internet coupons have become extremely popular with marketers.

According to the latest research, 76 per cent of all households in the UK have instant access to the internet, and 90 per cent of those users are on broadband; a large proportion of users are women, and the over-50s are spending more time online, making the medium very attractive to a broad set of brand owners.

According to the IPM, there was an unmistakable shift in the use of internet coupons by marketers in 2007, with an increase of 650 per cent in their use as a promotional device.

Today, the spread in popularity of internet coupons provided by companies like Groupon and VoucherCodes and brand owners like Pizza Express has accelerated consumer interest in searching for discounts across a wide range of products, tempted by 'two for one' and other offers.

All consumers need to do is download and print the voucher at home in order to use it at the point of purchase or input the unique voucher code online.

From a marketer's perspective, electronic coupons have several advantages over traditional paper coupons: they are highly targeted and easier to administer because it's online, they can generate measurable in-store sales as a direct result of online marketing and advertising spend, and they are cost-effective, extremely flexible, and fast to change in response to customer interest and demands.

There are three principal types of coupons used by marketers involved in this type of promotional activity:

- coupons for online redemption (promotion codes, offer codes and discount codes, for example), where the brand owner distributes promotional discount codes for consumers to use to receive a discount whilst shopping online;

- web-to-post coupons, where consumers visit a brand owner's website and enter their address, and possibly other information, in order to receive coupons via the post; and

- internet print-at-home coupons, where the consumer simply downloads and prints off the coupon. This can be provided by a manufacturer and redeemed at a retailer stocking the advertised product or can be provided by a retailer to be redeemed against a specific product or service. These electronic coupons are most commonly offered in a 'controlled' web environment, such as the coupon image not being shown on the screen to avoid possible online manipulation, and the number of prints allowed by the consumer being limited.

Despite the popularity of electronic coupons, brand owners and promoters continue to face several challenges in the use of this promotional device.

Legal and non-legal issues relating to coupons

Replication and copying

The opportunity exists to make multiple copies of internet print-at-home coupons by photocopying, scanning or reprinting the original coupon. Consumers can also print multiple copies if the internet coupon vendor doesn't have technology in place to limit the number of prints by a consumer.

The primary impact of coupon copying is the potential for unbudgeted redemption liability. In addition, replicated coupons may not have the same print quality as the original offer. Replicated coupons may not move efficiently through the redemption process, resulting in a slowdown at the point of sale, reduced checker productivity, and hard-to-handle issues that add costs to the clearing process.

Replication of coupon offers isn't unique to print-at-home coupons. Direct mail, in-store, magazine and other types of coupons are also susceptible to replication using computer software, colour copiers and printers.

Coupon attributes manipulation

This applies to things like face values, expiration dates and bar codes, which can all be altered, and so it's important for marketers to select internet coupon providers, vendors and agencies that use technology to utilize strict controls to protect the integrity of the scheme against counterfeiting.

Unintentional distribution

This applies to things like e-mail, online forums and online auction sites, which all have the potential to reach a wider base than originally planned.

As a result, coupons other than those intended by the promoter could be introduced into the marketplace. It's critical to choose the right internet coupon solution, as unintentional distribution and/or changes in design could result in an increase in promotion liability, inconsistent or incorrect product messaging or targeting, deductions resulting from discrepancies between a retailer's expected coupon receivables and a manufacturer's authorized reimbursement, and decreased productivity at the point of sale.

Print quality and readability by point-of-sale scanners

Print quality can be compromised by the type of printer used by consumers, resulting in coupons that may scan incorrectly at the point of sale or the retailer or manufacturer clearing house, resulting in damage to consumer confidence, delays at the checkout, and hard-to-handle issues that add to the cost or time of the clearing process. It's therefore critical to employ software capable of the proper rendering of coupon bar codes.

Tracking coupon prints and redemptions

One of the big advantages of e-coupons is their ability to be quantified and evaluated. However, if reporting data aren't accurate or timely, or are ambiguous, the marketer is in danger of drawing false conclusions on the success of the campaign.

It's important to the successful ongoing management of the coupon promotion to use applications that can measure the prints taken by consumers and combine this with reliable redemption data.

Retailer acceptance

Understandably, major retailers want to accept only legitimate coupons and need to be confident that the promoter has taken all possible best-practice measures, as defined by the IPM, in the management of the promotion.

There are a number of coupon protection strategies that the marketer can employ in order to protect the integrity of the promotion, and these include:

- *Set rolling expiration dates.* Limit the amount of time consumers have to copy or manipulate the coupon by setting rolling expiration dates. For example, setting the rolling expiration date to 14 days means the expiration date printed on the coupon will be set to 14 days from the day the coupon is printed unless it encroaches on the final expiration date set, which may be sooner.

- *Print the consumer's name on the coupon.* Whenever possible, the consumer's name or other forms of identification should appear on the face of the coupon to deter misuse.

- *Include a legal warning.* Enhance security messaging and include a form of words recommended by the IPM, such as 'It may not be used against any other product as this would constitute a breach of the terms of this offer. Only one coupon may be used against each such retail purchase. No photocopies accepted. Coupon is not transferrable' or other such words.

- *Take additional precautions for 'free' coupons.* Marketers should take extra precautions when running 'free product' offers. Your coupon partner should advise you of the extra measures to be taken to protect against fraud.

- *Mark unapproved coupons 'void'.* For coupons that aren't ready for distribution or still in design mode, mark all coupons and especially their bar codes with the word 'void' or a similar marking to avoid the coupon being leaked prior to the promotion launch date.

The IPM also recommends coupon design and layout as well as other matters such as bar code scanning, and for further guidance marketers should check its website.

Intellectual property issues

Sometimes in a promotion a promoter may refer to third-party businesses and their products or services. If so care must be taken to avoid infringing their intellectual property rights (IPRs).

Some IP issues of particular importance relating to promotions are discussed below. For a full discussion of IP rights, see Chapters 3–4.

Copyright

A brand owner shouldn't copy or deal with unlawful copies of another party's copyright material, such as photographic images or illustrations belonging to that entity, without a licence to do so.

In contrast, copyright in works created by the brand owner's own employees in the course of their employment will be owned by the brand owner.

If materials are created outside the brand owner, the brand owner should always ensure that copyright in materials created by third parties on its behalf is assigned to it before the promotion is launched. In this regard a careful review of third parties' terms and conditions before commissioning any work is essential.

Copyright can subsist in more than just printed materials. Therefore, if a brand owner's promotion involves audiovisual materials then it should ensure that it also owns (or has a sufficient licence to exploit) the copyright in any films or sound recordings used in the promotion.

If the promotion is broadcast on television or radio, depending on the contractual terms agreed with the relevant broadcaster the brand owner may also be able to obtain ownership of the copyright in the broadcast itself.

As discussed in Chapter 3, copyright arises from the expression or recording of the ideas and concepts behind the promotion and not in those ideas and concepts themselves. Consequently, if a promoter formulates a new type of competition or marketing campaign it can't use copyright to prevent competitors from using that campaign or competition concept in their own promotions. However, the promoter can prevent competitors from using elements or all of its promotion or competition if it can show that a substantial part of the copyright work(s) it owns has been copied and/or that copies of its works have been issued to the public without its authority.

Confidential information

In order to protect the integrity of the promotion or competition the marketer should insist on complete confidentiality from all those working on the promotion prior to its launch. The best way to achieve this is to ensure that people with access to the promotion know that it's commercial in confidence and where appropriate have entered into a confidentiality agreement. This applies equally to the promoter's own employees as well as sales promotion agencies and other third parties it has a business relationship with.

Trademarks and passing off

As discussed in Chapter 3, a brand owner should avoid trademark infringement by seeking permission to use third-party trademarks in any promotional material. This approach applies whether those trademarks are well known and highly recognizable brands or less well known marks; infringement will be restrained by the courts whether or not the mark infringed is owned by a global brand owner or a small company trading only locally.

As a result, the marketer should carry out registered trademark clearance searches at an early stage in the promotion planning process. Conversely, consideration should also be given to applying for registered trademarks in respect of key elements of the promotion such as logos and images of any characters associated with the promotion.

A marketer must also ensure that its promotion is not so similar in look and feel to the promotion or branding of a third party that it causes confusion in the minds of potential participants, who are led mistakenly to think that both marketers are associated with each other. If such a misconception can be shown to have influenced those persons to participate in the promotion it may lead to a claim for passing off.

For example, a passing-off action could arise if a retailer is running a special promotional offer on a range of products made by another company and the brand owner's promotion leads participants into incorrectly believing that that company has officially endorsed its promotional campaign.

The following list is a useful reminder of the points contained in this and other chapters that apply to running successful sales and price promotions:

- Ensure that the sales and price promotion complies with relevant legislation and the CAP and BCAP Codes, depending on the type of media, together with any specific rules relating to certain activities, such as promotions aimed at children and young people.

- Confirm that contracts are in place with relevant third parties, for example suppliers of prizes, confirming the number and quality of goods and/or the owners of any IP rights featured in material, confirming the use of such rights.

- Check that all instructions, restrictions on entry and terms and conditions are brought prominently to the attention of all participants.

- Remember to obtain final approval for promotional mechanics and promotional copy from in-house compliance officers and/or legal advice before incurring production costs for the sales and price promotions.

- Ensure that the copy makes sense and will be easily understood by all participants.

- Check that the sales and price promotion is compliant with data protection controls (Chapter 6), best-practice codes (Chapter 4) and IP laws (Chapter 3) in order to resist legal challenges from competitors.

- Be aware that a binding contractual agreement may arise from the relationship with participants, so ensure that all promotional literature allows for substitute goods if necessary.

References and further reading

Websites

Advertising Standards Authority adjudications [accessed 28 June 2011] http://www.asa.org.uk

CAP Code Clearance Guidance website [accessed 27 June 2011] http://www.copyadvice.org.uk

Charities Aid Foundation [accessed 28 June 2011] http://www.cafonline.org

Distance Selling Regulations [accessed 28 June 2011] http://www.bis.gov.uk/policies/consumer-issues/buying-and-selling/distance-selling

Institute of Promotional Marketing [accessed 28 June 2011] http://www.theipm.org.uk

Marketing Law [accessed 28 June 2011] http://www.marketinglaw.co.uk

The Times law site [accessed 25 June 2011] http://www.thetimes.co.uk/law

Books

Circus, P (2007) *Sales Promotion and Direct Marketing Law*, Tottel Publishing, Haywards Heath

DTI (2006) *A Guide for Businesses on Distance Selling*, Office of Fair Trading, London

Kolah, A (2002) *Essential Law for Marketers*, Butterworth-Heinemann, Oxford

Kolah, A (2005) *Maximising the Value of Licensing and Merchandising*, Electric Word, London

Kolah, A (2013) *High Impact Marketing that Gets Results*, Kogan Page, London

Mullin, R (2010) *Sales Promotion*, 5th edn, Kogan Page, London

Ofcom (2010) *The Communications Market*, Ofcom, London

"It's your lucky day!"

Prize promotions and incentives

Introduction

One of the most engaging and powerful aspects of business-to-consumer (B2C) and business-to-business (B2B) customer marketing and communications is prize promotions and incentives. They are also some of the most difficult things to get right, requiring an understanding of a web of complex competition, data protection and media laws and regulations. However, because they are complex tactics shouldn't mean you can't employ them in order to achieve powerful results.

Part of the reason why prize promotions and incentives have gained in popularity over the past decade is that marketers have been adjusting to a new era of deep customer engagement. Marketers have tacked on new functions, such as social media management, altered processes to better integrate advertising campaigns online, on television and in print and added staff with web expertise to manage the explosion of digital customer data. Yet this still isn't sufficient to keep pace with changing consumer behaviour.

As discussed in Guru in a Bottle® *High Impact Marketing that Gets Results,* to truly engage customers for whom 'push' advertising is increasingly irrelevant, brand owners and organizations must do much more outside of the confines of traditional marketing. At the end of the day, customers and clients no longer separate marketing from the product – it is the product! They don't separate marketing from their in-store or online experience – it is the experience! And in the era of engagement, marketing is the company or enterprise.

According to Jeremy Stern, Managing Director of PromoVeritas, one of the UK's leading promotions specialists, many marketing agencies are also lagging behind changes in consumer behaviour that has helped to make prize promotions and incentives so popular not just in the UK but all over the world. Jeremy Stern advises:

> *As a communications company, you get involved with consumer and trade interactions – often they involve a reward. These are 'promotions' and need to be run correctly and compliantly. B2B, social media, online or offline, text or post, it makes no difference. Getting it right requires an understanding of statutory and regulatory frameworks, self-regulation policies, and best practice as defined by certain trade bodies as well as embedding a company's ethics and policies in the running of such promotions.*

As discussed in Chapter 8, there are several key characteristics that distinguish prize promotions and incentives from sales or price promotions.

'A far bigger benefit can be given in a prize promotion than in a promotion where the benefit is available to everyone who participates,' observes Roddy Mullin, a marketing expert in this area.

> *There's a difficult balance to be struck in writing about prize promotions. On one hand, they are staggeringly successful. The chance to win a car, a holiday, or a substantial sum of money at little or no cost is permanently attractive to consumers. Reader's Digest has built its business on this basis, giving away nearly £3 million a year. On the other hand, they are a legal minefield. Too much stress on legal niceties can lead promoters to regard it as a no-go area. Too much stress on promotional effectiveness can lead promoters to forget the need for caution. Provided there's no change to the purchase price then a prize promotion is likely to be OK.*

The most common types of prize promotions are:

- prize draws;
- competitions;
- free draws;

- instant wins; and
- games.

As discussed in this chapter, each of these types of prize promotion is distinct in legal terms, is subject to different legal and code of practice restrictions, and offers different mechanisms for winning the prize (Table 9.1).

Table 9.1 Similarities and differences between typical promotional marketing tactics

Type of promotion	Characteristic
Competitions	Offer prizes for the successful exercise of a significant degree of mental or physical skill or judgment. Participants may be required to pay or make a purchase to enter.
Free draws	Make available prizes by distribution of random chances. No skill or judgment is always involved, and participants can be asked to pay or make a purchase to enter, provided the product hasn't been increased in price as a result.
Instant wins	Offer prizes by distributing a predetermined number of winning tickets. Consumers know instantly whether they have won or lost. No skill or judgment is involved, and consumers can't be asked to pay or make a purchase to enter.
Games	Forms of free draw or instant win that give the appearance of requiring skill but in fact rely on probability. They can be based on brand-name games such as Monopoly® or Trivial Pursuit® or generic games such as snakes and ladders. Because no significant degree of skill or judgment is called for, no purchase or payment can be required in order to enter.

As can be seen from Table 9.1, the distinctions aren't immediately obvious and, as new formats are created, the boundary lines between each of these marketing tactics are likely to become blurred even further.

The popularity of Facebook for running promotions is dealt with separately (see 'Facebook's promotions guidelines' later in this chapter).

As a rule of thumb, lotteries are a no-go area for commercial promoters. The only exceptions are small-scale lotteries held at a single event, such as a fundraising dinner, with non-cash prizes below £50 in total value and where the proceeds are entirely donated to charity.

Prize draws and lotteries

The National Lottery

The Committee of Advertising Practice (CAP) Sales Promotion Codes apply to advertisements for the National Lottery. In particular, they mustn't be likely to appeal to anyone less than 18 years of age by reflecting or being associated with youth culture.

The law on lotteries changed in September 2007 in the UK when the sections of the Gambling Act 2005 that regulate lotteries and prize competitions came into force. A separate regime applies in Northern Ireland, and qualified legal advice needs to be sought for running promotions in this part of the UK.

Other lotteries

Under the Gambling Act 2005, most types of lotteries are illegal in the UK except for the National Lottery and small, private, society and local authority lotteries.

Legal lotteries will generally require a licence, although there are exceptions, for example for small raffles. More guidance about these types of lotteries can be found on the Gambling Commission's website. The Gambling Commission is responsible for regulating gambling and betting under the Gambling Act 2005, which includes lotteries.

Definition of a lottery

The Gambling Act 2005 states that the three elements of a lottery are:

- the requirement to pay to participate;
- the allocation of prizes; and
- the determination of winners by chance.

Under the Gambling Act 2005 there are two types of lottery: simple lotteries, where prizes are allocated wholly by chance; and complex lotteries, where prizes are allocated by a series of processes, the first of which relies wholly on chance.

A random prize draw isn't a lottery if participants don't have to pay to enter. Such a prize draw is exempt from statutory control.

What is payment?

For the purposes of lotteries regulated under the Gambling Act 2005, payment includes:

- the payment of money, which would include a requirement to pay to collect the prize, although it would be acceptable to charge normal rates for delivery or, for example, to charge for road tax and insurance for a prize car;
- transferring money's worth; and
- paying for goods and services at a price or rate that reflects the opportunity to take part in an arrangement under which the participant might win a prize.

In light of the above, it's apparent that it's lawful to run a promotion whereby a consumer has to buy a product provided the price of the product isn't higher than it otherwise would have been. It's not permissible for a marketer to inflate the price of the item to cover the cost of the promotion.

It doesn't matter to whom the payment is made or who benefits from the payment. For example, paying for an entry fee that is then sent to the marketer may still be covered by the legislation.

However, Schedule 2 of the Gambling Act 2005 states that normal-rate telephone calls and postage (normal first- and second-class rates without special arrangements for delivery) don't constitute payment. On the other hand, a premium-rate phone call could constitute a payment.

The provision of personal data, for example as a result of filling out an online survey, isn't likely to be considered payment, although it would depend on whether the request for data was proportionate and whether the information was being obtained in circumstances where the marketer intended to transfer it or sell it to third parties, in which case a monetary value could be placed on this and it would then be considered 'payment'.

Free entry routes

Free entry routes won't be needed as frequently as in the past since the enactment of the Gambling Act 2005. However, it's still relevant in Northern Ireland and if premium-rate telephone lines are used as a means of entry to the promotion. In this latter situation, a free method of entry also needs to be provided and properly publicized, including entry via normal post and telephone calls. A free entry route must be no less convenient than a paid entry route.

In relation to online entry, the Gambling Commission takes the view that many people don't have access to the internet at home and so entering online is not free in all contexts. It appears that online promotions are acceptable, but a problem might exist where the main route to entry is via premium-rate calls or text messages, with the alternative being entering online.

If people have to visit their local library to access the web, they are more likely to call the premium-rate number. Therefore the Commission wouldn't consider the online entry a genuine no-purchase route, especially where the need for an immediate response was emphasized to entrants or the promotion was run only for a short period, such as in the evening when libraries are closed.

The Gambling Commission considers that participants who wish to use internet entry need at least three working days to do so, and the fact that participants may enter online must be made clear. If a marketer is in doubt about whether online entry meets the requirements, it should offer telephone or postal entry at normal rates.

Organizers also need to bear in mind that a promotional free draw will involve payment and be an illegal lottery if a charge is made to find out whether a prize has been won or to take delivery of that prize.

It's not clear what the Gambling Commission's view would be on, for example, prize holidays where travel to a UK airport isn't included and the winner has to pay that cost. Common sense would say that, as long as this is made clear to entrants before they go to the trouble of entering, it would be acceptable, as they may then choose not to enter.

A purchase-linked prize draw is permissible provided the price to be paid doesn't reflect the opportunity to win a prize; it doesn't matter how low the charge is, as the test is whether it involves any amount that can be regarded as a 'participation fee'.

This is a tricky legal area for promotions off the back of a new product launch, as there's no previous price to base the assessment on. Problems can also occur where there's a mixture of free entry and purchase linked to a prize draw. In cases of a new product, marketers should keep the price of the new product the same after the promotion, as otherwise it will be deemed that there's a payment to enter the prize draw.

Why use a free draw rather than a competition?

There are several reasons for issuing prizes at random to people who may never be customers:

- Free draws can be highly effective in generating interest, awareness and participation. In particular, free draws are a strong traffic builder for retailers and a proven readership builder for newspapers. The absence of tie-breakers means that free draws attract up to 20 times as many participants as do competitions.

- They are easy for the marketer to administer, are easy for consumers to enter, involve a fixed prize fund and are a quick and easy way of building a customer and prospect database.

- They can involve an implicit encouragement to purchase. This needs to be treated carefully. Newspapers invariably state (as they are required to) that consumers can check their tickets without buying the newspaper; petrol stations invariably state (as they are required to) that tickets are issued to all those who visit the petrol station, not just those who buy petrol. This is the 'plain paper entry' route. In practice, between 80 and 90 per cent of those who enter also make a purchase.

- They allow substantial opportunities for creative marketing!
Compared with competitions, which are the main alternative for those marketers seeking a mechanic with fixed costs, free draws require fewer rules and don't require questions but do allow free rein for games of every kind.

How prize draws work

For B2C prize draws, all you need to do is have a pile of cards on which entrants can write their personal details, a box for them to make their entries and a declared date on which the winner will be drawn from the box.

For B2B prize draws, it's even simpler – just provide a box into which entrants can drop their business cards. When you make the draw, it's important that it is done by an independent person and that it's done with witnesses so it's seen to be independent.

These type of 'out of the hat' prize draws are regularly used by retailers, motor dealers, and companies exhibiting at trade shows as a traffic builder and as a way of capturing data. Provided that the guidelines in the CAP Code are followed (see Chapter 4), these prize draws should be easy to execute as part of the marketing campaign. The other advantage is that they are one of the fastest and simplest forms of promotion to organize.

An alternative free prize draw is to issue consumers with a card printed with a unique set of random numbers. These numbers are openly displayed, not uncovered by opening a flap or scratching off a layer. The winning numbers are announced separately – on a board in a shop or in the pages of a newspaper. Consumers have to check the winning numbers against the number of their card and, if there's a match, they need to contact the promoter to claim the prize. 'Most newspaper cards operate in this way, with winning numbers displayed daily in the newspaper. There is a clear advantage of a double hit – first obtain the card and then check the winning numbers, although to be legal there mustn't be a cost to consumers for checking the winning numbers,' says Roddy Mullin.

Predetermined number cards are a variant on the random number system. Each card is uniquely numbered but, instead of the winning numbers being announced for consumers to check, cards must be returned to the promoter to be matched against predetermined winning numbers. This prize draw format is used by *Reader's Digest* and other direct mail operators, very often because it encourages consumers to respond to direct mail.

For further discussion on direct marketing, refer to Guru in a Bottle® *High Impact Marketing that Gets Results*.

A further alternative method is to distribute a series of different cards that have to be matched together to create a set. Only a limited number of the cards needed to complete the set are distributed. Once the set is complete, the win is instant. Petrol stations have often used this format to good effect with matching halves of banknotes, for example. The left-hand halves were plentiful but the right-hand halves were very rare.

These are some of the straightforward free draws, but such mechanics are also becoming increasingly sophisticated, for example an instant-win card that's also (when mailed in) a predetermined number card and provides an opportunity to match and complete a set. Numbers can be replaced by symbols or words and a whole range of other variants.

Roddy Mullin warns that marketers need to be circumspect in order to avoid fraud and ensure an equitable distribution of winning tickets:

> *You need to use a security printer to make sure that you don't have multiple winning tickets in circulation. A means of verifying the winning ticket via hidden but unique marks is also advisable. You need to carefully seed the winning tickets so that they don't all turn up in the same outlet at the same time. Also, you need to ensure that there's no one involved with the distribution of winning tickets who can take advantage of their knowledge. A good way of doing this is to ask an independent person to do the seeding. That way, you're protected if you are publicly accused of fixing the scheme.*

Competitions

If a promotion is to qualify as a prize competition, the winner must be determined by judgment, skill or knowledge.

There are many forms of competition. The main ones are:

- Order of merit: 'List the following five items in order of importance.'
- Complete a slogan: 'Complete this sentence in no more than 10 words.'
- Question plus slogan: 'Answer these five questions and complete this sentence in no more than 10 words.'
- Spot the difference: 'Identify 12 differences between photographs A and B.'
- Estimate: 'Estimate how many packs of this product will fit inside this car.'
- Spot the ball: 'Mark with an "X" where the ball is on this photograph.'
- Identify: 'Identify these famous people from the photographs of their eyes.'
- Be creative: 'Draw a picture, take a photograph or write a short story.'
- Treasure hunt: 'Use the clues to find the hidden treasure.'

By far the most common type of competition is the question-plus-slogan variety. It's the easiest to fit into the limited space available to communicate most competitions and the easiest to explain and judge. The benefit over a slogan-only competition is that the questions filter the number of slogans that have to be judged.

Skill-based competitions

Genuine prize competitions are permitted, even if they charge a premium for entry. A process won't be treated as relying wholly on chance – that is, it won't be considered to be a lottery – if it contains a requirement to exercise skill and judgment or knowledge that is reasonably likely to: prevent a significant proportion of people who take part from receiving a prize; or prevent a significant proportion of people who wish to take part from doing so. If either of these barriers to entry or success can be shown, the process won't be deemed to rely wholly on chance and the arrangement won't be a lottery.

A skills-based competition could be a crossword or a number puzzle, for example. You need to make sure that the skills-based competition isn't too easy and is sufficiently difficult. This is a grey area! The meaning of the words 'significant proportion' in the Gambling Act 2005 is important in order to distinguish between a competition and a lottery.

The Gambling Commission has issued limited non-binding guidance that what's 'significant' will depend on the context and the facts of the promotion, and it will take the term's ordinary, natural meaning. It's still unclear how you prove this – but the onus is on the marketer, and you should keep material and research documentation demonstrating you've taken steps to estimate the likely proportion of potential or actual participants who are or will be eliminated by the skill element. Where marketers seek to rely on the argument that significant proportions of potential entrants have been deterred, the Gambling Commission considers that it won't be sufficient to compare numbers of entrants with, for example, the audience figures for the television programmes or the readership figures for the newspaper carrying the competition.

The Gambling Commission will require evidence of the propensity of that audience to enter such competitions – so it's a higher burden of proof that's required. This issue is most likely to arise where entry is via premium-rate phone numbers.

The Gambling Commission takes the view that it will be obvious in most cases whether or not the competition requires a sufficient level of skill. It provides the example of a crossword puzzle, where entrants have to solve a large number of clues and where only fully completed entries are submitted. This will qualify as a prize competition even if those who successfully complete the puzzle are subsequently entered into a draw to pick the winner.

At the other extreme, there are many competitions that ask just one simple question, to which the answer will be widely and commonly known or which may be easy to find in the accompanying material. The Gambling Commission takes the view that such competitions would be illegal because they would constitute a lottery.

The Gambling Commission won't generally take action where a competition uses a multiple-answer format provided that:

- there are sufficient plausible alternative answers;
- the question is relevant to the context in which the competition is offered;
- the correct answer is not obviously given close to the question; and
- 'joke' answers are avoided.

It's important to ensure that competitions are run properly with independent judges and clear judging criteria. The Advertising Standards Authority (ASA) has upheld complaints where it has considered that competitions haven't been run fairly.

Bradford & Bingley plc (2008)

An internet advertisement by Bradford & Bingley building society was headlined 'Tell me about the "Property Woman of the Year" Awards.' The advertisement stated: 'Judging will be based on your financial nous, feedback from your tenants, how long it took to build your business, how you run it, and your personal drive and determination to succeed. We don't want much do we?'

The complainant, who was shortlisted for her region in that tier of the competition but didn't win, challenged whether the competition had been properly administered. She argued to the ASA that she hadn't been asked to provide any evidence that might objectively be compared with that of other competitors and believed the regional winners may have been chosen without verification.

The building society said it took its responsibilities under the CAP Code very seriously and had appointed a PR firm to advise on the best way to structure and promote its competition. It said the competition was advertised on its website, via a news release, and independently via the National Landlords Association's e-mail alert, and was open to any woman with a buy-to-let property, regardless of whether or not she held mortgages with the society.

The building society also said it had appointed a panel of three expert judges, including for the regional heats, and ensured some of them were independent of the firm. It also pointed to a full set of legal terms and conditions accessible from the website, and these set out the criteria on which competition entrants would be judged: financial acumen, how long it had taken to build up their business, how they ran their business including property conditions, and their personal drive and enthusiasm.

In total, 50 entries received were first checked in-house to ensure entrants had filled out the forms correctly and provided sufficient information. The next stage was that the entries from all those shortlisted in the regional heats were submitted to the judges, who were asked to score them based on criteria that distilled those set out in the competition rules into four easy-to-score categories: 'overcoming personal obstacles', 'clear business strategy explained', 'taking some form of risk in their venture' and 'overall success (evidence of making a reasonable profit on a property portfolio)'. The competition judges awarded scores of between one and five for each category, with five being the highest.

At stage two of the competition, once the regional shortlisted candidates had been scored and winners chosen for each region, the firm's PR company contacted the tenants of the regional winners to check their credibility and to obtain views on matters such as property upkeep.

A team from the building society also checked semi-finalists on their Mortgage Express database (MX) to establish if the accounts they held were properly conducted. If any of the regional winners didn't have properties with the society, then a Land Registry search was made. This information was then cross-checked by the PR company. Further information was then cross-referenced with the scores the judges had previously given to the eight semi-finalists, in order to arrive at the overall winner.

In evidence to the ASA, the building society said it accepted that whilst verification checks were carried out on semi-finalists (winners of the regional heats) they weren't carried out on all applicants, but said it believed this was a reasonable and proportionate way to have administered the competition.

They sent judges packs for the two independent judges, but not for the third in-house judge, detailing the scores given by them to those entrants shortlisted in the regional heats of the competition, which led to the choice of regional winners. One of the judges had destroyed her notes after the final, as she hadn't foreseen the need to keep them. However, the PR company's records of all three of the judges' scorings on the semi-finalists for the regional heats were submitted to the ASA adjudication panel.

The ASA found in favour of the complainant, as the building society hadn't administered the promotion according to the criteria stated in the advertisement and thereby hadn't dealt fairly with entrants throughout all stages of the competition.

A key finding against the building society was that the regional shortlists put before the judges were drawn from all entries in-house and that the process and criteria for regional shortlisting were unclear. It also found that the four scoring categories given to the judges didn't map clearly on to the criteria set out in the advertisement. For example, the advertisement didn't mention 'overcoming personal obstacles' or 'taking some form of risk in their venture' as judging criteria. In addition, 'feedback from your tenants' was a criterion that had been applied only to the regional winners to determine the overall winner from amongst them, and the ASA considered that the advertisement gave the misleading impression this criterion would be applied across the board and so the advertisement breached the CAP Code as it applied to promotions. The building society was warned to ensure the advertised judging procedures and criteria for its competitions matched those applied in practice in any future competitions.

How competitions work

Competitions tend to have a low level of entry. For example, over 0.5 per cent of opportunities to participate would be considered a good turnout! Competitions can be effective in creating awareness, interest and impact at the point of sale well beyond the actual number of entrants. These are legitimate sales promotion objectives, and they don't have a bearing on sales. On the other hand, a competition can be a useful way of drawing attention to a product's benefits and features, which can result in incremental sales, for example cooking utensils.

Research shows that the level of response to competitions is strongly influenced by the prizes on offer. Best practice is to fix the budget available from the beginning of the competition. There are also different schools of thought with respect to the nature of the prize on offer – a large one or several smaller ones. If the structure is too complicated, this will have the effect of dissipating the impact of the competition and increasing costs – something that marketers should avoid.

The size of the prize is also a factor to be carefully considered when designing a competition. The general rule of thumb is that holidays and cars are always top of the list of goodies because everyone likes them. It's sensible to add in the rules of the competition that there's no cash alternative for the prize (you're likely to have got this prize at a discount of its face value) and, if this is not stated, it can become problematical if demands made for a cash alternative are rejected, as the promoter in those cases can look unreasonable and attract negative publicity.

It's worth bearing in mind that a large number of entries is a reasonable test of attractiveness of a competition but not of its promotional effectiveness. The number of entries can be quite unrelated to the promotional objectives. Attracting entries depends on presenting the competition in the most compelling way to the desired audience and customer segments.

Prediction competitions

These are generally permitted if:

- no payment or purchase is required; or
- purchase is required but the product is sold at the 'normal' price; or
- payment or purchase is required but a compliant alternative entry route is available.

If the competition doesn't comply with any of the above, then it's likely to be deemed as 'betting' as defined by the Gambling Act 2005. The provisions under the Act are designed to ensure that prediction competitions, such as fantasy football games, are regulated as betting products. As a result these may only be offered under a relevant betting licence.

Alternative entry routes

In order to keep on the right side of the Gambling Act 2005, marketers must ensure that:

- each eligible individual has the option to participate by 'sending a communication' rather than paying;
- the communication is ordinary post or 'another method of communication which is neither more expensive nor less convenient than entering... by paying';
- the choice of alternative entry is publicized so as to be 'likely to come to the attention of each individual who proposes to participate'; and
- the prize allocation system 'does not differentiate between those who participate by paying and those who participate by sending a communication'.

Does the provision of data constitute payment?

An issue that the Gambling Commission had to take a view on was whether the provision of personal data constitutes 'money's worth'. According to news reports, there's a growing phenomenon of consumers selling their personal data to companies in order to make money from marketers! The Gambling Commission's view is that the provision of personal data won't constitute 'payment' provided the questions asked of entrants are proportionate. Where the situation would fall foul of the Gambling Act 2005 is where a large amount of data is required before entry to the competition draw takes place and particularly where data are obtained by the promoter in circumstances where it intends to sell them to third parties.

Prizes

Prize winners should receive their prizes within 30 days of the draw date or be told when they'll receive their prizes if later than 30 days after the closing date.

For instant-win promotions, participants should receive their winnings at once or should know immediately what they have won and how to claim without delay, unreasonable costs or administrative barriers. Instant-win tickets, tokens or numbers should be awarded on a fair and random basis, and verification should take the form of an independently audited statement that all prizes have been distributed, or made available for distribution, in that manner.

Marketers should consult the CAP Code for more advice about administering prize promotions and consider the following additional points when administering a prize promotion:

- Prizes should be awarded in accordance with the laws of chance and, unless winners are selected by a computer process that produces verifiably random results, by an independent person or under the supervision of an independent person.

- Each entry should carry an equal chance of winning the prize, ie the draw must be made from all the entries. It's not lawful to select an entry from a particular category of entrant and make the draw from there.

- Winners should be informed individually, rather than relying on their claiming the prize following publication of a list of winners.

- Participants must be able to retain conditions or easily access them throughout the promotion. With online competitions and draws, the winners should be able to retain and print off the prize draw rules for their records. It's good practice to ensure the rules have a print-friendly format.

Holidays as prizes

If a marketer wishes to award holidays as prizes, it's good practice to:

- Describe the prize as fully as possible to avoid disappointment. This could include details such as the quality of hotel, type of room, facilities, full board or half-board, and the number of nights in the resort.

- Fully explain any costs that the winner must bear, such as transport to and from airports or insurance.

- Explain any other factors that may influence a person's decision to enter the competition, for example that the hotel is unsuitable for people with disabilities, the holiday can be taken only within a limited time period or there are excluded dates such as school holidays or bank holidays.

- Make it clear that the responsibility for the holiday will lie with carriers or hotels. However, this won't reduce the marketer's duty to check partners such as travel agents or tour operators to ensure that they are reliable and won't let the winner down.

The Blue Elephant Restaurant (2009)

An online competition, to win a holiday to Thailand, stated: 'BLUE ELEPHANT Cocktail Competition 2009. Create your own unique cocktail with 'Mekhong' the original Thai spirit to win a Royal Orchid Holiday package to Thailand... PRIZE: THE WINNER – One Royal Orchid Holiday package to Thailand in a luxury 5 star hotel. Complimentary one course cooking class at Blue Elephant Cooking School. Complimentary dinner for two at the Blue Elephant in Bangkok... RULES: All the recipes that comply with the conditions of the competition are to be registered into the contest... The finals will be held at Blue Elephant restaurant.'

The winner of the first prize complained to the ASA claiming that the competition was misleading, because it didn't make clear the significant terms and conditions attached to the prize. The argument with the restaurant owners was around the holiday package plus a cooking class and dinner at the Blue Elephant restaurant in Bangkok for two.

The competition details stated the complimentary dinner was 'for two', and there were no terms and conditions stating the holiday package was for only one person. However, when the winner tried to arrange to receive her prize she found out that the only element of the prize that was for two people was dinner at the Blue Elephant restaurant in Bangkok. She was also told at that point that she would have to pay all airport taxes and surcharges for the flight, and the transfer from the airport in Phuket to the hotel, 100 kilometres away, which wasn't included in the prize. In addition, she was told she would have to bear the cost of travelling from her hotel in Phuket to dinner at the Blue Elephant restaurant in Bangkok, 500 miles away, and the only dates she could take the holiday were between May and September 2009.

Although the ASA conceded that the holiday package and cookery class were for one person and the dinner was for two people, it did uphold the complaint in that there were grounds for disappointment, failure to make clear the significant costs the prize winner had to pay and the restriction on the dates the winner could take the holiday.

The CAP Code clearly states that promotions should specify clearly, before or at the time of entry, how to participate, including significant conditions and costs, and any other major factors reasonably likely to influence consumers' decisions or understanding about the promotion. The CAP Code also stipulates that participants should be able to retain the conditions or have easy access to them throughout the promotion, and advertisements for promotions should specify all the significant conditions that were applicable.

The ASA panel considered the airport taxes and surcharges, airport transfers and travel from the hotel in Phuket to Bangkok for the meal as significant costs, and the restriction in the time of year was deemed to be a significant condition. It was notable that the online competition details made no mention of any of those conditions or costs, and also no terms and conditions were available for entrants to access at the time of entering the competition or at any subsequent point.

Terms and conditions

Clear and unambiguous terms and conditions are core to a competition's success. If marketing space restrictions mean that it's not possible to include all the terms within the body of the communication, then best industry practice is to include those terms that have a material bearing on whether a contestant decides to take part. Potential entrants can be directed to a different source for the rest of the terms, such as the company's website.

Some terms must be brought to participants' attention before they either buy the relevant product or enter the competition or draw.

Other points that should be considered for inclusion are whether:

- offers are subject to availability (see also the Consumer Protection from Unfair Trading Regulations 2008);
- a cash alternative to the prize is available;
- the winners are to appear in post-competition PR activities;
- the company or entrant owns the copyright in entries;
- entries will be returned;
- offers are available in conjunction with other offers;
- entry forms must be original and undamaged; and
- the company accepts no liability for entries that aren't submitted on time or in full, such as damaged entry forms or corrupted web pages.

It's also important to warn participants, if appropriate, that the judge's decision is final and that no correspondence will be entered into.

A promoter must explain how entries will be judged. What many marketers forget to recognize is that the terms and conditions of the prize draws and competitions create a contract between the promoter and the individual entrant. So a big question to ask is whether you have done enough to bring the terms and conditions to the notice and attention of the entrant

- Make sure the rules and the creative copy don't contradict each other.
- Conditions must be brought to the notice of the party to be bound before or at the time the contract is made.
- As the Blue Elephant case illustrates so well, significant conditions need to be provided before purchase or, if no purchase is required, before or at the time of entry or application in order to comply with the CAP Code.

Facebook's promotions guidelines

At the time of writing, social network giant Facebook has updated its promotions guidelines, which govern all communication about or administration of any contest, competition, sweepstake or other promotion anywhere in the world.

The big caveat here is that you need to comply with the relevant regulations within the jurisdiction in which you're running the prize promotion or competition, such as those provided by the ASA under the CAP Code, as well as Facebook's own 'internal' rules.

Owing to the increasing popularity of running prize promotions on Facebook, these changes are a 'must know' for marketers and should be constantly checked, as Facebook is likely to amend them in the future.

The 'internal' Facebook rules cover any operation of any element of the promotion, such as collecting entries, conducting a drawing, judging entries, notifying winners, or promoting, advertising or referencing a promotion in any way on Facebook, for example in advertisements, on a Facebook page or in a wall post. These rules apply to promotions that include a prize of monetary value and a winner determined on the basis of skill and those promotions based on chance.

The guidelines are contractually binding on all those using the social media site for the purposes of a promotion.

The likely consequences of breaking these 'internal' rules could include the summary removal from the Facebook website of any materials relating to the promotion in question or the disabling of the relevant page and the complete disabling of the marketer's account. Facebook makes it clear that its decision on whether its 'internal' guidelines have been violated is at its sole discretion. So it pays to play the game, so to speak!

It must also be borne in mind that even if a promotion is permissible under the Facebook guidelines this is no guarantee of lawfulness. The promotion may be contrary to other local laws or codes, so these should always be checked before embarking on a promotion on Facebook. Marketers should also comply with other Facebook terms and conditions, including the Facebook statement of rights and responsibilities and the Facebook advertisement guidelines.

The main 'internal' Facebook rules are:

- Promotions must include a complete release of Facebook by each entrant.
- Promotion must include an acknowledgement that the promotion is in no way sponsored, endorsed, administered or associated with Facebook.
- Facebook features or functionality can't be used as a promotion's registration or entry mechanism; for example, the act of liking a page or checking into a place can't automatically register or enter a promotion participant.
- You mustn't condition entry on the entrant liking a wall post or commenting on or uploading a photo on a wall.
- You mustn't use Facebook features or functionality, such as the 'like' button, as a voting mechanism for a promotion.
- You must not notify winners through Facebook.
- You mustn't use Facebook's name, trademarks or other intellectual property in connection with the promotion or mention the brand in the rules except in order to comply with the first two obligations above.

Consumer Protection from Unfair Trading Regulations 2008

The rules that affect prize promotions and incentives such as the CAP Code must also be read in conjunction with the law as it applies to unfair commercial practices. Under the Consumer Protection from Unfair Trading Regulations 2008, commercial practices will always be considered unfair where the promoter: claims to offer a competition or prize promotion without awarding the prizes described or a reasonable equivalent; and creates a false impression that the consumer has already won, will win or will on doing a particular act win a prize or other benefit when in fact there's no prize or benefit and extracts money from the consumer in relation to claiming the fictitious prize.

Under the Regulations 2008, a practice is an 'unfair commercial practice' if the practice contravenes the requirements of professional diligence. This is defined as a standard of special skill and care that a trader may reasonably be expected to exercise towards consumers, which is commensurate with either: honest market practice; or the general principle of good faith in the trader's field of activity.

Enforcement

Office of Fair Trading *v* Purely Creative Ltd and others (2011)

In order to be legal, a scratch card promotion must comply with certain hygiene factors:

- It needs to have a clearly identified minimal cost, no part of which reaches the promoter's pocket and which is de minimis in comparison to the value of the prize won, and should be unlikely to constitute a misleading or aggressive commercial practice.

- A requirement for payment, all or part of which the trader receives and uses to offset the cost of both the acquisition and the delivery of the prize, may create a misleading impression that a prize has been won, even if its value to the consumer substantially exceeds the cost of claiming it (for example, the consumer has bought the item, not won it).

The 'average consumer' is reasonably well informed, observant and circumspect, not ignorant, careless or hasty, and may not have read the entirety of the promotion small print. The test applied in this case was to consider the combined effect of misleading acts and omissions and then consider whether it would cause the average consumer's transactional decision.

Non-legal issues to consider with prize draws and competitions

A new breed of 'professional entrant' to competitions and prize draws in the UK threatens to affect tens of thousands of marketing campaigns unless action is taken now by promoters, warns Jeremy Stern. As a result of a squeeze on household incomes, coupled with the increasing cost of living, rising inflation and the 20 per cent VAT rate, the number of people seeking tax-free 'money for nothing' is set to explode.

Research by PromoVeritas shows that some 'professional compers' make on average at least 100 entries a week and will often have 10–20 mobile SIM cards to make it easier to enter multiple times for 'text to win'-type promotions. They also operate in syndicates, sharing entry forms, and group-buying promotional packs and tokens.

Some professional compers even resort to using false names and fake e-mails to improve their chances of winning, with the result that their actions make it increasingly difficult for marketers to pick bona fide winners or to get a return on investment from such marketing activities, which are frequently run to create a valuable database of future customers.

'And that's just the tip of the iceberg!' warns Jeremy Stern.

In the past, marketers would judge the success of a promotion by the numbers of entries their promotions would attract. Today, this is an increasingly irrelevant measure as it could include a flood of entries from 'hardcore compers' who are just out to win anything and everything and by whatever means is available to them.

Few brand owners or promotions agencies are aware of their techniques and even fewer seek to effectively guard against them, leading to a massive waste of time and budget with no corresponding spike in sales. We know of individuals who win prizes on an almost daily basis, most of which are then sold on eBay, which helps to fund their habit.

There are now a number of very popular subscriber-funded magazines and websites, such as Loquax.co.uk and Compersnews.com, that offer advice on how to win and list all available prize draws together with the answers to competitions and lists of prize-winning tie-breakers, which are often then reused to enter a current promotion!

But marketers are still falling down on compliance issues. Jeremy Stern observes:

Compared to other countries in Europe, we've a very liberal regulatory environment. We don't need government approval to run a draw or pay fees or taxes on the value of prizes as they do elsewhere. However, there's still a high level of ignorance amongst marketers on how to properly run the back end of their promotions and this creates weak spots in a marketing campaign with consequent risk to brand reputations and wasted budgets.

In summary, the following points should be observed:

- *General.* Review all statutory and non-statutory guidance, such as the CAP Codes.
- *Lotteries.* Does the event involve the distribution of prizes by chance to participants who have contributed by any means (in money or money's worth)? In some jurisdictions this can be an illegal lottery. To avoid this, ensure entry can be obtained without any form of financial contribution.
- *Competitions.* Ensure that the competition substantially involves some degree of skill to avoid categorization in some jurisdictions as an illegal lottery. In most countries, a competition is permitted, even where a purchase is required, if the competition is a true test of skill. Ensure that all relevant provisions of voluntary guidance have been complied with. Does any tie-breaker used require skill to solve or complete? This is necessary to avoid it being chance, which would classify the competition as an illegal lottery. Finally, are the terms of the competition clear and well publicized?
- *Prize draws.* Ensure that genuinely no contribution is necessary to enter the draw to avoid it being classified as an illegal lottery. You need to comply with the CAP Code.

References and further reading

Cases and judgments

Blue Elephant Restaurant, adjudication of the ASA (2009)
Bradford & Bingley plc, adjudication of the ASA (2008)
Office of Fair Trading *v* Purely Creative Ltd and others [2011] EWHC 106 (Ch)
Office of Fair Trading *v* Purely Creative Ltd and others [2011] WLR (D) 34

Websites

Compers magazines: http://www.Loquax.co.uk and Compersnews.com [accessed 14 June 2011]
Facebook promotion guidelines [accessed 14 June 2011] http://www.facebook.com/promotions_guidelines.php
Gambling Commission for legal regulations on running raffles, tombolas and sweepstakes [accessed 17 June 2011] http://www.gamblingcommission.gov.uk

Books

Circus, P (2007) *Sales Promotion and Direct Marketing Law*, Tottel Publishing, Haywards Heath
Kolah, A (2002) *Essential Law for Marketers*, Butterworth-Heinemann, Oxford
Kolah, A (2013) *High Impact Marketing that Gets Results*, Kogan Page, London
Mullin, R (2010) *Sales Promotion*, 5th edn, Kogan Page, London

"Let the Games commence!"

Sponsorship and hospitality

Introduction

You have to travel a long way back in history to find the roots of modern-day sponsorship and hospitality – in fact to Roman times! The idea of gladiators fighting to the death and of an amphitheatre where this could take place, watched by an enthusiastic audience, epitomizes the depths to which the Roman Empire was capable of sinking in 264 BC, the year of the first recorded gladiatorial event to be staged in public.

Yet to the Romans themselves the institution of the arena was one of the defining features of their civilization and, as we witnessed in the UK, it was a defining feature of the London 2012 Olympic Games too. The gladiatorial spectacle was staged by the Roman aristocracy, rather than the London Organising Committee of the Olympic Games (LOCOG), as a means of displaying their power and influence within the local community.

Advertisements for gladiatorial displays have survived at the ancient site of Pompeii, painted by professional sign-writers on house-fronts or on the walls of tombs clustered outside the city gates. The number of gladiators on display appeared to be the point of the exercise: the larger the number, the more generous the sponsor was perceived to be and the more glamorous the spectacle.

Most gladiators were slaves, owned by their sponsor and subjected to a rigorous training regime, sustained on a high-energy diet and receiving expert medical attention, as it was considered back then, to keep them in peak performance. Like today's athletes, football players and F1 racing drivers, those Roman slaves were an expensive investment by anyone's standards and not to be dispatched lightly.

Sponsorship has of course come a long way since then but has retained certain key features over the passage of time. For example, sponsorship is about making a lasting impression with an audience; it's an audacious way for a brand owner to stand head and shoulders above its rivals and can provide a point of differentiation and competitive advantage for its products and services that can't be achieved through advertising alone.

But unlike the situation in Roman times, when sponsorship was the preserve of the few, today there's a wide variety of sponsorship options so that it doesn't always have to be a fight to the death to get noticed.

Despite its scope and breadth, sponsorship isn't well understood compared with say advertising, although arguably sponsorship has been around a lot longer. Part of the reason is historical – most sponsoring organizations don't have a dedicated sponsorship department unless they're the size of an Olympic sponsor like Coca-Cola, Visa or McDonald's. As a result, 'sponsorship' has been added to the job specifications of many public relations, advertising, corporate communication, corporate affairs, human resources and sales and marketing professionals.

With the appropriate level of management expertise and resources in place, sponsorship and hospitality can deliver extremely powerful results, not just in terms of brand awareness but more importantly in helping to drive incremental sales.

However, it's not without its challenges. Sponsorship requires a high degree of technical competence compared with other forms of marketing communications. Tangible and intangible rights must be very carefully managed in order to extract the maximum value from the sponsorship property.

Understanding the legal framework around sponsorship and hospitality is therefore essential in getting the most from these activities and is the focus for the final chapter of this book.

Types of sponsorship

Typical sponsorship arrangements that can be entered into include:

- venue sponsorship;
- exclusive sponsorship;
- multi-sponsor format;
- secondary sponsorship;
- official supplier/partner status;
- personality sponsorship and endorsement;
- broadcast sponsorship;
- editorial sponsorship;
- advertiser-funded programming (AFP);
- community-linked sponsorship.

Venue sponsorship

Venue sponsorship is a relatively new development in the UK, although much more common in Europe and the United States. Notable examples in the UK include the Reebok Stadium in Bolton, Walkers Stadium in Leicester, Emirates Stadium in London, MEN Arena in Manchester and the former Millennium Dome, which is now the O2 Arena in the Docklands and recently used as a venue at the London 2012 Olympic Games.

In some cases, a venue sponsorship will form part of a naming rights deal, a hybrid of advertising and sponsorship rights where the sponsor's name is attached to the stadium or building. These rights sit on top of a pyramid of other tangible and intangible rights.

Exclusive sponsorship

The promotional value of being an exclusive team sponsor, such as Brit Insurance for the England cricket team and Shell for Ferrari F1, can be extremely powerful given the amount of broadcast media coverage each sport attracts.

In football, Barclays is the exclusive sponsor of the Premiership League, and this has opened up new communications opportunities with fans, customers and prospects on a scale that couldn't have been achieved in absence of the sponsorship investment.

Multi-sponsor format

A multi-sponsor format involves several sponsors benefiting from a basket of identical sponsorship rights or having different levels of sponsorship rights commensurate with the amount of sponsorship fees, benefits-in-kind and value-in-kind invested by the sponsor. Examples include the London 2012 Olympic Games, the FIFA World Cup and the FIA World Championships.

These types of sponsorship work particularly efficiently where a brand owner wants to reach a consumer audience on a global basis and relies heavily on broadcast coverage to do the job.

In the case of the Olympic Games, which doesn't permit any form of branding on athletes or hoardings within the line of camera view, sponsors must be creative in activating their sponsorship rights in other ways, such as on merchandise and at the point of sale within a retail environment.

For further discussion on best practice in this area, refer to Guru in a Bottle® *High Impact Marketing that Gets Results*.

From a rights holder's perspective, sponsorship clutter needs to be avoided. For example, the UEFA Champions League currently limits the number of its sponsors to six in order to deliver a higher level of media exposure for Heineken, PlayStation, MasterCard, UniCredit, Adidas and Ford of Europe.

Secondary sponsorship

This describes that status of a sponsor that provides a lower-level cash contribution that's counterbalanced by a larger benefit-in-kind or value-in-kind contribution to the rights holder. For example, Heineken enjoys primary sponsorship of the European Rugby Cup (the Heineken Cup), with a range of secondary sponsors, including FedEx, Amlin, Adidas and EDF, supporting the event.

Official supplier status

Under such an arrangement, an existing sponsor can receive enhanced rights as 'the official supplier' of a product or service category it wishes to associate with the event for marketing purposes. Alternatively, 'official supplier' status can be conferred on a brand owner that's not a full-blown sponsor of the event or property, indicating a lower level of commitment. For example, 'official supplier' status will almost always include category exclusivity, such as kit supply agreements entered into with sports brand owners like Nike and Adidas.

Personality sponsorship and endorsement

Many superstars have individual sponsorship deals in place where they endorse a particular product or service. For example, Hollywood actor George Clooney has a global endorsement deal with Nescafé for a range of its coffee products and coffee machines; and Mercedes-Benz has a multi-platform global marketing partnership with the 16-time Grand Slam champion Roger Federer, which covers the use of his image, personal appearances and product placement in a partnership that makes the tennis star a global ambassador for the brand.

Broadcast sponsorship

Broadcast sponsorship is typically the sponsorship of a television or radio broadcast on a commercial channel or the channel itself. In the case of the broadcast sponsorship of an event, the broadcast sponsor will enter into a separate arrangement with the broadcaster and may therefore be different to the event sponsor.

The event organizer may license the right to broadcast the event to a production company, which will then sub-licence these rights to broadcasters, or the rights holder may commission a producer but sell the broadcast rights itself directly to broadcasters.

Television and radio rights are commonly sold on an individual-territory basis and often before sponsors have been acquired. This is common in the case of television broadcasts, as a sponsor will usually make television exposure a condition of entering into any sponsorship agreement, such as UEFA's Champions League.

Broadcast sponsorship of a programme or series will confer on the sponsor rights to associate itself with each programme in 'bumpers' around the opening and closing credits, as well as in the advertisement breaks, and must comply with strict Ofcom regulations.

Editorial sponsorship

Editorial sponsorship is a bit like an 'advertorial', although the copy isn't generated by the brand owner but by a journalist working for the newspaper, magazine or website. For example, cricket correspondent Tom Collomosse's column in the *London Standard* is sponsored by Brit Insurance, although editorial control remains with the newspaper. The justification of this editorial sponsorship from the editor's point of view is that the money it generates covers the travel costs that allowed the reporter to attend the successful Ashes series in Australia in 2010, which he couldn't have done without the editorial sponsorship provided by Brit Insurance.

Advertiser-funded programming (AFP)

This form of sponsorship goes much deeper than simply an association with a particular programme. In AFP, the sponsor has input into the selection and treatment of the subject matter, although editorial control remains in the hands of the programme maker. An early example of this type of programming was 'Dinner Doctors', a six-part cooking series on Channel 5 aimed at young mothers, which included many recipes involving Heinz products but didn't involve any product placement, although this is now permissible under the new rules.

Community-linked sponsorship

To some extent this is corporate social responsibility (CSR) but under a different name. The nature of this type of sponsorship is different from that of other forms of sponsorship, because it satisfies a range of sponsor objectives that are more community rather than commercially based.

In this respect, a community-linked sponsorship, such as a brand owner funding a healthy eating programme in schools through educational literature, helps put a 'halo' around the brand rather than necessarily driving incremental sales, although the latter may occur as a result of the activity where messaging about healthy eating extends beyond the school gates and into the homes of families and can then influence their purchasing behaviour.

Rights and obligations of the sponsor

As already mentioned, sponsorship is a basket of tangible and intangible rights that the sponsor will need to activate in order to unlock the value of that sponsorship investment (Table 10.1).

Table 10.1   Tangible and intangible rights for a sponsor

Tangible rights	Description	Intangible rights	Description
Media exposure	This may be as a result of broadcast coverage of the sponsorship property and can be measured in terms of hours, minutes and seconds of broadcast media coverage.	Positive brand perception amongst desired audience and customer segments	This is important for all sponsors, as the perception of the brand amongst key stakeholder groups can have a dramatic impact on sales of its products and services.
Tickets	This is very often the easiest of rights to measure from a financial perspective, as each ticket has a face value and typically this will be discounted as part of the sponsorship package sold to the sponsor.	Tickets are the currency for networking opportunities with influencers, authorizers and specifiers hosted by the sponsor	Good old-fashioned face-to-face contact is extremely important in a 'wired world' where relationships are still important. Inviting existing customers or clients by providing them with tickets to an appropriate event can open the door to some strong ongoing networking opportunities.
Hospitality	Corporate entertainment at a venue or event is extremely powerful for customer relationship management.	Networking with customers and prospects can help oil the wheels of business development	These activities are subject to the Bribery Act 2010, which places a higher standard of ethical behaviour on organizations and its officers.

Table 10.1 *continued*

Tangible rights	Description	Intangible rights	Description
Advertising and signage	This is very important within a stadium or facility, where such signage can help to brand the location and demonstrate a link with the sponsor and the property in a high-impact way.	Prestige and reputational enhancement	Part of the allure of sponsorship for the brand owner is the feeling of prestige of being part of something that arouses passion amongst audiences it wants to reach.
Database access	Data about fans and prospects are extremely valuable, but have to be collected on a permission basis.	Open dialogue with audience and customer segments in a more meaningful way and on the back of something that they are genuinely passionate about	Given the long-term nature of sponsorship, there's a good opportunity to develop the database of customers and prospects in the future, subject to the Data Protection Act 1998.
Specialist knowledge or expertise	For example, if the sponsorship is in sport, education, environment or the arts then it's likely the sponsor will have access to specialist knowledge and expertise that it wouldn't have enjoyed in the absence of the sponsorship.	Teamwork with the rights owner that empowers the sponsor and deepens the relationship between the parties	There's a lot that business can learn from sponsorship in terms of teamwork, leadership and performance, and involving the coach of a successful sports team to work with the management of the sponsor can be an enlightening and fulfilling experience.
Conference or meeting and product showcase facilities	Facilities at the venue, such as a stadium, will have a commercial value and be part of the sponsorship package.	Convenience of location and access to facilities, which save the sponsor time and money	Given that there's an existing relationship between the sponsor and the rights holder, using conference facilities at a stadium for internal and external events should be much easier to organize.

Table 10.1 *continued*

Tangible rights	Description	Intangible rights	Description
Sampling and pouring rights	These are particularly valuable rights for an FMCG sponsor, as they can prevent a competitor's products being served or sampled at the venue.	Exclusivity and prestige	The opportunity to run sampling amongst a highly targeted customer segment, as well as positioning the product within an exciting and engaging environment without any competitor distractions, can be uplifting for the brand.
Personal appearances of celebrities, individuals and team members	This is another valuable tangible benefit, as high-profile athletes and celebrities can often be a big draw for clients and employees and add the 'wow' factor.	'Money-can't-buy' experiences using high-profile athletes and celebrities in their fields when engaging with customers and clients can be extremely memorable for the guests	Building good relationships with employees and third parties that are important to the business.
Content production	This is becoming extremely important, particularly 'behind the scenes' video stuff, as well as user-generated content by fans and others.	Building a strong relationship with supporters or fans	Making content exclusive to an audience by viral and mobile channels can be very powerful in keeping customers engaged with the brand and for building loyalty.
Marketing communications	Many sponsors expect to see a proportionate amount of activity by the rights holder in helping to activate the sponsorship in order to unlock its benefits.	Sounding board for ideas and buy-in to the 'brand world' of the sponsor by the rights holder	Sponsorship is all about great teamwork – and working with the rights holder's own in-house team or external agency(s) can be extremely cost-effective for the sponsor in its own marketing communications activities.

The rights and obligations of a sponsor will largely depend on the objectives it's trying to achieve as a result of becoming or continuing as a sponsor.

The provision of sponsorship funding doesn't automatically entitle a sponsor to any proprietary rights or control over a marketing opportunity. In order to maximize the marketing and brand-building opportunities, a licence to use proprietary rights for certain purposes must therefore be acquired.

The intellectual property (IP) rights to be licensed are diverse and include the name of the sponsored property, for example the team, event or venue and logo for promotional and merchandising activities, and in some cases the image or personality rights of sports personalities and celebrities may also be licensed to the sponsor. For a discussion on the use of trademarks and other IP rights, refer to Chapter 3.

The following isn't an exhaustive list of the rights and obligations of a sponsor but covers those terms most likely to be found in a sponsorship agreement.

Exclusivity

Sponsors may expect different levels of exclusivity dependent upon the level of sponsorship investment.

Duration of the agreement

The sponsorship agreement may or may not have a defined duration. In the case of a specified term, the circumstances and terms upon which the period can be extended should be defined. For example, in sports sponsorship, the average length of a football shirt sponsorship deal is three years. In contrast, a naming rights deal on a new football stadium could be as long as 15–20 years.

With respect to an event or television broadcast, a sponsor will want to ensure there are timetables specified for the occurrence of the relevant event or broadcast of the sponsored programme.

Termination

The sponsor should retain the right to terminate the sponsorship agreement prematurely if the rights holder goes into liquidation or fails to fulfil some or all of its obligations, such as failing to spend the sponsorship income on specified items, not obtaining additional sponsorship, not staging the event within a specific timescale, or having one event in a long-term campaign that doesn't meet specified criteria.

Any compensation payable in such a case must be expressly stated in the agreement. The consequences of termination or post-termination restrictions must also be specified carefully.

A sponsor may also wish to include a provision to terminate if the sponsored property has changed its image, for example if a famous athlete has tested positive for the use of banned drugs and a full investigation corroborates this finding.

Where certain elements of a sponsorship agreement are 'of the essence' of the sponsorship, for example the appearance of certain sports personalities at an event on specified television coverage, the sponsor should reserve the right to terminate the sponsorship agreement if these elements aren't delivered.

The fundamental matters giving rise to the sponsor's right to terminate should be cited as essential conditions within the body of the sponsorship agreement. If these fundamental matters aren't fulfilled, the right to terminate should be stated to be automatic and immediate. The alternative is to allow the rights holder a specified time to remedy the fundamental breach. If a condition isn't phrased in this way, damages for breach of contract may be held to be a sufficient remedy.

Any notice required to be given should allow both parties time to put alternative arrangements in place.

In the event of termination, there should be provisions preventing the parties from continuing to promote their connection with each other and other provisions dealing with the handover of materials, logistics and any forward commitments made by the incumbent sponsor that may bind the new sponsor.

Payment structures

The sponsorship agreement may structure the payment method in a number of ways depending on various factors such as cash flow, risk assessment and tax effectiveness.

Different methods of funding sponsorship include:

- *Fixed amount.* The sponsorship fee may be payable upfront or at fixed intervals, for example, in the case of F1, where payments are made for each of the individual grand prix races held. Repeat fees are normally subject to an annual increment calculated according to a specific formula or are renegotiable following an agreed period. Brand owners should avoid payment of the whole sponsorship fee in advance if a marketing opportunity is new and there's no guarantee that it will deliver as agreed or at all. In such a case, the brand owner should obtain an agreement to retain a proportion of the sponsorship fee until the agreed criteria have been fulfilled.

- *Conditional.* This arrangement is often appropriate where the sponsor wishes to be satisfied that certain participants will attend, certain performance targets will be met or specified television coverage will be obtained.

The sponsorship agreement must therefore cater for failure of one or more of the rights holder's obligations. A specified consideration should be attached to each of the key rights to be received by the sponsor so that, if one or more aren't received, the sponsorship fee is reduced accordingly or a refund is due to the sponsor.

- *Variable.* The sponsor may wish to provide additional funds to the sponsored party if certain events occur, for example a bonus being payable on the team securing promotion to the Premier League. However, a cap on the maximum payable by the sponsor should be considered if this arrangement is chosen.
- *Value-in-kind.* This involves the sponsor providing something that the rights holder would have had to buy in any event, such as IT or certain facilities that have a clear economic value. For example, for many years IBM has supplied the technology and human resources behind the Wimbledon Tennis Championships as part of its sponsorship of the tournament. The sponsorship agreement should specify any maintenance or insurance requirements as well as what will happen to any products or equipment after the event.

Event sponsorship rights

Given the huge choice of potential events available, the first decision a brand owner must take is whether to sponsor a single event, a seasonal or annual event or a one-off long-term project. In some cases, the decision will already have been made by cash constraints, provided the brand owner has been realistic about its cash flow requirements in each year of the event. Subject to cash restrictions, the choice will depend on whether the target benefits are to be achieved within a short period or the intention is to make a long-lasting impression. If the latter is the objective, the event must be capable of sustaining a prolonged marketing communications campaign.

In order to take full advantage of the sponsorship of an event, it will often be necessary to obtain licences from more than one party. In particular, regarding sports events, the relevant international or national sports federations may hold certain rights separately from the league organizing the event, the participating clubs and individuals, and the venue owner.

In addition to the exclusive or non-exclusive right to associate itself with the event and use the rights holder's trademarks in connection with its promotional activities, the sponsor may seek to gain added value from additional activities.

Such additional rights may include any of the following:

- rights to the appointment of a sponsor's representative on the board of the event;
- rights to be involved with the organization and management of the event;
- rights to supply and to insist that participants wear particular clothing;
- additional advertisements in the event programme and on boards and banners in and around the venue, preferably within view of television cameras and product display facilities;

- rights to take and publish its own photographs of the event, having obtained the consent of any individuals prominently featured;
- rights to use and publish official photographs of the event in marketing campaigns, in which case a licence of the copyright in the photographs will need to be acquired (along with the consent of the individuals);
- personal endorsement (personality rights) agreements with participating individuals;
- right to award prizes and trophies at major events;
- guaranteed television exposure;
- sponsorship of television and/or radio broadcasts;
- free tickets, hospitality rights and free parking; and
- marketing and merchandising rights in respect of the event name and logo.

Hospitality rights

The sponsor will typically be granted the non-exclusive right to use the event's hospitality facilities, including entrance tickets, reserved seating and use of office, catering and other facilities at the event venue. Such a right may or may not be at the expense of the sponsor, and the right may include access for corporate guests to meet sporting heroes or the cast of a film at a post-launch premiere party.

The sponsorship agreement should also set out any rights and limitations the sponsor may have to resell tickets, for example to the sponsor's customers or clients, or to use tickets for unconnected promotional activities, such as a competition with a national newspaper, magazine or radio station.

Postponement rights

Unless the date of the event is expressed in the agreement as 'essential', the rights holder may be entitled to postpone the event. If, as a consequence of postponement, it's necessary to amend the material contract terms, the sponsor should be allowed a reasonable period of time to review its position and if necessary withdraw from its sponsorship. Third-party contracts may also need to be extended or renegotiated.

A sponsor should consider insurance to cover any costs incurred as a result of the postponement of an event because of bad weather or an act of war (force majeure), which is unfortunately more than a theoretical risk today.

Duration of the agreement

In the case of one-off events, the sponsorship agreement will usually cover the event and any postponement, plus any post-event period during which the sponsor may continue its association with the event. Periodic events may be treated in the same way or as a series of events, with the sponsorship agreement also covering any period of inactivity in between events.

Cancellation rights

Whether cancellation of the event constitutes a breach of contract depends on the wording of the sponsorship agreement. A breach may entitle the sponsor to:

- damages for wasted expenses incurred as a result of a campaign to promote its products and services connected to the event;
- the whole or part of any sponsorship fees paid, depending on whether it can be shown to have received some benefit from these already; and
- damages for lost opportunity if that can be clearly demonstrated and is recoverable in law.

Renewal rights

If an event is seasonal or annual, the parties may wish to maximize the return on their investment in the relationship by agreeing to maintain their relationship for a minimum number of years or seasons. For example, the Emirates deal with Arsenal Football Club was signed in 2004 and is expected to run past 2021. It's therefore important to specify the minimum number of years or seasons upfront and if relevant include a provision in the agreement such that at the end of the initial period there's a recalculation of the sponsorship fees on renewal by reference to a specified formula.

Matching option rights

If the sponsor wants to have an ongoing relationship with a particular event but isn't prepared to commit upfront, then the sponsor should consider including an option to renew the sponsorship either on payment of an increased fee or through a matching rights option, which is designed to establish the market value of the event. In simple terms, the sponsor is granted an option to match the highest offer obtained by the sponsored party from any other bona fide potential sponsor.

Such options need safeguards to ensure that rights owners can't simply obtain a false offer from a third party in a bid to inflate a potential offer from the incumbent sponsor.

Where the sponsor has effectively helped create and fund a new event and build it into something prestigious, matching option rights are a particularly effective method of achieving a return on investment and a marketing advantage over its rivals by locking them out of entering into a fresh agreement with the rights holder should the sponsor wish to renew.

Clauses giving the sponsor a first right of refusal to renew the sponsorship contract must be carefully drafted to prevent a rights holder attempting to circumvent its terms.

In order to protect the sponsor, the option must include the following key clauses:

- a clear statement of precisely what it is the sponsor has the first option to accept;
- a time frame for negotiations – these should begin before the expiry of the existing agreement to enable a new agreement to be made; and
- a deadline for the acceptance of the new sponsorship package.

Rights and obligations of the property owner

With respect to a single event, the rights holder will typically accept the following non-exhaustive legal obligations to:

- make all the necessary arrangements for the event to take place;
- ensure that the venue has the necessary facilities to enable performance of all its obligations;
- comply with applicable regulations, whether national or particular to the type of event (for example, regulations of a sports governing body);
- not materially alter the format or schedule of the event, which would have an impact on the value of the rights acquired by the sponsor;
- fulfil all its obligations to third parties that provide goods, services or facilities for the event;
- not incur any unnecessary expense or liability for the sponsor outside any implied, usual or actual authority given by the sponsor to act on its behalf;
- use its sales and marketing capabilities to promote the event to agreed market and customer segments;
- guarantee that a particular level of television coverage will be provided;
- allow access by the sponsor to the venue before the event to install agreed display, product and/or sampling opportunities;
- provide special access for the sponsor and its guests to VIP areas and also include privileged parking rights near to where the hospitality is taking place;
- appoint secondary sponsors, where appropriate, to work alongside the main sponsor;
- indemnify the sponsor against any expense or liability arising from breach of any warranties given under the terms of the sponsorship agreement;
- maintain necessary insurance cover, for example for the cancellation or postponement of the event and for third-party liability; and

● not assign the benefit of any of the obligations under the sponsorship agreement to a third party without the agreement of the sponsor.

Management of intellectual property rights

Sponsorship is a complex web of IP rights belonging to the rights holder, the sponsor and increasingly the broadcasters of the event, which need to be coordinated and managed. Figure 10.1 provides a schematic view of some of the IP rights involved in a televised football match.

Figure 10.1 Tangled web of IP rights in the television broadcast of a football match

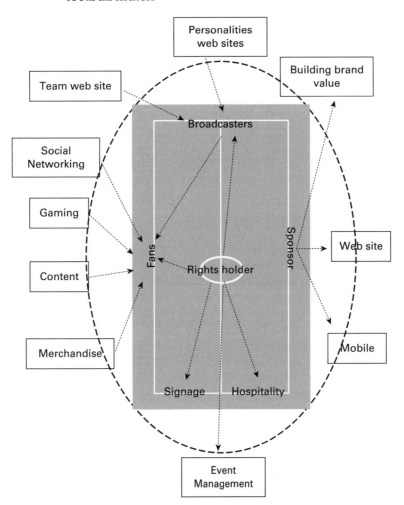

As discussed in Chapter 3, some of the most valuable IP rights are trademarks, copyright and personality rights.

Trademarks

The rights holder and sponsor should ensure that their respective trademarks are registered in all territories relevant to the event, particularly if this is broadcast internationally. The event logo and identity and other marks should be registered separately. If the event logo was created by independent designers, assignment of their rights in the mark should be made to the event rights holder.

The sponsor will require a licence to use the rights holder's logo or event name on its products and marketing literature and in promotional and advertising campaigns. In return, the event organizer will want a non-exclusive licence to use the sponsor's trademark for specified purposes, which typically include advertising promotions and related public relations activities.

Licensees of official licensed merchandise may also be interested in using both the event logo and the sponsor's trademark, and such deals need to be carefully negotiated, for example ensuring that the brand guidelines and sign-off procedures for the use of those marks are followed.

Copyright

A sponsor may also want to use photographs or film footage in a future promotional marketing campaign, but will need to ascertain who owns the copyright in such works in order to start to negotiate a licence for the use of that content.

Personality and image rights

The publication of photographs featuring star players and celebrities requires careful consideration.

Personality rights are recognized in a number of jurisdictions outside the UK, including the United States, France, Italy and Germany, where greater protection is available for celebrities with respect to the use of their image.

There's no such legal protection for privacy under UK law, although many lawyers argue that the protection of privacy exists through the back door as a result of the Human Rights Act 1998. As discussed in previous chapters, the unauthorized use of a person's image may also be actionable under the tort of passing off or defamation and in an action for malicious falsehood.

In the United States, the situation is very different. For example, in New York, an individual's personality rights are protected as well as their right of publicity.

The safest route for a marketer is always to get written permission for the use of the photograph or broadcast material for its own marketing and promotional purposes, although a copyright licence fee for the use of such material may be required.

Various industry codes of practice contain guidance on the use of an individual's image. For example, the Broadcast Committee of Advertising Practice (BCAP) Code provides that living persons mustn't be portrayed or referred to in television advertisements without their permission.

For a detailed discussion on the BCAP and CAP Codes, refer to Chapter 4.

Marketers must be careful when using 'stock' or 'library' footage of celebrities or sports personalities, as the copyright in the image is one issue, but the use of the image or likeness of a famous person and the commercial context of that use are a completely separate matter.

IP rights in an event itself

The provision of funds by a sponsor doesn't give rise to any proprietary rights to that event, except for large events such as the London 2012 Olympic Games, which are subject to the London Olympic Games and Paralympic Games Act 2006.

In terms of IP rights, performances of a dramatic nature, which include works of dance or mime, are protected by copyright, but there's no IP right in sport, as this isn't generally considered to be dramatic works under the Copyright, Designs and Patents Act 1988. Instead, sponsorship rights are 'controlled' contractually through the agreements entered into by the organizer of the event (the rights holder).

Competition law

Article 101 of the Treaty on the Functioning of the European Union (TFEU) (formerly Article 81 of the EC Treaty) prohibits agreements that prevent, distort or restrict competition in the EU and that have an appreciable effect on trade between EU member states.

Provided sponsorship is organized in a fair, open and transparent way and the rights owner doesn't abuse a dominant position in the market, there'll generally be no grounds for intervention under EU competition rules. Nevertheless, one particular issue that will give rise to competition concerns is a requirement that only equipment or goods of a certain manufacturer can be used during an event. Sponsorship shouldn't result in the grant of an exclusive right for a manufacturer to supply a market with its products in such a way as to exclude competitors. So, for example, a league or championship couldn't enter into a sponsorship with the supplier of certain sports equipment and insist that every player and team had to use that brand of equipment in order to compete in the league or championship.

The European Commission takes the view that, unless the 'official supplier' label can be justified on technical grounds, then granting the right to its use may mislead consumers by unjustifiably attributing a label of quality to the products.

It must be clear from the label that the relationship concerns a sponsorship/supply arrangement, and doesn't close off the market to other manufacturers.

Broadcast sponsorship regulation

In the UK, regulator Ofcom is responsible for ensuring that section 9 of the Broadcasting Code (2011) is observed by broadcasters as it applies to commercial references in television programming, which includes sponsorship of television content by a sponsor. Sponsorship isn't permissible on the BBC, as this is funded through the television licence fee and sponsorship of its programmes would be incompatible with its public service broadcasting remit.

Terminology used in the Broadcasting Code (2011)

- *'Television programming'*. This is taken to mean all broadcast content apart from spot advertising and teleshopping.
- *'Sponsor'*. This is any public or private undertaking or natural person other than the broadcaster or programme producer who is funding the programming with a view to promoting its products, services, trademarks and/or activities.
- *'Sponsor reference'*. This is any reference to the sponsor's products, services or trademarks.
- *'Sponsored programming/channel'*. This is programming that has had some or all of its costs met by a sponsor and includes AFP. Sponsored programming covers a single programme, a single channel, a programme segment or a block of programmes.
- *'Sponsorship credit'*. This is an announcement that informs the viewer when content is sponsored and by whom.
- *'Costs'*. In relation to broadcast sponsorship, this refers to any part of the costs connected to the production or broadcast of the programming.

Current position as to television sponsorship

Subject to certain rules, programme and channel sponsorship is permitted where the primary purpose of the sponsor is the promotion of its products, services, trademark or activities. Under the rules, sponsors can fund programmes at any stage of the production process; for example, a broadcaster may sell the sponsorship of a programme that it has commissioned or produced itself or an advertiser may directly fund the production of content on that channel (AFP). In addition, sponsors now have the flexibility to fund blocks of programmes, programme segments or entire television channels.

The rules attempt to strike a balance between allowing a brand owner the promotional benefit of being associated with the content it's sponsoring and ensuring that sponsorship arrangements don't lead to a blurring of the boundaries between editorial and advertising, surreptitiously or otherwise, which can be taken as a form of 'viewer deception'.

For example, the line is drawn preventing a sponsored programme overtly promoting a sponsor's individual products and services.

The rules require broadcasters to retain editorial independence over sponsored content, as well as ensuring that the audience is told when content is sponsored, and prevent unsuitable sponsorship from reaching the small screen.

When a reference to the sponsor within a sponsored programme meets the definition of 'product placement', then Ofcom licensees must comply with the rules around product placement as discussed in Chapter 5.

What hasn't changed under the new regime is that sponsorship of news and current affairs isn't permitted.

However, short specialist reports that accompany news, such as sport, travel and weather reports, can be sponsored provided that such content doesn't itself include material that constitutes news or current affairs. Such programme inserts should also look distinct from the rest of the news output, and this can be achieved by using different presenters and a different set so that viewers aren't under any misapprehension as to the sponsored content that's being presented within the show.

Compliance issues

Both the BCAP and the CAP Codes provide a list of prohibited categories of advertisers, which are barred from undertaking any form of programme or channel sponsorship. These include:

- political parties;
- tobacco brands;
- prescription-only medicine brands;
- guns and gun clubs; and
- adult sexual services.

In addition, the BCAP Code prevents any deviation from the content and scheduling rules. For example, a children's programme can't be sponsored by a product that's high in fat, sugar or salt. This has led to the government being accused of double standards in the wake of the controversy of Coca-Cola and McDonald's being global partners of the Olympic Games and permitted to exploit this association to children and young people, as well as seeking protection under draconian archaic sponsorship protection laws granted by Parliament under the Olympic Symbol etc (Protection) Act 1995.

Commissioning of programmes that attract sponsorship

Brand owners can legitimately get involved in the commissioning and creation of programmes, although such arrangements shouldn't lead to the creation of content that's a vehicle for the purpose of nakedly promoting its commercial interests or the distortion of editorial content for that purpose.

The broadcaster must ensure that it retains ultimate editorial control over the programmes it transmits in order to prevent the viewer from being exploited by such overt commercialization of television programme content.

Reference to the sponsor within programming

There are limited circumstances in which a sponsor or its interests may be referred to during a programme as a result of a commercial arrangement with the broadcaster or programme maker. For example, in the case of a product placement arrangement or when the sponsorship arrangement is identified, it must also comply with the relevant product placement rules, as discussed in Chapter 5.

An incidental reference to the brand owner that isn't part of any commercial arrangement is also caught by section 9 of the Broadcasting Code (2011), for example when a product is acquired for use as a prop or when a reference to one of the sponsor's products is unintentionally included in a programme as a result of filming on location.

Advertiser-funded programming

In the case of AFP where the sponsor has been involved in the creation of the programme, any reference to the sponsor or its commercial interests is likely to be considered to be deliberate and therefore subject to the product placement rules. References to generic products or services that are associated with the sponsor may also be treated as product placement depending on the circumstances.

For example, a generic reference to a product that's synonymous with the brand owner is more likely to be treated as product placement than a generic reference to a product that's not associated with a particular brand.

Programme credits

Broadcast sponsorship must be clearly identified by means of sponsorship credits, and these must make clear: the identity of the sponsor by reference to its name or trademark; and the association between the sponsor and the sponsored content.

Viewers should be told when a programme is sponsored and the identity of the sponsor. The sponsor's association with the sponsored content must be clear to the audience in all sponsorship credits.

Broadcasters are free to use various and different creative messages to identify sponsorship arrangements, for example 'sponsored by...', 'in association with...' or 'brought to you by...'.

However, care should be taken to avoid ambiguous statements that may lead to viewer confusion over the nature and purpose of the announcement.

Sponsorship messages shouldn't suggest that the sponsorship arrangement has in any way compromised the requirements of the BCAP Code.

To ensure that viewers are made aware when a programme is sponsored, credits must be broadcast at the beginning, during or at the end of the programme. To help ensure transparency, credits may be broadcast at each of these junctures as well as the 'bumpers' in the programme.

The rules on undue prominence apply, and excessively long sponsorship credits or frequent internal credits are likely to be unacceptable under the BCAP Code.

For sponsored content other than programmes, such as programme segments or television channels, sponsorship credits should be broadcast at appropriate points during the schedule to ensure viewers are able to identify sponsored content. For example, where a programme segment or item is sponsored – such as a cookery spot in a magazine format or a sports programme – credits could be broadcast at the time the segment or item is shown.

Distinction between sponsorship and editorial content

Viewers should be able to distinguish at all times between editorial content and paid-for commercial references. As a result, particular care is required when a sponsorship credit is broadcast during a programme to ensure that it's not confused with editorial content.

The rules permit the use of programme elements in sponsorship credits, and this can include a presenter or character actor appearing in sponsorship credits, but broadcasters must exercise caution to avoid blurring the distinction between sponsorship credits and editorial content.

Sponsorship credits must be distinct from advertising

The rules provide that: sponsorship credits broadcast around sponsored programmes mustn't contain advertising messages or calls to action; and sponsorship credits mustn't encourage the purchase or rental of the products or services of the sponsor or a third party.

Sponsorship credits are an intrinsic part of the sponsored content (albeit distinct from editorial), and their purpose is to identify sponsorship arrangements: they're not a platform for a sponsor to sell its products or services to the viewer.

The focus of the credit must be the sponsorship arrangement itself. Such credits may include explicit reference to the sponsor's products, services or trademarks for the sole purpose of helping to identify the sponsor and/or the sponsorship arrangement.

Article 10(1)(b) of the Audiovisual Media Services Directive 2010/13/EU provides that sponsored programmes 'must not directly encourage the purchase or rental of goods or services, in particular by making special promotional references to those goods or services'. Sponsorship credits should therefore fulfil the role of identifying the sponsorship arrangement and not be capable of being confused with advertising by focusing on the products or services of the sponsor.

Ofcom adjudication of Aviva sponsorship of ITV1 drama 'Downton Abbey' (2011)

The sponsorship credits featured a 'mini-drama' involving a character called Gary. Each credit throughout the episode reflected a development in the story line of Gary's motorbike accident, his recovery, his inability to return to work and his decision to retrain for a new career.

One of the sponsorship credits consisted of the following: Gary and his wife are sitting on the sofa. Gary is reading a document. His wife asks: 'What are you doing now?' Gary responds: 'It's my insurance policy. I think I'm still covered if I do that course!' His wife asks: 'Will you have to wear a uniform?' and Gary laughs. The Aviva logo and the caption: 'Aviva Income Protection Sponsors Drama Premieres. Reconstruction. Inspired by actual events' appeared on a yellow strapline across the bottom of the screen.

Ofcom ruled that the sponsorship credit was in breach of Rule 9 of the Broadcasting Code (2011), as it referred to a benefit of Aviva's Income Protection Policy and so it was an 'advertising message'.

Channel sponsorship

The BCAP Code permits the sponsorship of programmes, programme segments and channels. Ofcom recognizes that the sponsorship of entire channels may raise specific issues in relation to compliance with the sponsorship rules and has produced guidelines to assist broadcasters when entering into channel sponsorship arrangements. There are certain rules that may render the sponsorship of some channels unacceptable, such as a news and current affairs channel like Sky News. However, channel sponsorship is possible where the channel broadcasts some news and current affairs content, such as ITV1.

However, broadcasters need to ensure that channel sponsorship arrangements don't result in the sponsorship of programmes that can't be sponsored or appear to apply to such programmes.

When assessing whether a channel can be sponsored, Ofcom will take into account the following factors: the amount of content to be sponsored on the channel; and whether a channel broadcasts content that consists wholly or mainly of programmes that can be sponsored.

In the above example of ITV1, channel sponsorship may be permitted. As a rule of thumb, programmes should normally account for around 75 per cent or higher of the channel's output. Channels that broadcast a significant amount of programme content that is incapable of being sponsored (25 per cent or higher) are unlikely to be capable of being sponsored by a brand owner.

Identifying channel sponsorship arrangements

The BCAP Code requires sponsorship to be clearly identified, and it's important that credits for channel sponsors make clear what's sponsored – the channel and not the programmes – and the identity of the channel sponsor.

Unlike most television programmes, channels don't have a clearly defined beginning and end at which credits can naturally be placed. Broadcasters will need to exercise judgement as to when and where to identify channel sponsorship to ensure that section 9 of the Broadcasting Code (2011) and the BCAP Code requirements on transparency and distinction are met, whilst avoiding undue prominence for the sponsor. For example, natural breaks in the broadcast schedule such as after commercial breaks and between programmes would provide suitable junctions at which to place channel sponsorship messaging.

However, care needs to be taken to avoid confusion if a programme sponsorship credit is also broadcast near to a channel sponsorship credit. Channel sponsorship credits, like programme sponsorship credits, must be distinct from both editorial and advertising content. Channel sponsorship may be identified when channel 'idents' are broadcast. However, the size and duration of credits should be limited to avoid giving undue prominence to the sponsor.

Legal issues around hospitality within sponsorship

One of the many reasons why brand owners undertake sponsorship is to entertain their key customers, clients and stakeholders. Outside of brand image, awareness and credibility, hospitality is an important benefit. For example, in cultural and arts sponsorships in particular, where name awareness and media promotion levels are traditionally much lower than those provided by high-profile sports sponsorships, the ability to offer exclusive entertainment opportunities is often crucial.

Providing tickets and hospitality to a memorable event and creating a 'money can't buy' experience for guests are priceless for long-term relationship building. Not least, these occasions also offer something that's more attractive and outstanding than anything done by a brand owner's peers in its market segment.

Despite the obvious attractions of hospitality, legislators are tightening up the rules around it for fear of the spread of bribery and corruption, although the approaches taken aren't always consistent given cultural differences that exist throughout the EU and beyond.

For example, offering hospitality and gifts is very much part of the tradition in the Middle East and Asia but is less acceptable in a Western culture, where in some cases it can be illegal.

An organization set up to fight global corruption, Transparency International, defines bribery as 'the offering, promising, giving, accepting or soliciting of an advantage as an inducement for an action which is illegal, unethical, or a breach of trust. Inducements can take the form of gifts, loans, fees, rewards or other advantages (such as taxes, services and donations).'

Adjudication of the Financial Services Authority in the Aon case (2009)

In 2009, insurance giant Aon was fined a record £5.25 million by the Financial Services Authority (FSA) for failing to take reasonable care to counter risks of bribery and corruption. As shirt sponsor of Manchester United Football Club, Aon was pulled up for various issues, which included providing lavish travel and entertainment linked to foreign public officials who were clients. Between January 2005 and September 2007 Aon failed to assess properly the risks involved in its dealings with overseas firms and individuals who helped it win business and failed to implement effective controls to mitigate those risks. As a result of Aon's weak control environment, the firm made various suspicious payments, amounting to approximately US$7 million to a number of overseas firms and individuals.

Since the discovery of its failings in 2007, the firm has cleaned up its act to the extent that the FSA now regards its systems and controls in this area as a model of best practice for the rest of the insurance sector.

In the UK, the Bribery Act 2010 required commercial organizations as well as those in the public sector to have in place an anti-fraud and bribery policy together with codes of practice for the prevention of bribery by 1 July 2011.

This sent a shudder through many marketing and communication departments responsible for managing corporate hospitality and sponsorship, as initially it was thought that influencing clients to gain new deals or retain existing contracts could be considered an illegal activity.

The timing couldn't have been worse – bosses had started to measure the success of sponsorship not just in terms of how many decision makers, at what level, were being entertained as guests but also what business leads and new business were being generated as a result.

However, the interpretation of the new rules appears to have been exaggerated out of all proportion, according to Justice Secretary Kenneth Clarke QC. 'It's normal business hospitality to get to know your customers better.

No one is going to call that dishonest. Most of the provisions in the Bribery Act 2010 won't make the slightest difference to any reputable company. They won't have to spend millions of pounds on new control systems, which the compliance industry will tell them they need,' he said, promising that a common-sense approach to the enforcement of the new rules will prevail.

Bribery Act 2010

Many of the offences under the Bribery Act 2010 refer to 'improper performance', and broadly the test is how a reasonable person in the UK would expect a person to behave, ignoring any local custom or practice unless the law of the relevant country allows or requires that practice.

There are two general bribery offences that can be committed by a person or organization: offering a bribe; and accepting a bribe.

The Bribery Act 2010 deals only with bribery and not with other forms of white-collar crime.

The relevance from a hospitality perspective is that an offence will be committed if a person:

- intends to influence an official in his or her relevant capacity;
- intends to get or keep business or a business advantage; and
- offers or promises, directly or indirectly, a bribe to the official (or another person at the official's request or with his or her agreement) and the written law that applies to the official doesn't allow or require him or her to be influenced.

A brand owner commits an offence if it allows anyone connected with it ('an associated person') to bribe another person, intending to get or keep business or a business advantage for the organization. An 'associated person' is defined as 'a person who performs services by or on behalf of the relevant commercial organization' such as a public relations or sponsorship agency. However, it's a defence for a brand owner to prove it had in place adequate procedures to prevent persons associated with it from engaging in this conduct.

It's also an offence to bribe a 'foreign public official', and broadly this means any person outside the UK who holds any legislative, administrative or judicial position, exercises a public function for any country or public agency or enterprise or is an official or agent of a public international organization.

The maximum penalty for an offence under the Bribery Act 2010 is 10 years' imprisonment and/or an unlimited fine.

In the case where the brand owner fails to prevent a bribery offence from being committed and hadn't taken reasonable steps to prevent such activities from taking place so that on the balance of probabilities bribery and corruption were likely to occur, then the court will impose a fine.

The Ministry of Justice has laid out six principles to help brand owners in complying with the new duties and obligations under the Bribery Act 2010:

- *Principle 1: Proportionate procedures.* The action to be taken by a brand owner should be proportionate to the risks it faces and to the size of its own business. On this basis, a brand owner might need to carry out a thorough audit to prevent bribery if its organization is large and operates in an overseas market where bribery is known to be commonplace, compared with a brand owner that has a much smaller organization and operates in markets where the incidence of bribery is exceptionally rare.

- *Principle 2: Top-level commitment.* Those at the top of an organization are in the best position to ensure their organization conducts business without bribery. The executive management team running the business will want to show that it's been active in making sure that all employees as well as the key people who do business with it understand that it doesn't tolerate any form of bribery.

- *Principle 3: Risk assessment.* A brand owner will need to consider the bribery risks it might face. For example, it may want to do some research into markets and customer segments in terms of customs, traditions and culture to protect itself from being implicated in activities that could be in breach of the Bribery Act 2010.

- *Principle 4: Due diligence.* The Ministry of Justice guidance states: 'Knowing exactly who you are dealing with can help to protect your organisation from taking on people who might be less than trustworthy. You may therefore want to ask a few questions and do a few checks before engaging others to represent you in business dealings.'

- *Principle 5: Communication.* Communicating ethical and anti-corruption policies and procedures to employees and others who perform services for the brand owner will raise awareness and help to deter bribery by making clear the basis on which the company or organization does its business. It may be prudent to provide additional training or awareness raising amongst all employees.

- *Principle 6: Monitoring and review.* The risks faced and the effectiveness of procedures may change over time, and so a brand owner may want to keep an eye on the anti-bribery steps it has taken so that it can keep pace with any changes in the bribery risks it faces when it enters new market segments.

The Ministry of Justice guidance on the issue of hospitality states: 'Bona fide hospitality and promotional or other business expenditure which seeks to improve the image of a commercial organisation better to present products and services or establish cordial relations is recognised as an established and important part of doing business and it is not the intention of the Bribery Act 2010 to criminalise such behaviour.'

In other words, hospitality will be acceptable if it's reasonable and proportionate depending on the circumstances. It shouldn't be overlooked that providing sponsorship itself could be taken as a form of bribery if it's judged to be an undue influence or providing a benefit to a foreign public official related to obtaining or retaining business.

One notable case that caused controversy occurred in 2007 when Nike sent a couple of tickets to the opening match of the Rugby World Cup in Paris to the European Commission's trade office in Geneva, along with the offer of free transport in its company van to Paris.

Adjudication by the European Ombudsman in the Nike case (2007)

In September 2007, Nike offered two officials working for Peter Mandelson, the European Commissioner for Trade at that time, VIP tickets to see the opening game of the Rugby World Cup in Paris. The officials were allowed to accept the offer and also travelled in a car provided by Nike staff from Brussels to Paris.

In December, Friends of the Earth wrote to the European Commission (EC) asking whether the decision was in line with staff rules. The group wasn't satisfied with the EC's response and brought a complaint to the European Ombudsman, arguing that the two officials could be involved in a conflict of interest because they'd been working on anti-dumping duty cases involving sports shoes made in China and Vietnam. Friends of the Earth pointed out that the EC's own guidance for staff stated that 'as a general rule of thumb you decline all such offers that have more than merely symbolic value'.

The European Ombudsman found that the evidence didn't suggest that accepting gifts had led to an actual conflict of interest and accepted that the decision to impose anti-dumping duties on imports of sports footwear from Asia was taken a year before the tickets were offered by Nike and there were no ongoing anti-dumping investigations directly relevant to the company. Nonetheless he found that there was an 'apparent conflict of interest' because it couldn't be ruled out that the two officials would deal with anti-dumping cases in the future.

In a letter sent on 20 April 2007, the European Ombudsman, Nikiforos Diamandouros, offered the EC, as an alternative to a verdict of maladministration, a 'friendly solution' that involved the EC in admitting that it shouldn't have allowed the two officials to accept the invitation and also undertaking to change its internal staff rules so that officials wouldn't be allowed to accept such hospitality in the future.

For its part, the EC issued a statement saying it 'understood the need to guard against both real and apparent conflicts of interest in order to maintain public trust and confidence and to protect staff from unjustified suspicion'.

It should be noted that most anti-bribery legislation, such as that enacted in the UK, has extra-territorial aspects, and this is important in relation to multinational sponsorships by a brand owner with a global operation. The key question is whether the hospitality is provided with the relevant criminal intention at its root.

The lavishness of any hospitality is only one factor to be taken into account in determining relevant criminal intent. The safest approach to take is that corporate hospitality shouldn't be lavish or too frequent and should be appropriate to the business relationship with the attendees.

The Ministry of Justice guidance note does provide some helpful examples in making such an assessment. One example indicates that an invitation to foreign clients to attend a Six Nations match at Twickenham as part of a public relations exercise designed to cement good relations or enhance knowledge in the organization's field is extremely unlikely to be a breach of the Bribery Act 2010. However, the outcome might be different in the case of an invitation to a foreign public official, as the required intention would be different, as can be seen in the Nike case.

The following checklist for brand owners will assist in keeping hospitality within a sponsorship programme legal:

- Establish a company policy on ethical behaviour, including the giving and receiving of hospitality and gifts based on the principles of transparency, honesty and openness about such dealings.

- Consider imposing limits on the value and type of hospitality to be provided to guests so that it's compatible with the scale and prestige of the sponsored event.

- Ensure recipients clearly understand that hospitality is provided on a no-obligation/no-expectation basis.

- Ensure payment for hospitality is made to the services supplier rather than making cash reimbursements to the invitees.

- Consider any hospitality to foreign public officials very carefully and question whether this should be done at all.

- Create a standard procedure for handling requests from within the company or organization for tickets and hospitality as part of the company's sponsorship programme – this should cover the motivation for the hospitality, whether it's standard practice, who's invited, whether it may have an impact on any decision making in the future, whether it's in alignment with company policy to offer such hospitality and whether such provision would stand up to public scrutiny or scrutiny in a court of law.

- Consider training all employees and incorporating these procedures into the staff handbook.

- Ensure that all marketing communications agencies know and acknowledge in writing that they will follow the procedures as they relate to sponsorship and hospitality on behalf of the company or organization.

- Ensure that all dealings with customers and prospects are clearly logged so there's a paper trail of all correspondence and contact linked to the sponsorship activity.

References and further reading

Cases and judgments

Aon case, adjudication by the Financial Services Authority (2009), reported on the FSA's website [accessed 23 April 2012] http://www.fsa.gov.uk

Aviva broadcast sponsorship of ITV1's 'Downton Abbey', adjudication by Ofcom (2011)

Nike case, adjudication by the European Ombudsman (2007), reported on the news website European Voice [accessed 23 April 2012] http://www.europeanvoice.com

Websites

European Sponsorship Association [accessed 19 April 2012] http://www.sponsorship.org

Global Anti-Corruption Alliance has useful information on its website [accessed 22 April 2012] http://www.transparency.org

Ministry of Justice, Guide to the Bribery Act 2010 [accessed 18 April 2012] http://www.justice.gov.uk/guidance/bribery.htm

Journals and reports

Journal of Brand Strategy, published by Henry Stewart Publications

Ofcom (2011) Guidance notes: commercial references in television programming

Books

Collett, P and Fenton, W (2011) *The Sponsorship Handbook*, Jossey-Bass, San Francisco

Ferrand, A, Torrigiani, L and Povill, A (2007) *Routledge Handbook of Sports Sponsorship*, Routledge, London

Kolah, A (2001) *How to Develop Effective Naming Rights Strategies*, SportBusiness, London

Kolah, A (2003) *Maximising the Value of Sponsorship*, SportBusiness, London

Kolah, A (2004) *Maximising the Value of Hospitality*, SportBusiness, London

Kolah, A (2006) *Advanced Sports Sponsorship Strategies*, SportBusiness, London

Kolah, A (2007) *Sponsorship Works: A brand marketer's casebook*, Electric Word, London

Kolah, A (2013) *High Impact Marketing that Gets Results*, Kogan Page, London

Index

NB: page numbers in *italic* indicate figures or tables

Endorsements

The marketing world is beset with both legal restrictions and great opportunities. Here is the jargon free, concise and straightforward advice required to navigate a successful path... and made a fun read with the help of some great cartoons! **Andrew Marsden, Chairman, UK Advertising Standards Authority Code Review**

Readable, relevant and instructive, Guru in a Bottle is an excellent guide through the legal maze which creates the selling and marketing opportunities and pitfalls of operating in today's global marketplace. I highly recommend it. **Sir Dominic Cadbury, Chancellor, Birmingham University**

Within the context of digital and m-marketing, having a strong grip on the shifting legal and regulatory framework across the European Union is vital. This book, written by a leading authority, provides an invaluable reference for all agencies working in this space and is written in a highly accessible way. **Dusan Hamlin, Joint CEO, M&C Saatchi Mobile**

This may well be the book that saves your career. It should be compulsory reading for anyone braving today's wide open world of PR and marketing. **David Gallagher, Senior Partner/CEO Europe, Ketchum Pleon**

All too often, marketers make crucial decisions without being aware of the legal issues involved. This book can change that. It is an essential guide by one of the leading experts in the field. **Professor Jaideep Prabhu, Judge Business School, Cambridge University**

The second edition of this leading work on the subject makes an extremely valuable contribution to understanding how the law establishes the framework within which marketers must operate but can also provide a source of competitive advantage. An outstanding and well researched resource delivered in a highly accessible way. **Sir Paul Judge, President, Chartered Institute of Marketing**

The Guru in a Bottle series is a great resource that tackles complex subjects and makes them human. Essential Law for Marketers, *written by Brand*

Republic blogger Ardi Kolah, makes it easy to navigate the complexities of UK and European laws and regulations that impact all of sales and marketing practitioners. Kolah has pulled this off with humour – always a tough job. Definitely one to own. **Gordon McMillan, Editor, Brand Republic**

With the rapid changes in digital technologies, sales and marketing practitioners need to keep up to date with best practice that also stays within UK and European laws and regulations. The Guru in a Bottle series and this second edition has just made this task much easier, in addition to putting fun back into sales and marketing. Essential reading for all businesses and organizations wanting to use emerging channels such as m-marketing. **Phil Jones, Managing Director, Real Time Consultancy**

Mandatory reading for anyone wanting to ensure that their creativity does not lead them to the wrong side of the law, and their clients' carefully planned marketing program coming to an unexpected sudden halt, with the grief of product withdrawals and induction into the marketing halls of shame. **Michael Payne, former IOC Global Marketing/Broadcaster Director and advisor to Bernie Ecclestone**

A great reference work for experienced practitioners and beginners alike who want to avoid the pain of reading impenetrable law books. It's a welcome departure from other publications on the market today. **Matt Fanshawe, Group Chief Operation Officer, Havas EHS**

A great book for business owners who need a quick guide to the legal pitfalls that exist when marketing their products. Written in an easily accessible style by an expert in the field, this is a great book to add to your business bookshelf. It's also useful for PR, marketing and business students who need a good foundation. **Alison Theaker, coach and former Head of Education, Chartered Institute of Public Relations**

This excellent book helps the reader to keep abreast of the latest developments in the ever-changing European legal and regulatory landscape. Highly recommended. **Allan Karlsen, Northern Europe Regional Director, Genworth Financial**

Essential Law for Marketers *is exactly what it says on the tin... It's an excellent book and I wish we'd published it.* **Daryn Moody, Publisher, Journal of Brand Strategy**

The first edition of Essential Law for Marketers *was a breath of fresh air for anyone involved in marketing who wanted a clear, easy to understand and jargon-free explanation of where they stand legally in relation to planned activities. This second, fully revised and differently organized edition has all the benefits of the first edition but with full and easily understood updates on the complicated world of EU legislation. Our well-thumbed and regularly used copies of the first edition are ready to be replaced by this wonderfully updated and revised book. It really is an essential day-to-day reference for anyone in the marketing community.* **Chris Protheroe, President & Group Managing Director, The Copyright Promotions Licensing Group**

Ardi the guru has done it again! The second edition of Essential Law for Marketers *is thoroughly comprehensive, with lots of legal case examples, helpful checklists and anecdotes in a clear and easy to read style. It is bang up to date with new sections on the impact of social media, direct electronic marketing, cookies, the Bribery Act 2010, the latest EU Directives and more. An essential read for all modern-day marketers.* **Keith Arundale, Visiting Fellow, Kingston University Business School, London**

Despite all the promises by politicians to reduce the burden of regulation on business, the law surrounding marketing continues to get more complex. To play the game well, a good marketer must understand the rules on everything from data privacy to hospitality. This book explains and elucidates the relevant regulation with wit and insight. Don't launch a thing without it. **Hugh Burkitt, CEO, The Marketing Society**

With his multi-skill set and publishing experience, you'll not find a better placed person to package the law into such a highly informative and accessible resource. **Nick Lawrie, Director, Press Association**

For the majority of sales and marketing practitioners, the way UK and European law applies to their everyday work remains a mystery and yet it's probably the most important consideration when considering a new product launch; the ability to acquire new customers and clients as well as the deployment of a range of new channels that can be highly precise in reaching the desired customer or client segments. This book provides a simple to read, easy to follow path for those with one year's experience or more in understanding the rules of engagement – and makes this a lot of fun along the way. Essential reading. **David Haigh, CEO, Brand Finance plc**

The law can be a minefield when you're a marketer, and too many in our industry can have no idea how to navigate it. Fortunately, Ardi Kolah's new book provides expert guidance on keeping on the right side of the law – if you work in marketing, you should buy it today. **Francis Ingham, Director General, PRCA**

The definitive work on the subject that any self-respecting sales and marketing practitioner should download! **Alistair Gosling, CEO, The Extreme Sports Company**

Shareholders rightly demand that companies protect value through the proper application of law. This requires marketing employees to work within a legal construct so that they can protect value. This seminal work provides the framework and should be mandatory reading for all in marketing. **Raoul Pinnell, former Chairman, Shell Brands International**

Leaving no legal loophole unexposed, this book is a must have for marketers. Authoritative yet accessible, comprehensive yet manageable and legally precise yet marketing orientated, the Guru in a Bottle has designed the text well and is capable of tackling the complex and changing legal minefield in a hugely interesting way which engages the reader. **Professor Vince Mitchell, Sir John E Cohen Professor of Consumer Marketing, Cass Business School, City University**

Ardi Kolah is an extremely accomplished marketing guru whom I have known and worked with for many years. This second edition of his much-respected book is a must-buy for all marketing practitioners. Congratulations on another cracking good textbook. **Malcolm McDonald, Emeritus Professor, Cranfield School of Management, Bedford**

As a relative newcomer to sales and marketing, I found this beautifully written book extremely valuable and the best book on the subject I have read. **Captain Mike Davis-Marks, OBE Royal Navy Director of Naval Recruiting and former Director of Public Relations**

If there's one thing that Ardi is brilliant at it's marketing, and in the increasingly litigious world in which we live, this book is essential reading for all those marketers who need to get a quick grip of the law. **Dr Ann Limb OBE, DL**

This modern update seamlessly builds upon the guidance of the first edition, giving marketers confidence when working in the digital economy. Getting to grips with broad policy changes can be a minefield, especially when dealing with international firms. The Guru series is the guiding hand you need to leap the barriers and tackle the challenges of the digital age. A pivotal figure in the marketing world, Ardi Kolah demonstrates more expertise than any other in his field. He continues to guide and innovate, driving progress for thousands of industry leaders. This book is an essential weapon in the arsenal of any marketer, its invaluable instruction keeping technical leaders safe in business and future proofing their legal knowledge. An absolute must-read. **Richard Teideman, CEO, London Creative**

Written in an engaging and accessible style, Ardi Kolah's updated Essential Law for Marketers *provides a timely and comprehensive introduction to the legal framework, its obligations and pitfalls, for all those active in the industry. Recommended reading.* **Frank Saez, Managing Director, SMG Insight/ YouGov**

As the title suggests this is essential reading for all marketers, whether strategic or tactical, based at head office or facing off to clients or customers. In this ever changing world, marketers must not only be aware of the legal implications of their actions but understand how they can navigate their way through the broad range of actions that enable us to answer a customer's needs. Ardi Kolah successfully guides the reader through the maze, acting as a personal lawyer and allowing the marketer to feel confident that they are doing the 'right' thing for their organization, client and customer. **Alan Osborne, Product Development Leader, Genworth Financial**

With many different attempts by marketers to give their advice as to how to approach the science of applied common sense, this latest book by Ardi Kolah is an absolute must in helping to navigate the jungle of how the law is applied to marketing. It's one thing to have a great marketing idea but it's another to make sure it remains within the ever increasing complexities of the law of land. This book not only provides insight and intellect, but delivers it in a manner and style that recognizes that most marketers don't have a law degree! A must-read. **Howard Kosky, Chairman, markettiers4dc Group of companies**

All sales and marketing students must get hold of a copy of this excellent book as it dispels the myth that learning how to navigate the complexities of UK and European laws and regulations requires a legal mind. Written by a world recognised marketing expert, this book lifts the lid on what can be a dry and dull subject by bringing it alive along with the Guru in a Bottle style that has become very popular internationally. **Rosie Phipps, Principal, Oxford College of Marketing**

Ardi is one of the brightest minds in the industry and he brings to life this most complex of areas in an easily digestible and interesting way. This book has already become an essential companion to all marketers and this second edition covers everything you will need to know... ever! **Dan McLaren, Founder, UK Sports Network**

The latest Guru in a Bottle book, Essential Law for Marketers *is perhaps Ardi Kolah's finest work yet. It delicately balances the comprehensive legal information savvy marketers must know in this modern world with easily digestible insights of key information. If you are a professional marketer then you must read this book and, more importantly, keep it near your desk; a legal issue may not come up today but it certainly will tomorrow. Then the real value of having read Guru in a Bottle and keeping your copy nearby will be crystal clear.* **Steve Madincea, Founder and Group Managing Director, PRISM (WPP plc)**

A comprehensive, readable and accessible account of everything a marketer should know about the law as it affects daily practice. **Stephen Jolly, Fellow, Judge Business School, University of Cambridge**

The first edition of this book was essential reading for professional marketers who sought to understand legislation and how it affected them, while also discovering how the law might offer their organizations competitive advantage. This second edition has transformed that knowledge, through the restructuring of the content and cartoons into a practical tool which is now an instant guide to the very latest key sales and marketing legal issues. Essential reading for all marketers no matter what aspect of the profession they address. **John Flynn, Master of The Worshipful Company of Marketers**

Working in events and sales means Essential Law for Marketers *will provide me with knowledge and a better understanding of how to sell my products and services to my clients, whilst learning how to maximise sponsorship opportunities.* **Minaxi Mistry, CEO, Yellow Brick Events**

In our transparent 24/7 world communicators need to be able to respond quickly to news and opportunities, and our campaigns need to 'stand out' in order to be recognized. As consultants we want our work to be known for all the right reasons, and therefore having an understanding of legal implications and requirements is crucial to both campaignsand business success. Ardi Kolah provides not only a reassuring voice but a comprehensive insight into all aspects of law in marketing and public relations. If you are to buy one book on the subject, this is it. **Elisabeth Lewis-Jones, CEO of Liquid, Past President of the CIPR and Chairman of the PRCA Council**

As someone deeply involved with marketing but not being a marketer I'm delighted that Ardi Kolah has written such a clear book on the legal minefield that surrounds the profession. I will be consulting it frequently. **Dr Michael Jackson, CEO, ShapingTomorrow.com**

All SMART marketers will refer to this book time and time again. **Rupert Leigh, CEO, A Public Nuisance**

Sales and marketing competency is critical for survival within the charity sector, so it is vital we understand not just the legal constraints, but also the immense opportunities out there to engage more effectively with our existing and potential supporter base. This excellent book, written by the leading authority on the subject, is essential reading for anyone wishing to fully exploit their brand. **Richard Leaman, CB, OBE, CEO Guide Dogs for the Blind UK**

Legal maxims and tales of model citizens riding the Clapham Omnibus mean little to those aren't legal scholars. Yet the laws governing sales, marketing and advertising apply to all. Guru in a Bottle is an indispensable, practical and ingenious guide for 21st Century marketers tackling real-world issues in a competitive marketplace. **Cedric Perrier, CEO, Media & Entertainment Group**

Whether you are in sales, marketing or corporate communications, soon or later, you'll need this book. **Fabrizio Falzarano MBA, marketer at Canon Europe**

Ardi's Guru in a Bottle titles are great guides to achieving our potential, and being able to understand complicated subjects like the law without being intimidated by them. And the great cartoons by Steve Marchant make the books an entertaining learning experience as well as an effective one. **David Lloyd, cartoonist of 'V for Vendetta'**

A great book to help you get to grips with the complexities of UK and European laws and regulations whilst implementing your PR and marketing campaigns. A 'go to' book to keep you at the top of your game. **Sam Mercer, director, Hopscotch Consulting**

This is an impressive work and will qualitatively add to the knowledge base in this area. Law firms and their clients will find this an invaluable resource in not just knowing the UK and European laws and regulations that impact sales and marketing but using this knowledge for competitive advantage. **Ashraf Mohammed, former partner, Davies Arnold Cooper**

Most people in marketing have no background in law and vice versa. Both professions are focussed on language, but they use words in very different ways. Lawyers seek clarity and accuracy in communicating with other lawyers. Marketers communicate with simplicity to a much wider audience. They are very different ways of thinking. Very few people can master both of these, but Ardi Kolah is one of those few. He explains the essentials of law to the marketing community with clarity and simplicity, guiding the reader through the swamps of liability in a brilliantly accessible way. **Quentin Langley, Senior Lecturer, University of Bedfordshire**

This book will be very quickly seen as an essential part of the toolkit of every professional marketer. All marketing and sales professionals at all levels can now safely navigate the minefield of law. A refreshingly jargon-free zone, Guru in a Bottle approaches a hugely important and complex subject from a clear and positive perspective – improving the performance of sales and marketing activities. Having spent more than 15 years in the communications industry, I have read some of the most outrageous claims and statements from organizations who frankly should know better. Now they can. Finally, in a world of hyperbole and over-claim, I would say that this is probably the best book of its type in the world! Now turn to section two – 'Making statements in sales and marketing' – to check that previous sentence! **Simon Mottram, Director, Financial Services, YouGov**

This should be an essential companion for every law abiding marketer! **Nigel Moore, Director of Marketing, Royal College of Obstetricians**

If you are looking for answers about essential law in marketing this is the book for you. Its jargon-busting style and easy to read format together with plenty of examples make it an informative and enjoyable experience to read. For the self-directed learner this book will make a huge difference. **Andrew Griffiths, Director, Coral Leadership.**

Too many brand reputations have been damaged through a failure to understand the legal framework in which marketing must operate. It's time that today's marketers recognized that staying abreast of the latest legal rules of engagement is not a burden, but an important source of both competitive advantage and marketing efficiency. Ardi Kolah's updated edition of Essential Law for Marketers *is therefore an important and welcome contribution that should be read and understood by student and professional alike.* **Craig Hurring, Director of Communications and Marketing, CFA Society of the UK**

This book is written by someone who knows what they are talking about; a practitioner who speaks with knowledge and authority and who thinks about the marketing profession deeply. What we have here is an invaluable toolkit for marketers who need to know the law. It's written in an accessible way, packed with practical advice and examples. It should be on every practitioner's shelf and taken down and used until the pages fall out. **Professor Anne Gregory, Director, Centre for Public Relations Studies, Leeds Business School, Leeds Metropolitan University**

No matter how experienced a marketer you are there is absolutely no way that you will have grasped the Byzantine intricacies of contract, copyright and new media law. This very accessible book is not just a guide, it is essential if you want avoid the horror and expense of litigation. It is also the knowing friend who will scream 'no!!!!' just as you think that you are about to make your fortune and maybe stop you losing it. Essential Law for Marketers *is exactly what it says on the cover and may make you sleep more easily in your bed.* **Jerry Hayes, Barrister-at-Law and former Member of Parliament**

Only few years ago, most lawyers frowned on those in their profession who indulged in sales and marketing. It was later seen as a necessary evil. All lawyers now recognize that to survive and thrive, sales and marketing needs to be at the heart of their business. But we are not naturally good at it and until recently there has been an unfulfilled need for a simple, easy to follow guide, a Guru whose effortless wisdom will walk you around the elephant traps and to your destination. Ardi Kolah has produced just such a book. It is a no-fuss explanation of UK and European law that makes it easy to understand the relevant legal framework around such activities. This second edition, written by the acknowledged authority on the subject, takes an innovative approach in a highly readable way; it's set to become a best seller in the UK and Europe amongst lawyers and their clients. **Sailesh Mehta, Barrister-at-Law, Red Lion Court, London**

Clarity of sales communication is essential but the relationship between perception and truth is getting ever cloudier. Clever wording, attractive claims, distorting facts and figures lead to a minefield of risk and legality with the potential for legal sanctions and significant brand damage. So where should marketers and managers turn for the latest advice and guidance, and how do they know where the ever moving boundaries are? I can find no better place than between the pages of this book. Here is a really comprehensive primer covering all the key issues you need to be aware of as a marketer, corporate manager, regulator, legal professional or lay person. This one volume sets the stage for the next decade in an easy to read format that's a model of clarity. I recommend it to you having squeezed it into my collection of key reference. Enjoy, I did! **Dr Peter Cochrane OBE, former Chief Technology Officer, BT**

This is a fantastic reference book, written in the language of the layman rather than that of a lawyer. It's very clear and well laid out, which makes it easy to navigate and to digest. An excellent companion for all clients and agencies alike. **David Peters, Head of Sponsorship, Carat Sponsorship**

A 'must-read' for any non-law savvy sales and marketing professional, especially given the current environment where any wrong move, no matter what the intent, can be scrutinized. **James Hirst, Business Development Director, Clear**

Law is often considered an afterthought for many marketing professionals; a subject that only comes into play when things go wrong or is best left to the legal department. However, this book is an eye-opening tome of information that sheds light on how law can, and must, be an essential part of a marketing plan and strategy, and how it can be a tool for best practice and increased competitive advantage. Guru in a Bottle offers a highly practical, comprehensive and comprehensible guide to all the aspects of law that a marketer will encounter throughout a successful career. The format of the book ensures that it can be enjoyably consumed in a flowing logical way and easily referred to later when needed. I would recommend this book to all marketers and other professionals at all stages of their careers, whether students or business leaders. **Jeff Zaltman, Managing Director, Flying Aces**

In an increasingly litigious world, the line between success and failure is often demarcated by the practical legalities of a particular campaign. This book removes wishful thinking to reveal the legal guidelines in a compelling, jargon-free way with case law examples. Professional marketers should buy this book, read and refer to it – before their competitors do! **Steve Dobson, founder, Unusual Hotels of the World**

I see this book becoming my 'go to' companion for all things marketing. The style and layout of the book allows me to dip in and out whenever I feel the need. Essential Law for Marketers *should be on every business professional's bookcase.* **Jonathan Walsh, director, Hayes Fuels**

This valuable little book succeeds in distilling highly complex but essential law for marketers into delicious little sips. It is reliably accurate and thoroughly researched, yet can be readily understood by someone entirely new to the law. **Professor Penny Darbyshire, Kingston Law School**

What few marketers fail to appreciate is that in the right hands, the law can be a powerful weapon for achieving sales and marketing advantage. Rather than being a drag on creativity, understanding how the law can be used to support such activities can lift your thinking to a new level and achieve surprising results. This book is a blueprint for doing just that. **James Hilton, Joint CEO, M&C Saatchi**

In any democracy a just law must be an accessible, comprehensible one. That is fundamental. But accessibility means quite different things to different people. Law that passes the lawyer's test of comprehensibility is often enough a mysterious thicket to those without legal training. To be fair to lawyers, many do attempt to translate the inevitable complexities and jargon into plain English. To be realistic, however, few succeed. Even fewer manage it without over-simplification. Ardi Kolah is to be congratulated on this work, which brings to his subject a clear and coherent structure and some crisp and accurate explanations. Each of the different kinds of marketing activity its readers will be undertaking has its own chapter. At the same time, the book also manages to cover the use of design rights and other intellectual property rights to gain and preserve market share. The book's account of the relevant legal rules is organized logically and simply, using language that is easy to understand. I am confident this second edition will prove a deserved success. **Mark Warby QC, 5 RB Chambers, London (UK)**